PARTICIPATION AND THE MYSTERY

PARTICIPATION AND THE MYSTERY

*Transpersonal Essays in Psychology,
Education, and Religion*

JORGE N. FERRER

STATE UNIVERSITY OF NEW YORK PRESS

Cover image courtesy of NASA.

Published by
STATE UNIVERSITY OF NEW YORK PRESS
Albany

© 2017 State University of New York

For information, contact
State University of New York Press
www.sunypress.edu

Production, Laurie D. Searl
Marketing, Michael Campochiaro

Library of Congress Cataloging-in-Publication Data

Name: Ferrer, Jorge N. (Jorge Noguera), 1968– author.
Title: Participation and the mystery : transpersonal essays in psychology, education, and religion / by Jorge N. Ferrer.
Description: Albany, NY : State University of New York Press, [2017] | Includes bibliographical references and index.
Identifiers: LCCN 2016031415| ISBN 9781438464879 (hardcover : alk. paper) | ISBN 9781438464862 (pbk. : alk. paper) | ISBN 9781438464886 (e-book)
Subjects: LCSH: Transpersonal psychology. | Spirituality—Psychology. | Psychology, Religious.
Classification: LCC BF204.7 .F47 2017 | DDC 150.19/87—dc23
LC record available at https://lccn.loc.gov/2016031415

10 9 8 7 6 5 4 3 2 1

CONTENTS

ACKNOWLEDGMENTS

This book is the product of more than a decade of thinking deeply about the implications of a participatory worldview for contemporary psychology, education, and religion. As usual with any book of this kind, I owe an immense debt of gratitude to the countless individuals who generously offered me their critical input after reading earlier versions of these chapters. I am also grateful to those who took the time to write reviews of my previous books or engage my work through various personal or scholarly exchanges. These contributions not only helped to improve the presentation of my ideas, but also saved this work from many conceptual imprecisions and oversights.

In particular, I want to thank the following friends, scholars, and colleagues (in alphabetical order): John Abramson, George Adams, Ramón V. Albareda, Bruce Alderman, A. H. Almaas, Rosemarie Anderson, Masoud Arez, Christopher Bache, Natalia Barahona Noseda, Father Bruno Barnhart, William B. Barnard, Michael Bauwens, Duane R. Bidwell, Nicholas G. Boeving, Andrew F. Burninston, Elias Capriles, Craig Chalquist, William C. Chittick, Christopher Clarke, Brendan Collins, Randy Conner, Andrew Cooper, Paul F. Cunningham, Edward J. Dale, Marylin C. J. Daniels, Michael Daniels, Douglas Duckworth, Sean Esbjörn-Hargens, Roland Faber, Gabriel Fernandez, Charles Flores, Robert K. C. Forman, Anthony Freeman, Paul D. Freinkel, Harris Friedman, Octavio García, Ann L. Gleig, Gerry Goddard, Ellen Goldberg, Stanislav Grof, M. S. Haar Farris, Glenn Hartelius, John Heron, Michael Hollick, Pablo Ianiszewski, Lee Irwin, Karen Jaenke, Don Hanlon Johnson, Stephen Kaplan, Sean Kelly, Michael King, Jürgen Kremer, Jeffrey J. Kripal, Gregg Lahood, Brian L. Lancaster, Beverly Lanzetta, Michael Lerner, Agustín López Tobajas, David Lorimer, David Loy, Sinesio Madrona, Juan Antonio Martinez de la Fe, Robert McDermott, Douglas McDonald, Vicente Merlo, Alfonso Montuori, Michael Murphy, David Nicol, José Antonio Noguera, Jay Ogilvy, Raimon Panikkar, Agustín Pániker, William Parsons, Jordi Piguem, Daryl S. Paulson, Iker Puente,

Kaisa Puhakka, Peter Reason, Kenneth Ring, Oliver Robinson, Marina
T. Romero, Donald Rothberg, John Rowan, Matthew D. Segal, Jacob
H. Sherman, Bahman A. K. Shirazi, Larry Spiro, Olga R. Sohmer,
Joseph Subbiondo, Nahuel Sugobono, Becca Tarnas, Richard Tarnas,
Steve Taylor, Jenny Wade, Harald Walach, Michael Washburn, and Ken
Wilber.

Special gratitude goes to my coauthors of chapter 5, Marina T.
Romero and Ramón V. Albareda, for permission to reproduce their work
in this anthology.

Inspiring dialogues with my students at California Institute of Integral Studies (CIIS) in San Francisco have significantly enriched the
contents of this book. At CIIS, I also learned a great deal from chairing
the doctoral research of Zayin Cabot, Samuel A. Malkemus, and Alex
Rachel, who in their own unique ways are taking participatory thinking
in new and exciting directions.

I would like to particularly thank Anna F. Doherty, whose editorial
magic blessed many of the chapters of this book and makes the English
prose of this Spaniard more elegant and idiomatic. I am also grateful to
my research assistants, Elisabeth Teklinski and Jennifer Spesia, whose
generous and meticulous help with numerous editorial and formatting
tasks allowed me to complete this book at its proper time. Special kudos
go to Elisabeth for her thorough consolidation and revision of the book's
references, as well as the arduous labor of cross-checking the text's cita-
tions against the reference list.

While most of the contents of this book derive from work previously published, all have been thoroughly revised and updated. In
addition to numerous new references, endnotes, and minor changes, all
the chapters include original materials; the book also incorporates an
entire new chapter (chapter 7), an important Postscript clarifying the
evolution of my thinking, and two Appendices respectively discussing
A. H. Almaas's (2014) Diamond Approach and S. Taylor's (2017) soft
perennialism from the perspective of the participatory approach. Redun-
dancies between chapters have been eliminated, except for a few cases
in which the same passage was essential for the argumentative line of
more than one chapter.

Lastly, special thanks to the late Nancy Ellegate, Senior Acquisition Editor of the State University of New York (SUNY) Press, as well
as to her assistant Jessica Kirschner, Senior Production Editor Laurie
Searl, and the SUNY Press creative and administrative team, for their
steadfast support in the publication of this work.

ॐ

Permission to use material from the following publications has been granted:

Chapter 1. Ferrer, J. N. (2011). Participatory spirituality and transpersonal theory: A 10-year retrospective. *The Journal of Transpersonal Psychology*, 43(1), 1–34.

Chapter 2. Ferrer, J. N. (2014). Transpersonal psychology, science, and the supernatural. *The Journal of Transpersonal Psychology*, 46(2), 152–186.

Chapter 3. Ferrer, J. N. (2008). What does it mean to live a fully embodied spiritual life? *International Journal of Transpersonal Studies*, 27, 1–11.

Chapter 4. Ferrer, J. N. (2003). Integral transformative practice: A participatory perspective. *The Journal of Transpersonal Psychology*, 35(1), 21–42.

Chapter 5. Ferrer, J. N., M. T. Romero, and R. V. Albareda. (2005). Integral transformative education: A participatory proposal. *Journal of Transformative Education*, 3(4), 306–330.

Chapter 6. Ferrer, J. N. (2011). Teaching the graduate seminar in comparative mysticism: A participatory integral approach. In W. Parsons (ed.), *Teaching mysticism* (173–192). American Academy of Religion Series. New York, NY: Oxford University Press.

Chapter 8. Ferrer, J. N. (2002). *Revisioning transpersonal theory: A participatory vision of human spirituality*. Albany, NY: State University of New York Press.

Chapter 9. Ferrer, J. N. (2011). Participation, metaphysics, and enlightenment: Reflections on Ken Wilber's recent work. *Transpersonal Psychology Review*, 14(20), 3–24.

Chapter 10. Ferrer, J. N. (2010). The plurality of religions and the spirit of pluralism: A participatory vision of the future of religion. *International Journal of Transpersonal Studies*, 28(1), 139–151.

Ferrer, J. N. (2012). The future of world religion: Four scenarios, one dream. *Tikkun: Culture, Spirituality, Politics*, 27(1), 14–16, 63–64.

Coda. Ferrer, J. N. (2004). A secret poem for you. *International Journal of Transpersonal Studies*, 23, 91–93.

INTRODUCTION

This book largely derives from various articles and book chapters (published 2003–2014) applying participatory thinking to questions central to the fields of transpersonal psychology, integral and contemplative education, contemporary spirituality, and religious studies. Each chapter stands on its own and can be read independently; however, as chapter 1 offers an updated overview of my participatory approach (Ferrer, 2002, 2008; Ferrer & Sherman, 2008a), readers unacquainted with my work or participatory thinking in general may want to begin there. While this book can serve as a perfect introduction to my participatory perspective, I have also designed it to be a resource for those who wish to deepen their understanding of participatory approaches to psychology, education, and religion.

First and foremost, it is important to clarify that nowhere in this book do I claim—or seek—to represent the ideas of the increasing number of authors working under a participatory banner.[1] Although for style reasons I often mention *the* participatory approach, this expression refers exclusively to my own participatory perspective. As with any other, this perspective is shaped not only by inevitable limitations, but also by particular features and values—such as the adoption of an enactive cognitive approach, the rejection of a representational paradigm of cognition, the rejection of naive objectivism and pregiven referents in spiritual discourse, a challenge to neo-Kantianism and associated metaphysical agnosticism, the affirmation of a plurality of spiritual worlds and ultimates, and the recommendation of a pragmatist emancipatory epistemology for transpersonal and religious studies. These values may or may not be endorsed by other participatory thinkers. As Jacob H. Sherman and I wrote in the introduction to *The Participatory Turn* (2008b), a participatory sensibility to spirituality and scholarship can and does manifest in a rich multiplicity of ways.

The first part of the book focuses on transpersonal psychology and theory and consists of four chapters.[2] The opening essay, "Participatory Spirituality and Transpersonal Theory," examines the evolution of the participatory approach in transpersonal studies and related disciplines since the publication of my first book, *Revisioning Transpersonal Theory* (Ferrer, 2002). After an introduction to participatory spirituality (which stresses the embodied, relational, and creative dimensions of spiritual practice), I discuss three ways this approach has been understood in the transpersonal literature: as a disciplinary model, theoretical orientation, and paradigm or paradigmatic epoch. I then review the influence of the participatory turn in transpersonal studies, consciousness studies, integral education, and religious studies. After responding to integral, archetypal, and participatory critiques, I conclude with some reflections about the nature and future of the participatory movement.

Chapter 2, "Transpersonal Psychology, Science, and the Supernatural," is more philosophical in nature. I critically discuss the scientific status of transpersonal psychology and its relation to so-called supernatural claims, focusing in particular on Friedman's (2002, 2013a) proposed division of labor between a "scientific" transpersonal psychology and "non-scientific" transpersonal studies. This chapter demonstrates that despite Friedman's aim to detach transpersonal psychology from any particular metaphysical worldview, turning the field into a modern scientific discipline effectively binds transpersonal psychology to a naturalistic metaphysical worldview that is hostile to most spiritual knowledge claims. After identifying several problems with Friedman's account of science and neo-Kantian skepticism about "supernatural" factors in spiritual events, I introduce the perspective of a participatory metaphysical pluralism and consider the challenge of shared spiritual visions for scientific naturalism. Finally, a participatory research program is outlined that bridges the naturalistic/supernaturalistic split by embracing a more liberal or open naturalism—one that is receptive to both the ontological integrity of spiritual referents and the plausibility of subtle worlds or dimensions of reality. This chapter is personally important for me, as for the first time in my scholarly work I discuss some of my own entheogenic experiences.

Chapter 3, "Toward a Fully Embodied Spiritual Life," identifies *embodiment* as a central feature of participatory approaches to spiritual practice and understanding. I discuss the meaning of embodied spirituality (based on the integration of all human attributes, including the body and sexuality) and contrast it with the disembodied spirituality (based on dissociation or sublimation) that prevails in human religious history. Then I describe what it means to approach the body as a living partner with which to cocreate one's spiritual life, and outline ten features of a fully embodied spirituality. The chapter concludes with some reflections about the past, present, and potential future of embodied spirituality.

Building on the arguments of the previous chapter, chapter 4, "A New Look at Integral Growth," proposes that most psychospiritual practices in the modern West suffer from favoring growth of mind and heart over the physical and instinctive aspects of the human experience, with many negative consequences. I argue that past prescriptions for an Integral Transformative Practice (ITP)—such as those from Murphy (1993) and Wilber (2000a, 2000b; Wilber, Patten, Leonard, & Morelli, 2008)—can easily perpetuate such a mind-centered direction of growth, in that they inherently ask a person's mind to pick from and commit to already constructed practices. I identify the need for an approach that will permit all human dimensions to cocreatively participate in the unfolding of integral growth. As one possible solution, I then present a participatory approach to integral practice based in the novel practice of "interactive embodied meditation," which involves mindful physical contact between practitioners seeking to access the creative potential of all human dimensions. This chapter stresses the relational and creative dimensions of participatory spirituality.

The second part of the book explores the implications of participatory thinking for integral and contemplative education. Chapter 5, "The Four Seasons of Integral Education," coauthored with Marina T. Romero and Ramón V. Albareda, is the more theoretical of the three chapters of this part, and outlines a general participatory educational framework inspired by nature's four seasons. Together, we argue that although a consensus is emerging among holistic educators about the need for educational approaches that incorporate all human dimensions into the learning process, most contemporary attempts at implementing this vision fall back into cognicentrism—they still privilege the use of the mind and its intellectual capabilities. The chapter then introduces a participatory framework to integral transformative learning in which all human dimensions—body, instinct, heart, mind, and consciousness—are invited to cocreatively participate in the unfolding of the educational process. The metaphor of "the four seasons" is used to illustrate this multidimensional approach, as well as to suggest concrete ways in which learners can support the various stages of the integral creative cycle. After identifying three central challenges of integral education—lopsided development, mental pride, and anti-intellectualism—the chapter concludes with some reflections about the importance of reconnecting education with its transformative and spiritual dimensions.

The following two chapters offer different practical illustrations of the participatory pedagogy presented in chapter 5. Chapter 6, "Teaching

Mysticism from a Participatory Perspective," describes a participatory pedagogics that engages multiple epistemic faculties in the teaching of a doctoral seminar in comparative mysticism. After a brief account of the academic context, structure, and content of the seminar, I introduce the seminar's participatory pedagogy, contrasting it with two other approaches to integral education: mind-centered and bricolage. Next, I discuss six pedagogical strategies employed in the course: guided visualization and contemplative inquiry; ritual and somatic grounding; mandala drawing; dialogical inquiry as spiritual practice; meditative reading of texts; and role play and multidimensional presentations. Finally, I argue that this type of pedagogy paves a methodological middle way between engaged participation and critical distance in the teaching and study of mysticism. In conclusion, I stress the integrative thrust of participatory knowing and reflect on the future of participatory approaches in the teaching of religion.

Chapter 7, "Embodied Spiritual Inquiry," introduces a radical second-person approach to contemplative learning and education. In the context of a cooperative research paradigm (Heron, 1996; Heron & Reason, 2001), Embodied Spiritual Inquiry applies the interactive embodied meditation practice introduced in chapter 4 to intersubjectively access different ways of knowing (e.g., bodily, vital, emotional, contemplative) and mindfully investigate collaboratively decided questions. After briefly situating Embodied Spiritual Inquiry in the context of prevalent second-person approaches to contemplative education, this chapter describes the methodology, epistemology, and inquiry structure of "Embodied Spiritual Inquiry" as a graduate course. I also discuss the contextual, transformational, and participatory validity of this inquiry approach, and conclude by addressing the radical nature of Embodied Spiritual Inquiry insofar as its emphasis on (1) intrapersonal epistemic diversity, (2) embodiment and "bodyfulness," (3) deep relationality, and (4) transpersonal morphic resonance.

The last part of the book consists of three chapters applying participatory thinking to central questions in the modern study of spirituality, mysticism, and religious studies. Chapter 8, "Stanislav Grof's Consciousness Research and the Modern Study of Mysticism," focuses on Grof's (1985, 1988a) account of the spiritual insights that occur during special states of consciousness facilitated by psychedelics and holotropic breathwork (i.e., sustained hyperventilation combined with evocative music and bodywork). I demonstrate that Grof's research provides crucial empirical evidence to settle one of the most controversial issues in the modern study of mysticism—the question of mediation in spiritual knowledge. Grof interprets his findings as supporting a neo-Advaitin, esotericist-perspectival version of the perennial philosophy. However, I argue that a more pluralist participatory vision of human spirituality can harmoniously house Grof's experiential data while avoiding certain shortcomings of perennialism. In conclusion, I suggest that a participatory account of Grof's work not only brings forth richer spiritual landscapes, but also has emancipatory potential for spiritual growth and practice.

Chapter 9, "Participation, Metaphysics, and Enlightenment: Reflections on Ken Wilber's Integral Theory," discusses a number of key issues in contemporary spiritual discourse emerging from engagement with the latest theoretical work of the integral philosopher Ken Wilber (2006). The chapter begins with a response to the defense of Wilber's work in the wake of the participatory critique developed in *Revisioning Transpersonal Theory* (Ferrer, 2002), addressing the question of the cultural versus universal nature of Wilber's Kosmic habits (i.e., cocreated ontological realities). I then offer a critique of Wilber's integral postmetaphysics and contrast this approach with participatory spirituality. Finally, I discuss the nature of enlightenment, as well as meditation, integral practice, and spiritual individuation. The chapter concludes with some concrete directions in which to move forward the dialogue between participatory and integral thinking.

The last chapter, "Religious Pluralism and the Future of Religion," first uncovers the subtle spiritual narcissism that has characterized historical approaches to religious diversity. I begin by discussing the merits and shortcomings of the main forms of religious pluralism that have been proposed as its antidote: ecumenical, soteriological, postmodern, and metaphysical. Then, I show how a participatory pluralism allows an appreciation of religious diversity that eschews the dogmatism and competitiveness involved in privileging any particular tradition over the rest, without falling into cultural-linguistic or naturalistic reductionisms. The second part of the chapter explores different scenarios for the future of religion—global religion, mutual transformation, interspiritual wisdom, and spirituality without religion—and proposes that such a future may be shaped by spiritually individuated persons engaged in processes of cosmological hybridization in the context of a common spiritual family. I conclude by suggesting that this approach is capable of reconciling the human longing for spiritual unity, on the one hand, and the developmental and evolutionary gravitation toward spiritual individuation and differentiation, on the other.

A Postscript has been added to discuss several conceptual changes in my thinking since the introduction of the participatory approach. These changes, in particular, are (1) the substitution of the term *indeterminate* for *undetermined* to refer to the mystery or creative force of the cosmos and reality; (2) the adoption of an open naturalism that questions, and potentially bridges, the naturalistic/supernaturalistic gap; and (3) the deconstruction of the transcendence/immanence dichotomy through the postulation of a multiverse or multidimensional cosmos that can house a rich variety of subtle worlds. I have also included a Coda introducing one of my father's poems to evoke some central aspects of participatory spirituality in relation to the world of nature.

The book closes with two appendices. Appendix 1 discusses similarities and differences between participatory spirituality and Almaas's (2014) new turning of the Diamond Approach. Although Almaas's work arguably incorporates some central theses of the participatory approach, I identify ways in which his new Diamond Approach is still constrained by certain perennialist and hierarchical assumptions, as well as by Almaas's overlooking of the enactive or cocreative nature of his own personal spiritual trajectory and realizations. Differences between Almaas's individual soul and the spiritually individuated participatory self are also addressed.

Appendix 2 examines S. Taylor's (2017) recent attempt to reconcile perennialism and participatory spirituality in terms of a *soft perennialism* that proposes strong phenomenological similarities in spiritual awakening processes, a common experiential spiritual landscape, and an immanent spiritual force. After discussing the merits of soft perennialism, I identify three possible shortcomings in S. Taylor's project: (1) intrasubjective reductionism, (2) the reintroduction of hierarchical gradations of spiritual traditions and states, and (3) the danger of reification of an experiential realm and perpetuation of the myth of the given.

Taken together, my hope is that these chapters provide a wide-ranging introduction to participatory spirituality and establish its potential to advance thinking in the fields of transpersonal psychology, integral education, contemporary spirituality, and religious studies.

PART ONE

TRANSPERSONAL PSYCHOLOGY

ONE

PARTICIPATORY SPIRITUALITY AND

TRANSPERSONAL THEORY

My contribution to the participatory turn in transpersonal studies was formalized in 2002, when *Revisioning Transpersonal Theory* (*Revisioning* hereafter) was published shortly after R. Tarnas's (2001) preview of the book.[1] The book had two general goals: (1) to critically examine some central ontological and epistemological assumptions of transpersonal studies, and (2) to introduce a participatory alternative to the neo-perennialism dominating the field thus far. At that time, R. Tarnas (1991) had already laid the foundations of a spiritually informed participatory epistemology, Kremer (1994) had developed a participatory approach to Indigenous spirituality, and Heron (1992, 1996, 1998) had introduced a participatory inquiry method as a relational form of spiritual practice and articulated a participatory ontology and epistemology. Nonetheless, the prevalent transpersonal models conceptualized spirituality in terms of replicable inner experiences amenable to be assessed or ranked according to purportedly universal developmental or ontological schemes.

Revisioning reframed transpersonal phenomena as pluralistic participatory events that can occur in multiple loci (e.g., an individual, a relationship, or a collective) and whose epistemic value emerges—not from any preestablished hierarchy of spiritual insights—but from the events' emancipatory and transformative power on self, community, and world. On a scholarly level, I sought to bridge transpersonal discourse with relevant developments in religious studies (e.g., in comparative mysticism or the interreligious dialogue), as well as with a number of modern trends in the philosophy of mind and the cognitive sciences, such as Sellars's (1963) critique of a pregiven world entirely independent from human cognition and Varela, Thompson, and Rosch's (1991) enactive paradigm of cognition.[2]

In the wake of increasing interest from other scholars in the participatory perspective, I subsequently explored the implications of the participatory turn for such areas as transpersonal science and research programs (see chapter 2), embodied spirituality (see chapter 3), integral transformative practice (see chapter 4), integral education (see chapters 5 and 6), contemplative education and spiritual inquiry (see chapter 7), consciousness research and integral theory (see chapters 8 and 9), religious pluralism and the future of religion (see chapter 10), and contemporary religious studies (Ferrer & Sherman, 2008a), among others. Most of these developments are included in this book.

More than fifteen years after the publication of *Revisioning*, the main aim of this chapter is to assess the current status and ongoing impact of the participatory turn in transpersonal studies.[3] Although ample reference is made to the work of many other participatory thinkers, the analysis focuses on the impact of my work. After an outline of the participatory approach to transpersonal and spiritual phenomena, I identify three ways it has been received in transpersonal scholarship: as disciplinary model, theoretical orientation, and paradigmatic epoch. Then I examine the influence of the participatory turn in transpersonal and related disciplines, respond to several criticisms of my work, and conclude by reflecting on the nature and future of the participatory movement. My hope is that this chapter provides not only an introduction to participatory transpersonalism, but also a collection of scholarly resources for those interested in exploring or pursuing a participatory orientation in transpersonal scholarship.

AN OUTLINE OF PARTICIPATORY SPIRITUALITY

Developed over time (e.g., Ferrer, 1998a, 1998b, 2000a, 2000b, 2001), published as a book (Ferrer, 2002), and expanded in an anthology (Ferrer, 2008; Ferrer & Sherman, 2008a), the participatory approach holds that human spirituality essentially emerges from human cocreative participation in an undetermined mystery or generative power of life, the cosmos, or reality. More specifically, I argue that spiritual participatory events can engage the entire range of human epistemic faculties (e.g., rational, imaginal, somatic, vital, aesthetic) with both the creative unfolding of the mystery and the possible agency of subtle entities or energies in the enactment—or "bringing forth"—of ontologically rich religious worlds.

In other words, the participatory approach presents an enactive[4] under-standing of the sacred that conceives spiritual phenomena, experiences, and insights as *cocreated events*. By locating the emergence of spiritual knowing at the interface of human multidimensional cognition, cultural context, subtle worlds, and the deep generativity of life or the cosmos, this account avoids both the secular post/modernist reduction of reli-gion to cultural-linguistic artifact and, as discussed below, the religionist dogmatic privileging of a single tradition as superior or paradigmatic.

The rest of this section introduces eight distinctive features of the participatory approach—spiritual cocreation, creative spirituality, spiri-tual individuation, participatory pluralism, relaxed spiritual universalism, participatory epistemology, the integral *bodhisattva* vow, and participatory spiritual practice—which other chapters in this book discuss in greater detail.

Dimensions of Spiritual Cocreation

Spiritual cocreation has three interrelated dimensions—intrapersonal, interpersonal, and transpersonal.[5] These dimensions respectively estab-lish participatory spirituality as embodied (spirit within), relational (spirit in-between), and enactive (spirit beyond), discussed below (see Table 1.1, page 12).

Intrapersonal cocreation consists of the collaborative participation of all human attributes—body, vital energy, heart, mind, and conscious-ness—in the enactment of spiritual phenomena. This dimension is grounded in the *equiprimacy principle*, according to which no human attri-bute is intrinsically superior or more evolved than any other. As Romero and Albareda (2001) pointed out, the cognicentric (i.e., mind-centered) character of Western culture hinders the maturation of nonmental attri-butes, making it normally necessary to engage in intentional practices to bring these attributes up to the same developmental level the mind achieves through mainstream education (see chapters 4 and 5). In prin-ciple, however, all human attributes can participate as equal partners in the creative unfolding of the spiritual path, are equally capable of sharing freely in the life of the mystery here on Earth, and can also be equally alienated from it. The main challenges to intrapersonal cocreation are cognicentrism, lopsided development, mental pride, and disembodied attitudes to spiritual growth. Possible antidotes to those challenges are the integral *bodhisattva* vow (see below and chapter 3), integral practices (see chapter 4), the cultivation of mental humility (see chapter 5), and

Table 1. A Map of Participatory Spirituality

	Principles	Challenges	Antidotes	Tests	Regulative Goals	Direction
Transpersonal Cocreation	Equiplurality	Disempowerment Indoctrination Spiritual Narcissism Spiritual Materialism **Objectivist Spiritualities**	Inner Spiritual Authority Right to Inquire Heretical Courage **Creative Spiritualities**	Egocentrism Test	Openness to SPIRIT BEYOND	Enlightenment →
Interpersonal Cocreation	Equipotentiality	Spiritual Pride Spiritual Inflation Isolation Elitist Exclusivism **Hierarchical Spiritualities**	Spiritual Humility Deep Dialogue Cooperative Spiritual Inquiry **Relational Spiritualities**	Eco-Socio Political Test	Collaborative Communion with SPIRIT IN-BETWEEN	Engagement ↑
Intrapersonal Cocreation	Equiprimacy	Lopsided Development Spiritual Bypassing Dissociation Cognicentrism Mental Pride **Disembodied Spiritualities**	Integral Practices Mental Humility Integral Bodhisattva Vow **Embodied Spiritualities**	Dissociation Test	Groundedness in SPIRIT WITHIN	Enlivenment ←

embodied approaches to spiritual growth (see chapters 3 and 7). Intrapersonal cocreation affirms the importance of being rooted in *spirit within* (i.e., the immanent dimension of the mystery) and renders participatory spirituality essentially *embodied* (cf. Heron, 2006, 2007; Lanzetta, 2008; Washburn, 2003a).

Interpersonal cocreation emerges from cooperative relationships among human beings growing as peers in the spirit of solidarity, mutual respect, and constructive confrontation (see chapter 4; Heron, 1998, 2006). It is grounded in the *equipotentiality principle*, according to which "we are all teachers and students" insofar as we are superior and inferior to others in different regards (Bauwens, 2007; Ferrer, Albareda, & Romero, 2004). This principle does not entail that there is no value in working with spiritual teachers or mentors; it simply means that human beings cannot be ranked in their totality or according to a single developmental criterion, such as brainpower, emotional intelligence, or contemplative realization. Although peer-to-peer human relationships are vital for spiritual growth, interpersonal cocreation can include contact with perceived nonhuman intelligences, such as subtle entities, natural powers, or archetypal forces that might be embedded in psyche, nature, or the cosmos (e.g., Heron, 1998, 2006; Jung, 2009; Rachel, 2013; R. Tarnas, 2006). The main challenges to interpersonal cocreation are spiritual pride, psychospiritual inflation, circumstantial or self-imposed isolation, and adherence to rigidly hierarchical spiritualities. Antidotes to those challenges include collaborative spiritual practice and inquiry (see chapters 4 and 7), intellectual and spiritual humility (see chapter 5), deep dialogue (see chapter 6), and relational and pluralistic approaches to spiritual growth (see chapters 4 and 10). Interpersonal cocreation affirms the importance of communion with *spirit in-between* (i.e., the situational dimension of the mystery) and makes participatory spirituality intrinsically *relational* (cf. Heron, 1998, 2006; Heron & Lahood, 2008; Lahood, 2010a, 2010b).

Transpersonal cocreation refers to dynamic interaction between embodied human beings and the mystery in the bringing forth of spiritual insights, practices, states, and worlds (Ferrer, 2002, 2008). This dimension is grounded in the *equiplurality principle*,[6] according to which there can *potentially* be multiple spiritual enactions that are nonetheless equally holistic and emancipatory.[7] For example, a fully embodied liberation could be equally achieved through Christian incarnation (Barnhart, 2008) or Yogic integration of *purusa* (consciousness) and *prakriti* (nature) (Whicher, 1998); likewise, freedom from self-centeredness at the service of others can be attained through the cultivation of Mahayana Buddhist *karuna* (compassion) or Christian *agape* (selfless love) in the context of radically different ontologies (Jennings, 1996). This principle frees participatory spirituality from allegiance to any single spiritual system and paves the way for a genuine, ontologically and pragmatically grounded, spiritual pluralism. The main challenges to transpersonal cocreation are spiritual disempowerment, indoctrination, spiritual narcissism, and adherence to naive objectivist or universalist spiritualities. Antidotes include the development of one's inner spiritual authority and the affirmation of the right to inquire (Heron, 1998, 2006), heretical courage (Cupitt, 1998; Sells, 1994), and enactive and creative spiritualities (Ferrer, 2002; Ferrer & Sherman, 2008b). Transpersonal cocreation affirms the importance of being open to *spirit beyond* (i.e., the subtle dimensions of the mystery) and makes participatory spirituality fundamentally inquiry-driven (Heron, 1998, 2001, 2006) and *enactive* (Ferrer, 2000b, 2002, 2008; Ferrer & Sherman, 2008a).

Although all three dimensions interact in multifaceted ways in the enactment of spiritual events, the creative link between intrapersonal and transpersonal cocreation deserves special mention. Whereas the mind and consciousness arguably serve as a natural bridge to subtle spiritual forms already enacted in history that display more fixed forms and dynamics (e.g., cosmological motifs, archetypal configurations, mystical visions and states), attention to the body and its vital energies may grant greater access to the more generative immanent power of life or the mystery (Ferrer, 2002; Ferrer & Sherman, 2008a). From this approach, it follows, the greater the participation of embodied dimensions in religious inquiry, the more creative one's spiritual life may become and a larger number of creative spiritual developments may emerge.

A Creative Spirituality

In the infancy of participatory spirituality in the 1990s, spiritual inquiry operated within certain constraints arguably inherited from traditional religion. As Eliade (1959/1989) argued, many established religious practices and rituals are "re-enactive" in their attempt to replicate cosmogonic actions and events. Expanding this account, I have suggested that most religious traditions can be seen as "reproductive" insofar as their practices aim to not only ritually reenact mythical motives, but also replicate the enlightenment of their founder or attain the state of salvation or freedom described in allegedly revealed scriptures (see chapter 3).

Although disagreements about the exact nature of such states and the most effective methods to attain them abound in the historical develop-ment of religious ideas and practices—naturally leading to rich creative developments within the traditions—spiritual inquiry was regulated (and arguably constrained) by such pregiven unequivocal goals.

Participatory enaction entails a model of spiritual engagement that does not simply reproduce certain tropes according to a given historical a priori, but rather embarks upon the adventure of openness to the novelty and creativity of nature or the mystery (Ferrer, 2002; Ferrer & Sherman, 2008a; Heron, 2001, 2006). Grounded on current moral intuitions and cognitive competences, for instance, participatory spiritual inquiry can not only undertake the critical revision and actualization of prior reli-gious forms, but also the cocreation of novel spiritual understandings, practices, and even expanded states of freedom (see chapters 3 and 9).

Spiritual Individuation

This emphasis in creativity is central to *spiritual individuation*, that is, the process through which a person gradually develops and embodies her unique spiritual identity and wholeness. Religious traditions tend to promote the homogenization of central features of the inner and outer lives of their practitioners, for example, encouraging them to seek the same spiritual states and liberation, to become like Christ or the Bud-dha, or to wear the same clothes (in the case of monks). These aspira-tions may have been historically legitimate, but after the emergence of the modern self (C. Taylor, 1989), our current predicament (at least in the West) arguably calls for an integration of spiritual maturation and psychological individuation that will likely lead to a richer diversity of spiritual expressions (see chapters 9 and 10). In other words, the partici-patory approach aims at the emergence of a human community formed by spiritually differentiated individuals.

It is important to sharply distinguish between the modern hyper-individualistic mental ego and the participatory selfhood forged in the sacred fire of spiritual individuation. Whereas the disembodied modern self is plagued by alienation, dissociation, and narcissism, a spiritually individuated person has an embodied, integrated, connected, and perme-able identity whose high degree of differentiation, far from being isolat-ing, actually allows him or her to enter into a deeply conscious com-munion with others, nature, and the multidimensional cosmos. A key difference between modern individualism and spiritual individuation is thus the integration of radical relatedness in the later. Similarly, Almaas (1988, 1996) distinguished between the narcissistic ego of modern individualism and an essential personhood or individual soul that integrates autonomy and relatedness; for a discussion of the differences between Almaas's individual soul and the spiritually individuated participatory self, see Appendix 1.

Participatory Pluralism

The participatory approach embraces a pluralistic vision of spirituality that accepts the formative role of contextual and linguistic factors in religious phenomena, while simultaneously recognizing the importance of nonlinguistic variables (e.g., somatic, imaginal, energetic, subtle, archetypal) in shaping religious experiences and meanings, and affirming the ontological value and creative impact of spiritual worlds.

Participatory pluralism allows the conception of a multiplicity of not only spiritual paths, but also spiritual liberations, worlds, and even ultimates. On the one hand, besides affirming the historical existence of multiple spiritual goals or "salvations" (Ferrer, 2002; Heim, 1995), the increased embodied openness to immanent spiritual life and the spirit-in-between fostered by the participatory approach may naturally engender a number of novel holistic spiritual realizations that cannot be reduced to traditional states of enlightenment or liberation. If human beings were regarded as *unique* embodiments of the mystery, would it not be plausible to consider that as they spiritually individuate, their spiritual realizations might also be distinct even if potentially overlapping and aligned with each other?

On the other hand, participatory pluralism proposes that different spiritual ultimates can be enacted through intentional or spontaneous participation in an undetermined mystery, spiritual power, or generative force of life or reality. Whereas I take these enactions to be ultimate in their respective spiritual universes, this consideration in no way relativizes the various traditions' ultimates—nor does it posit a supra-ultimate spiritual referent beyond them. In contrast, I hold that participatory enaction allows one to not only move away from representational and objectivist accounts of spiritual cognition, but also avoid the problematic *dualism of the mystery and its enactions*.[8] Hence, the participatory perspective does not contend that there are two, three, or any limited quantity of pregiven spiritual ultimates, but rather that the radical openness, interrelatedness, and creativity of the mystery or the cosmos allows for the participatory cocreation of an indefinite number of ultimate self-disclosures of reality and corresponding religious worlds.[9] Participatory approaches, that is, seek to enact with body, mind, heart, and consciousness a creative spirituality that lets a thousand spiritual flowers bloom.

A More Relaxed Spiritual Universalism

The pluralistic spirit of the participatory approach should not eclipse its "more relaxed" spiritual universalism—although eschewing dubious equations among spiritual ultimates (e.g., the Tao is God or Buddhist emptiness is structurally equivalent to the Hindu Brahman), the participatory approach affirms an underlying undetermined mystery or creative spiritual power as the generative source of all spiritual enactions (Ferrer, 2002, 2008). This shared spiritual dynamism should be distinguished from any Kantian-like noumenon or "thing-in-itself" endowed with inscrutable qualities and from which all spiritual ultimates are always incomplete, culturally conditioned, or cognitively constrained phenomenal manifestations (e.g., Hick, 1989). In contrast, the enactive epistemology of the participatory approach does away with the Kantian two-worlds dualism by refusing to conceive of the mystery as having objectifiable pregiven attributes (such as personal, impersonal, dual, or nondual) and by affirming the radical identity of the manifold spiritual ultimates and the mystery, even if the former do not exhaust the ontological possibilities of the latter. Put simply, the mystery cocreatively unfolds in multiple ontological directions (see chapter 9 and Postscript).

Moreover, the relationship between pluralism and universalism cannot be consistently characterized in a hierarchical fashion, because while there are "lower" and "higher" forms of both universalism and pluralism (e.g., more or less rigid, sophisticated, encompassing, explanatory), "*the dialectic between universalism and pluralism, between the One and the Many, displays what it may well be the deepest dynamics of the self-disclosing of the mystery*" (Ferrer, 2002, p. 191). In a similar vein, Puhakka (2008) offered some important reflections on the dialectic between "unity vs. diversity" (p. 8) in the context of the historical evolution of transpersonal discourse, with which I fully concur.

Participatory Epistemology and Critical Theory

It cannot be stressed strongly enough that participatory pluralism does not entail the uncritical or relativistic endorsement of past or present religious understandings or forms of life. Put differently, the participatory rejection of an objectifiable pregiven spiritual ultimate referent does not prevent qualitative distinctions in spiritual matters. To be sure, like beautiful porcelains made out of amorphous clay, traditions cannot be qualitatively ranked according to their accuracy in representing some imagined (accessible or inaccessible) original template. However, this account does not mean discernment cannot be cultivated regarding more (or less) evocative, skillful, or sophisticated artifacts.

In addition, whereas the participatory turn renders meaningless the postulation of qualitative distinctions among traditions according to a priori doctrines or a prearranged hierarchy of spiritual insights, these comparative grounds can be sought in a variety of practical fruits (e.g., existential, cognitive, emotional, interpersonal). Specifically, I have suggested two basic guidelines: the *egocentrism test*, which assesses the extent to which spiritual traditions, teachings, and practices free practitioners from gross and subtle forms of narcissism and self-centeredness; and the *dissociation test*, which evaluates the extent to which the same foster the integrated blossoming of all dimensions of the person (Ferrer, 2002, 2008; see also chapters 9 and 10). Given the many abuses and oppressions perpetuated in the name of religion, it may be sensible to add an *eco-socio-political test*, which assesses the extent to which spiritual systems foster ecological balance, social and economic justice, religious and political freedom, class and gender equality, and other fundamental human rights (cf. Heron, 2006).[10]

Two important qualifications must be made regarding these guidelines: First, some spiritual paths and liberations may be more adequate for different psychological and cultural dispositions (as well as for the same individual at distinct developmental junctures), but this does not make them universally superior or inferior. The well-known four yogas of Hinduism (reflection, devotion, action, and experimentation) come quickly to mind in this regard, as do other spiritual typologies that can be found in other traditions (Beena, 1990; H. Smith, 1994). Second, the participatory emphasis on overcoming narcissism and self-centeredness, although arguably central to most spiritual traditions, may not be shared by all. Even more poignantly, most religious traditions would likely not rank too highly in terms of the dissociation or the eco-socio-political tests; for example, gross or subtle forms of repression, control, or strict regulation of the human body and its vital/sexual energies (vs. the promotion of their autonomous maturation, integration, and participation in spiritual knowing) are rather the norm in most past and present contemplative endeavors (see chapter 3). Likewise, many religions have had a demonstrably negative environmental impact (e.g., L. E. Nelson, 1998a); supported violence, militarism, and authoritarian regimes (Juergensmeyer, 2000; Victoria, 2006); and brought about serious violations of human rights (Ghanea-Hercock, 2010) even though they have also provided vital resources to secure them (Banchoff & Wuthnow, 2011). Thus, the integrative and socially engaged thrust of the participatory turn is foundational for the development of a participatory critical theory of religion.

More positively, these tests normatively point toward the universal ideal of a *socially responsible integrated selflessness*, which (although the attainability of a fully integrated selflessness is open to question) can act as a regulative principle à la Habermas's (1984) "ideal speech situation." The idea of integrated selflessness is thus capable of providing procedural criteria for critical discernment in spiritual matters, that is, concerning how qualitative distinctions in spiritual discourse might be made. From this evaluative principle, applicable standards, rules, or tests to assess spiritual choices and practices can be derived. In addition to self- and peer-assessment (e.g., Heron, 1996, 1998), one might consider the use of standardized tests such as the Narcissistic Personality Inventory or NPI (Raskin & Terry, 1988). In addition, the thoughtful combination of other tests may indicate the degree of psychosomatic integration of spiritual states, for example measures of transcendence (e.g., Akyalcin, Greenway, & Milne, 2008; Friedman, 1983) used with measures of body intelligence and awareness (e.g., Anderson, 2006).

To sum up, the emancipatory epistemology of the participatory approach assesses spiritual paths according to the degree to which they foster both an overcoming of self-centeredness and a fully embodied integration. These two attributes make individuals not only more sensitive to the needs of others, nature, and the world, but also more effective cultural and planetary transformative agents in whatever contexts and measure life or the mystery calls them to be.

Integral Bodhisattvas

Since the conscious mind is the seat of most individuals' sense of identity, an exclusive liberation of consciousness can be deceptive insofar as one can believe that one is fully free when, in fact, essential dimensions of the self are underdeveloped, alienated, or in bondage—as the dysfunctional sexual behavior of numerous modern spiritual teachers attest (e.g., Butler, 1990; Edelstein, 2011; Kripal, 2002). As discussed

above, participatory spirituality seeks to foster the harmonious engagement of all human attributes in the spiritual path without tensions or
dissociations. Despite his downplaying the spiritual import of sexuality
and the vital world, Sri Aurobindo (2001) was correct when he wrote
that the liberation of consciousness cannot be equated to an integral
transformation entailing the spiritual alignment of all human dimensions (pp. 942ff).

With this in mind, I have proposed an integral *bodhisattva* vow in
which the conscious mind renounces its own full liberation until the
body, the heart, and the primary world can be free as well from alienating
tendencies that prevent them from sharing freely in the unfolding life
of the mystery here on Earth (Ferrer, 2006, 2007). Needless to say, to
embrace an integral *bodhisattva* vow is not a return to the individualistic
spiritual aspirations of early Buddhism because it entails a commitment
to the *integral* liberation of all sentient beings, rather than only of their
conscious minds or conventional sense of identity. Likewise, as the above
description reflects, my use of the term *bodhisattva* does not suggest a
commitment to early Buddhist accounts of liberation as extinction of
bodily senses and desires and release from the cycle of transmigratory
experience (*samsara*; S. Collins, 1998; P. Harvey, 1995; see also chapters
3 and 9).

Participatory Spiritual Practice

In addition to many classical spiritual skills and values (e.g., mindfulness, compassion, unconditional love), participatory spiritual practice
cultivates the embodied, relational, and enactive (i.e., creative, inquiry-driven, and world-constituting) dimensions of spiritual cocreation.
This emphasis can be found in some traditional practices, many contemporary revisions of traditional practices, and a number of innovative
spiritual developments. Examples include the following. Whereas some
traditional practices (e.g., kabbalistic, contemplative, Indigenous, esoteric) are participatory in many regards (see Ferrer & Sherman, 2008b;
Lahood, 2007a), in their modern (re-)articulations one can find more
explicit and robust affirmations of participatory values. In this context
I locate, for example, Ray's (2008) embodied reconstruction of Buddhist meditation and Rothberg's (2006, 2008) relational expansion of
Buddhist practice, contemporary postural yoga (Horton, 2012; Singleton, 2010) and Whicher's (1998) integrative account of Patanjali's yoga,
modern Eastern and Western approaches to Tantra (Urban, 2003), and

Schroeder's (1995) and Vennard's (1998) engagements of the body and sexuality in Christian prayer, among many others.

In addition, the last few decades have witnessed the emergence of a variety of novel participatory spiritual practices, such as Albareda and Romero's interactive embodied meditations (see chapter 4), Heron's (1998, 2006) cooperative spiritual inquiry, and my own Embodied Spiritual Inquiry (see chapter 7; Osterhold, Husserl, & Nicol, 2007), which was also proposed as an effective method to foster the integration of spiritual experience (Bailey & Arthur, 2011). Other bodies of practice with important participatory elements include Grof's Holotropic Breathwork (S. Grof & C. Grof, 2010), Almaas's (2002, 2014) Diamond Approach, feminist and women spirituality approaches (e.g., Eller, 1993; T. King, 1992), modern forms of entheogenic spiritual inquiry (e.g., Bache, 2000; Ball, 2008), Sri Aurobindo's integral yoga (Mukherjee, 2003), some contemporary somatic approaches (e.g., D. Johnson, 1995), relational approaches to spirituality (e.g., Achterberg & Rothberg, 1998; Bauwens, 2007; Lahood, 2010a; Welwood, 2000), and modern engagements of sexuality as spiritual path (e.g., Bonheim, 1997; Wade, 2004), among others. With this outline of participatory spirituality established, the discussion now turns to understandings of the participatory approach in the field of transpersonal studies.

THE PARTICIPATORY APPROACH: MODEL, ORIENTATION, PARADIGM, OR EPOCH?

To date, transpersonal scholars have understood the participatory approach in three main ways: as a disciplinary model, theoretical orientation or perspective, and paradigm or paradigmatic epoch. This section briefly examines each case.

Disciplinary Model

The participatory approach is considered a theoretical model within the discipline of transpersonal psychology. In *Shadow, Self, Spirit*, for example, M. Daniels (2005) included the participatory approach as one of the chief theories or models in the field, together with Maslow's metamotivational theory, Jung's analytical psychology, Assagioli's psychosynthesis, Grof's holotropic model, Sri Aurobindo's integral psychology, Wilber's structural-hierarchical model, Washburn's spiral-dynamic model, and Wright's feminist theory. After discussing some major differences among these models (e.g., on immanence, transcendence, or the self), M. Daniels aligned his own perspective with Sri Aurobindo's and the spiral-dynamic and participatory models, highlighting their convergence in the affirmation of an embodied, integrative spirituality. Other scholars who have referred to the participatory approach as transpersonal or spiritual model include Almendro (2004), M. King (2009), Péter (2009), and Friedman, Krippner, Riebel, and Johnson (2010).

Theoretical Orientation

In addition, the participatory approach is understood as a larger theoretical orientation or perspective transcending the disciplinary boundaries of psychology and operating in a variety of transpersonal disciplines (Walsh & Vaughan, 1993), a multidisciplinary transpersonal orientation (Boucouvalas, 1999), or even beyond the boundaries of transpersonal studies (e.g., Ferrer & Sherman, 2008b; Lahood, 2007a). In this spirit, Washburn (2003b) described three major transpersonal theoretical orientations—structural-hierarchical (Wilber), spiral-dynamic (Washburn), and participatory (Ferrer)—noting that the participatory orientation challenges the other two in their claims to exclusive or complete spiritual truth.[11] Washburn also discussed feminist and ecological approaches, but suggested that they are perspectives "defined more in terms of a particular focus of inquiry (women spirituality, the sacredness of nature) than in terms of a theoretical orientation that would guide inquiry" (p. 3). As perspectives, feminism and ecology can be equally applied by advocates of the structural, dynamic, and participatory orientations.

Similarly, Goddard (2005, 2009) identified three major theoretical orientations in the field: neo-perennialist (Wilber), neo-Jungian (Washburn), and pluralistic-participatory (R. Tarnas, Ferrer), which neatly correspond to Washburn's categorization. In contrast to Washburn (2003b), however, Goddard included feminist, ecological, and shamanic perspectives within the participatory orientation. Goddard's work seeks to reconcile the differences among these orientations through the development of an archetypal integrative model, to which I return below. Finally, Cunningham (2011a) described the participatory approach as a transpersonal theoretical orientation located in-between the perennial philosophy at one end of the continuum and empirical scientific approaches based upon mechanist, materialistic, and reductionist assumptions at the other end.

Paradigm or Paradigmatic Epoch

The participatory turn has also been understood as a paradigm or para-digmatic epoch. *Revisioning* introduced the participatory approach as a "participatory turn" in transpersonal and spiritual studies—a paradigmat-ic shift breaking with transpersonal theory's prevalent epistemological strategies (inner empiricism) and ontological assumptions (perennial-ism). In the foreword to *Revisioning*, R. Tarnas (2002) offered a powerful paradigmatic account of the participatory approach, framing it as the second conceptual stage of the paradigm shift initiated by Maslow's and Grof's launching of the discipline of transpersonal psychology. In this regard, R. Tarnas wrote:

> If the founding works of transpersonal psychology by Maslow and Grof constituted its declaration of independence, then this book may well be seen as its emancipation proclamation, its "new birth of freedom." For here transpersonal theory is liberated from that mortgage to the past, those constraining assumptions and principles inherited from its Enlightenment and modern scientific origins. (p. xv)

Other authors who have written about the participatory turn as a con-ceptual revolution include Kripal (2003), Jaenke (2004), and C. Clarke (2009).

Building on R. Tarnas's (2002) proposal, the transpersonal anthro-pologist Lahood (2007a) described two turns in transpersonal scholar-ship. The first began with the birth of transpersonal psychology in the late 1960s and can be defined as "an attempt to integrate psychologies East and West; an attempt to map the farthest shores of conscious-ness . . . ; and the merging of pragmatic science and spiritual concerns" (2). Lahood characterized this turn with a commitment to religious uni-versalism (or perennialism) and included the work of Maslow, Grof, and Wilber as representative. The second turn is the participatory one (as exemplified by Lahood in the works of R. Tarnas, Heron, and Ferrer), which represents a departure from transpersonal psychology's allegiance to perennialism and emphasizes the embodied, relational, and pluralistic dimensions of transpersonal events. In this regard, Hartelius, Harrahy, Crouch, Thouin, and Stamp (forthcoming) situated the participatory perspective within a wider second-wave transpersonalism that stresses the embodied, embedded, diverse, and transformative aspects of transpersonal psychology.

In a subsequent essay, Lahood (2008) extended this account into three paradigmatic epochs of transpersonalism. Epoch one is the *pre-transpersonal movement* or "psychedelic revolution" of the 1960s and 1970s, leading to the hybridization of Eastern spirituality and entheogenic states and culminating with Maslow's and Grof's formalization of the movement. Epoch two, the *neo-perennial era*, goes from 1977 to the mid-1990s and is dominated by Wilber's work, which seeks to integrate Western and Eastern philosophy, psychology, and religion into an evolutionary framework structured according to a supposedly universal teleological process whose ultimate aim is an integral nondual realization. Epoch three, the *participatory turn*, begins in the early 1990s with R. Tarnas's (1991) analysis of Grof's consciousness research and is formalized in the writings of Heron (1992, 1998, 2006) and Ferrer (2002), both of whom Lahood named as articulating cogent alternatives to transpersonal neo-perennialism.

Similarly, Dale (2014) situated the "pluralistic-participatory movement" (p. 108) as the prevalent growing force (*agglomeration*, in his term) in transpersonal scholarship in the twenty-first century, after Wilber's hierarchical neo-perennialism and the East-West synthesis of the 1960s and 1970s that spawned the birth of transpersonal psychology. According to Dale, only the pluralistic-participatory movement correlates with the nonlinear paradigm in contemporary science (i.e., moving beyond mainstream psychology's linear statistical averaging), which provides the best explanation of transpersonal inquiry and development. Although participatory pluralism "is yet to arrive at its period of greatest influence" (p. 116), Dale stated, "a chronological ascendancy in period of dominance is also a striking characteristic of the agglomerations identified" (p. 116).[12]

In addition, Dale (2014) distinguished between empirical-positivist and participatory/non-Cartesian research approaches in transpersonal psychology. According to Dale, *empirical positivism* derives from analytical philosophy and is linked to the empirical work of Transcendental Meditation (TM) researchers (e.g., Alexander, Heaton, & Chandler, 1994) and Wilber's (2000c, 2006) integral approach, while *participatory non-Cartesianism* stems from continental philosophy and is associated with the work of Heron (1992, 2006), R. Tarnas (1991), Ferrer (2002), and Hartelius (Hartelius, 2006; Hartelius & Ferrer, 2013), among others. In an important paper, Cunningham (2015) elaborated further on these two transpersonal epistemic cultures.

Whereas it may be valid to conceive the participatory approach as disciplinary model, theoretical orientation, research approach, or even conceptual revolution (or paradigm), my sense is that epochal claims may have been premature. It is one thing to argue that the participatory approach is an increasingly prevailing perspective or that it represents a conceptual revolution with regard to prior transpersonal theorizing—it is quite another to claim that it inaugurated a new paradigmatic era in transpersonal thinking. Before entertaining this possibility seriously, a thorough analysis of the actual impact of participatory thought on transpersonal scholarship seems necessary. The next section begins to explore the scope of such an influence.

THE IMPACT OF THE PARTICIPATORY TURN

Participatory perspectives in philosophy, religion, and the human sciences predate the publication of *Revisioning* and any possible influence of my work should be seen in this larger context.[13] Before reviewing the impact of the participatory approach, it is helpful to note the relationship of mutual inclusivity between transpersonal theory and the participatory turn. On the one hand, as discussed above, the participatory approach can be seen as a theoretical model, orientation, or paradigm within the field of transpersonal studies. On the other hand, transpersonal studies is only one among other scholarly disciplines—such as anthropology (Lahood, 2007c), Indigenous studies (Bastien & Kremer, 2004; Marks, 2007), or comparative mysticism (Ferrer & Sherman, 2008b; Freeman, 2007)—impacted by the participatory turn. That said, this section follows the footprints of the participatory perspective in four bodies of knowledge: transpersonal studies, consciousness studies, integral and holistic education, and religious studies.[14]

Transpersonal and Integral Studies

In recent years an increasing number of transpersonal and integral scholars have aligned their works in varying degrees with different aspects of the participatory approach. I locate here, in chronological order, the works of Heron (1998, 2001, 2006), R. Tarnas (2001, 2006), Jaenke (2004), Paulson (2004), M. Daniels (2005), O'Connor (2005), Hollick (2006), Hartelius (2006, 2015a, 2015b, 2016; Hartelius & Ferrer, 2013), Bauwens (2007), Kremer (2007), Lahood (2007b, 2007c), Irwin (2008),

Kelly (2008), Lancaster (2008), Rothberg (2008), Sherman (2008; Ferrer & Sherman, 2008a), Alderman (2011, 2012a, 2012b), Rachel (2013), Segall (2013), R. S. Brown (2013), Brooks, Ford, & Huffman (2013), Cabot (2014, 2015), Dale (2014), and Cunningham (2015), and S. Taylor (2017), among others.[15]

In general, *Revisioning* is often credited with freeing transpersonal thinking from the constraints of Wilber's neo-perennialism and associated hierarchical rankings of spiritual traditions, states, and orientations (e.g., Jaenke, 2004; Lahood, 2007b; Lancaster, 2004; R. Tarnas, 2001), as well as for articulating a more embodied, relational, and pluralistic approach to spiritual growth and understanding (e.g., Dale, 2014; M. Daniels, 2005, 2009; Heron, 2006; Lahood, 2008). As Lahood (2007a) pointed out, many scholars in the field adapted the participatory use of the language of events (vs. experiences) to refer to transpersonal phenomena (e.g., Irwin, 2008; Kremer, 2007; G. Palmer & Hastings, 2013; Wade, 2004). Likewise, the participatory approach to spiritual diversity and pragmatic emancipatory epistemology are endorsed in many transpersonal works (e.g., Alderman, 2011, 2012a, 2012b; Dale, 2014; Friedman et al., 2010; Hollick, 2006; Lancaster, 2004).

This spread of participatory thinking has begun to affect Wilber's writing and that of his colleagues and critics alike. Despite Wilber's (2002) early dismissal of *Revisioning* as expressing "a green-meme approach to spirituality" (see below), his most recent work Wilber (2006) incorporated a number of participatory insights and constructions. As M. Daniels (in Rowan, Daniels, Fontana, & Walley, 2009) indicated, for example, the cocreated nature of the spiritual path, the language of participation, and the use of the myth of the given in spiritual critical discourse are central features of the participatory approach introduced in my early work (e.g., Ferrer, 2000a, 2000b, 2001, 2002). Although Wilber has assimilated aspects of the participatory approach into his integral theory, from a participatory perspective many problems remain (see chapter 9; Hartelius, 2015a, 2015b; Hartelius & Ferrer, 2013). Furthermore, in a series of important essays, Alderman (2011, 2012a, 2012b) offered the most successful attempt yet to reconcile Wilberian and participatory perspectives on enaction and spiritual pluralism. DiPerna (2012) coined the term *participatory integration* to name the paradigm shift necessary to develop a Wilberian-integral approach to religious studies. Other integral scholars employing participatory ideas in their theorizing include McIntosh (2007), who used *Revisioning*'s enactive approach and epistemological critique to elaborate a more pluralistic "integral reality framework" that seeks to counter some of the problems of Wilber's model, and Ferendo (2007), who presented the participatory perspective on integral practice (see chapter 4) as complementary to Wilber's approach.

In the rest of this section, I illustrate various ways in which the participatory perspective has been engaged in transpersonal works through three examples. Firstly, in *The Science of Oneness*, Hollick (2006) proposed the adoption of Heron's (1996, 1998) cooperative inquiry to produce reliable inner knowledge, and devoted two chapters to argue that Heron's and Ferrer's participatory approaches lay the foundations for "a new, inclusive and holistic model of spirituality that speaks to the spirit of present age" (p. 345). For Hollick, participatory spirituality not only accommodates the diversity of spiritualities better than other models, but also stresses embodied, ethical, cocreative, relational, and cooperative dimensions of the spiritual path that he considers crucial in present times. The emerging "holistic model of human spirituality" (p. 352), Hollick concluded, should be able to

> draw upon the ancient wisdom of the shamanic, polytheistic, monotheistic and transcendent religious traditions; welcome the devotional, intellectual, detached, engaged, solitary, social, exoteric, esoteric, transcendent, immanent and other spiritual paths; and embrace the cocreative, participatory view of our relationship with Spirit. (pp. 352–353)

Secondly, Lahood (2007a) edited two issues of the journal *ReVision* to explore the emergence of a participatory worldview in transpersonal studies, anthropology, Indigenous studies, and ecopsychology, among other disciplines. With the title, *The Participatory Turn, Part 1 and 2*, the *ReVision* monographs not only engage extensively with my own work, but also include significant participatory developments by authors such as R. Tarnas (2007), Heron (2007), Kremer (2007), Abram (2007), Lahood (2007b, 2007c), Bauwens (2007), Conner (2007), and Marks (2007).

Finally, M. Daniels (2009; see also M. Daniels 2013) proposed that the participatory perspective represents a third vector (which he calls "extending") in transpersonal development beyond the standard "ascending" (i.e., geared to otherworldly transcendence) and "descending" (i.e., geared to this-worldly immanence) ones. M. Daniels argued that previous formulations of the "descending" current tended to conflate two fundamentally distinct perspectives: depth psychological, whose focus is the exploration and integration of unconscious material (e.g.,

Jung, Washburn, Grof), and relational-participatory, which stresses the spiritual connection with others and the world. "Such relational, participatory thinking," he wrote, "is exemplified in Indigenous spiritualities, feminist spirituality (e.g., the connected self), transpersonal ecology (ecocentrism), relational spiritualities, and Ferrer's (e.g., 2002) participatory vision (emancipation from self-centeredness, cocreative participation)" (p. 97). M. Daniels (2009) concluded by making a strong case for the import of an "all-vector" transpersonal theory and practice; after surveying a number of spiritual models, he highlighted the participatory approach and Sri Aurobindo's integral yoga as the two spiritual orientations conferring equal prominence to all three vectors (ascending, descending, and extending).

I close this section by noting the growing presence of the participatory perspective in related fields such as Gestalt-transpersonal therapy (Lahood, 2015; L. Williams, 2006), psychosynthesis (Faith, 2007; H. Palmer & Hubbard, 2009), enneagram studies (Bailey & Arthur, 2011), Jungian psychology (Brown, 2017; Ianiszeskwi, 2010), archetypal cosmology (B. Tarnas, 2016), imaginal psychology (Voss, 2009), relational psychoanalysis (R. S. Brown, 2016), resource focused counseling and psychotherapy (Wilson, 2017), addiction recovery (Eng, 2016), ecopsychology (W. W. Adams, 2010a, 2010b; H. Walker, 2012), classical singing (Freinkel, 2015), occupational science (M. Collins, 2010), and relational and peer-to-peer approaches to spiritual growth (Bauwens, 2007; Heron, 2006; Lahood, 2010a, 2010b).

Consciousness Studies

The participatory perspective in also present in certain scholarly sites dedicated to the study of consciousness. In 2006 Anthony Freeman, managing editor of the *Journal of Consciousness Studies*, published a provocative essay in this journal arguing that, in light of the participatory critique of a subtle Cartesianism in transpersonal theory (Ferrer, 2002), Dennett's heterophenomenology (an agnostic third-person approach to first-person experiential reports) should be welcomed as the most coherent and suitable methodology for transpersonal psychology (Freeman, 2006). Freeman's essay triggered a lively debate on the epistemological status of transpersonal psychology, the nature of transpersonal inquiry, and appropriate methods for the study of human consciousness, with responses by Tart (2006), W. A. Adams (2006), and Hartelius (2006)—the latter of which, in my view, provides the most effective rejoinder to Freeman's claims. For an important related paper, see Walach and Runehov (2010).

This is not the place to sum up this rather technical debate and I refer the interested reader to the original papers; my aim here is simply to point out the sites where the participatory perspective is present in the study of consciousness. In this vein, the participatory approach is also discussed in works on the nature of consciousness (Lancaster, 2004), in the context of the anthropology of consciousness (Lahood, 2007c, 2008), and as an important element of a general theory of enaction (Malkemus, 2012).

Integral and Holistic Education

The presence of the participatory turn in integral and holistic education cannot be denied: Gidley (in Molz & Gidley, 2008) named the five main approaches to integral theory and education as *macro-integral* (Wilber), *meso-integral* (Laszlo), *microintegral* (Steiner), *participatory-integral* (Ferrer), and *transversal-integral* (Nicolescu, Morin). The participatory approach to integral education was first introduced in a coauthored article (Ferrer, Romero, & Albareda, 2005) that presented a pedagogical vision in which all human dimensions (body, heart, vital energy, mind, and consciousness) cocreatively participate at all stages of the learning process in interaction with the generative power of life or the cosmos (see chapter 5).

Since the initial article in 2005, this approach rapidly disseminated in scholarly circles.[16] For example, Subbiondo (2006) articulated ten principles of integral education drawn from a course of my design based on the participatory approach. Participatory integral education was also featured in the UCLA's *Spirituality in Higher Education Newsletter* (HERI Spirituality Project Team, 2005), in an important Higher Education Administration dissertation on the integration of contemplative and student-centered education (Seitz, 2009), and, more recently, in an anthology on the academic teaching of mysticism (Parsons, 2011). Further, a leading authority of holistic education, J. R. Miller (2006) included "participatory" as one of the central features of his "timeless learning" educational philosophy and adopted the more relaxed universalism proposed in *Revisioning* as its underlying spiritual framework (see also M. Anthony, 2008).

In addition to the general introduction of participatory thinking to integral education, Embodied Spiritual Inquiry—an approach I developed over the last decade (see chapter 7)—is gaining notice as a pedagogical method seeking to put into practice the principles of participatory integral education. In this context, Embodied Spiritual Inquiry students learn, through the practice of mindful physical contact, to collaboratively construct knowledge from multidimensional experience (e.g., somatic, vital, emotional, mental, and contemplative). Using Albareda and Romero's interactive embodied meditations (see chapter 4) as inquiry tools, students investigate questions selected by participants in the context of a cooperative research paradigm (Heron, 1996). Embodied Spiritual Inquiry has been also presented as an integral, second-person, contemplative pedagogy beyond not only first-person but also second-person, presence/awareness and mental/dialogical types of contemplative education (see chapter 7; Ferrer, 2011; Ferrer & Sohmer, 2017). Two Embodied Spiritual Inquiry case studies—which discuss Embodied Spiritual Inquiry's pedagogical approach, epistemology, and research process—have been published so far: Osterhold et al. (2007) on the nature of relational spirituality and Sohmer, Baumann, and Ferrer (forthcoming) on the nature of human boundaries and the experiential differences between dissociation, merging, and integration. Embodied Spiritual Inquiry is also the focus of *Transformative Inquiry: An Integral Approach* (Nakagawa & Matsuda, 2010), an anthology of writings based on the presentation of this approach at Ritsumeikan University in Kyoto, Japan.

Religious Studies

The participatory turn has received increasing attention in the field of religious studies. In alignment with my goals in writing the book, *Revisioning* was reviewed in religious studies journals (e.g., G. Adams, 2003; Fuller, 2002; Parsons, 2003). In addition, the religious scholar Kripal (2003) endorsed the book's major theses while cautioning about the potential danger that a historically dubious "moral perennialism" (i.e., the assumption of an ethical convergence in mysticism) might sneak through the back door of the participatory vision.[17] In a later essay on mysticism, Kripal (2006a) highlighted the participatory critique of experientialism (i.e., the reduction of spiritual phenomena to intrasubjective experience) and recommendation to talk about the mystical in terms of participatory events including but transcending inner experience. Also in the context of the study of mysticism, Freeman (2007) presented the participatory approach as an effective middle path to resolve the long-standing impasse between essentialists and constructivists. Left (2003), supporting the idea of enacted spiritual shores, pointed out that the participatory approach "provides a new framework for appreciating [her] similar attempt to revision the tradition of Jewish mysticism" (p. 344).

Attention to the participatory perspective in religious studies increased following the publication of *The Participatory Turn* (Ferrer & Sherman, 2008b), which explicitly focused on the contemporary study of religion. Besides the anthology's essays—which engaged traditions such as Sufism (Chittick, 2008), Kabbalah (Lancaster, 2008), Christianity (Barnhart, 2008; Lanzetta, 2008), Hinduism (McDermott, 2008), engaged Buddhism (Rothberg, 2008), Bergsonian vitalism (Barnard, 2008), and Western esotericism (Irwin, 2008) from various participatory standpoints—book reviews quickly appeared in journals such as *Tikkun* (Gleig & Boeving, 2009), *Network Review: Journal of the Scientific and Medical Network* (C. Clarke, 2009), *Journal of Transpersonal Psychology* (Chalquist, 2009), *Resurgence* (Reason, 2010), *Sophia* (Goldberg, 2010), *Journal of Contemporary Religion* (G. Adams, 2011), *Spiritus: A Journal of Christian Spirituality* (Gleig, 2011a), *Alternative Spirituality and Religion Review* (Gleig, 2011b), *Journal for the Study of Spirituality* (M. King, 2012), and *Journal of Integral Theory and Practice* (Alderman, 2012b).

Interest is continuing: The 2010 Annual Meeting of the American Academy of Religion (AAR) featured a well-attended wildcard session on *The Participatory Turn* (Gleig, Ferrer, Sherman, Barnard, Lanzetta, Irwin, & Kripal, 2010) and a second panel engaging contemplative studies from a participatory perspective was presented at the 2011 AAR Annual Meeting (Grace, Sherman, Ferrer, Malkemus, Klein, & Lanzetta, 2011). More recently, I was invited to present the participatory approach to critical subjectivity at the University of San Diego's Conference on Contemplative Studies (Ferrer, 2014a).

Furthermore, in his study of the mystical dimensions of psychic phenomena, Kripal (2010) argued for the participatory nature of paranormal events in that "they appear for us but rely on our active engagement . . . to appear at all or gain meaning" (p. 269; see also Voss, 2013). The Buddhist scholar Duckworth published a paper in the journal *Sophia* presenting participatory pluralism as a less sectarian alternative to Tibetan Buddhist inclusivism (Duckworth, 2014a), as well as a paper in *Journal of the American Academy of Religion* re-envisioning Buddhist understandings of emptiness and Buddha-nature from a participatory perspective (Duckworth, 2014b). In addition, the cultural philosopher Ogilvy (2013)

wrote that the "new polytheism" with which he characterized participatory pluralism represents not only a "spirituality that does justice to
the multi-cultural condition of a globalized world" (p. 47), but also the
best response to the criticisms of religion crafted by the so-called new
atheists (Dawkins, 2006; Dennett, 2006; Harris, 2004; Hitchens, 2007).
In the context of Christian spirituality, Devenish (2012) wrote, "I have
discovered that one of the most meaningful ways of talking about spiritual knowing is something called 'participative knowing'" (p. 43). In a
recent essay, Bidwell (2015) argued not only that participatory theory
can explain the phenomenon of simultaneous, multiple religious identity,
but also that "framing spiritual identity as a participatory event . . . can
generate possibilities for a Buddhist-Christian dialogue less constrained
by . . . doctrinal, ontological, and anthropological tensions" (p. 109).
Finally, *The Participatory Turn* is an important focus of, or provides the
methodological framework for, doctoral dissertations such as Haar Farris's
(2010) or Cabot's (2011), as well as for Gleig's (2012) research into new
religions movements.

To return to the question raised above, I suggest that while the
participatory perspective has definitively gained prominence in transpersonal studies and related fields, it is likely too early to regard it as a paradigmatic epoch in transpersonal scholarship. Although the number of
transpersonal authors influenced by participatory thinking is increasing,
it should be obvious that transpersonal studies is today a richly pluralistic field populated by many other theoretical orientations of equal or
greater influence (see Caplan, Hartelius, & Rardin, 2003; Cunningham,
2007, 2011a; M. Daniels, 2005; Friedman & Hartelius, 2013a; Rothberg
& Kelly, 1998).

CRITICAL PERSPECTIVES

Having reviewed the spread of the participatory turn in terms of those
who have accepted and adapted it, I now consider the main critical
perspectives on my work, which fall into three areas: Wilberian-integral,
archetypal, and participatory.

Wilberian-Integral

Two critical responses to *Revisioning* were issued from the camp of Wilberian integral studies although one of those authors (Paulson, 2002, 2003,
2004) later retracted his critique. First, Paulson (2002) claimed that

anything of value in the book had been already said by Wilber, and the rest was, citing a personal communication from Wilber, "a condensation of three decades of postmodern wrong turns" (para. 43). The following year, however, Paulson (2003) retracted these views, stating:

> When I first read this book I hated it, but I have read and studied it for 2 years and find it one of the best books ever written on transpersonal psychology. . . . This is not a Washburn or Wilber spin off but something entirely different. (para. 1)

Since then, Paulson (2004) seems to have moved to more participatory shores, as suggested by the following remark: "Wilber's integral philosophy . . . is a ready-made system, not one codeveloped by the individual participating in life through lived experience. It thus falls short of a participatory integral philosophy" (p. 140).

The second critical response came from Wilber, who first indicated that

> the view he [Ferrer] is representing is basically a green-meme view of psychology and spirituality . . . it is simply a matter of personal inclination: if you resonate with green-meme values, you will resonate with Ferrer; if you resonate with second-tier values [i.e., such as those of Wilber's own integral theory], you will not. At this point, no amount of argument, evidence, facts, or rhetoric will make you change your mind. . . . Ferrer's book basically marks the end of the transpersonal movement. (cited in Paulson, 2002, para. 43)

This passage is disconcerting: In addition to ostensibly making his perspective invulnerable to criticism, Wilber implied that disagreement with his model necessarily stems from operating at a purportedly lower developmental or evolutionary stage.

More substantially, Wilber (2002) charged *Revisioning* with falling into performative self-contradiction (i.e., critiquing hierarchical rankings while upholding the superiority of its own participatory approach) and promoting what he calls a flatland where no qualitative distinctions can be legitimately made.[18] Although I agree with Wilber's analysis of the contradictions of antihierarchical stances, the critique does not apply to my work. As discussed above, my proposal does not privilege any tradition or type of spirituality over others on *doctrinal, objectivist, or ontologi-*

cal grounds (i.e., saying that theism, monism, or nondualism corresponds to the nature of ultimate reality or is intrinsically superior), but it does offer criteria for making spiritual qualitative distinctions on *pragmatic and transformational grounds*. The crucial difference is that these rankings are not ideologically based on a priori ontological doctrines or putative correspondence to a single nondual spiritual reality, but instead ground critical discernment in the practical values of selflessness, embodiment, and integration. I stand by these values, not because I think they are universal (they are not), but because I firmly believe that their cultivation can effectively reduce personal, relational, social, and planetary suffering. Thus, my response to Wilber's charge is that one can critique these standards, but the participatory approach cannot be consistently pigeonholed as relativist or self-contradictory.[19]

Archetypal

In an important work, Goddard (2009) endorsed central aspects of the participatory approach and its critique of Wilber's theory while offering four serious criticisms. First, Goddard proposed that participatory enaction is epistemologically valid at the first levels of spiritual awakening—where there is still a creative polarity between the individual and the mystery—but not at the final one, which reveals an "Absolute Identity . . . where there is nothing left to participate with anything" (p. 614). Although Goddard's archetypal model is more cocreative, flexible, and less linear than Wilber's theory, it ultimately supports Wilber's monistic nondual spirituality as the universal, mandatory final stage of spiritual realization.[20] As with Wilber's rankings, however, Goddard offered no convincing evidence or argument to support this doctrinal stance.

Second, Goddard (2009) took issue with participatory pluralism, stating that to claim a multiplicity of spiritual ultimates is not less biased than to posit one single Ultimate—this critique apparently emerges from a misapprehension. As stated above, participatory pluralism is grounded in a "more relaxed spiritual universalism" (Ferrer, 2002, p. 183) that, recognizing a shared undetermined mystery or spiritual power underlying all cocreated spiritual ultimates, avoids both the distortions of perennialism and the privileging of the One or the Many as utterly superior: "[T]he everlasting dialectical movement between the One and the Many in the self-disclosing of Spirit makes any abstract or absolute hierarchical arrangement between them misleading" (Ferrer, 2002, p. 191). Thus, the participatory approach does not seek to "refute(s) an Ultimate beyond all possible ultimates"

(p. 623), as Goddard believed; rather, it rejects both the reification of such an underlying power into a supra-ultimate that can be hierarchically posited over the rest of spiritual ultimates (see Postscript), and the dubious perennialist equivalences among religious ultimates. Instead, the participatory approach provides an enactive understanding of the mystery free from the objectivist assumptions and doctrinal hierarchical implications of perennialist approaches (see Ferrer, 2000a, 2002, 2008).

Third, and more intriguing, Goddard (2009) contrasted the perennialist return to the Ground of Being with what in his view is the participatory enthroning of Becoming. Favoring the perennialist view, he wrote, "participation itself returns to the Ground. . . . We cannot logically say of any entity that it participates with the Ground" (p. 623). I believe that Goddard is onto something here. In contrast to the perennialist return to the ground—derived from the Neo-Platonic "metaphysics of emanation and return" of mystics such as Pseudo-Dionysius and Bonaventure (Harmless, 2008)—I take the view that the mystery unfolds from a primordial state of undifferentiated unity toward one of infinite differentiation-in-communion.[21] Even if a return to the Ground were to be the final goal of cosmic evolution, this can be conceived in ways that maintain the existence of participatory individualities (cf. Almaas, 2014; Bache, 2000).

Finally, Goddard (2009) claimed that the participatory view does not allow for "different levels of insight, clarity and ethical comportment in the spiritual sphere" (p. 616) and that, although fiercely critiquing spiritual rankings, the participatory approach also has its own. As the second charge is addressed in my response to Wilber above, I focus here on Goddard's first point. I am puzzled by Goddard's claim since my emphasis in overcoming self-centeredness and dissociation obviously entails ethical qualitative distinctions. As for levels of spiritual insight, although I accept the ones mapped by the traditions in the context of their particular aspirations, I do feel cautious about the legitimacy of making noetically based cross-cultural rankings; after all, the very insights that one tradition considers identical with ultimate liberation (e.g., Advaita Vedanta's realization of the Self) other traditions (e.g., Buddhism) regard as an unequivocal sign of delusion and ignorance (Ferrer, 2002). Therefore, I believe it more appropriate and productive to look at practical and transformational outcomes in the cross-cultural assessment of spiritual knowledge claims.

Participatory

Critiques of aspects of the participatory turn also come from those who see its merit. In a significant paper, Lahood (2008) claimed that my metaphor of an "ocean with many shores" (originally used to convey a plurality of enacted spiritual ultimates that nonetheless may share an overcoming of self-centeredness) results in a kind of "cosmological multiculturalism" that isolates the various spiritual worlds (cf. Friedman, 2013a). For Lahood, the problem with this otherwise liberating account is that it builds rigid boundaries among the various spiritual universes, not accounting for the possibility of "cosmological hybridizations," that is, the mixture or amalgamation of religious forms often leading to new insights and traditions. Lahood concluded by saying that "Ferrer's Ocean of Many Shores . . . should really be constituted of hybrid spiritscapes: Oceans of many hybrids of hybrids" (p. 180).

Lahood (2008) is correct in noting that in its breaking with transpersonal (neo-)perennialism, my early work (Ferrer, 2002) stressed the autonomy and diversity of spiritual worlds and ultimates. However, Lahood's account fails to capture the participatory rejection of the radical separateness of spiritual cosmologies:

> My defense of many viable spiritual paths and goals does not preclude the possibility of equivalent or common elements among them. In other words, although the different mystical traditions enact and disclose different spiritual universes, two or more traditions may share certain elements in their paths or goals. . . . In this context, Vroom's (1989) proposal of a "multicentered view of religion" that conceives traditions as displaying a variety of independent but potentially overlapping focal points should be seriously considered. (Ferrer, 2002, pp. 148–149)

The fact that traditional practices enact particular spiritual worlds (e.g., Patanjali's traditional yoga leads to the experiential corroboration of the Samkhya dualistic metaphysics) does not mean that those universes are entirely isolated from one another. In other words, plurality is not necessarily equivalent to fragmentation (cf. Dale, 2014). Although I did not originally use the language of "hybridization," the participatory emphasis on interreligious interaction and (ensuing) emergence of novel spiritual expressions naturally embraces such syncretistic possibilities (see chapter 10). Even further, in light of Lahood's (2010a) account of the hybrid nature of transpersonalism, the participatory approach itself can be seen as the upshot of a cosmological hybridization between Eastern, Western, and Indigenous traditions, on the one hand, and contemporary spiritual, philosophical, and scientific orientations, on the other. In any event, following Lahood's (2008) welcomed elucidation of this important phenomenon, in an essay on the future of religion I discussed types of spiritual hybridizations (conceptual, practical, and visionary) and concluded with the following:

> The future of religion will be shaped by spiritually individuated persons engaged in processes of cosmological hybridization in the context of a common spiritual family that honors a global order of respect and civility. (Ferrer, 2010, p. 146)

In sum, criticism of the participatory approach mostly stems from either adherence to alternative ontological or metaphysical frameworks such as perennialism, or arguable misapprehensions of participatory claims, some of which may be rooted in ambiguities of my early presentation of the approach. In this chapter, I hope to have clarified both those possible ambiguities and the nature of such ontological disagreements.

CONCLUSION

This investigation yields four conclusions regarding the nature of the participatory perspective, which together suggest and support a vision for the future. First, during the past decade there has been a growing literature on the participatory perspective in transpersonal studies and related disciplines such as consciousness studies, holistic and integral education, and religious studies. Second, whereas the participatory approach can be reasonably conceived as disciplinary model, theoretical orientation, research approach, and even conceptual revolution or paradigm, its proposed status as paradigmatic epoch is as yet uncertain. Given the rich diversity of theoretical perspectives in transpersonal scholarship (Cunningham, 2007, 2011a; M. Daniels, 2005; Friedman & Hartelius, 2013a; Rothberg & Kelly, 1998), it is likely that the field will continue to house a number of mutually enriching orientations—such as spiral-dynamic, structuralist, perennialist, participatory, archetypal, social-scientific, and so on—which arguably illuminate different aspects of transpersonal phenomena and their study. Although transpersonal scholars have taken important steps in exploring the differences, complementarities, and possible integration of these theoretical orientations (e.g., Dale, 2014; M. Daniels, 2005, 2009; Goddard, 2005, 2009; Ianiszeskwi, 2010; Washburn, 2003b), further work is necessary in order to achieve a fuller and more cohesive understanding of transpersonal phenomena.

Third, although participatory spirituality provides resources for critical discernment in spiritual matters, it is misleading to consider the participatory movement (or any particular participatory approach) a spiritual tradition that could be situated above all others. In contrast, participatory spirituality might be better understood as a spiritual orientation (i.e., toward embodiment, integration, relationality, and creative inquiry) that can be found in various degrees within many existing traditions (see Ferrer & Sherman, 2008b), that is increasingly alive in the ongoing contemporary renewal of traditions (e.g., Fox, 2002; Horton & Harvey, 2012; Lerner, 2000; Ray, 2008; Urban, 2003; Whicher, 1998), and that may also give rise to new spiritual expressions (see chapters 3 and 4; Heron, 1998) and shape the emergence of novel religious or spiritual traditions.

Four, and perhaps most significant, the current state of participatory scholarship leads me to characterize the participatory movement more as a network of independent thinkers sharing a scholarly/spiritual sensibility (e.g., about the cocreated nature of spiritual knowledge, the centrality of embodiment and multidimensional cognition, or the import of religious pluralism) than as a school of thought or discipline formalized through traditional scholarly structures (cf. Cabot, 2014). Although participatory associations, programs, journals, and book series may be launched in the future, this network-nature of the participatory movement is advantageous in at least the following two regards. On the one hand, a network promotes the transdisciplinary dissemination of the participatory perspective, preventing the scholarly isolation that afflicts many schools of thought and tends to limit the scope of their action to in-house disciplinary conversations among their members. In a similar vein, arguing against an American Psychological Association (APA) division for transpersonal psychology, Krippner suggested that the creation of the APA division of humanistic psychology reduced the influence that a more diffuse movement operating throughout extant APA groups might have had on the discipline of psychology (Schroll, Krippner, Vich, & Mojeiko, 2009, pp. 42–43).

On the other hand, the inherently pluralistic character of a net-work can house greater theoretical diversity than a school of thought, which often achieves its identity through commitment to specific para-digmatic assumptions or conceptual frameworks. Thus, a network-type organization is not only coherent with the pluralistic ethos of the par-ticipatory movement, but also fecund in the sense of not imposing a priori theoretical constraints via premature commitments to particular models or the aspiration to converge into a unified theory. Lastly, the decentralized nature of a network is consistent with the critique of hier-archical and authoritarian tendencies in society and religion issued by many participatory thinkers (e.g., Heron, 1998, 2006), as well as with related proposals for peer-to-peer modes of knowledge production, access, and distribution (Bauwens, 2007).

In closing, I extend an invitation to scholars to add their voices and perspectives to the conversation and to expand participatory thinking in new directions and into new fields. I proceed with the conviction that the participatory approach provides helpful understandings and practical tools to facilitate a more fertile interreligious interaction, empower indi-viduals in the embodied cocreation of their spiritual path, and, perhaps most fundamentally, participate more fully in the mystery out of which everything arises.

TWO

TRANSPERSONAL PSYCHOLOGY, SCIENCE, AND THE SUPERNATURAL

Should transpersonal psychology be a scientific discipline? Do transpersonal psychologists need to pledge to the exclusive use of empirical methods in their research and scholarship? A number of contemporary transpersonal scholars have so argued (see M. Daniels, 2001, 2005; Friedman, 2002, 2013a; MacDonald, 2013). Although with different emphases, they propose that transpersonal psychology should focus on the scientific study of the naturalistic (i.e., physical and psychological) aspects of transpersonal phenomena, staying away from not only supernatural or metaphysical considerations, but also nonempirical approaches such as hermeneutics or contemplative methodologies. Their explicit aim is to free transpersonal psychology from religious ideologies, secure the field's metaphysical neutrality, and thus enhance its social and academic legitimacy as a scientific discipline.

While I argue against the pursuit of these aims in this chapter—and in particular against Friedman (2002, 2013a) as their strongest advocate—I also recognize the value of a scientific approach. First, although I have elsewhere critiqued the "empiricist colonization of spirituality" (i.e., the import of empiricist standards such as falsifiability to spiritual inquiry; see Ferrer, 1998b, 2002), I also think that transpersonal psychology would benefit from more scientific studies. To discern the transformative outcomes, neurobiological correlates, and phenomenology of transpersonal events, among other possible empirical findings, is hugely important; quantitative and qualitative approaches should be regarded as equally vital for the field (see Anderson & Braud, 2011, 2013).[1] Second, I agree with Friedman (2002, 2013a) that transpersonal psychology should neither become a religion nor be exclusively tied to any particular spiritual tradition or metaphysical worldview. With this goal in mind, some of my past works sought to expel spiritual ideologies underlying transpersonal models through a participatory framework that does not privilege any spiritual tradition or orientation over others on doctrinal, ontological, or metaphysical grounds (i.e., saying that theism, monism, or nondualism corresponds to the nature of ultimate reality). Those writings also offered criteria for making qualitative distinctions regarding spiritual matters, based on pragmatic and transformational grounds such as selflessness, embodied integration, and eco-socio-political justice (Ferrer, 2002, 2008). Third, although accounts of the scientific method from the transpersonal defenders of science more closely resemble what one would find in a science textbook than the activities of a practicing scientist, these authors are not naive scientists. Rather, these scholars present a philosophically informed scientific approach that properly acknowledges science as but one path to knowledge, the provisional nature of scientific products, and the hermeneutic dimension of science (i.e., data are theory laden; Friedman, 2002, 2013a; MacDonald, 2013).

In this chapter, however, I show that the scientific approach can be—and indeed has been—taken too far. I first argue that these scholars (e.g., M. Daniels, 2001, 2005; Friedman, 2002, 2013a; MacDonald, 2013) underestimate how the powerful ways in which modern science is embedded in a naturalistic metaphysics betray their goal to free the discipline from fidelity to any metaphysical worldview. Then, after identifying serious problems with these authors' adherence to a neo-Kantian epistemology and associated metaphysical agnosticism, I show the residual scientism afflicting their proposals for a scientific transpersonal psychology. Next, I present the critical metaphysical pluralism of the participatory approach and discuss the challenge of shared spiritual visions for scientific naturalism. Finally, as a possible direction to relax the field's metaphysical tensions, I offer an example of a participatory research program that bridges the modern dichotomy between naturalism and supernaturalism (though I later argue against the need for either term, they are appropriate when discussing this so-called divide). I conclude by arguing that although transpersonal psychology should encourage scientific studies, the field should not be defined or limited by its allegiance to any single inquiry approach, epistemology, or metaphysical worldview.

SCIENCE, NATURALISM,
AND METAPHYSICAL AGNOSTICISM

In two important manifestos, Friedman (2002, 2013a) proposed to restrict the term *psychology* to refer to the scientific study of transpersonal phenomena and to use the broader category *transpersonal studies* for nonempirical approaches.[2] Friedman's main motivation appears to be detaching transpersonal psychology from specific metaphysical worldviews, such as those espoused by religious traditions. Because metaphysical statements cannot be empirically tested, Friedman argued, a scientific transpersonal psychology should remain agnostic about metaphysical and supernatural claims and concentrate instead on the naturalistic study of the physical and the psychological (cf. MacDonald, 2013).

Leaving aside the circularity of this argument, a more serious issue emerges when considering that, *as generally understood and practiced in modern times,*[3] science entails a *naturalistic metaphysics* associated with an ontological materialism and reductionism that is antithetical to "supernatural" worldviews (De Caro & Macarthur, 2000, 2004a; J. Dupré, 1995; Ellis, 2009; Mahner, 2012). In other words, far from being metaphysically neutral, modern science endorses the naturalistic "view that all that exists is our lawful spatiotemporal world" (Mahner, 2012, p. 1437). Metaphysical naturalism, Mahner (2012) added, should be considered essentially constitutive of science—"a tacit metaphysical supposition of science, an ontological postulate" (p. 1438) without which science would no longer be science (cf. Schafersman, 1997). As B. H. Smith (2009) compellingly argued, even proponents of a more ontologically neutral *methodological* naturalism (which excludes any appeal to supernatural beings or forces for scientific research and theorizing) tend to fall into a *metaphysical* naturalism that denies the existence of any entity or force other than material or physical ones.

While Friedman (2002, 2013a) has been silent on this subject, MacDonald (2013) duly conceded that naturalistic science, like religion, is based on unverifiable metaphysical assumptions. As J. Dupré (1995) pointed out, "It is now widely understood that science cannot progress without powerful assumptions about the world it is trying to investigate, without, that is to say, a prior metaphysics" (p. 1). One of science's main metaphysical assumptions, MacDonald continued, is the commitment to an "ontological materialism or naturalism" (p. 316) that favors reductionist explanations, for example, seeking to explain spirituality through

neurobiological mechanisms.[4] MacDonald understands that this commitment has the same assumptive epistemological status as what he calls
a "transcendental reductionism" that views "transpersonal phenomena
as ontologically real and of a source and quality that is not reducible
to material processes" (p. 318). However, he unwarrantedly concluded
that such a predicament, instead of encouraging metaphysical pluralism or neutrality, renders "the criticism of reductionism . . . as holding
little value in advancing transpersonal science" (p. 318). The upshot of
this move is that any talk about transcendent or supernatural realities
should be "viewed in purely experiential terms" (p. 321) with "anything that is available to human experience [being] a legitimate focus
of scientific study" (p. 321). Although such a radical empiricism (after
James, 1912/2003) is salutary, experientialism—the reduction of spiritual
phenomena to human experience—generates a plethora of problems for
transpersonal psychology. As I have examined those problems elsewhere
(Ferrer, 2002), the present discussion focuses on other issues.

In *The Empirical Stance* (2002), the philosopher of science van
Fraassen showed that the common association of scientific empiricism with naturalistic and materialistic metaphysical theories is not
only unwarranted, but also misleading and ideological. Essentially, van
Fraassen argued, whenever empiricism is linked to any metaphysical or
philosophical position telling what the world is like, one cannot avoid
falling into ideological false consciousness: "There is no factual thesis
itself invulnerable to empiricist critique and simultaneously the basis for
the empiricist critique of metaphysics" (p. 46). To be consistent, van
Fraassen maintained, empiricism should be regarded as a methodological
stance—that is, an attitude, orientation, or approach free from necessary specific beliefs or theses about reality and thus potentially open to
both secular and religious worldviews.[5] His concluding passage merits
reproduction at length:

> Each of the "isms" I mention here [i.e., materialism, natural-
> ism, secularism] has at some point appropriated for itself all
> the credit for the advances of science, in order to claim its
> liberating power and moral authority. Each has at some point
> intimated that it consists in nothing more than full-fledged
> acceptance of what science tells us about the world. Coupled
> with this, a little paradoxical, comes the insistence that sci-
> ence would die if it weren't for the scientists' conscious or
> unconscious adherence to this philosophical position. All of

this is false; in fact, it is in philosophy that we see the most glaring examples of false consciousness and they occur precisely at this point. (pp. 194–195)

Similarly, J. Dupré (2004) explained how the naturalistic opposition to supernatural agents or explanations often degenerates into a physicalism endorsing a monistic metaphysical worldview that is in conflict with empiricism (i.e., *monistic* in the sense that everything in existence consists of and can be explained in terms of a single substance: physical matter).[6] Since the completeness of physics is not empirically warranted, J. Dupré added, such monism is a supernatural myth at odds with empiricist standards. The problems with physicalism and materialism as metaphysical doctrines are exacerbated by the many failures of reductionism in biology, genetics, ecology, and psychology (J. Dupré, 1995). In addition, important contemporary trends in complexity theory, nonlinear science, and neuroscience not only postulate diverse forms of downward causation but also challenge the epistemic superiority of reductionist explanations (e.g., Andersen, Emmeche, Finnemann, & Christiansen, 2000; Beauregard, 2007). In this context, transpersonal psychologists may be especially interested in Fingelkurts and Fingelkurts's (2009) thorough rebuttal of the fifteen most frequent arguments used to reduce religious experience to neurobiology. "The only conclusion from observed neuroscientific studies," they summarized, "is that religious experience is *reflected* in brain activity and that the brain somehow *mediates* some aspects of religiosity" (p. 312). As the nonlinear scientist A. Scott (2004) wrote, "Reductionism is not a conclusion of science but a belief of many scientists" (p. 66).

Other scholars support J. Dupré's (1995, 2004) concerns and highlight the problems raised by this naturalistic metaphysical worldview for religion. Habermas (2008), for example, wrote the following: "The ontologization of natural scientific knowledge into a naturalistic worldview reduced to 'hard facts' is not science but bad metaphysics" (p. 207). He added that with its naturalistic worldview, "scientism enters into a genuine relation of competition with religious doctrine" (p. 245). This naturalism becomes a "*quasi*-religion" (Plantinga, 2011, p. x) in its answering (even if in the negative) questions concerning the existence of God or the intrinsic meaning of life. Critiquing the "religious" temperament of naturalistic empiricism, Irwin (2008) pointed out, "Those who fail to recognize the truth of this empiricism are condemned to ignorance; 'salvation' lies in embracing the materialist belief that all religious causality is reducible to biology, evolutionary psychology, and/ or sociocultural conditioning" (pp. 197–198). Metaphysical naturalism further assumes "that when religious people claim to have had super- natural experiences that defy rational explanations they are mistaken in some way" (McCutcheon, 1999, p. 127). The naturalistic paradigm, in Byrne's (1999) words, "far from being a neutral description . . . assumes the falsity and/or irrationality of religious thought and practice" (p. 251).

It is also important to consider that, as Bilgrami (2010) explained, science's adoption (in the seventeenth century) of a naturalist metaphys- ics that voids the natural world of spiritual or divine presence was not, contra widespread belief, a scientific necessity—rather, it was historically motivated by powerful political and economic factors (see also Nagel, 2012).[7] To be sure, as R. Tarnas (1991) pointed out, the disenchantment of the natural world was overdetermined by a plethora of philosophical, social, political, and psychological factors. Reflecting this complexity, powerful political alliances between key ideologues of the Royal Society of London and commercial interests, intersecting with strictly scientific considerations, seem to have played a key role in the triumph of a natu- ralistic worldview (cf. Kubrin, 1980). After all, Bilgrami wrote, "from an anima mundi, one could not simply proceed to take at whim and will" (p. 42), but a disenchanted world devoid of value, purpose, or divinity could be easily turned into "natural resources" to be recklessly exploited.

Beyond its ideological underpinnings, the systematic deflation- ary bracketing of supernatural claims can have a fatal consequence for transpersonal research, effectively blinding researchers from the actual presence of supernatural (i.e., standing outside of the currently known or accepted natural world) agents or forces at play in the shaping of spiritual and transpersonal events. After all, as Mahner (2012) stressed, the "no-supernatural principle" (p. 1442) is not only a methodological but also a metaphysical supposition of modern science (cf. B. H. Smith, 2009). Even in philosophy, all varieties of naturalism are joined in their rejection of supernatural agents such as gods, angels, or spirits (see De Caro & Macarthur, 2000, 2004a).[8]

However, as Northcote (2004) persuasively argued, the method- ological suspension of the validity of supernormal claims (e.g., about metaphysical entities or levels of reality), far from warranting objectivism or scholarly neutrality in the study of religion, may actually constitute a bias against "the possibility that people's thinking and behaviour are indeed based on various supernormal forces . . . a bracketing approach will falsely attribute mundane sociological [or biological] explanations to behaviour that is in actuality shaped by supernatural forces" (p. 89). Accordingly, Northcote issued a call for a more symmetrical dialogue between Western naturalistic and alternative perspectives in the appraisal of supernormal claims. In the same vein, B. H. Smith (2009) wrote:

> The exclusion—and implied denial of the possibility of the existence—of entities or forces other than those currently comprehended by natural science amounts both to a metaphysical claim and to a possibly significant intellectual confinement. . . . Metaphysical naturalism . . . may close the doors to what would otherwise be recognized as properly scientific inquiry. (p. 123)

Wallace (2000) made a similar point regarding scientific materialism: "If there are any nonphysical influences on physical events, unquestioning acceptance of this belief [in the causally closed nature of the physical world] will ensure that those influences will not be recognized" (p. 25). Thus, I argue that unless one subscribes ideologically to a naturalistic metaphysics, it may be prudent—and heuristically fertile—not to reject a priori the possibility of effective causation from the various metaphysical sources and subtle psychic influences described by religious and spiritual practitioners.[9]

In light of modern science's metaphysical commitments, it is evident that Friedman's (2002, 2013a) proposal fails to meet its own standards. Scientific naturalism is not only *thoroughly* metaphysical, but also arguably shaped by economic interests perpetuating an eco-pernicious, disenchanted worldview that imposes methodological blinders on transpersonal researchers. As the famous dictum goes, "Epistemology drives metaphysics," and so, whether in science or transpersonal psychology, metaphysical skepticism is usually rooted in an allegiance to neo-Kantian epistemology, to which I now turn.

ON TRANSPERSONAL NEO-KANTIANISM

Both Friedman (2002, 2013a) and MacDonald (2013) advised that transpersonal psychology should remain metaphysically agnostic toward any ontological reality beyond the physical and psychological, and simply focus on the scientific study of human experience.[10] This apparently cautious stance, however, is dependent on the validity of neo-Kantian frameworks that bracket the existence of supernatural and metaphysical sources of spiritual and transpersonal phenomena. Although Kant's actual views on this matter are far from clear (Perovich, 1990), neo-Kantian frameworks assume that innate or deeply seated epistemic constraints in human cognition render impossible and therefore illicit any knowledge claim about metaphysical realities. In other words, metaphysical (noumenal) worlds *may* exist, but the only thing accessible is the human situated phenomenal awareness of them.[12]

Friedman (2002) is explicit about his commitment to neo-Kantian dualism. After stating that "science can directly study phenomena but not underlying noumena" (p. 182), he restricted transpersonal psychology to the scientific study of "transpersonal phenomena"—removing any talk about possible "transcendent noumena" from its scope (p. 182).[13] A scientific transpersonal psychology, then, should be skeptical and agnostic about the existence of any transcendent referent and stick with the study of human experience. By "transcendent," however, Friedman means different things in different essays. Initially, he reified "the transcendent" into a single ineffable and transcategorical mystical ultimate: "I consider it [the transcendent] to be the ultimate holistic concept that can only be experienced, if at all, in a direct and unmediated fashion unhampered by any specific limitation" (p. 182). Later he reformulated this notion as "anything that is supernatural and metaphysical (e.g., that might be outside of space and time)" (2013a, p. 307). In both accounts, Friedman argued, transpersonal psychology should remain metaphysically agnostic because the transcendent is transconceptual, that is, "beyond categories" (2013a, p. 183).

One of the problems with this account is that there is no such thing as "*the* transcendent" in the singular, but instead a rich variety of alleged spiritual worlds and ultimates that, while some are indeed said to be transconceptual, can nonetheless be theorized in numerous ways—as hundreds of religious texts attest. (For a reconceptualization of what has been commonly called "transcendent," see this volume's Postscript.) In addition, many allegedly supernatural spiritual phenomena are *thoroughly conceptual* and so they escape Friedman's (2002, 2013) demarcation criterion concerning scientific transpersonal psychology's scope of study. Consider, for example, spiritual visions such as Ezekiel's Divine Chariot, Hildegard's visionary experience of the Trinity, or Black Elk's Great Vision, as well as spiritual realms such as Buddha lands, the Heavenly Halls of Merkavah mysticism, and the many subtle worlds posited by Western esoteric schools or shamanic traditions. These realms and visionary referents are far from being formless or "beyond categories" *and* are claimed to exist beyond physical and psychological domains. While Friedman's portrayal of the transcendent may be consistent with certain apophatic mysticisms (Sells, 1994), it is by no means inclusive of the variety of ways in which supernatural realities have been understood and described.

In addition, scientific transpersonal psychology cannot study the transcendent, Friedman (2013a) claimed, because "any direct, nonmediated knowing would not be conceptual but another ilk outside of the parameters of science" (p. 306). Direct knowledge, however, can be conceptualized. Right this moment I am having a direct experience of the hot chocolate I am drinking, but this does not prevent me from describing it (e.g., as warm, spicy, bittersweet) and thus potentially study it. To be sure, such an experience, like allegedly transcendent ones, has mediated elements (e.g., cultural predispositions), but they are rather insignificant compared to its direct qualities (i.e., no cultural influence will make my hot chocolate taste like cold orange juice; cf. S. B. King, 1988). As Wilber (1995) put it, "I find myself in *immediate* experience of *mediated* worlds" (p. 601).

The entire mediated-unmediated dichotomy, however, is ultimately parasitic of neo-Kantian epistemology: On the one hand, there is an unfathomable noumenon or "thing-in-itself," and, on the other, a variety of mediating factors or mechanisms through which such a reality becomes phenomenally accessible. These factors (e.g., deep structures, paradigms, conceptual frameworks, languages, cognitive schemes, neural-physiological mechanisms), so the neo-Kantian story goes, not only operate at conscious and unconscious levels of awareness, but also limit and shape in fundamental ways what can be possibly known about the world. Central to the notion of mediation is the claim that it is *only* through these constructions and mechanisms that human beings can make intelligible the raw input of an otherwise inscrutable reality.

As discussed elsewhere (Ferrer, 2002), after disposing of the Kantian two-worlds metaphysical doctrine and related dogmas such as the scheme-content dualism (Davidson, 1984), these so-called mediating factors—far from being limiting or distorting—can be seen as the vehicles through which reality or being self-manifests through the human (cf. Schilbrack, 2014a). Mediation is thus transformed from an obstacle into *the very means that enable human beings to directly participate in the self-disclosure of the world*. R. Tarnas (1991) gets to the heart of the matter:

> All human knowledge of the world is in some sense determined by subjective principles [mediating factors]; but instead

of considering these principles as belonging ultimately to the separate human subject, and therefore not grounded in the world independently of human cognition, this participatory conception held that these subjective principles are in fact an expression of the world's own being, and that the human mind is ultimately the organ of the world's own process of self-revelation. (pp. 433–434)

Friedman (2002) has also overlooked the religious implications of his transpersonal neo-Kantianism. After his rightful plea against the use of transpersonal psychology "to promulgate any specific religious or spiritual folks traditions" (p. 176; cf. Friedman, 2009), he wrote that his claim regarding the cognitive inaccessibility of transcendent noumena is "congruent with . . . the Judaic emphasis on the essential mystery of God's unknowability and the Taoist emphasis in the *Tao Te Ching* (*Book of Changes*) that those who speak about the Tao do not know of what they speak" (p. 182). However, many (arguably most) mystical traditions—from Advaita Vedanta to Raja Yoga to most Buddhist schools to many forms of Christian mysticism—do defend the possibility of directly knowing such an ultimate referent or reality (cf. R. King, 1999). Incidentally, Friedman's inclusion of Taoism as supporting his view is dubious since claims for immediate dynamic attunement to the Tao in this tradition are well known (e.g., Kohn, 2001).

My aim here is not to argue for any particular epistemic viewpoint but merely to show the inescapability of metaphysical (and perhaps even religious) commitments in human inquiry, whether scientific or not. Actually, since the impossibility of directly knowing God is especially central to Judaism (as *Ain Sof* or primordial divinity), Gnosticism, and certain Christian and Muslim apophatic mysticisms, one could charge Friedman's (2002) proposal with inadvertently accomplishing exactly what he seeks (and implicitly claims) to avoid: he confines transpersonal research within the epistemological and metaphysical strictures of particular Western religious traditions.[13]

In sum, the legitimacy of metaphysical agnosticism and skepticism is contingent on the validity of a neo-Kantian dualistic metaphysics, which further undermines the professed metaphysical neutrality of transpersonal scientism. In effect, Friedman's (2002) account creates an implicit hierarchy not only between particular Western traditions (which got it right) and most other religious traditions (which got it wrong), but also, as the next section stresses, between Western and non-Western epistemic frameworks.

Western Ethnocentrism and Epistemic Colonialism

Neo-Kantian skepticism is not only empirically unwarranted, but also requires the ethnocentric dismissal of the cognitive claims of most of the world spiritual practitioners. This is evident in the way it explicitly or implicitly dismisses supernatural claims made by spiritual practitioners as precritical, ingenuous, dogmatic, or even primitive and superstitious. In the context of religious studies, Irwin (2008) caustically wrote about such an attitude:

> Causality attributed to nonempirical sources, neither measurable nor scientifically testable, must be relegated to the dust bins of history as quaint misbeliefs held by "folk" believers, whose poor intuitions have led them astray into the murky subterranean depths of the unconscious, social repression, and the denied stirrings of primal needs and desires. (p. 198)

In other words, since the world's Indigenous and contemplative traditions have not undergone the Kantian revolution of the modern West, their cognitive claims should not be taken seriously. Instead, traditional supernatural claims should be taken symbolically, critically filtered through Western epistemologies, or translated into Western scientific or academic categories.

Consider how Friedman's (2002, 2013a) neo-Kantianism led him to believe that noumenal or ultimate reality is unavoidably inaccessible to human cognition. This claim contradicts most contemplative and Indigenous epistemic frameworks, which explicitly assert such an access (e.g., Forman, 1989; R. King, 1999; A. Klein, 1986; Irwin, 1994). The problem here is that assuming neo-Kantianism is right elevates a highly questionable Western epistemology (see, e.g., Davidson, 1984; Schilbrack, 2014a; Schrader, 1967; R. Tarnas, 1991) as superior to all other Western and non-Western epistemic frameworks.

Of course, the reevaluation of non-Western emic frameworks in contemporary debates does not settle the contested issues (Ferrer & Sherman, 2008a); rather, it simply but crucially highlights the fact that Western epistemologies may not be the last arbiters in the assessment of religious knowledge claims, and in particular of those emerging from long-term spiritual practice or ritual. As R. King (1999) stated:

> My point is not that Western scholars should necessarily accept the emic [epistemological] perspectives over which

they are claiming the authority to speak, but rather that they
at least entertain the possibility that such perspectives are a
legitimate stance to adopt and engage them in constructive
debate. (p. 183)

Komarovski's (2015) work offered a superb example of the possibilities of
such a constructive engagement. In his detailed study of Tibetan Buddhist
mystical experience, he demonstrated how the use of Tibetan Buddhist
theories paves the way to "transcending the Eurocentric framework of
the debate on this issue [i.e., (un)mediated mystical experience] between
scholars siding with Katz or Forman" (p. 245).[14] This approach, then,
entails more than merely taking emic claims as inspirations for "real"
scientific research (which Friedman accepts)—one must also consider
the relevance of emic epistemic frameworks to alternatively understand
ways of knowing and assess knowledge claims.

Friedman (2013a) sees value in adopting emic perspectives in
cross-cultural encounters but only to a point. Since such perspectives
are based on supernatural assumptions, he considered such an approach
"potentially dangerous for those who desire to maintain their so-called
scientific objectivity through keeping an etic perspective. However, having an emic perspective can be useful, if the etic perspective can also
be kept intact" (p. 303). In other words, non-Western standpoints are
to be appreciated insofar as they do not challenge Western frameworks
and their supposedly "objective" standards.[15] Friedman's (2013a) account
of transpersonal psychology's mission gives the show away. He stated:
"Transpersonal psychology can be seen as an attempt to *replace traditional
spiritual and folk psychological worldviews with perspectives congruent with
those of modern science*, that can develop scientifically through empirical
research" (p. 310; italics added). Emic perspectives and categories, that
is, should be not only translated but also ultimately replaced by Western
scientific ones.[16]

In counterpoint to Friedman's (2013a) suggestion, an increasing number of anthropologists, scholars of religion, and transpersonal
thinkers refuse the translation of religious terms into Western scientific
concepts. In addition to Stoller's (Stoller & Olkes, 1987) participatory rejection of ethnographic realism in anthropology and Viveiros de
Castro's (2014, 2015) influential plea to take seriously the plausibility of Amerindian ontology, many contemporary scholars endorse the
application of emic categories in the study of religion and spirituality.
For example, Saler (2000) suggested that scholarship could benefit from

the use of folk categories (e.g., the Hindu concept of *dharma*) as tools of anthropological analysis (cf. Lancaster, 2013). Transpersonal scholar Rothberg (2000) made an even stronger case in the context of spiritual inquiry:

> To interpret spiritual approaches through categories like "data," "evidence," "verification," "method," "confirmation," and "intersubjectivity" may be to enthrone these categories as somehow the hallmarks of knowledge. . . . But might not a profound encounter with practices of spiritual inquiry lead to considering carefully the meaning of other comparable categories (e.g. *dhyana, vichara, theoria, gnosis,* or *contemplatio*) and perhaps to developing understandings of inquiry in which such spiritual categories are primary or central when we speak of knowledge? To assume that the categories of current western epistemology are adequate for interpreting spiritual approaches is to prejudge the results of such an encounter, which might well lead to significant changes in these categories. (pp. 175–176)

These and others scholars are persuasively arguing that importing Western epistemic categories to analyze and account for the validity of knowledge claims from all cultures, ways of knowing, and domains of reality is highly questionable (cf. Roth, 2008). Most religious and spiritual endeavors, I should add, are aimed not so much at describing or explaining human nature and the world, but at engaging and transforming them in creative and participatory ways (Apffel-Marglin, 2011; Ferrer & Sherman, 2008b; Hollenback, 1996; Viveiros de Castro, 2014, 2015), and may therefore call for different validity standards than those emerging from the rationalistic study of the natural world.

In closing this section, a number of questions arise: Might not the very goals and assumptions of Western research programs be revised in the encounter with non-Western understandings? Should not a truly postcolonial scholarship be open to be transformed *at depth* by transcultural methodological interactions? Can scholars dance between etic and emic, insider and outsider stances, in their approach to spiritual phenomena, particularly those involving supernatural or metaphysical claims? Paraphrasing Kripal (2006b), I propose that it is as important to let go of the pride of the insider and embrace the "gnosis of the outsider" as it is to let go of the pride of the outsider and embrace the "gnosis of the insider." To this end, transpersonal scholarship may need to navigate successfully between the Scylla of uncritical acceptance of all emic claims ("romanticism" and "going native") and the Charybdis of assuming Western epistemological superiority ("colonialism" and "epistemic violence").

I suggest that transpersonal psychology will be *fully* free from epistemic colonialism only when it stops taking for granted Western frameworks such as neo-Kantianism or scientific empiricism as absolutely privileged in the study of the world's traditions (even if science can be considered a superior approach to study particular empirical aspects of religion, e.g., brain activity and cognitive capacities functioning; see Lancaster, 2004, 2013). Postcolonial transpersonal approaches should not be motivated by politically or spiritually correct attitudes (often rooted in cultural guilt) but by a blend of epistemological boldness and humility that embraces the potential value of different epistemic frameworks, while concurrently acknowledging the limits of the analytic rationality cultivated in the modern West. The next section elaborates on this critical point.

Neo-Kantianism, Disembodiment, and Existential Alienation

Thinkers as diverse as Bordo (1987), Leder (1990), Nagatomo (1992), Varela et al. (1991), and Yasuo (1987) have suggested that the process of increasing dissociation between mental and somatic worlds, which arguably characterized important strains of the modern Western trajectory, was an important source of both the postulation and the success of the Cartesian mind-body doctrine. The overcoming of Cartesian dualism, therefore, may not be so much a philosophical but a practical, existential, and transformative task.

In a similar vein, I propose that the Kantian two-worlds doctrine (and its associated epistemic skepticism) is largely dependent on the estrangement of the human mind from an embodied apprehension of reality. As contemporary cognitive science shows, "Our sense of what is real begins with and depends crucially upon our bodies. . . . As embodied, imaginative creatures, *we never were separated or divorced from reality in the first place*" (Lakoff & Johnson, 1999, p. 17, p. 93).[17] If this is correct, then it becomes entirely understandable that the decline of embodied participation in human inquiry, arguably precipitated by the disconnection between mind and body, may have undermined the sense of being in touch with the real, engendering the Kantian mentalist dualism of a merely phenomenal world and an always inaccessible noumenal reality.[18]

As R. Tarnas (1991) suggested, this epistemic dualism contributes in fundamental ways to the existential estrangement of the modern self. By placing the individual inexorably out of touch with the "real" world, the alienating Cartesian gap between subject and object is epistemologically affirmed and secured: "Thus the cosmological estrangement of modern consciousness initiated by Copernicus and the ontological estrangement initiated by Descartes were completed by the epistemological estrangement initiated by Kant: a threefold mutually enforced prison of modern alienation" (p. 419). R. Tarnas's analysis brings to the foreground the pernicious implications of this dualism for human participation in spiritual knowledge:

> The Cartesian-Kantian paradigm both expresses and ratifies a state of consciousness in which experience of the unitive numinous depths of reality has been systematically extinguished, leaving the world disenchanted and the human ego isolated. Such a world view is, as it were, a kind of metaphysical and epistemological box. (p. 431)

One of the central issues at stake in this discussion is whether some kind of personal engagement and even transformation—such as body-mind integration, triumph over mental pride, or the development of contemplative competences—are needed for the enactment, apprehension, and assessment of certain truth claims (see Evans, 1993; Ferrer & Sherman, 2008a; Kasulis, 2002; Kripal, 2006b; Taber, 1983). After all, most contemplative traditions hold that in order to ascertain their most fundamental insights, practitioners need to develop cognitive competences beyond the structures of linguistic rationality. In the end, as Kripal (2006b) reminded us, "Rationalism and reductionism . . . are also state-specific truths (that is, they are specific to highly trained egoic forms of awareness), but their states of mind are more easily reproduced and communicated, at least within our present Western cultures" (pp. 141–142).

Indeed, modern Western education emphasizes the development of the mind's rational and intellectual powers, paying little attention to the maturation of other ways of knowing. A common outcome is that most individuals in the Western culture reach adulthood with a conventionally mature mental functioning but with poorly or irregularly developed somatic, emotional, aesthetic, intuitive, and spiritual intelligences (see chapters 4 and 5; Emmons, 1999; Gardner, 1983/1993). Can the modern mind admit that its mastered epistemic competencies may not be the final or necessarily superior cognitive plateau, and yet maintain and even sharpen its critical look toward oppressive, repressive, and untenable religious beliefs and ideologies?

These issues are central for assessing contemporary proposals for a scientific transpersonal psychology, which, following the mandates of modern science, posit the replicability and public nature of observation to be paramount. If specific types of personal transformation are necessary to enact or access particular spiritual referents, such a replicable public nature is then naturally limited to those who have transformed themselves in those specific ways. Although conventional science makes cognitive demands to its practitioners (e.g., years of study, practical lab trainings), the demands of a personally transformative inquiry are obviously greater and rather unconventional from mainstream scientific or philosophical perspectives (for notable exceptions, see Kasulis, 2002; Taber, 1983; Wallace, 2000).

Although Friedman (2002, 2013a) supported Tart's (1972) proposal for state-specific sciences, in which researchers may be required to undergo meditative training to study transpersonal phenomena, he restricted those phenomena to human experiences and remarked that such a training "is not dissimilar to the years of mastery required by researchers in areas of conventional science" (Friedman, 2002, p. 185). These statements suggest that Friedman is discussing meditative skills training aimed at mapping states of mind, not the personal, existential, and even ontological transformation most traditions consider necessary to apprehend what have traditionally been understood as supernatural or metaphysical referents (see L. Dupré, 1996; Hollenback, 1996; Lanzetta, 2008). In the next section, I turn to a closer examination of Friedman's account of science.

TRANSPERSONAL SCIENCE OR SCIENTISM?

Avoiding the hardest form of scientism, Friedman (2013a) repeatedly stated that the nonscientific approaches he seeks to expurgate from transpersonal psychology are "neither intrinsically more or less valuable than science" (p. 308). However, a strong scientism and positivism animate Friedman's assumptions that (1) modern science is less metaphysically biased and more progressive than other inquiry traditions, (2) a definite boundary can be drawn between science and nonscience, and (3) there is unity in the scientific method (for a lucid account of scientism, see Sorell, 1991). Each of these assumptions is problematic.

First, Friedman's (2002, 2013a) claim that scientific approaches are free (or freer) from the metaphysical baggage that in his view afflicts philosophical and religious traditions reveals his faith in the positivist dream of science as the unproblematic path to nondogmatic knowledge. After all, as Sorell (1991) concluded his study, "The *new* scientism in philosophy is a kind of naturalism" (p. 177). In the same spirit, Friedman's insistence that scientific research into the transcendent is implausible closely follows the understanding in classical logical positivism that metaphysical claims or "statements alluding to some transcendental reality [are] meaningless, since they could not be verified" (Tauber, 2009, p. 92). In addition, Friedman (2013a) characterized science as distinctively progressive: "Scientific strategy facilitates progress, rather than stagnation, and differentiates transpersonal psychology as a science from traditional worldviews and religions, as well as philosophy" (p. 304). This statement suggests that Friedman wants to have it both ways: On the one hand, he wants to avoid the charge of scientism by stating that he does not regard science as superior to religion or philosophy; on the other, he claims that epistemic progress is exclusive of science (why then would not science be cognitively superior?). As history shows, however, many scientific disciplines—from anatomy to astronomy to acoustics—do not show any substantial progress for decades whereas many nonscientific ones (e.g., literary criticism or military strategy) arguably do (Laudan, 1996). Thus, "progress" as specific to science (and missing from nonscience) will not do. Although the case for "progress" is a thorny one in all inquiry traditions, one might argue that not only philosophical but also spiritual traditions show signs of epistemic progress, for example, in their understanding of liberation, response to new historical demands, or invention of novel methods to more effectively achieve their ends. In any event, it is important to remember, "faith in progress" as a distinguishing feature of science was another canon of the positivist doctrine that Friedman resuscitates (see Tauber, 2009, p. 50).

Second, Friedman's (2002, 2013a) division between scientific transpersonal psychology and nonscientific transpersonal studies is questionable because no definite demarcation criterion between science and nonscience (or pseudoscience) has ever been successfully established. After a thorough review of proposed demarcation criteria (including method, verifiability, and falsifiability), Laudan (1996) wrote, "No demarcation line between science and nonscience, or between science and pseudo-science . . . would win assent from a majority of philosophers" (p. 211). The demarcation problem, Laudan concluded, is an ideological pseudoproblem:

> If we would stand up and be counted on the side of reason, we ought to drop terms like "pseudo-science" and "unscientific" from our vocabulary; they are just hollow phrases which do only emotive work for us. As such, they are more suited to the rhetoric of politicians and Scottish sociologists of knowledge than to that of empirical researchers. (p. 222)

Furthermore, although relocating psychology within the science camp,[19] Friedman (2002, 2013a) perpetuates the classical Two Cultures split (Snow, 1959/1964) between the sciences (physics, chemistry, and biology) and the humanities (sociology, psychology, and anthropology) that contemporary sociology of knowledge and science studies have so effectively dismantled: "Science no longer resides outside the humanities as some distant colony of academic inquiry" (Tauber, 2009, p. 11). Even though the positivist picture of science still dominates "*popular* conceptions of science" (p. 12), Tauber (2009) continued, "science has been dethroned from its special positivist pedestal, and a One Culture mentality has emerged to challenge the Two Culture picture of science and society" (p. 12). Once scientism is *fully* exorcised from science, Tauber argued, science can be reintegrated within the larger tradition of humanistic inquiry from which it originated.[20]

Third, Friedman's (2002, 2013a) portrayal of science as possessing a singular method with invariant qualities that can be set against "nonscientific" approaches resurrects another long-gone positivist dream. The very failure to demarcate between science and nonscience was largely due to, and intensified by, the vast diversity of so-called scientific practices. For Laudan (1996), the lack of agreement about the features of "*the* scientific method" means that the "unity of method" thesis should be regarded as refuted. As Duhem (1954/1991) showed, accounts of the scientific method "bore little resemblance to the methods actually used by working scientists" (Laudan, 1996, p. 214)—a conclusion extensively corroborated today by research into actual scientific practice (e.g., Shapin, 2010; for a balanced review of science studies, see Tauber, 2009). Despite the exaggerations of some postmodern constructionists, Tauber (2009) concluded, "Historical and sociological studies have demonstrated beyond the reasonable doubt that the working *practices* of scientific disciplines are both incompletely and inaccurately portrayed by the methodologies to which scientists officially subscribe" (p. 130).

What is more, J. Dupré (1995, 2004) pointed out that scholars typically use the rhetoric of science's methodological unity to ideologically dismiss (perhaps with good reasons) disciplines whose knowledge claims they consider to be far-fetched, unreliable, or dogmatic. As J. Dupré (2004) wrote, however,

> If one thinks of the daily practice of a theoretical physicist, a field taxonomist, a biochemist, or a neurophysiologist, it is hard to believe that there is anything fundamentally common to their activities that constitutes them all as practitioners of the Scientific Method. (p. 42)

In addition, J. Dupré (1995) argued, such a "disunity of science" is not a temporary state of affairs to be overcome in the future by superior cognitive or technological achievements, but "rather reflects accurately the underlying ontological complexity of the world" (p. 7).[21] Summing up the issues with both the demarcation project and the unity of science, De Caro and Macarthur (2004b) wrote:

> [S]cience has no essence and . . . the very idea of a sharp division between what is scientific and what is not is highly questionable. Indeed, the *ideal* of the unity of sciences is an unrealized and unrealizable dream. The point is not just that there is no single method or set of methods that is properly called the scientific method, but, more than this, that there is no clear, uncontroversial, and useful definition of science to do the substantial work scientific naturalists require of it. (p. 15)

Taken together, these assumptions about science disclose a positivist scientism in Friedman's (2002, 2013a) proposal that I find counterproductive for the integrity and appropriate epistemological legitimation of transpersonal psychology. In the end, as Walach (2013) pointed out, "at least part of the transpersonal enterprise is in fact an implicit or explicit *challenge to the entire history and set of methodologies by which science and scientific psychology* is done" (p. 68). Before exploring alternatives to Friedman's project, I briefly consider its implications for transpersonal research.

SCIENTIFIC TRANSPERSONAL RESEARCH PROGRAMS

In a section suitably titled, "What is left for transpersonal psychology to study," Friedman (2013a) reiterated that transpersonal psychology should exclusively research the physical and psychological aspects of transpersonal phenomena. Arguably controverting his earlier support of qualitative methods, Friedman (2013a) further claimed that transpersonal psychology should not research lived transpersonal experiences and instead study the expansion of one's "self-concept" or mental-linguistic understanding of one's identity (e.g., using his Self-Expansiveness Level Form; Friedman, 1983, 2013b). Since Friedman's (2013a) overriding goal is "to conceptualize and operationalize a transpersonal approach devoid of metaphysical assumptions" (p. 204), this focus on the self-concept is justified because he believes that the "notion of self as experienced can be equated to consciousness itself, and is a metaphysical notion every bit as obscure as transcendence" (p. 205).

To be sure, researching the self-concept is a legitimate endeavor, but as a transpersonal scholar I am mostly interested not in what people "think" about their identity but how they actually "experience" it. In my view, the "self-concept" is a construct whose value to measure or assess transpersonal states or growth is dubious. While the self-concept can change after a lived expansion of consciousness, it can also expand, for example, after reading an evocative spiritual book—think of Watts's (1966/2011) *The Book: On the Taboo Against Knowing Who You Are*—or after becoming intellectually familiar with transpersonal psychology, the notion of the ecological self, and so forth. Transpersonal psychologists should seek to assess transpersonal states through the study of changes in felt-sensed self-identity, not of mental views about such identity. Friedman's belief that only the self-concept can be researched is mistaken—changes in lived self-identity can be identified via qualitative methods, for example, longitudinal phenomenological studies of meditation practice. Friedman might respond that phenomenological reports necessarily refer to the self-concept, but it is one thing to report one's views on self-identity, and quite another to report one's lived experience of such an identity (see van Manen, 1990).

Interestingly, Friedman (2013a) claimed to embrace not only James's (1912/2003) radical empiricism but also Tart's (1972) state-specific sciences—approaches that consider data from both outer and inner (or introceptive) senses. Contra mystical claims, however, Friedman quickly added that nonduality and other spiritual states are terms without empirical referents and therefore they lie beyond the scope of scientific transpersonal psychology. The issue at stake here is what Friedman considers to be "inner data." After including phenomenological and electroencephalographic data, he qualified the kind of empirical data that in his view a community of meditators can produce: "Insofar as some in such community might have what could be described as transcendent experiences, those would be outside the realm of science to study directly (i.e., I would see these direct experiences as noumenal, not phenomenal)" (p. 309). Once again, Friedman's neo-Kantianism traps him in an epistemic box that is hermetically sealed by its own critical presuppositions—this time, one that James's radical empiricist openness to direct nonlinguistic experience actually overcomes (Blum, 2014; E. Taylor & Wozniak, 1996). All the above suggests the need to explore transpersonal epistemologies and research programs free from neo-Kantian assumptions and exclusive allegiance to a naturalistic metaphysics—a task for the rest of this essay.

PARTICIPATORY METAPHYSICAL PLURALISM

Integrating the work of Davidson (1984), R. Tarnas (1991), and Varela et al. (1991), among others, participatory approaches eschew the Kantian two-worlds dualism by regarding human beings as vehicles for the creative self-unfolding of reality and the enaction (or "bringing forth") of directly knowable spiritual worlds, realms, or domains of distinctions (e.g., Ferrer, 2002, 2008; Ferrer & Sherman, 2008b; Hartelius & Ferrer, 2013; Irwin, 1996, 2008). Whereas perennialism (and confessional and theological stances) posits a single or primary transcendent reality (Ferrer, 2000a, 2002) and modern science subscribes to a naturalistic worldview that brackets, denies, or reduces supernatural referents (De Caro & Macarthur, 2004a, 2010), participatory pluralism allows for a multiplicity of enacted spiritual worlds that can in principle be accounted for in both naturalistic and supernaturalistic fashions:

> [T]o embrace a participatory understanding of religious knowledge is not *necessarily* linked to confessional, religionist, or supernaturalist premises or standpoints. . . . [V]irtually all the same participatory implications for the study of religion can be practically drawn if we were to conceive, or translate the term, *spirit* in a naturalistic fashion as an emergent creative potential of life, nature, or reality. . . . Whether such creative source is a transcendent spirit or immanent life will likely be always a contested issue, but one, we believe, that does not damage the general claims of the participatory turn. (Ferrer & Sherman, 2008a, p. 72)

Thus, whereas both perennialism and scientism commit transpersonal psychology to a single metaphysical worldview—transcendentalist and naturalistic, respectively—participatory frameworks free the field from such univocal vows and invite researchers to remain open to multiple metaphysical possibilities. As M. Daniels (2005) pointed out, "It is vital that we remain pluralistic at this time and do not fall into the trap of committing the discipline as a whole to any particular ontology" (p. 231). The participatory approach, Hartelius (2016) wrote, allows for the coexistence of "multiple ontological claims regarding ultimacy . . . because they are claims to relational phenomenal, not self-existent objective-like referents" (p. v).

It is important to stress that participatory pluralism also disputes the idea of a single, pregiven nature world that is perceived differently by the various species and human cultures (see Megill, 1994). This stance is aligned with Viveiros de Castro's (2014, 2015) challenge of the superiority of scientific "mononaturalism," which acknowledges different representations of the same pregiven world, over Amerindian "multinaturalism" conceiving that different embodiments and cognitive apparatus bring forth ontologically distinct worlds. In his own words: "Multinaturalism does not suppose a Thing-in-Itself partially apprehended through categories of understanding proper to each species. . . . What exists in multinature are not such self-identical entities differently perceived but immediately relational multiplicities" (2014, p. 73).

Returning to strictly religious matters, while dispensing with dubious equations among spiritual ultimates (e.g., the Tao is God or Buddhist emptiness is structurally equivalent to the Hindu Brahman), participatory pluralism affirms an undetermined mystery or creative power as the generative source of all spiritual enactions (Ferrer, 2002, 2008).[22] As I argue in chapter 1, however, this shared spiritual dynamism should be sharply distinguished from any Kantian-like noumenon or "thing-in-itself" endowed with inscrutable qualities in relation to which all spiritual ultimates are always incomplete, culturally conditioned, or cognitively constrained phenomenal manifestations (e.g., Hick, 1989). In contrast, an enactive participatory epistemology (Ferrer, 2002, 2008; Malkemus, 2012) does away with the Kantian dualism by not only refusing to conceive of the mystery as having objectifiable pregiven attributes (e.g., personal, impersonal, dual, nondual), but also affirming the radical identity of the manifold spiritual ultimates and the mystery—even if the former do not exhaust the generative ontological possibilities of the latter. In other words, the mystery cocreatively unfolds in multiple ontological directions (see also chapter 9 and Postscript).

The question rightfully arises: Would not such a participatory account be another metaphysical worldview competing for supremacy? After all, no spiritual vision or conceptual framework is metaphysically neutral, and the undetermined nature of the mystery espoused by the participatory approach can be seen as especially consistent with Buddhism's emptiness and apophatic mystical accounts (Duckworth, 2014b; Ferrer, 2002). My use of the term *undetermined*, however, is eminently performative—that is, it seeks to evoke the sense of not-knowing and intellectual humility that I find most fruitful in approaching the creative power that is the source of our being (Ferrer, 2008). Rather than affirming negatively (as the term *indeterminate* does), *undetermined* leaves open the possibility of both determinacy and indeterminacy within the mystery, as well as the paradoxical confluence or even identity of these two apparently polar accounts (for further discussion, see Postscript). As Duckworth (2014a) observed regarding this proposal, metaphysical biases are thus neutralized for the most part; such an "undetermined ultimate precludes emptiness from being the final word on reality because, being undetermined, ultimate reality can also be disclosed as theistic in a personal God. And importantly, this 'God' is not a lower reality than emptiness" (pp. 346–347). Irwin (2008) concurs: "The participatory model is not based on preconceptions about the validity of (or relationship to) any particular metaphysical view, but seeks to elucidate this view as yet another example of authentic spiritual encounter" (p. 200).

In addition, the participatory approach bridges the *epistemic gap between human experience and reality* that is intrinsic to neo-Kantianism. This alienating gap is not only problematized by the aforesaid disembodied origins of Kantian dualism, but also bridged by Davidson's (1984) dismantling of the scheme-content dualism, R. Tarnas's (1991) participatory epistemology, elements of Bhaskar's (1989) critical realism and James's (1912/2003) radical empiricism, as well as modern embodied cognitive science (e.g., Chemero, 2009; Clark, 1997; Varela et al., 1991). Many of these approaches, Schilbrack (2014a) argued, restore metaphysics as a viable form of contemporary cognitive inquiry.[23]

At this juncture, it is important to distinguish between two different meanings of the term *metaphysics*. On the one hand, the notion of metaphysics in Western philosophy is generally based on the distinction between appearance and reality, with a metaphysical statement being one claiming to portray the "Reality" presumably lying behind the realm of appearances (van Inwagen, 1998). In addition to this use, on the other hand, many religious traditions talk about metaphysical worlds to refer to subtle levels, realms, or dimensions of reality existing beyond the sensible world or within the ontological depths of human consciousness (see chapter 9 and Postscript). Schilbrack (2014a) cogently argued that dropping Kantian assumptions renders religious metaphysical claims of direct access to the nature of reality cognitively viable in a modified first sense that is free from two world dualisms (*superempirical*, in his term); I propose that it also allows *entertaining the plausibility of a deep and ample multidimensional cosmos in which the sensible world (as narrowly conceived by modern naturalism) does not exhaust the possibilities of the Real.*[24]

The consequences of this move for transpersonal research are arguably profound: Stripping the supernatural of its monolithic and trans-categorical clothes allows a re-consideration of the existence of diverse subtle worlds of energy/consciousness. Intersubjective agreement about these worlds can then be pursued in special states of consciousness (after all, ordinary consciousness was evolutionarily shaped to optimize survival in the physical world). The import of not dismissing a priori the existence, or the possibility to apprehend, such realms is exemplified by the phenomenon of "shared visions" discussed in the next section.

THE EPISTEMOLOGICAL CHALLENGE OF SHARED VISIONS

In 2008, I spent one month in a Shipibo *vegetalista* center in the jungle near Iquitos, Peru, drinking the entheogenic brew called ayahuasca every other day (for ayahuasca studies, see Metzner, 2014; Shanon, 2002). At one of my first ayahuasca sessions, I was struck by the vision of a number of nonphysical entities (animal, human, and other-than-human) wandering in the *maloca* (traditional ceremony shed). Perhaps the most striking vision concerned certain entities well known in Indigenous medicine circles.

The vision began with my perception of a thick energetic thread of white light clearly emerging from the healer's mouth during the singing of an *icaro* (ayahuasca healing song). When I visually followed the thread to the farther corners of the *maloca*, I realized that it was attached to several nonphysical entities entering into the ceremonial shed. Although of humanoid shape (i.e., they had a head, body, arms, and legs), the entities were appreciably taller than humans and apparently made of a fuzzy white light that concealed any identifiable traits beyond their general form.

The "astral doctors," as I later learned these entities are usually called,[25] moved with apparent volitional precision around a room, for example, situating themselves in front of the ceremony's participants and extending their arms to make contact with specific areas of participants' bodies, especially the heart and the vital center. When my turn arrived, their contact resulted in dramatically tangible energetic adjustments of incredible finesse in those centers, accompanied by the feelings of deeply healing, profound gratitude, and instinctive trust in the benevolent nature of the entities. This experience led to a new understanding of the healing power of (at least that particular) ayahuasca ceremony as emerging from the complex interplay of the medicine, the healer, the *icaro*, and the astral doctors.

The next morning, when I asked the healer about my visions, he nodded his head and verbally corroborated the presence of "astral doctors" at the ceremony. Fascinated by the intersubjective agreement about such "open-eye" visions, I decided to interview the center director and Shipibo elder Guillermo Arévalo (see Ferrer, 2013).[26] During the interview, after distinguishing between ayahuasca visions emerging from personal imagination and those of a more transpersonal or shared nature, Arévalo stated that he and other healers often contrasted their perceptions searching for intersubjective agreement:

> We can plan to discuss these perceptions before a ceremony and then talk about it afterwards. In many cases, I ask another shaman sitting in the same ceremony what he saw in order to gain certainty through such agreement. If there is no clear agreement, we can try to achieve it at the following ceremony. (cited in Ferrer, 2013, p. 17)

Overall, this procedure struck me as remarkably similar to the scientific emphasis on public observation and replicability with one (arguably huge) difference—these healers were discussing entities that scientific naturalism would consider fictitiously supernatural.

The most astonishing shared visionary event I participated in, however, occurred some years earlier at a San Pedro (*wachuma*) ceremony in Urubamba, Peru (for studies on the Peruvian cactus San Pedro, see Heaven, 2012; Sharon, 1990). Several hours into the ceremony, and totally unexpectedly, I began seeing in front of my open eyes what looked like red, energetic spiderwebs of great complexity that elastically responded to my physical contact. I was so taken by the clarity and interactive nature of the vision that I approached the only other participant—a young U.S. woman who was drinking San Pedro for first time—and, pointing in the direction of the webs, asked her (without describing what I was seeing) whether she could see anything there. To my shock, she described the red, energetic spiderwebs exactly in the ways I was seeing them. What is more, the other participant and I could interactively play with those energy fields. When I asked Victoria (the healer), she not only corroborated she was seeing them, but also stated that such energetic visions were a common occurrence in San Pedro ceremonies. The red spiderwebs marked the beginning of nearly two hours of breathtaking external visionary experiences (I later titled the entire episode "Harry Potter Meets the Matrix")—blue and green energies curatively entering my body, contact with benevolent Indigenous spirits, and perceptions of energy vortices of diverse colors in the room, some of which stemmed from Victoria's "power objects."

Because San Pedro preserves one's critical capabilities intact (at least in my twelve-year experience with this plant), I had my "researcher hat" on during most of the visionary journey. In disbelief about the shared nature of the visions, I repeatedly asked both the other participant and the healer to describe the specificities of their visions in order to verify whether they matched my perceptions. Invariably, when pointed in the direction of my vision and asked "what do you see there?," they accurately described the color, shape, and directional movements of the various energetic fields I was seeing. This event strongly suggested to me that San Pedro allowed human sight to perceive or enact subtle energetic dimensions of reality; actually, one can often feel San Pedro organically retraining human sight, for example, refocusing it on the space in between objects or forms. From this space, in my experience, subtle visions emerge.[27]

The literature is not entirely silent on this type of experience. Indigenous people widely claim that their medicines allow access to an enhanced sensory faculty granting direct perception of subtle energies and spiritual entities—called, for example, "true seeing" by the Matsigenka of Southern Peru (Shepard, 2014), "second sight" by the Thonga of Mozambique, or "stargazing" by the Navajo (E. Turner, 1992). Elements of the phenomena I experienced have been also documented in the scholarly literature on entheogenic and healing visions. In addition to Shanon's (2002, pp. 69–85) reports of a variety of ayahuasca "open-eye visualizations," one of the most powerful examples of shared vision I am familiar with is described in Edith Turner's (1992) research into *ihamba*, a Zambian Ndembu healing ceremony in which the healer extracts an invisible spirit (supposedly visible as an ivory tooth) from the patient's body. Whereas thirty years earlier her husband the anthropologist Victor Turner's (1967) "scientific" ethnographic account famously portrayed Ndembu healers as therapeutically skilled sleight-of-hand magicians and denied ontological status to the "extracted" invisible spirit, E. Turner's (1992) participation in the ritual (which included ingestion of a non-hallucinogenic leaf medicine called *nsompu*) reportedly opened her to the reality of the Ndembu spiritual world. Central to this discussion, she saw the following and later reported that *three healers and the patient shared the same vision*:

> Suddenly Meru [the patient] raised her arm, stretched it in liberation. And I *saw* with my own eyes a giant thing emerging out of the flesh of her back. The thing was a large gray blob about six inches across, a deep gray opaque thing emerging as a sphere. . . . The gray thing was actually out there, visible, and you could see [the healer] Singleton's hands working and scrabbling on the back—and then the thing was there no more. Singleton has it in his pouch, pressing it with his other hand as well. (p. 149)

Intriguingly, only the five people ingesting the non-hallucinogenic medicine saw the "giant thing"; the rest of the group saw only the tooth, which, E. Turner (1992) concluded, should be considered the physical manifestation (vs. a mere symbol) of the immaterial spirit. She stressed: "I repeat that I did not merely intuit the spirit emerging from Mera's back but saw it, saw it with my open eyes" (pp. 189–190). This fascinating account powerfully shows how social-scientific reports shaped (limited?) by naturalistic assumptions can be problematized through participatory research open to Indigenous cosmologies, emic epistemologies, and ostensibly supernatural factors (cf. Irwin, 1994).

What to make of these phenomena? Naturalistic scholars may easily dismiss *inner* or *individual* visions of this kind as private, subjective, or brain hallucinations.[28] However, what about *intersubjectively shared outer visions* such as the ones above described?[29] In general, as Sacks (2012) indicated, the "shareable" (p. ix) nature of sensory claims is what distinguishes successful perception from hallucination. In their discussion of hallucinations, for example, Aleman and Larøi (2008) asked: "What happens in the brain when people see things others do not see . . . ?" (p. 147). Moreover, whether in science or philosophy intersubjective agreement or consensual validation is considered the final mark of "objectivity" or "reality," so what to make of shared visual perceptions of supernatural phenomena such as nonphysical entities or spirits? The naturalistic mind may understandably appeal to the notion of "collective" or "public hallucinations," such as rainbows, mirages, reflections in the water, and the like (see van Fraassen, 2008).[30] Unlike the ayahuasca astral doctors, however, rainbows do not autonomously move, intentionally touch people, and palpably alter a person's embodied experience. Unlike the *wachuma* visions of energetic webs and vortices, mirages neither respond pliantly to physical contact nor do they persist when viewed from different angles. In addition, unlike E. Turner's (1992) vision of the *ihamba* spirit, water (or mirrored) reflections do not emerge from a human body at the climax of an extraction healing ritual.

BEYOND NATURALISM AND SUPERNATURALISM: TOWARD A PARTICIPATORY RADICAL EMPIRICISM AND RESEARCH PROGRAM

The failure of "public hallucinations" models to account naturalistically for these phenomena leads me to conclude that the above participant-observation reports not only present a powerful challenge to scientific naturalism (and materialism), but also suggest the existence of subtle worlds or dimensions of reality coexisting with the physical domain. Equally important, these phenomena raise the possibility of intersubjective testing of so-called supernatural claims through a radical empiricist epistemology (after James, 1912/2003) that challenges the scientist attachment of "empirical validity" to "naturalistic sensory evidence." After all, spiritual practitioners following similar contemplative and ritual techniques generally reach intersubjective agreement about spiritual insights and realities, even if the falsification of those claims is not possible (Ferrer, 2002).

Even if one were to endorse a naturalistic metaphysics, Stroud (2004) names the appropriate question in his 1996 American Philosophical Association (APA) presidential address: "What is and what is not to be included in one's conception of nature" (p. 22). Although not fond of supernatural claims, Stroud recommended an "open naturalism" that "is not committed in advance to any determinate and therefore potentially restrictive conception of what is so" (p. 35). Such an open naturalism simply "says that we must accept as true everything we find we have to accept in order to make sense of everything that we think is part of the world" (p. 35). It may be important to remember here that the rational plausibility of so-called supernatural forces or entities is contingent on one's conscious or unconscious metaphysical commitments. As Ellis (2009) indicated, there is an inescapable logical circle here: "A postulated existent is ontologically plausible if and only if it fits into an adequate metaphysical theory. And a metaphysical theory is adequate if and only if it accommodates all of the things that we truly believe in" (p. 19).

In this light, I propose that transpersonal psychology should overcome the naturalistic/supernaturalistic divide, retire both terms, and endorse a more liberal or *open naturalism*—one that not only studies the physical and psychological dimensions of transpersonal phenomena, but also is free from materialism and reductionism, thus being open to both the ontological integrity of spiritual referents and the plausibility of subtle worlds or dimensions of reality. Once free from a priori allegiance to any particular metaphysical worldview (whether scientist or religionist), researchers can consider multiple methodological standpoints (emic and etic, insider and outsider), epistemologies (objectivist, constructivist, participatory), and metaphysical frameworks (scientific naturalism, perennialism, participatory pluralism) in the discernment of the most cogent account of the perceived phenomena.

Openness to the heuristic value and potential validity of alternate epistemic and metaphysical frameworks does not snare researchers in relativistic dilemmas. The attempt to rise above the inevitable biases of Western frameworks should not degenerate into a vulgar relativism incapable of offering grounds for qualitative distinctions or cross-cultural criticism. This unfortunate outcome can be avoided by dialogically evaluating all knowledge claims—etic and emic, insider and outsider, naturalistic and supernaturalistic—through validity standards of both dominant and marginal Western and non-Western epistemologies in whatever measure may be appropriate according to the context of the inquiry and the type of knowledge claims. In this scenario, the dividing line between sound and weak scholarship should not be traced between Western and non-Western epistemologies—or naturalistic and supernaturalistic claims—but between methodologies that lead to *radically empirical intersubjectively testable outcomes and/or discernible pragmatic consequences* and those which do not.[31]

In light of the discussion so far, questions arise for further research to consider. Can transpersonal research programs be open to all accounts, "naturalistic" and "supernaturalistic"? Might such a dialogical approach eventually deconstruct the binary opposition and disclose different ways to "think the world" beyond the naturalistic/supernaturalistic divide?[32]

What is lost and what is gained if transpersonal psychologists employ such an epistemologically and metaphysically pluralistic approach? Might this approach lead to a more flexible, expansive, or liberal open naturalism free from materialism—one that takes seriously the plausibility of subtle worlds or dimensions of reality? Could this open naturalism be capable of disrupting Western epistemic violence and fostering a more symmetrical dialogue—perhaps even collaborative inquiry—between transpersonal researchers and the world's spiritual practitioners? For now, my provisional stance is that each case (knowledge claim) needs to be assessed independently. No a priori or generic hierarchical relationship between so-called naturalist and supernaturalist accounts—and related etic and emic, outsider and insider, Western and non-Western accounts—can be legitimately established to ascertain the most accurate account of what truly transpires in a spiritual or transpersonal event (e.g., a Kalua tantric ritual or a Shipibo ayahuasca ceremony).

There is no methodological reason why transpersonal psychologists cannot research shared external visions. Such a research program could entail the intake of a visionary medicine—such as San Pedro or ayahuasca—by a team of researchers focusing their attention on the possible occurrence of external visions.[33] This type of research could be also developed in collaboration with traditional practitioners such as shamans or healers. At a first stage (preparation), coresearchers would agree to contrast their perceptions both during and after ceremonies while being mindful of peer-pressure influences, unconscious group collusion, and other potential methodological pitfalls (see Heron, 1996, 1998). The second stage (journey) would consist of the actual intake of the medicine and ensuing group visionary journey. At a third stage (internal comparison and interpretation), coresearchers would contrast their experiences and search for intersubjective agreement in their visions. Were shared visions identified, coresearchers would discuss their ontological nature from a pluralistic epistemological perspective that would not impose a priori metaphysical limits to the nature of the inquiry outcomes. Multiple methodological standpoints, epistemologies, and metaphysical frameworks could be considered to discern the more appropriate account of the perceived phenomena. At a final stage (external comparison and reinterpretation), coresearchers could look for contrasts between the group's inquiry outcomes and available Western and non-Western literature about the meaning and ontological nature of the shared visions.

To be sure, actual research is necessary to assess the epistemic fertility and methodological soundness of such a research program. Contra

Friedman's (2002, 2013a) proposal, however, I suggest that transpersonal psychologists should be able to carry out these types of research and still rightfully call themselves *psychologists*.

CONCLUSION

Transpersonal psychology should indeed encourage scientific studies, but Friedman's (2002, 2013a) division of labor between a "scientific" transpersonal psychology and "nonscientific" transpersonal studies is neither cogent nor salutary. To turn transpersonal psychology into a modern scientific discipline achieves precisely what Friedman seeks to avoid, that is, binding transpersonal psychology to a singular naturalistic worldview with a metaphysical status equivalent to religious supernaturalism. Although transpersonal psychologists should definitively remain vigilant against the infiltration of metaphysical or religious ideologies in the field, scientific naturalism as an alternate ideology should not be the exception. Whereas it might be impossible to carry out scholarship without metaphysical assumptions, it is important to be explicitly self-critical about them and avoid presenting naturalistic science as less metaphysically biased or as the only path to progressive knowledge. The alternative, I propose, is to work with a larger naturalistic inquiry framework that is open to the viability of a multiverse or multidimensional cosmos in which modern science's narrow "naturalistic" world does not necessarily exhaust the possibilities of the real.

Transpersonal scholars should also scrutinize the neo-Kantian assumptions lying beneath skepticism and agnosticism toward the ontological status of certain spiritual realities. It is fundamental to be aware that such a stance, far from warranting neutrality or impartiality, is the fruit of a Western, dualistic, and arguably disembodied epistemological ethos that automatically renders suspect many spiritual claims about the nature of knowledge and reality. In their attempts to promote the scientific legitimacy of the field, some transpersonal psychologists have prematurely committed to a neo-Kantian dualistic epistemology that is in fact ideologically tied to a naturalistic, and often materialistic, metaphysics. Whether such a narrowly conceived naturalistic worldview will ultimately be cogent is unknown (I strongly suspect that it will not), but transpersonal scholars should note the metaphysical presuppositions of such a methodological agnosticism; in this way, they can avoid assuming or defending its purportedly metaphysically neutral status and thereby falling prey to one of science's most prevalent ideologies (van Fraassen, 2002).

As a possible way forward, I have suggested the following steps:

1. recognizing the inevitability of metaphysics in both science and religion;

2. minimizing parochialism via working with inquiry frameworks that are open to both "naturalistic" and "supernaturalistic" accounts of spiritual phenomena even if this approach may ultimately lead to the overcoming of such a binary opposition (e.g., in the form of an open naturalism);

3. developing methodological approaches that dialogically engage emic and etic claims, as well as Western and non-Western epistemologies, in the understanding and assessment of spiritual knowledge claims;

4. approaching religious traditions in the spirit of a participatory pluralism that is open to the ontological richness of religious worlds without reducing them to any single transcendentalist or naturalistic worldview; and

5. critiquing oppressive and repressive inner and outer systems of domination, selfishness, dissociation, and violence within, between, and among human beings, other sentient beings, and the world.

Methodologically, I firmly believe that such an approach calls for transpersonal psychology to embrace empirical (quantitative and qualitative; linear and nonlinear), theoretical (e.g., hermeneutic, comparative, integrative, critical, feminist, postcolonial), and contemplative/visionary methods. As Lancaster (2013) argued, "The defining feature of transpersonal psychology is that it integrates across all the levels [neuroscientific, cognitive and neuropsychological, psychodynamic, and spiritual/mystical] in its approach to understanding the mind and processes of transformation" (p. 225). Following Lancaster's suggestion, it is time to work toward a metaphysically, epistemologically, and methodologically plural transpersonal psychology that, bridging previously polarized camps (e.g., science and religion, modern and postmodern, or empiricism and hermeneutics), may well become one of the first truly holistic disciplines of the twenty-first century.

THREE

TOWARD A FULLY EMBODIED
SPIRITUAL LIFE

"Embodied spirituality" has become a buzzword in contemporary spiritual circles, yet the concept has not been dealt with in a thorough manner.[1] What is really meant when people say that spirituality is "embodied"? Is there a distinct understanding of the body underlying this expression? What does distinguish "embodied" from "disembodied" spirituality in practice? What are the implications for spiritual practice and spiritual goals—and for the very approach to spiritual liberation—of taking embodiment seriously?

Before attempting to answer these questions, two caveats are in order. First, although the following reflections seek to capture essential features of an emerging spiritual ethos in the modern West, by no means do I claim that they represent the thinking of every spiritual author and teacher who today uses the term *embodied spirituality*. It should be obvious that some authors may focus on or accept only some of these features, and that the following account inevitably reflects my own standpoint, with its unique perspective and consequent limitations. Second, this chapter engages in the task of a "creative interreligious hermeneutics" that not only freely—and admittedly somewhat impetuously—weaves together spiritual threads from different religious traditions, but also at times revisions them in light of modern spiritual understandings.[2] Although this procedure is still considered anathema in mainstream academic circles, I am convinced that only through a critical fusion of past and present global spiritual horizons can a trustworthy tapestry of contemporary embodied spirituality began to be stitched.[3]

WHAT IS EMBODIED SPIRITUALITY?

The expression "embodied spirituality" can be rightfully seen as redundant and perhaps even hollow. After all, is not all human spirituality "embodied" insofar as it necessarily transpires in and through embodied men and women? Proponents of embodied spiritual practice, however, assert that important trends of past and present spiritualities are "disembodied" (e.g., Masters, 2010; Ray, 2008; Washburn, 2003a). What does "disembodied" mean in this context?

Regarding prevalent Western and Eastern spiritual history, I suggest that "disembodied" does not denote that the body and its vital/primary energies were ignored in religious practice—they definitely were not—but rather that they were (most often) not considered legitimate or reliable sources of spiritual insight in their own right. In other words, body and instinct have not generally been regarded as capable of collaborating as equals with heart, mind, and consciousness in the attainment of spiritual realization and liberation (no matter how differently these goals have been understood and enacted). What is more, as I document below, many religious traditions and schools believed that the body and the instinctive world (and aspects of the heart, such as certain passions) were actually a hindrance to spiritual flourishing—a view that often led to the repression, regulation, or transformation of these worlds at the service of the "higher" goals of a spiritualized consciousness. This is why disembodied spirituality often crystallized in a "heart-chakra-up" spiritual life that was based preeminently in the mental or emotional access to transcendent states of consciousness and that tended to overlook spiritual sources immanent in the body, nature, and matter.[4]

Embodied spirituality, in contrast, views all human dimensions—body, vital, heart, mind, and consciousness—as equal partners in bringing self, community, and world into a fuller alignment with the mystery out of which everything arises. Far from being an obstacle, this approach sees the engagement of the body and its vital/primary energies as crucial for not only a thorough spiritual transformation, but also the creative exploration of expanded forms of spiritual freedom. The consecration of the whole person leads naturally to the cultivation of a "full-chakra" spirituality that seeks to make all human attributes permeable to the presence of both transcendent and immanent spiritual sources.[5] This account does not mean that embodied spirituality ignores the need to emancipate body and instinct from possible alienating tendencies; rather, it means that *all* human dimensions—not just somatic and primary ones—are recognized as possibly alienated but also equally capable of sharing freely in the unfolding life of the mystery here on Earth.

The contrast between sublimation and integration can help to clarify this distinction. In *sublimation*, the energy of one human dimension is used to amplify, expand, or transform the faculties of another dimension. For example, a celibate monk may sublimate sexual desire as a catalyst for spiritual breakthrough or to increase the devotional love of the heart, or a tantric practitioner may use vital/sexual energies as fuel to catapult consciousness into disembodied, transcendent, or even transhuman states of being.[6] In contrast, the *integration* of two human dimensions entails a mutual transformation, or sacred marriage, of their essential energies. For example, the integration of consciousness and the vital world makes the former more embodied, vitalized, and even eroticized, and grants the latter an intelligent evolutionary direction beyond its biologically driven instincts (see chapter 4). Roughly speaking, it could be said that sublimation is a mark of disembodied spirituality, and integration is a goal of embodied spirituality. This is not to say, of course, that sublimation has no place in embodied spiritual practice. The spiritual path is intricate and multifaceted, and the sublimation of certain energies may be necessary—even crucial—at specific junctures or for certain individual dispositions. To turn sublimation into a permanent goal or energetic dynamic, however, may be a fast lane to disembodied spirituality.

In addition to spiritualities that blatantly devalue body and world, a more subtle type of disembodied orientation sees spiritual life as emerging exclusively from the interaction of human immediate experience and transcendent fields or states of consciousness (cf. Heron, 1998). In this context, spiritual practice is aimed either at accessing such overriding realities ("ascent" paths, such as classic Neo-Platonic mysticism) or at bringing such spiritual consciousness down to earth to transfigure human nature and the world ("descent" paths, e.g., those illustrated by important aspects of Sri Aurobindo's [1993] integral yoga). The shortcoming of this "monopolar" understanding is that it ignores the existence of a second spiritual pole—immanent spiritual life—that, as I elaborate below, is intimately connected to the vital world and stores the most generative power of the mystery. To overlook this spiritual source leads practitioners—even those concerned with bodily transformation—to neglect the significance of the vital world for a creative spirituality, as well as to seek to transcend or sublimate their sexual energies. A *fully* embodied spirituality, I suggest, emerges from the creative interplay of both consciousness and energy—that is, transcendent and immanent spiritual sources—in complete individuals who embrace the fullness of human experience while remaining firmly grounded in body and earth.

To be sure, religious attitudes toward the human body have been profoundly ambivalent, with the body being regarded as a source of bondage, sinfulness, and defilement on the one hand, and as the locus of spiritual revelation and divinization on the other. The history of religions houses tendencies that fall along a continuum of disembodied to embodied goals and practices. Examples of disembodied trends include the asceticism of Brahmanism, Jainism, Buddhism, monastic Christianity, early Taoism, or early Sufism (Bhagat, 1976; Wimbush & Valantasis, 2002); Hindu views of the body as unreal (*mithya*) and the world as illusion (*maya*; L. E. Nelson, 1998b); Advaita Vedanta's consideration of the "bodiless liberation" (*videhamukti*) achievable only after death as "higher" than a "living liberation" (*jivanmukti*) inexorably tainted by bodily karma (Fort, 1998); early Buddhist accounts of the body as a repulsive source of suffering, of *nirvana* as the extinction of bodily senses and desires, and of "final *nirvana*" (*parinirvana*) as attainable only after death (S. Collins, 1998); the Christian view of the flesh as the source of evil and of the resurrected body as asexual (Bynum, 1995); the "isolation" (*kaivalyam*) of the universal Self from body and world in Samkhya-Yoga (Larson, 1969); the tantric transmutation of sexual energy to attain union with the divine in Kashmir Saivism (Mishra, 1993) or to be attuned to the creative flow of the Tao in Taoist self-cultivation (Yasuo, 1993); the Safed Kabbalists' obsession with the sinfulness of masturbation and nocturnal emissions (Biale, 1992), or the Lurianic repudiation of the body as "preventing man from [achieving] perfection of his soul" (as cited in Fine, 1992, p. 131); the Islamic consideration of the hereafter (*al-akhira*) as being immeasurably more valuable than the physical world (*al-dunya*; Winter, 1995); and the Visistadvaita Vedanta's claim that complete liberation entails the total cessation of embodiment (Skoog, 1996).

Likewise, examples of embodied trends include the Zoroastrian view of the body as part of human ultimate nature (A. Williams, 1997); the Biblical account of the human being as made in the "image of God" (Genesis; Jónsson, 1988); the tantric affirmation of the nonduality of sensual desire and awakening (Faure, 1998); the early Christian emphasis on incarnation, as in the Biblical "the Word became flesh" (John 1:14; Barnhart, 2008); the goal of attaining Buddhahood in this very body (*sokushin jobutsu*) of Shingon Buddhism (Kasulis, 1990); the Jewish religious enjoyment of all bodily needs and appetites in the Sabbath (Westheimer & Mark, 1995); the radical embrace of sensuality in the

Sufi poetry of Rumi or Hafez (Barks, 2002; Pourafzal & Montgomery, 1998); the Taoist vision of the body as a symbolic container of the secrets of the entire universe (Saso, 1997); the somatic connection to immanent spiritual sources in many Indigenous spiritualities (e.g., Lawlor, 1991); Soto Zen's insistence on the need to surrender the mind to the body in order to reach enlightenment (Yasuo, 1987); the Islamic esoteric saying of the Shi'ite Imams, "Our spirits are our bodies and our bodies our spirits" (*arwahuna ajsaduna wa ajsaduna arwahuna*; Galian, 2004, para. 53); and the long-standing Judeo-Christian advocacy for social engagement and justice in the spiritual transformation of the world (e.g., Forest, 1993; Heschel, 1996), among many others.

Many apparently embodied religious orientations, however, conceal highly ambivalent views toward sensuality and the physical body. For example, Taoism did not generally value the physical body in itself, but only because it was believed to be a dwelling place for the gods; Taoist sexual practices often involved rigorous self-restraint, inhibitory rules, and a depersonalization of sexual relationships that disdained the cultivation of mutual love among individuals (J. J. Clarke, 2000; Schipper, 1993). Also, whereas the Jewish Sabbath is a day for the consecration of sexual intercourse between husband and wife, many traditional teachings (e.g., the *Iggeret ha-Kodesh*) prescribed the need to engage in such a union without pleasure or passion, as it was supposedly carried out in the Orchard before the first sin (Biale, 1992). What is more, much of the Vajrayana Buddhist appreciation of the "gross" physical body as a facilitator of enlightenment lay in considering it the foundation of a more real, nonphysical, "astral body" or "rainbow body" (P. Williams, 1997). In a similar fashion, Hindu Tantra regarded body and world as real, but some of its rituals of identification with the cosmos entailed the purification and visualized destruction of the "impure" physical body to catalyze the emergence of a subtle or divine body from the very ashes of corporeality (e.g., the *Jayakhya Samhita* of Tantric Vaisnavism; Flood, 2000). In short, although certain religious schools generated spiritual goals more inclusive of embodiment, in living practice a fully embodied spirituality that engages the participation of all human attributes in cocreative interaction with both spiritual consciousness and immanent life was, and continues to be, an extremely rare pearl to find.

An examination of the numerous historical and contextual variables behind the tendency toward disembodied spirituality goes beyond the scope of this chapter, but I would like to mention at least a possible underlying reason (see Ferrer et al., 2004; Romero & Albareda, 2001).

The frequent inhibition of the primary dimensions of the person—somatic, instinctive, sexual, and certain aspects of the emotional—may have been necessary at certain historical junctures to allow the emergence and maturation of the values of the human heart and consciousness. More specifically, this inhibition may have been essential to avoid the reabsorption of a still relatively weak, emerging self-consciousness and its values into the stronger presence that a more instinctively driven energy once had in human collectivities. In the context of religious praxis, this tendency may be connected to the widespread consideration of certain human qualities as being spiritually more "correct" or wholesome than others; for instance, equanimity over intense passions, transcendence over sensuous embodiment, chastity or strictly regulated sexual practice over open-ended sensual exploration, and so forth. What may characterize the present moment (at least in the modern West), however, is the possibility of reconnecting all these human potentials in an integrated way. In other words, having developed self-reflective consciousness and the subtle dimensions of the heart, it may be the moment to reappropriate and integrate the more primary and instinctive dimensions of human nature into a fully embodied spiritual life.[7] The next section explores the distinctive understanding of the human body implicit in embodied spirituality.

THE LIVING BODY

Embodied spirituality regards the body as subject, as the home of the complete human being, as a source of spiritual insight, as a microcosm of the universe and the mystery, and as pivotal for enduring spiritual transformation.

Body as Subject

To see the body as subject means to approach it as a living world, with all its interiority and depth, its needs and desires, its lights and shadows, its wisdom and obscurities. Bodily joys and sorrows, tensions and relaxations, longings and repulsions are some of the means through which the body can speak to us. By any measure, the body is not an "It" to be objectified and used for the goals or even spiritual ecstasies of the conscious mind, but a "Thou"—an intimate partner with whom the other human dimensions can collaborate in the pursuit of ever-increasing forms of liberating wisdom.

Body as the Home of the Complete Human Being

In this physical reality, the body is a human being's home, a locus of free-dom that allows people to walk their own unique path, both literally and symbolically. Once the dualism of matter and spirit is fully overcome, the body can no longer be seen as a "prison of the soul" or even as a "temple of spirit." The mystery of incarnation never alluded to the "entrance" of spirit into the body, but to its "becoming" flesh: "In the beginning was the Word, and the Word was God. . . . And the Word became flesh" (John 1:1, 14). Would it then perhaps be more accurate to appreciate the human body as a *transmutation* of spirit into fleshy form, at least dur-ing physical existence? Through the ongoing incarnation of innumerable beings, life aims at the ultimate union of humanity and divinity *in the body*. Perhaps paradoxically, a complete incarnation can bring a peace-ful and fulfilling death because human beings can then depart from this material existence with a profoundly felt sense of having accomplished one of the most essential purposes in being born into the world.

Body as Source of Spiritual Insight

The body is a divine revelation that can offer spiritual understanding, discrimination, and wisdom. First, the body is the uterus for the concep-tion and gestation of genuine spiritual knowledge. Bodily sensations, for example, are foundational stepping-stones in the embodied transforma-tion of spirit's creative energies through each human life. In the absence of severe blockages or dissociations, this creative energy is somatically transformed into impulses, emotions, feelings, thoughts, insights, visions, and, ultimately, contemplative revelations. As the Buddha famously said, "Everything that arises in the mind starts flowing with a sensation in the body" (cited in Goenka, 1998, p. 26).

Furthermore, listening deeply to the body can lead to the real-ization that physical sensations and impulses can be genuine sources of spiritual insight (see chapters 5 and 7). In certain Zen schools, for example, bodily actions constitute crucial tests of spiritual realization and are seen as the ultimate verification of sudden illumination or *satori* (Faure, 1993). The epistemological relevance of embodiment in spiritual matters was also passionately asserted by Kazantzakis (1965):

> Within me even the most metaphysical problem takes on
> a warm physical body which smells of sea, soil, and human

sweat. The Word, in order to touch me, must become warm flesh. Only then do I understand—when I can smell, see, touch. (p. 43)

Perhaps even more important, the body is the human dimension that can arguably reveal the ultimate meaning of incarnated life. Being physical itself, the body stores within its depths the answer to the mystery of material existence. The body's answer to this conundrum is not given in the form of any grand metaphysical vision or Theory of Everything, but gracefully granted through states of being that render life naturally profound and meaningful. In other words, the meaning of life is not something to be discerned and known intellectually by the mind, but to be felt in the depths of the flesh.

Body as Microcosm of the Universe and the Mystery

Virtually all spiritual traditions hold that there is a deep resonance among the human being, the cosmos, and the mystery. This view is captured in the esoteric dictum "as above so below" (Faivre, 1994); the Platonic, Taoist, Islamic, Kabbalistic, and tantric understanding of the person as microcosm of the macrocosm (see Chittick, 1994a; Faure, 1998; Saso, 1997; Shokek, 2001; Wayman, 1982); and the Biblical view of the human being made "in the image of God" or *imago Dei* (Jónsson, 1988). For the Bauls of Bengal, the understanding of the body as the microcosm of the universe (*bhanda/brahmanda*) entails the belief that the divine dwells physically within the human body (McDaniel, 1992). The Jesuit thinker Pierre Teilhard de Chardin (1968) put it this way: "My matter is not a *part* of the Universe that I possess *totaliter*; it is the *totality* of the Universe possessed by me *partialiter*" (p. 12).

All these perceptions portray an image of the human body as mirroring and containing the innermost structure of both the entire universe and the ultimate creative principle.[8] In a number of traditions, this structural correspondence between the human body and the mystery has shaped mystical practices in which bodily rituals and actions were thought to affect the very dynamics of the Divine—a pursuit that was perhaps most explicitly described in Kabbalistic theurgical mysticism (Lancaster, 2008). This mystical orientation does not imply that the body is to be valued only because it represents or can affect "larger" or "higher" realities—such a view subtly retains the fundamental dualism of material body and spirit. Embodied spirituality recognizes the human body as a pinnacle of spirit's creative manifestation and, consequently, as overflowing with intrinsic spiritual meaning.

Body as Essential for an Enduring Spiritual Transformation

The body is a filter through which human beings can purify polluted energetic tendencies, both biographical and collectively inherited. As the body is denser in nature than the emotional, mental, and conscious worlds, changes occurring in it are more lasting and permanent. In other words, an enduring psychospiritual transformation needs to be grounded in somatic transfiguration. The integrative transformation of the somatic/ energetic worlds of a person effectively short-circuits the tendency of past energetic habits to return, thus creating a solid foundation for more thorough and stable spiritual transformation.

FEATURES OF EMBODIED SPIRITUALITY

In light of this expanded understanding of the human body, I offer a consideration of ten features of embodied spirituality.

A Tendency toward Integration

Embodied spirituality is integrative insofar as it seeks to foster the harmonious participation of all human attributes in the spiritual path without tensions or dissociations. Despite his downplaying the spiritual import of sexuality and the vital world, Sri Aurobindo (2001) was correct when he said that the liberation of consciousness should not be confused with an integral transformation that entails the spiritual alignment of all human dimensions. As I propose in chapter 1, this recognition suggests the need to expand the traditional Mahayana Buddhist bodhisattva vow (i.e., to renounce one's own complete enlightenment until all sentient beings attain liberation) to encompass an integral bodhisattva vow in which the conscious mind renounces its own full liberation until the body and the primary world can be free as well. Since the conscious mind is the seat of most individuals' sense of identity, an exclusive liberation of consciousness can be deceptive insofar as one can believe that one is fully free when, in fact, essential dimensions of the self are underdeveloped, alienated, or in bondage. Needless to say, to embrace an integral *bodhisattva* vow is not a return to the individualistic spiritual aspirations of early Buddhism because it entails a commitment to the integral liberation of all sentient beings, rather that only of their conscious minds or conventional sense of identity. Likewise, as the above description reflects, my use of the term *bodhisattva* does not suggest a commitment to early Buddhist accounts of liberation as the extinction of bodily senses and desires and release from the cycle of transmigratory experience or *samsara* (S. Collins, 1998; P. Harvey, 1995; see also chapter 9).

The preceding account does not require or assume an ontological dualism between mind and body, or between consciousness and vital energy. Once differentiated, all these human attributes can be unevenly developed as well as either integrated or dissociated (see chapter 4); nonetheless, I maintain their ontological continuity (cf. Viveiros de Castro's [2015] account of Amerindian mind/body continuity). In other words, mind/body experiential *duality* does not necessarily entail ontological *dualism*, even if the former can naturally lead to the conceptual postulation of the latter (see chapter 2).

Realization through the Body

Although their actual practices and fruits remain obscure in the available literature, the Hindu sect of the Bauls of Bengal coined the term *kaya sadhana* to refer to a realization through the body (McDaniel, 1992)— embodied spirituality explores the development of this realization as appropriate for the contemporary world. With the notable exception of certain tantric techniques, traditional forms of meditation are practiced individually and without bodily interaction with other practitioners. Modern embodied spirituality rescues the spiritual significance not only of the body but also of physical contact. Due to their sequential emergence in human development (from soma to instinct to heart to mind), each dimension grows by taking root in the previous ones, with the body thereby becoming a natural doorway to the deepest levels of the rest of the human dimensions. Therefore, the practice of contemplative physical contact in a context of relational mindfulness and spiritual aspiration can have a profound transformative power (see chapters 4 and 7).

In order to foster a genuine embodied practice, it is essential to make contact with the body, discern its current state and needs, and then create spaces for the body to engender its own practices and capabilities—devise its own yoga, so to speak. When the body becomes permeable to both consciousness and life energy, it can find its own rhythms, habits, postures, movements, and charismatic rituals. Interestingly, some ancient Indian texts state that yoga postures (*asanas*) first emerged spontaneously from within the body and were guided by the free flow of its vital energy or *prana* (Sovatsky, 1994). A creative indwelling spiritual life resides within the body—an intelligent vital dynamism that is waiting to emerge and orchestrate the unfolding of one's becoming fully human.

Bodyfulness: Awakening of the Body

The permeability of the body to spiritual consciousness and immanent life leads to its gradual awakening. In contrast to meditation techniques that focus on mindfulness of the body, this awakening can be more accurately articulated in terms of *bodyfulness* (Ferrer, 2006; cf. Caldwell, 2014). In bodyfulness, the psychosomatic organism becomes calmly alert without the intentionality of the conscious mind. Bodyfulness may reintegrate in the human being a lost somatic capability that is seemingly present in panthers, tigers, and other "big cats" of the jungle, who can be extraordinarily aware without intentionally attempting to be so. As Caldwell (2014) explained, "some of what could be considered as under the rubric of bodyfulness has been articulated in the name of mindfulness" (p. 76). However, she continued: "[although] mindfulness will sometimes involve body practices . . . and begins to approach aspects of bodily life . . . the body itself is capable of awakened states that go beyond these methods and practices" (p. 76). A possible future horizon of bodyfulness was described by Sri Aurobindo's spiritual consort Mirra Alfassa (known to her followers as The Mother) in terms of the conscious awakening of the very cells of the organism (see Satprem, 1992).

Resacralization of Sexuality and Sensuous Pleasure

Whereas mind and consciousness constitute a natural bridge to transcendent spiritual states, the body and its primary energies constitute a natural bridge to immanent spiritual life. Immanent life is spiritual *prima materia*—that is, spiritual energy in a state of transformation, still not actualized, saturated with potentials and possibilities, and the source of genuine innovation and creativity at all levels. As Romero and Albareda (2001) pointed out, sexuality and the vital world are the first soils for the organization and creative development of the immanent dimension of the mystery in human reality. For this reason (and others), it is crucial that sexuality be lived as a sacred land free from fears, conflicts, or ideologies imposed by the mind, culture, religion, and even spiritual beliefs. When the vital world is reconnected to immanent spiritual life, the primary drives can spontaneously collaborate in one's psychospiritual unfolding without needing to be sublimated or transcended.

Due to its captivating effect on human consciousness and the egoic personality, sensuous pleasure has been viewed with suspicion—or even demonized as inherently sinful—by most religious traditions. In a context of embodied spiritual aspiration, however, it becomes fundamental to rescue, in a nonnarcissistic manner, the dignity and spiritual significance of physical pleasure. In the same way that pain contracts the body, pleasure relaxes it, making it more porous to the presence and flow of both immanent and transcendent spiritual energies. In this light, the formidable magnetic force of the sexual drive can be seen as attracting consciousness to matter, facilitating both its embodiment and grounding in the world and the development of an incarnational process that transforms both the individual and the world. Furthermore, the recognition of the spiritual import of physical pleasure naturally heals the historical split between sensuous love (*eros*) and spiritual love (*agape*), and this integration fosters the emergence of genuinely human love—an unconditional love that is simultaneously embodied and spiritual (Romero & Albareda, 2001).[9]

The Urge to Create

In *Cosmos and History*, Eliade (1959/1989) made a compelling case for the "re-enactive" nature of many religious practices and rituals, for example, in their attempt to replicate cosmogonic actions and events. Expanding this account, I suggest that most religious traditions are "reproductive" insofar as their practices aim to not only ritually reenact mythical motives, but also replicate the enlightenment of their founder (e.g., the awakening of the Buddha) or attain the state of salvation or freedom described in allegedly revealed scriptures (e.g., the *moksa* of the Vedas). Although disagreements about the exact nature of such states and the most effective methods to attain them abounded in the historical development of religious practices and ideas—naturally leading to rich creative developments within the traditions—spiritual inquiry was regulated (and arguably constrained) by such predetermined unequivocal goals.

Embodied spirituality, in contrast, seeks to cocreate novel spiritual understandings, practices, and expanded states of freedom in interaction with both immanent and transcendent spiritual sources. The creative power of embodied spirituality is connected to its integrative nature.

Whereas through the mind and consciousness one tends to access subtle worlds and transcendent states already enacted in history that display forms and dynamics (e.g., specific cosmological motifs, archetypal configurations, mystical visions), connection to the vital/primary world gives greater access to the generative power of immanent spiritual life.[10] Put simply, the more that all human dimensions actively participate in spiritual knowing, the more creative spiritual life becomes.

Although many variables were clearly at play, the connection between vital/primary energies and spiritual innovation may help to explain two interesting conundrums: first, why human spirituality and mysticism have been to a great extent "conservative"—that is, heretic mystics are the exception to the rule, and most mystics firmly conformed to accepted doctrines and canonical scriptures (see Katz, 1983b); and second, why many spiritual traditions strictly regulated sexual behavior, and often repressed or even proscribed the creative exploration of sensual desire (e.g., S. J. Cohen, 1993; Faure, 1998; Feuerstein, 1998; Weiser-Hanks, 2000). I am not proposing that religious traditions regulated or restricted sexual activity *deliberately* to hinder spiritual creativity and maintain the status quo of their doctrines. In my reading, all evidence seems to point to other social, cultural, moral, and doctrinal factors (e.g., P. Brown, 1988; Parrinder, 1996). What I am suggesting, in contrast, is that the religious, social, and moral regulation of sexuality may have had an unexpected debilitating impact on human spiritual creativity across traditions for centuries. Although this inhibition may have been necessary in the past, an increasing number of individuals today may be prepared for a more creative engagement of their spiritual lives.

Grounded Spiritual Visions

As discussed above, most major spiritual traditions posit the existence of an isomorphism among the human being, the cosmos, and the mystery. From this correspondence, it follows, the more dimensions of the person that are actively engaged in the study of the mystery—or of phenomena associated with it—the more complete her knowledge will be. This completion should not be understood quantitatively but rather in a qualitative sense. In other words, the more human dimensions creatively participate in spiritual knowing, the greater will be the *dynamic congruence* between inquiry approach and studied phenomena and the more *grounded in, coherent with,* or *attuned to* the ongoing unfolding of the mystery will be the enacted knowledge.

In this regard, it is likely that many past and present spiritual visions are to some extent the product of dissociated ways of knowing—ways that emerge predominantly from accessing certain forms of transcendent consciousness but in partial or total disconnection from more immanent spiritual sources. For example, spiritual visions holding that body and world are ultimately illusory (or lower, or impure, or a hindrance to spiritual liberation) arguably derive from states of being in which the sense of self mainly or exclusively identifies with transcendent consciousness, getting uprooted from the body and immanent spiritual life. From this existential stance, it is understandable (and perhaps inevitable) that both body and world are seen as illusory or defective. This account is consistent with the Kashmir Saiva view that the illusory nature of the world belongs to an intermediate level of spiritual perception (*suddhavidya-tattva*), after which the world begins to be discerned as a real extension of the Lord Siva (Mishra, 1993). Indeed, when somatic and vital worlds are invited to participate in the spiritual life, making human identity permeable to not only transcendent forms of awareness but also immanent spiritual energies, then body and world become spiritually significant realities that are recognized as crucial for human and cosmic spiritual fruition.

In-the-World Nature

We are born on Earth. I passionately believe that this is not irrelevant, a mistake, or the product of a delusional cosmic game whose ultimate goal is to transcend our embodied predicament (cf. Romero & Albareda, 2001). Perhaps, as some traditions claim, human beings could have been incarnated in more subtle worlds or dimensions of reality, but the fact that we did it here must be significant if we are to engage the human life in any genuinely wholesome and meaningful manner. To be sure, at certain crossroads on the spiritual path it may be necessary to go beyond our embodied existence in order to access essential dimensions of our identity (especially when external or internal conditions make it difficult or impossible to connect with those dimensions in our everyday life). However, to turn this move into a permanent spiritual *modus operandi* can easily create dissociations in one's spiritual life leading to a devitalized body, an arrested emotional or interpersonal development, or lack of discernment around sexual behavior—as the sexual transgressions of many past and present Western, Eastern, and Indigenous spiritual teachers illustrate (see Feuerstein, 2006; Forsthoefel & Humes, 2005; Peluso, 2014; Storr, 1996).

If one lives in a closed and dark house, it is natural that one may feel pushed periodically to leave home in search of the nourishing warmth and light of the sun. An embodied spirituality, however, invites us as human beings to open the doors and windows of the body so that we can always feel complete, warm, and nurtured at home, even if we may want at times to celebrate the splendor of the outside light. The crucial difference is that our excursion will not be motivated by deficit or hunger, but rather by the meta-need to celebrate, cocreate with, and revere the ultimate creative mystery. It is here in our home—earth and body—that individuals can develop fully as complete human beings without needing to "escape" anywhere to find their essential identity or feel whole.

Resacralization of Nature

One does not need to hold a spiritual worldview to recognize the miracle of Gaia (i.e., Earth as a living organism). Imagine that you are traveling throughout the cosmos, and after eons of dark and cold outer space, you find Gaia, the blue planet, with its luscious jungles and luminous sky, its warm soil and fresh waters, and the inextricable wonder of embodied conscious life. Unless one is open to the reality of alternate physical universes, Gaia is the only place in the known cosmos where consciousness and matter coexist and can achieve a gradual integration through participating sentient beings. The inability to perceive Gaia as paradise may simply be a consequence of a collective condition of arrested incarnation.

When the body is felt as our home, however, the natural world can be reclaimed as our homeland. This double grounding in body and nature not only heals at its root the estrangement of the modern self from nature, but also overcomes the spiritual alienation—often manifesting as floating anxiety—intrinsic to the prevalent human condition of arrested or incomplete incarnation. In other words, having recognized the physical world as real, and being in contact with immanent spiritual life, a complete human being discerns nature as an organic embodiment of the mystery. To sense our physical surroundings as the mystery's body offers important resources for an ecologically grounded spiritual life.

Social Engagement

In a fundamental way, we humans *are* our relationships with both the human and nonhuman world, and this recognition is inevitably linked with a commitment to social transformation. To be sure, this commitment can take many different forms, from more direct, active social or political action in the world (e.g., social service, spiritually grounded political criticism, environmental activism; see Lerner, 1994; Loy, 2008; Rothberg, 2006) to more subtle types of social activism involving distant prayer, collective meditation, or ritual (Nicol, 2015). While there is still much to learn about the actual effectiveness of subtle activism, as well as about the power of human consciousness to directly influence human affairs, given the current global crisis, embodied spirituality cannot be divorced from a commitment to social, political, and ecological transformation— whatever form this may take.

Integration of Matter and Consciousness

Disembodied spirituality is often based on an attempt to transcend, regulate, or transform embodied reality from the "higher" standpoint of consciousness and its values (Ferrer et al., 2004). Matter's experiential dimension as an immanent expression of the mystery is generally ignored. This shortsightedness leads to the belief—conscious or unconscious—that everything related to matter is unrelated to the mystery. This belief, in turn, confirms that matter and spirit are two antagonistic dimensions. It then becomes necessary to abandon or condition the material dimension in order to strengthen the spiritual one. The first step out of this impasse is to rediscover the mystery in its immanent manifestation; that is, to stop seeing and treating matter and the body as not only alien to the mystery but as something that distances human beings from the spiritual dimension of life. Embodied spirituality seeks a progressive integration of matter and consciousness that may ultimately lead to what might be called a state of "conscious matter" (Romero & Albareda, 2001, p. 10). A fascinating possibility to consider is that a fuller integration of energy and consciousness in embodied existence may gradually open the doors to extraordinary longevity or other forms of metanormal functioning attested to by the world's mystical traditions (see Murphy, 1993).

CONCLUSION

I conclude this chapter with some reflections about the past, present, and potential future of embodied spirituality. First, as even a cursory study of the lives of spiritual figures and mystics across traditions suggests, the spiritual history of humanity can be read, in part, as a story of the joys and sorrows of human dissociation. From ascetically enacted mystical ecstasies to world-denying monistic realizations, and from heart-expand-ing sexual sublimation to the moral struggles (and failures) of ancient

and modern spiritual teachers, human spirituality has been characterized by an overriding impulse toward a liberation of consciousness—a
liberation that has too often been at the cost of the underdevelopment,
subordination, or control of essential human attributes such as the body
or sexuality. This account does not seek to excoriate past spiritualities,
which may have been at times—although by no means always—perfectly
legitimate and perhaps even necessary in their particular times and contexts, but merely to highlight the historical rarity of a fully embodied
or integrative spirituality.

Second, in this chapter I have explored how a more embodied
spiritual life can emerge today from participatory engagement with both
transcendent sources of consciousness and the sensuous energies of the
body. Ultimately, embodied spirituality seeks to catalyze the emergence
of more complete human beings—beings who, while remaining rooted
in their bodies, earth, and immanent spiritual life, have made all their
attributes permeable to transcendent spiritual energies, and who cooper-
ate in solidarity with others in the spiritual transformation of self, community, and world. In short, a complete human being is firmly grounded
in spirit-within, fully open to spirit-beyond, and in transformative communion with spirit in-between (see chapter 1).

Finally, embodied spirituality can access many spiritually significant
revelations of self and world, some of which have been described by
the world's contemplative traditions, and others whose novel quality
may require a more creative engagement to be brought forth. As Tarnas
(2002) wrote, a "spiritual dynamism in the human person embedded in
a spiritually alive cosmos. . . . empowers, and challenges, the human
community's participatory cocreation of spiritual realities, including new
realities still to unfold" (p. xv). In this context, the emerging embodied spirituality in the West can be seen as a modern exploration of
an incarnational spiritual praxis in the sense that it seeks the creative
transformation of the embodied person and the world, the spiritualiza-
tion of matter and the sensuous grounding of spirit, and, ultimately, the
bringing together of heaven and earth. Who knows, perhaps as human
beings more fully embody both consciousness and energy—a twofold
incarnation, so to speak—we can then realize that it is here, in this
plane of concrete physical reality, that the cutting edge of spiritual transformation and evolution is taking place. For then the planet Earth may
gradually turn into an embodied heaven, a perhaps unique place in the
cosmos where beings can learn to express and receive embodied love,
in all its forms.

FOUR

A NEW LOOK AT INTEGRAL GROWTH

In an age of spiritual confusion, a consensus is growing among transpersonal authors and spiritual teachers about the importance of an integral growth of the person—that is, a developmental process that integrates all human dimensions (body, instincts, heart, mind, and consciousness) into a fully embodied spiritual life (e.g., Leonard & Murphy, 1995; Masters, 2010; Murphy, 1993; Rothberg, 1996, 1999; Welwood, 2000; Wilber, 2000a, 2001). This emerging understanding stems in large part from an awareness of the many pitfalls of a lopsided development, such as spiritual bypassing (Masters, 2010; Welwood, 2000), spiritual materialism and narcissism (Caplan, 1999; Lesser, 1999; Trungpa, 1987), offensive spirituality and spiritual defenses (Battista, 1996), ethical and psychosexual problems in the guru-disciple relationship (Butler, 1990; Edelstein, 2011; Kripal, 1999), difficulties in integrating spiritual experiences (Bragdon, 1990; S. Grof & C. Grof, 1989), and a devitalization of the body and inhibition of primary-sexual energies (Romero & Albareda, 2001), among others.

    Although the idea of an integral spiritual life as firmly grounded in psychosomatic integration can be found in the world's religious literature—for example, in Sri Aurobindo's (1993) synthesis of yogas and the Christian doctrine of incarnation (e.g., Barnhart, 2008; Burns, 2002)—few efforts exist in contemporary Western culture that are aimed at the development of an effective praxis to actualize this potential in human lives. More specifically, little attention is usually given to the maturation of the somatic, instinctive, sexual, and emotional worlds, and the unfolding of genuine integral growth in spiritual practitioners seems to be the exception to the rule. As several authors have noted, even spiritual leaders and teachers across traditions display an uneven development; for example, high level cognitive and spiritual functioning combined with ethically conventional or even dysfunctional interpersonal, emotional, or sexual behavior (e.g., Feuerstein, 1991; Kripal, 2002; Wilber, 2001). A related outcome of this unbalanced development is that many honest spiritual efforts are undermined by conflicts or wounds at somatic, sexual, or emotional levels. Too often, spiritual seekers struggle with tensions existing between their spiritual ideals and their instinctive, sexual, and emotional drives, recurrently falling into unconsciously driven patterns or habits despite their most sincere, conscious intentions.

Furthermore, a lopsided psychospiritual development may have detrimental implications not only for human flourishing, but also for spiritual discernment. As I discuss in chapter 3, spiritual visions considering body and world to be ultimately illusory (or lower, or impure, or a hindrance to spiritual liberation) arguably derive from states of being in which the sense of self mainly or exclusively identifies with transcendent consciousness, getting uprooted from the body and immanent spiritual life. From this existential stance, it is understandable (and perhaps inevitable) that both body and world are seen as ultimately illusory or defective. However, when the somatic and vital worlds are invited to participate in spiritual life, one's sense of identity becomes permeable to not only transcendent but also immanent spiritual sources, turning body and world into sacred realities that can be appreciated as fundamental for human and perhaps even cosmic spiritual evolution.

Is it actually possible to integrate harmoniously the many needs, desires, dynamics, and understandings of the various human dimensions? Can human beings in fact cultivate the voice and wisdom of the body, instincts, heart, mind, and consciousness without generating internal tensions or dissociations? And, perhaps most importantly, *how* can one lie down and walk a truly integral spiritual path that respects the integrity of the many voices dwelling within? In other words, how can individuals foster the maturation of these dimensions—not only honoring their nature but also facilitating their creative participation in a spiritual life?

To explore these questions, this chapter opens with a brief review of some contemporary proposals for an Integral Transformative Practice (ITP). I then outline a participatory perspective on integral growth that may complement and expand these accounts. Finally, I introduce Holistic Transformation, an integral approach created by Albareda and Romero (1991; Romero & Albareda, 2001) that may offer a practical answer to some of the difficulties besetting individuals seeking to develop an integral life in the modern West. The chapter concludes with some reflections on ITPs as participatory, embodied spiritual practices.

INTEGRAL TRANSFORMATIVE PRACTICE (ITP):
CONTEMPORARY PROPOSALS

The three main contemporary ITP proposals are Murphy (1993), Leonard and Murphy (1995), and Wilber (2000a, 2000b, Wilber, 2006; Wilber et al., 2008).[1] In this section, I discuss each of these proposals in turn, while keeping in mind that they overlap one another.

The first and foremost ITP proposal is from Michael Murphy (1993), who, inspired by Sri Aurobindo's integral vision and synthesis of yogas, cofounded (with Richard Price) the Esalen Institute in 1962 to advance the development of the whole person.[2] In *The Future of the Body*, Murphy offered not only a compelling case for the evolutionary significance of ITPs, but also the most extended discussion to date regarding their guiding principles and potential benefits.

After outlining four possible shortcomings of conventional transformative practices—reinforcement of traits, perpetuation of limiting beliefs, subversion of balanced growth, and partial focus on specific experiences—Murphy (1993) presented a rich inventory of exercises, techniques, and practices that can be used to foster a more integral development. His suggestions include the following: Sensory Awareness and the Feldenkrais method for somatic awareness and self-regulation; depth psychotherapy, athletic training, and somatic disciplines for increasing vitality; empathic visualizations, mutual self-disclosure, and self-examination for the growth of love; psychotherapy, philosophical reflection, and study of philosophy, myths, artistic works, or religious symbols for mental cognition; witness meditation, the cultivation of mystical states, and karma yoga for individuation and the sense of self. (This list is only a representative sample of the various human attributes and practices presented by Murphy, and readers are encouraged to read his work to properly appreciate the extent of possibilities.) Murphy then described a set of five interdependent virtues and traits he considers vital for integral development—honesty, creativity, courage, balance, and resilience—stressing that "the cultivation of any virtue or capacity can facilitate more than one creative attribute" (p. 579). Finally, Murphy convincingly argued that these practices must be suited for each practitioner's unique dispositions, and, therefore, "There can be no single or 'right' kind of integral discipline with a universally applicable and strictly specified set of techniques" (p. 579).

The second ITP proposal was presented in *The Life We Are Given* (Leonard & Murphy, 1995), in which Murphy joined George Leonard—

another pioneer of the Human Potential Movement—to define ITPs as "a complex and coherent set of activities that produce positive changes in . . . the body, mind, heart, and soul" (p. 12) of individuals and groups. Leonard and Murphy's ITP program is based on the combination of aerobic exercise, a low-animal-fat diet, mentoring and community support, positive affirmations, and, most importantly, the regular practice of what they call the *ITP Kata*. Drawing on such disciplines as hatha yoga, martial arts, and modern exercise physiology, the ITP Kata begins with a series of balancing and centering movements, followed by a period of transformational imaging (i.e., the intentional use of mental imagery to promote body health, heart openness, creativity, or other qualities selected by the practitioner), and ends with a time for meditation that combines self-observation with contemplative prayer. The ITP Kata can be completed in forty minutes, but its duration can be extended according to individual needs and desires.

Leonard and Murphy's (1995) ITP program embraces the Greek principle of *antakolouthia* or "mutual entailment of the virtues," according to which the cultivation of any skill at any level—somatic, emotional, mental, and so on—has a beneficial impact on other levels. This cross-training synergy is one of the chief guiding principles of ITP: due to the interdependence of all human dimensions, mental, emotional, and physical practices are expected to have an impact on the entire organism. According to Murphy (as cited in A. Cohen 1999), the ultimate goal of ITPs is "integral transformation" (p. 90) or "integral enlightenment" (p. 90), that is, "the flowering, in all our parts, of all our attributes, of all the various capacities we have, of this latent divinity" (p. 90).

Finally, the integral philosopher Ken Wilber (2000a, 2000b) has also offered some important reflections on ITPs. Drawing on Gardner's (1983/1993) theory on multiple intelligences, Wilber pointed out that the various developmental lines—cognition, morals, affects, sexuality, self-identity, and so forth—are relatively autonomous, in the sense that a person does not develop evenly along all of them. Wilber (2001) wrote, "*Thus, a person can be at a relatively high level of development in some lines* [such as cognition], *medium in others* [such as morals], *and low in still others* [such as spirituality]" (p. 130).

Wilber (2000a, 2000b) originally used the term *ITP* to refer not only to Leonard and Murphy's (1995) integral program but also to any set of practices that cultivates all human dimensions. A consideration added by Wilber is that the fruits of these practices should not be confused with the attainment of absolute realization. However, Wilber regarded ITPs as facilitation factors for achieving what he considers the ultimate goal of human life: nondual enlightenment or One Taste. Echoing Richard Baker Roshi, Wilber (2000b) stated that enlightenment is an accident, and that although these practices cannot cause it, they can make one more prone to it: "The idea behind ITPs is simple: in an attempt to become more 'accident-prone,' the more dimensions of the human body-mind that are exercised, then the more transparent to the Divine they become, and thus the more accident prone the individual is" (p. 39).

Wilber (2000b) offered his own inventory of practices to exercise the basic human dimensions. To this end, he first suggested envisioning six columns representing the physical, emotional-sexual (*prana* or *chi*), mental or psychological, contemplative or meditative, community, and nature dimensions. Then he offered a variety of possible practices to train each dimension: aerobic exercise, weight lifting, and healthy diet for the physical; yoga, qi gong, and tai chi chuan for *prana*; psychotherapy, visualizations, and affirmations for the psychological; *zazen, vipassana,* or centering prayer for the contemplative; community service, compassionate care, and engagement with others for the community; and recycling, hikes, and nature celebration for nature. Wilber stated that "the idea of ITP is simple, pick at least one practice from each column and practice them concurrently. The more dimensions you practice, the more effective they all become, the more you become one big accident-prone soul" (p. 39). Finally, Wilber aptly cautioned readers not only that ITPs can become narcissistic games for egoic control, but also that their "pick and choose" (p. 126) nature can easily degenerate into the spiritual "cafeteria model so prevalent in our culture" (p. 126).

Changing the terminology, Wilber later recommended an Integral Life Practice (ILP) in which practitioners select ready-made practices from different modules corresponding to trainable human capacities, such as body, mind, spirit, sex, and relationships (Wilber, 2006; Wilber et al., 2008). Although Wilber and his associates expanded the range of modules and practices, the basic principle of what Wilber held to be "the first fully integral practice" (Wilber, 2006, p. 202) remains the same: "pick one practice for each module and exercise them concurrently" (p. 202). Wilber particularly endorsed what they considered ILP's "gold star practices" (p. 203), many of which involve acceptance and instruction in Wilber's integral theory. For example, the "gold star practice" for the mind is to study the Integral (AQAL) Framework (or the downloading in the practitioner's mind of Wilber's Integral Operating System); for spirit, starred practices include Integral Inquiry (i.e., a Wilberian synthesis of selected meditative practices) and The 1-2-3 of God (i.e., Wilber's reduction of the multiplicity of ways in which the mystery has been enacted into three perspectives: I, we, and it).

To sum up, contemporary ITP programs are largely based on an eclectic mixture of practices and techniques selected from the many somatic, psychological, and spiritual disciplines available today in the modern West. Through these programs, practitioners design their own personalized integral training to exercise their various attributes. According to their proponents, ITPs may ultimately lead to an integral enlightenment (Murphy) or optimize the emergence of a nondual One Taste (Wilber).

A PARTICIPATORY PERSPECTIVE ON INTEGRAL GROWTH

In this section, I offer some reflections on integral growth that may complement and expand contemporary proposals. As discussed above, modern ITP programs consist of a combination of techniques or practices imported from Western and Eastern traditions and schools. I concur with Wilber's (2000b) caution about the potential spiritual "cafeteria model" (noted above), and here I would like to suggest that there may be a more subtle, and potentially more pernicious, pitfall implicit in the very attempt to develop an integral life in the modern West.

Briefly, ITP programs can easily turn into a mentally devised integral training in which the practitioner's mind decides what are the best practices or techniques to develop her body, sexuality, heart, and consciousness. Consider, for example, what Wilber (2006) wrote about his proposed ILP: "Although we have what we consider 'gold star practices' in each module, the whole point of a modular approach is that you can select from among dozens of legitimate and time-tested practices in each module" (p. 202). This consideration may be naturally appealing for the highly individualistic (and consumerist) modern self, but the question that is left unanswered (and unasked) is, Who is the "you" making those selections? In most cases, it is very likely that this "you" is no other than the mental ego with which most modern individuals identify (Washburn, 1995). In addition to the aforementioned doctrinal elements embedded in the system, Wilber's ILP can thus easily turn into a mentally devised integral training in which the practitioner's mental ego is in charge of selecting somatic, vital-sexual, emotional, and relational practices.

This outcome is both understandable and perhaps not entirely unavoidable. After all, modern Western education focuses almost exclu-

sively on the development of the rational mind and its cognitive functions, with little attention given to the maturation of other dimensions
of the person (see chapter 5). As a result, most individuals in the modern
West arguably reach their adulthood with a fairly mature mental functioning, but with poorly developed somatic, instinctive, and emotional
intelligences. Given the extreme cognicentrism of Western culture, the
mental direction of integral growth seems nearly inevitable.

Types of Cognicentrism

Before proceeding farther, it is important to distinguish between four
types or levels of cognicentrism. The first is *cultural* and refers to the ethnocentrism (or epistemic narcissism) of both Western and non-Western
societies, in which one's cultural framework, thinking, or worldview
becomes—by default—the privileged context for engaging cross-cultural
differences. This type of cognicentrism is equivalent to what Roth (2008)
termed *cognitive imperialism* in contemplative studies (see also Sherman,
2014b) and, in the context of the East-West encounter, it is the source
of both Orientalism (J. J. Clarke, 1994) and Occidentalism (Buruma &
Margalit, 2004).[3]

The second type considers one particular *state of consciousness* as
optimal for mental health and as the final arbiter for demarcating between
reality and illusion; thus, one state of consciousness becomes the only
(or foremost) cognitive modality for the achievement of "sound knowledge" about the "objective" world. Both James (1961) and Harner (1980)
discussed this second form of cognicentrism regarding the widespread
prejudice in Western thought against the psychological and epistemic
value of nonordinary states of consciousness—a prejudice that implicitly
or explicitly promotes the ordinary state of wakeful consciousness as
superior and most preferred. It is important to note that the elevation
of any nonordinary state (e.g., dreaming or mystical awareness) as cognitively superior in any general sense also falls into this category. The
participatory approach favors a holistic or ecological view that not only
grants cognitive value to all states of consciousness, but also discerns that
certain states may be more appropriate than others in the enaction and
apprehension of different aspects or domains of reality.

The third cognicentrism refers to the favored position of the
rational-analytical mind (and its associated instrumental reason and
Aristotelian logic) in the modern Western world over and above other
ways of knowing (e.g., somatic, vital, emotional, aesthetic, imaginal,

visionary, intuitive, contemplative; e.g., see Jaggar, 1990; Lutz, 1988). As discussed in chapter 5, this cognicentrism is the root of the prevalent, mind-centered approach to education in the West and raises serious challenges to the implementation of genuinely integral pedagogies.

The last—and arguably deepest—type of cognicentrism is *mental pride*, or the mind's intrinsic disposition (at least in the modern West) to consider itself the most important or only player in the search for knowledge and understanding (Romero & Albareda, 2001; see also chapter 5). Although mental pride can be regarded as both a source and an outcome of other forms of cognicentrism, in modern Western culture most of these types reinforce each other in positive feedback loops. For example, mental pride strengthens the elevation of ratio-nal-analytical faculties, while the cultural, scientific, and technological successes of the application of instrumental reason (which are many and hugely important) deepen the rooting of mental pride in the Western psyche.

Although these four types of cognicentrism are related in multi-farious ways, in this and next chapter I mostly allude to the third and fourth types (for discussions of the first and second types, see chapters 2 and 10). This usage of the term *cognicentrism* does not of course sug-gest that the other human dimensions are not cognitive in the sense of not being able to apprehend knowledge or creatively participate in its elaboration. In addition, it follows that I am not reducing the mind's faculties to rational-analytical ones; the human mind has also intuitive, imaginal, and aesthetic powers, among others.

The Challenge of Cognicentrism to Integral Growth

The greatest tragedy of cognicentrism is that it generates a vicious circle that justifies itself. Because modern education does not create spaces for the autonomous maturation of the body, the instincts, and the heart, these worlds cannot participate in the developmental path unless they are mentally or externally guided. Yet, insofar as they are always mentally or externally guided, these human dimensions cannot develop autono-mously, and thus the need for their mental or external direction becomes permanently justified (see chapter 5; Romero & Albareda, 2001).

Complicating this situation further is that, after many generations of mind-centered education and life—often combined with the cultural control or inhibition of the body, instincts, sexuality, and passions—these nondiscursive worlds may be not only undeveloped but frequently wounded, distorted, or manifesting regressive tendencies (Romero & Albareda, 2001). Thus, when such an individual seeks guidance in these worlds, the first thing that she typically finds is a layer of conflicts, fears, or confusion that perpetuates the deep-seated belief that these worlds need to be mentally regulated in order to be wholesome or growth-promoting. What is normally overlooked, however, is an essential primary intelligence that lies beneath this layer; if accessed, this primary intelligence can heal the root of the conflict while fostering the development and maturation of these worlds from within.

What is needed, then, is to create spaces in which these human dimensions can heal and mature according to their own developmental principles and dynamics—not according to the ones that the mind thinks are most adequate (Romero & Albareda, 2001). Only when body, instincts, sexuality, and heart are allowed to develop autonomously will they be able to sit at the same table with the conscious mind and cocreate a truly integral personal and spiritual life. In developmental terms, one could say that, before being integrated, these human dimensions need to be differentiated.

Integral Growth, Integral Practice, and Integral Training

In this section, I offer a tentative definition of integral growth, and suggest the heuristic need to discriminate between integral practice and integral training as two essential but distinct elements of integral growth.

- *Integral growth* is a developmental process in which all human dimensions—body, instincts, heart, mind, and consciousness—collaboratively and cocreatively participate as equals in the multidimensional unfolding of the human being. This process can be understood as having two basic elements: integral practice and integral training.

- *Integral practice* fosters the autonomous maturation of all human dimensions, preparing them to manifest their own intelligence, to be harmoniously integrated, and to cocreatively participate in the developmental process. Integral practice engenders and brings forth novel potentials, qualities, and capabilities at all levels.

- *Integral training* exercises all human dimensions according to their own developmental principles and dynamics. Integral

      training exercises and strengthens potentials, qualities, and
      capabilities that emerge from integral practice at all levels.

The distinction between integral practice and integral training is crucial. In a way, modern ITP programs seem more geared to training or exercising already known skills than to facilitating conditions for the emergence of novel qualities and capabilities, some of which may be unique to the individual. An exclusive or predominant reliance on training, however, may parallel the "masculine" paradigm of Western education, which is essentially based on skills acquisition and the mental direction of learning (see chapter 5). When integral growth is primarily based on integral training, both the mental colonization of other human dimensions and the mental direction of the process become nearly unavoidable. At best, a mentally structured ITP program may promote the integral health of the person, but, although they usually overlap, integral health should not be confused with integral growth and transformation. At worst, the mental management of the other human dimensions may repress or abort their genuine voice, intelligence, and wisdom—and, in the long run, have detrimental consequences for integral health. Although intentional training is important, it is therefore fundamental to complement that training with the more "feminine" creation of spaces that facilitate the organic birthing or emergence of the infinite potentials dwelling within human nature.[4]

      Furthermore, to avoid the risk of aborting the natural unfolding of unique potentials and developmental dynamics, *integral practice needs to precede integral training*. Most psychospiritual practices and techniques are intentional in that they shape and direct human experience and growth in specific directions (Fenton, 1995). While surely beneficial in many regards, however, engaging intentional practices before the maturation of somatic, instinctive, and emotional worlds may not only hinder the emergence of their most unique potentials, but also leave untouched many wounds or conflicts (which in turn is a fast road to spiritual bypassing, as Masters [2010] persuasively argued). Before the design of an integral training program, then, these somatic, instinctive, and emotional worlds need to enter a process of healing, maturation, and germination according to their own developmental principles. Otherwise, integral programs can lead, in the long run, to a psychospiritual life that is dissociated, devitalized, stagnated, conflicted, or lacking genuine creativity.

      An example may help to clarify the above consideration. There are many practices and techniques for the cultivation of the body, from hatha yoga to aerobic training to weightlifting. Clearly, these practices can be of value and effectively promote health and growth for many individuals at specific junctures of their development. The risk of cultivating the body exclusively through these techniques, however, is that insofar as they are either selected by the mind or regulated by external standards (e.g., regarding the body's position, posture, movement, or appearance), these practices can potentially block the emergence of somatic autonomous intelligence. In other words, these practices may prevent the body from engendering from within the very positions, movements, and attitudes that may be more natural and vital for its optimum development. Although appropriate in cases of low muscular tone, for example, weightlifting may foster the pride of the body, and build an energetic armor making the physical organism impermeable to both the vital energy and the presence of consciousness (cf. D. Johnson, 2005).

To foster a genuine somatic growth, it is crucial to make contact with the body, discern its current state and needs, and then create spaces to engender its own practices and capabilities—devise its own yoga, so to speak. As Sovatsky (1994) pointed out in his rendition of yoga as *ars erotica*, yoga postures (*asanas*) first emerged spontaneously from within the body and its vital energy: "guided by its inner intelligence, prana moves the body exactly as it needs to be moved" (p. 96).[5] Indeed, as Leonard and Murphy (1995) stressed, "there is a profound wisdom in the body, in the pulsing of the blood, the rhythm of the breath, the turning of the joints" (p. 145), and when the body becomes permeable to both vital and conscious energies, it can find its own rhythms, habits, postures, movements, and charismatic rituals. The founder of the field of Somatics, D. Johnson (2005), similarly wrote, "Our most primal sources of intelligence lie within bodily experience" (p. 251).

In short, this process can be outlined in four roughly consecutive stages: (1) connecting with the current state of the body; (2) listening to its needs, calls, and creative urges; (3) regulating its healing and maturation through developing or selecting practices that respond to those needs, calls, or creative urges; and (4) training emerging skills and capabilities according to somatic developmental dynamics. The same could be said for the development of other human dimensions.

Two important clarifications need to be made here. First, it is essential to sharply differentiate this approach from a self-comforting integral practice in which the mind is in control of the process. In contrast, this approach demands the mental ego to humbly let go of its control, first by being at the service of the maturation of the other dimensions, and then by genuinely opening itself to learn from them. When the mind can let go of its pride, rigorous practices can gradually emerge from within. Second, this integral approach does not render existing practices useless or obsolete. On the contrary, it is perfectly possible that, once the body, instincts, and heart mature and can communicate with the conscious mind, they may call individuals to engage already established disciplines. What I am suggesting, however, is that although the cultivation of these dimensions has traditionally followed external standards devised by exceptionally gifted human beings (and often refined by generations of communities), an increasing number of individuals may now be ready for a more creative engagement of their integral growth and lives. In any event, the starting point cannot be the mental imposition of a given practice upon the body, sexuality, heart, or consciousness simply because the mind has somehow adopted the belief that it is the best or most beneficial. A creative indwelling life resides within—an intelligent vital dynamism that it is waiting to emerge to orchestrate that never-ending process of becoming fully human (cf. Heron, 1998; Masters, 2010).

To close this section, I offer three interrelated guiding principles of integral growth, as follows.

1. Integral growth is cocreated by all dimensions of human nature. A genuine process of integral growth cannot be exclusively directed by the mind, but emerges from the collaborative participation and creative power of all fundamental human dimensions: body, instincts, heart, mind, and consciousness.

2. Integral growth unfolds from within. When the various human dimensions mature and cocreatively participate in a developmental path, integral growth organically develops from within. A genuine integral growth that is grounded in the individual's unique potentials does not follow a pregiven path already traveled by others, nor can it be directed by external standards. External sources of guidance can be essential reference points at certain junctures of the journey, but the path toward the emergence of human beings' most unique capabilities cannot be directed from outside of them.

3. Integral growth balances the "feminine" and the "masculine." Integral growth combines the more "masculine"

elements of the exercise and training of skills, with the more "feminine" elements of gestating and giving birth to new qualities and capabilities from within. To optimize the grounding of the process in the most vital potentials of the individual, the "feminine" dimension needs to precede the "masculine" one.

HOLISTIC TRANSFORMATION:
TOWARD A NEW INTEGRAL PRAXIS

In this section, I present Albareda and Romero's Holistic Transformation (Romero & Albareda, 2001; Malkemus & Romero, 2012). They offer one example of an innovative integral approach that may complement and expand contemporary proposals while avoiding the pitfalls identified in the previous section.

Originally developed in Spain, Holistic Transformation is an approach to integral growth and healing that is not based on already existing practices or techniques.[6] Holistic Transformation emerges from more than four decades of practically based inquiry, with the help of the experience of hundreds of individuals in healing and psychospiritual processes. According to Romero and Albareda (2001), its main purpose is to facilitate natural conditions that allow each person, free from the potential constraints that are subtly imposed by psychospiritual models and ideals, to lay down her path of integral growth.[7] Through this work, they added, practitioners learn to self-regulate a process in which the fundamental dimensions of their being—body, instincts, heart, mind, and consciousness—autonomously mature and are gradually integrated. As I explain below, this goal is pursued through simple but potent practices seeking to open these dimensions to both the vital energy and what they call the "energy of consciousness" (p. 6). Romero and Albareda claimed that, when these fundamental dimensions become aligned to these energies, a new energetic axis emerges that guides integral development from within, not according to external standards or ideals.

Before describing the general structure of the work, however, it is important to say a few words about the central place that sexuality and life-energy have in a creative integral growth in general, and in Holistic Transformation in particular (see also Malkemus & Romero, 2012).[8] Besides the energy of consciousness, Romero and Albareda (2001) proposed that there is an immanent spiritual source in the cosmos: the *dark energy*. The adjective "dark" does not have here any negative connotation, but simply refers to an energetic state in which all potentialities are still undifferentiated and, therefore, cannot be seen by the "light" of consciousness. The dark energy is considered to be spiritual life inherently dwelling within the manifest, and the source of genuine innovation and creativity at all levels (cf. Heron, 1998). In other words, the dark energy is spiritual *prima materia*—that is, spiritual energy in state of transformation, still not actualized, saturated with potentials and possibilities. In human reality, they added, this energy is the source of felt-sensed vitality and natural wisdom, as well as the organizing principle of embodiment, sexuality, and instinctive life. For these authors, the energy of consciousness and the dark energy are ultimately the same energy, but in different states: whereas the dark energy is dense, amorphous, and undifferentiated, the energy of consciousness is subtle, luminous, and infinitely differentiated.

What is the creative value of accessing this dark energy for the spiritual life? Elsewhere I argued that human spirituality is participatory in the sense that it can emerge from (1) the active participation of all human essential dimensions (i.e., body, instincts, heart, mind, and consciousness); and (2) human cocreative interaction with an undetermined mystery or generative power of life, the cosmos, or reality (Ferrer, 2002, 2008). Here I want to stress that these two dimensions of participation are intimately intertwined. In other words, the more human dimensions actively participate in spiritual knowing, the more creative spiritual life becomes. As I indicate in chapter 3, in the same way that the mind and consciousness arguably serve as a natural bridge to transcendent forms of awareness, the body and its vital energies serve as a natural bridge to immanent spiritual life. Whereas through the mind and consciousness it is possible to tap into subtle worlds and spiritual states already enacted in history that display more fixed forms and dynamics (e.g., cosmological motifs, archetypal configurations, mystical visions),[9] attention to the body and its vital energies allows greater access to the more generative power of life or the mystery—the *dark energy*, in Romero and Albareda's (2001) terms.

Hence, I propose that *engagement with the body and its vital energies is essential for a genuine and creative integral spirituality*. On the one hand, to be *genuine*, integral spiritual growth needs to be grounded in each person's vital seeds—those energetic potentials (or genetic dispositions, in scientific jargon) that render each person a unique individual and are stored at the deepest levels of the vital world. On the other hand, to be *creative*, integral growth needs to emerge from human interaction with spiritual power in its generative state, which can be most directly accessed through engagement with embodied vital energy.

As for the significance of sexuality, Romero and Albareda (2001) stated:

> Sexuality is, potentially, [one of the] the first soil[s] for the organization and creative development of the dark energy in human reality. That is why it is so important that sexuality is an "open" soil based on natural evolutionary principles, and not on fears, conflicts, or artificial impositions dictated by our minds, cultures, or spiritual ideologies. (p. 13)

Due to the general inhibition of primary and sexual energies throughout Western history, they continued, a layer of accumulated conflicts, wounds, and fears exists between the modern self and the essence of the dark energy. In addition to individual dynamics, a nearly universal ingredient of this layer is organically embedded shame.

Organic shame, which should be sharply distinguished from psychological shame (and can exist without it), manifests through unconscious energetic contractions in the body that block the flow of the dark energy and its creative power within us. In a process of integral growth, Romero and Albareda (2001) pointed out, it is fundamental to heal this conflictive sediment and reconnect with the creative essence of the dark energy. When bodily embedded shame is cleared out (and the heart is freed from struggle and the mind from pride), this energy naturally flows and gestates within the person, undergoing a process of transformation through body and heart, ultimately illuminating the mind with a knowing that is both grounded in and coherent with the mystery. Because of the dynamically creative nature of mystery, as well as the historically and culturally situated human condition, this knowing is never final but always in constant evolution (Ferrer, 2002).

Although Holistic Transformation can take many forms, the usual format involves a group of individuals who commit to work together for a week-long intensive retreat, a course of three weekends, or a cycle of six or seven months. These cycles typically include one weekend encounter a month, supervised work between these encounters, and a concluding week-long intensive retreat. Despite the group format and the dimension of community that naturally emerges from the work, Holistic

Transformation is not primarily focused on group dynamics (which are addressed if necessary) and should be better understood as fostering individual work within a group context.

Essentially, Holistic Transformation is composed of four elements or processes: (1) interactive embodied meditations, (2) multidimensional contemplative practices; (3) individualized integral practices; and (4) integrative work in everyday life. Although these four processes tend to unfold sequentially to some extent, they also often overlap and the progression can vary significantly among individuals.

Interactive Embodied Meditations

With the notable exception of certain tantric methods, traditional meditation techniques are practiced individually and without bodily interaction with other practitioners.[10] One of Holistic Transformation's major innovations is that it features a variety of contemplative practices that, in a structured and respectful setting, are developed in *mindful physical contact* with other individuals.

Interactive embodied meditations are the starting point of the work. Through them, practitioners collaboratively experiment with several forms of contemplative contact among the various energetic centers of the human body: feet and legs for the body as the physical structure that provides support and containment; lower abdomen and pelvic area for the vital center, sexuality, and instincts; chest, back, arms, and hands for the heart and emotions; head and forehead for the mind; and the crown of the head for consciousness (see Malkemus & Romero, 2012). Based on several decades of lived inquiry with hundreds of individuals, Albareda and Romero maintain that these physical areas are entryways into the depths of these human attributes and associated ways of knowing.[11] As Malkemus and Romero (2012) put it, "There are a number of basic ways of knowing that are rooted in different regions of the human body" (p. 34).[12]

To optimize the emergence of richer information about and from these centers, two clearly differentiated roles are established in each practice: an *agent* role, which initiates and develops the contact, and a *receptive* role, which receives the contact. Since the experience of the same practice can drastically change (and therefore offer different data) depending on the role, practitioners usually begin their processes by exploring their experience in both roles. Regardless of their role, practitioners are encouraged to sustain an attitude of nonintentional, open receptivity to their own experience throughout the practice, like the one cultivated through mindfulness meditation and other contemplative techniques.

The general aim of these practices is to allow practitioners to experientially discern the deep energetic state of their various essential dimensions—body, vital, heart, mind, and consciousness—as well as their mutual integration or dissociation. In other words, they seek to provide practitioners with an "experiential radiography" of their structural and energetic organization as the foundation of their integral growth.

In this context, physical contact is considered essential because Albareda and Romero regard the body as the natural doorway to the deepest levels of the rest of the human attributes (see Malkemus & Romero, 2012). In their view, due to their consecutive emergence in human development—from soma to instinct to heart to mind—each dimension grows by taking root in the previous one(s). This developmental sequence should not be confused with a hierarchy, where dimensions that emerge later in time are seen as necessarily higher, more evolved, or more integrative than earlier ones. One of the orienting principles of Holistic Transformation is that all human dimensions, especially when mature, are equally valuable for individual and collective health, growth, and evolution (I call this the equiprimacy principle; see chapter 1). Since the biological organism is the first dimension that emerges after conception, however, Albareda and Romero consider it necessary to engage the human body in order to access the deepest energetic potentials and dispositions not only of the body, but also of instinct, heart, and mind. Leonard and Murphy (1995) shared a similar view: "Body, mind, heart, and soul [are] coequal manifestations of the human essence. But where deep down human change is concerned, there is no more effective teacher than the body" (p. 145).

As an example, I offer a description of a practice exploring the connection between heart and mind/consciousness. One of the actions that the person in the agent role can develop during this practice is a meditative contact between her forehead and the center of the back or chest of the person in the receptive role. The sustained contact between the embodied energetic centers of mind/consciousness and the heart can lead to a variety of important psychospiritual insights for both practitioners. In the context of Holistic Transformation, however, Albareda and Romero claim that this apparently simple contact can help: first, the receptive person to access the essential energetic state of her heart; and second, both agent and receiver to experientially learn about the quality of the connection between their hearts and their minds/consciousness (e.g., along polar realities such as differentiation/undifferentiation, integration/dissociation, harmony/struggle, clarity/confusion, or autonomy/dependency).[13] In order to gain more precise information through experiential contrasts, individuals can repeat the same practice a number of times or with different variables (e.g., with different people or genders, only in one role, for an extended time, in a different setting).

Before proceeding farther, two points need to be emphasized. First, although these practices can be naturally used to explore relational dynamics, their typical use at the first stages of Holistic Transformation is not interpersonal, but intrapersonal. In other words, in a consensually arranged "contract," practitioners function as satellites or mirrors for each other, facilitating the perception of their own potentials, dynamics, or energetic states. Interactive embodied meditations, then, should be distinguished from any kind of intentional hands-on healing, energetic, or body work. In practical terms, this means that regardless of their role as receiver or agent, practitioners attempt to remain mindfully anchored to their own experience during the practices, letting go as much as possible of any concern or intention regarding their partner's experience. This focus on one's own experience is facilitated by the participants' commitment to stop the practice at any given moment if necessary. One example might be during cases of physical contraction, fear, or confusion that the practitioner may not be ready to explore deeply or handle constructively. If the agent knows that the receiver will stop the practice if needed, then she will be able to develop the action without distracting preoccupations regarding the receiver's experience. And if the receiver knows that the agent will stop the practice if needed, then she will be able to receive the action without distracting preoccupations regarding the agent's experience.[14] Once practitioners have gained adequate knowledge of their essential attributes, intersubjective relationality can also become the focus of the practices. In other words, the intrapersonal emphasis is especially important in the first stages of the process. As practitioners gradually become clearer about their energetic dispositions and necessary boundaries, these practices can also be safely used to explore mutuality, interpersonal dynamics, relational forms of spirituality, and intersubjective contemplation (see chapter 7; Osterhold et al., 2007; Sohmer et al., forthcoming).

Second, whereas Romero and Albareda (2001) claimed that interactive meditations merely facilitate the direct perception of the deep energetic state of the various human attributes, these practices may shape human experience in specific directions. After all, some form of intentionality is arguably inevitable in any human activity, and even nonintentional practices such as *wu-wei* ("without doing"), *shinkan taza* ("sitting-only"), or zazen take place within particular contexts of spiritual aspiration (see Faure, 1993; Loy, 1988; Shaw, 1988; Slingerland, 2000).

Multidimensional Contemplative Practices

After introducing the interactive embodied meditations, Albareda and Romero present in their workshops a number of contemplative practices to facilitate a more nuanced, focused, or intentional exploration or transformation of the practitioners' somatic, instinctive, emotional, psychological, and spiritual dimensions. Many of these practices are also carried out in interactive embodied contact with other practitioners in both agent and receptive roles. No matter which role is chosen, practitioners cultivate a contemplative attitude of open presence, nonintentional receptivity, and unconditional acceptance toward their moment-to-moment experience.

The structure of these multidimensional practices is extremely diverse, but most are oriented by the following aims: (1) the differentiation, maturation, and integration of human essential dimensions (body, instincts, heart, mind, and consciousness); (2) the development of these dimensions to be porous to both immanent and transcendent spiritual sources; (3) the differentiation, maturation, and integration of "masculine" (agent) and "feminine" (receptive) capabilities at all dimensions; (4) the healing and transformation of wounds, conflicts, or dissociations stored at deep energetic layers of these dimensions; (5) the creation of spaces for the natural emergence of new capabilities, qualities, or potentials from within those dimensions; (6) the practice in the development of these emerging capabilities, qualities, or potentials; and (7) the integration of polar realities, such as mind/body, sexuality/spirituality, masculine/feminine, individual/community, or strength/gentleness.

Although space does not allow me to discuss all of these goals here, it is important to highlight two distinctive elements of these practices. The first is the differentiation and integration of human dimensions and polar realities. Albareda and Romero consider that the various human dimensions (body, instincts, heart, mind, and consciousness) and polar realities (masculine/feminine, sexuality/spirituality, individual/community, etc.) mature through processes of differentiation and integration. These processes, they claim, lead not only to the strengthening of each integrated dimension or polar reality, but also to the emergence of novel human qualities. When strength and gentleness are integrated, for example, strength can be fully strength because its incorporated gentleness prevents it from becoming aggression, gentleness can be fully gentleness because its incorporated strength prevents it from becoming weakness, and their integration brings forth a number of new qualities such as passionate nonattachment, forceful humbleness, or tender instinct. The "heart-anger" described by Masters (2000), in which "openly expressed anger and compassion mindfully coexist" (p. 34), can be seen as another example of a novel quality emerging from the integration of instincts, an undivided heart, and consciousness.

The second element is the special attention given to vital-sexual energies. Given their possible centrality for a genuine and creative integral growth, a number of contemplative practices focus on exploring and, if necessary, transforming the vital-sexual dimension. According to Washburn (1995, 2003a), the power of the Ground or primordial source of life—the *dark energy*, in Albareda and Romero's terms—undergoes a primal repression in early childhood that allows the resolution of the preoedipal stage and the emergence of a differentiated mental ego. Despite its benefits, primal repression not only causes "a loss of plenipotent energy, fully alive corporeality, imaginal creativity, and rootedness in the Ground" (Washburn, 2003a, p. 19), but also confines the power of the Ground to the sexual system and genito-pelvic area of the body. "In restricting the power of the Ground to an instinctual organization," Washburn (1995) explained, primal repression "makes the instincts the gateway to spirit" (p. 199). For Washburn, then, a genuine spiritual regeneration can only occur when this previously repressed primary energy is reawakened and gradually assimilated into a higher level of instinctual-spiritual integration.

Due to the tremendous—indeed potentially overwhelming—power of the primary energy, as well as the layer of wounds and conflicts usually stored therein, Albareda and Romero consider it fundamental that this reawakening occurs gradually and carefully to permit the appropriate assimilation of this energy. This is in part why Holistic Transformation practices focused on this level do not involve ordinary sexual behavior, which tends to not only activate more energy than most people can integrate, but also to evoke biographical and cultural associations that may interfere with connecting to the deepest essence of this energy. With this in mind, Albareda and Romero have developed a set of original contemplative embodied practices, which, in a safe and respectful environment, are directed to allow practitioners to gently reawaken their primary energy and slowly integrate it (see Malkemus & Romero, 2012). These practices—some of which focus on the vital center or involve the most primal senses of taste and smell—seek to facilitate the gradual assimilation and creative transformation of this energy through body, heart, mind, and consciousness. In this context it may be appropriate to mention the importance given in this work to alternating cycles of *experience* (i.e., direct access to experiential contents or energies) and *assimilation* (i.e., gestation and elaboration of the experiences through meditation, nature walks, meditation movement, dance, expressive arts, verbalization, or journal writing).

Although the aim of these primal contemplative practices is diverse and, as described below, becomes individualized in the process, they are devised to free the body from its organically embedded shame; heal or transform a number of wounds, conflicts, or inhibitions stored at energetic levels; allow a more fluid movement of the primary energy through body, heart, mind, and consciousness; align the primary energy and the energy of consciousness; integrate sexuality and spirituality; cultivate the "masculine" (agent) and "feminine" (receptive) aspects of the primary energy, which are considered essential for a healthy and creative life regardless of gender or sexual orientation; and foster the activation, gestation, and creative transformation of the primary energy in order to bring forth novel qualities and potentials at somatic, emotional, psychological, and spiritual levels.

As with the basic meditations, practitioners can repeat any given practice with the same or different parameters, partner(s), role, duration, place, and so on, in order to gain further precision and experiential contrasts, train new capabilities or qualities, or foster the vitalization, differentiation, and maturation of certain dimensions or potentials. Where possible, many of these practices are carried out in nature, and the work also features contemplative practices specifically designed to be developed in contact with nature's healing and transformative resources.

Individualized Integral Practices

Since each individual is similar to others in some regards, but singularly different in others, Holistic Transformation includes both common and individualized practices. At a certain moment in the process, practitioners start to design their own individualized practices, first with the guidance of the facilitators and then on their own. Individualized integral growth properly begins when practitioners, out of a clear awareness of their present limitations and potentialities, define and walk their own personal integral path. According to Albareda and Romero, individualized practices are essential: only through them can practitioners access the deepest domains of their unique being and hence ground their integral process in their own vital potentials.

It is fundamental to stress that even though the facilitators may offer practical advice about the design of personal practices, *the integral growth process is primarily regulated by the practitioner's own multidimensional experience.* In other words, the specific form of a given practice is organically shaped or inspired by whatever happens somatically, energetically, emotionally, mentally, or spiritually in the previous practice (e.g., difficulties or tensions, desires or impulses, confusion or questions, insights or inspirations, visions or spiritual openings). This is why integral growth unfolds through a route that can never be predetermined and that takes as many forms and directions as the individuals involved.

In order to illustrate the dynamics of the inner guidance of this process, Romero and Albareda (2001) offered the following image.

> Imagine that we face two magnets and keep them at a certain distance. Unless other forces are present, a magnetic field will be generated that will arrange any metallic object that enters the field across identical lines.
>
> Now imagine that one magnet is the dark energy and the other the energy of consciousness. This situation generates a new energetic movement in the interior of the person. The movement affects the individual just as a magnetic field influences metallic objects. Essentially, the individual is impelled toward a new order *from within.* Under this influence, and depending on a variety of factors, an individual can have two kinds of experiences: First, she can experience dissociation, which reveals those personal structures or energetic tendencies that preclude or hinder the alignment of both energies, for example, conflicts, blockages, struggles, fears, empty holes, and so forth. In this case, the individual can become aware of, relate to, and start to transform those elements. It must be stressed that the orientation of this process is neither external to the individual nor provided by already learned schemes. Rather, the orientation naturally emerges out of the new energetic axes generated by the alignment of the dark energy and the energy of consciousness.

Second, an individual can experience connection without resistance between the dark energy and the energy of consciousness. Such an experience can become an inner reference point for that person to lay down [his/her] path, even in those moments when it may seem very hard or impossible. It will also be an experience of profound regeneration and pacification of both the primary and the spiritual worlds of the individual. Both types of experiences are necessary to develop [an integral] path. (p. 10)

According to Albareda and Romero, most Holistic Transformation practices can be seen as structures that facilitate the organic emergence of experiential contents (e.g., energetic blockages, deep emotions, psychological insights). Once the various parameters of a practice have been clearly established (e.g., structure, type of meditative contact, persons, roles, boundaries, duration), practitioners let go of their intentions and expectations, and simply remain present, open, and receptive to their experience. Arguably, one of the main catalysts for the emergence of experiential materials may be the embodied contact between consciousness and the other energetic centers. Albareda and Romero believe that human consciousness has the capability to "impregnate" the energetic seeds of a person's somatic, instinctive, and emotional dimensions, catalyzing a process of conception, gestation, and emergence of new life within. In their view, this process has two different but not mutually exclusive outcomes. On the one hand, it can engender new qualities, capabilities, or potentials within these worlds ("feminine" phase), some of which may require intentional development, elaboration, training, and communal legitimization to become fully incorporated in the person ("masculine" phase). On the other hand, and perhaps more strikingly, the presence of consciousness can impregnate so deeply the essence of those worlds that they can become aligned with the conscious spiritual orientation of the person, spontaneously and creatively collaborating in her integral growth (Romero & Albareda, 2001).

Integrative Work in Everyday Life

When Holistic Transformation is offered in cycles of six or seven months, participants are encouraged to carry on with their practices between monthly encounters, to strengthen their process and facilitate its integration into their everyday lives. A dimension of community naturally emerges from this social network that can also be more intentionally cultivated through a variety of social gatherings and group activities. The presence of a community of support and the importance of integrating one's personal transformation into everyday life are both central to Holistic Transformation.

In addition to a creative transformation of everyday life, a more focused creative project (e.g., educational, artistic, intellectual, healing, community building, organizational, ecological, religious) can either guide the process of some practitioners or naturally emerge from its culmination. The number of social, educational, and cultural projects that have emerged from Holistic Transformation during the last decades is vast, so I simply mention here a few examples: an educative project for female prisoners; various university graduate courses; an alternative governmental political and social project in the Canary Islands, Spain; a project for the integration of immigrant women; several innovative therapeutic modalities, including one based on human-animal interaction; an educative project for the youth in a religious community; an institutionally incorporated approach to childbirth called Welcome to Life; several alternative community and ecological projects; and a large variety of artistic projects, exhibitions, and shows (sculpture, photography, painting, visual and plastic arts, music, and cartoons), including a dance performance called Eros & Spirit: Evolution from Within, presented in 2002 at the Brava Theater for the Women in the Arts in San Francisco. Finally, Romero, Malkemus, and myself have taught many graduate courses at California Institute of Integral Studies (CIIS), San Francisco, over the past fifteen years, including my course, "Embodied Spiritual Inquiry." As I discuss in chapter 7, Embodied Spiritual Inquiry also came to refer to both a second-person, contemplative, pedagogical approach and a participatory spiritual practice in itself.

CONCLUSION

Modern ITP proposals can be seen as important efforts to explore and foster in the modern West an embodied spirituality that is not only free from the tensions and contradictions of a lopsided development, but also grounded in the maturation and integration of all human attributes. In this chapter, however, I have identified two potential pitfalls of ITPs. First, given the generally underdeveloped condition of the somatic, instinctive, and emotional worlds of the individual (at least in the modern West), intellectually designed ITP programs can perpetuate the mental colonization of these worlds, preventing their autonomous maturation and paradoxically undermining the very possibility of a multidimensional, cocreative integral growth. Second, given the hypermasculine thrust of modern Western life and education, an emphasis on the training of these human dimensions through already existing practices may hinder the more "feminine," organic emergence of their most unique qualities and potentials.

Therefore, modern ITP proposals must be complemented with participatory approaches that (1) foster the autonomous maturation of all human dimensions according to their own developmental dynamics; and (2) balance the exercise of human attributes with the creation of spaces for the coming into being of novel qualities and inner potentials. I believe that only then may a genuine integral growth—one that is both grounded in human's most vital potentials and cocreated by all human essential dimensions—have some possibility to unfold.

To illustrate this participatory perspective on integral growth, I have introduced Holistic Transformation, an integral approach cocreated by Albareda and Romero (1991; Romero & Albareda, 2001; Malkemus & Romero, 2012). In this work, practitioners learn to first make contact with the present state of their somatic, instinctive, emotional, mental, and conscious worlds, and then design practices to foster their maturation, vitalization, and integration. Through a variety of innovative, embodied, and interactive contemplative practices, practitioners seek to access the creative power of their vital energy and gradually align it with the energy of consciousness. This alignment is said to bring forth an energetic axis in the person that orients her integral growth from within. The form and structure of individualized integral practices, for example, emerges not from external sources, but from the practitioner's somatic, vital, emotional, mental, and conscious experience. Although systematic research to assess the effectiveness of these practices is needed, Holistic Transformation's multidimensional, organic unfolding of integral growth holds a promise to short-circuit the danger of egoic or mental control of ITPs. Besides possibly engendering unique developmental paths, the Holistic Transformation process entails or culminates in the transformation of everyday life and the world through a variety of personal, cultural, social, and ecological creative projects.

To conclude, I propose that from a participatory perspective, ITPs may facilitate not only Zen-like nondual realizations, but also many other spiritually significant enactions of self and world. Some of these enactions have been described by the world's religious traditions, while the novel quality of others may require a more creative engagement to be brought forth. In the wake of the historical religious repression of sexuality and the body (see chapter 3), it is likely that more integral enactments of the mystery may hold many surprises on spiritual matters. As Kripal (2007) pointed out, even though human beings share a psychosomatic foundation that may lead to cross-cultural similarities in spiritual experience, historical and sociocultural variables can shape different forms of enlightenment of the body—or, to use Murphy's (1993) expression, "integral enlightenment" (as cited in Cohen, 1999, p. 90). In any event, I believe that ITPs can be seen as modern explorations of a more embodied and participatory spirituality, whose cultivation may lead to not only questioning many traditional religious doctrines, but also transgressing outdated injunctions (and proscriptions) for what counts as a "spiritually correct" practice.

PART TWO

INTEGRAL EDUCATION

FIVE

THE FOUR SEASONS OF
INTEGRAL EDUCATION

(with Marina T. Romero and Ramón V. Albareda)

This chapter introduces a participatory approach to integral transformative education in which all human dimensions—body, vital, heart, mind, and consciousness—are invited to participate cocreatively in the unfolding of learning and inquiry.[1] After some preliminary considerations about the basic elements of an integral curriculum and the horizontal and vertical dimensions of integral education, the first part of the chapter situates this participatory perspective in relation to two other approaches to integral education: mind-centered/intellectualist and bricolage/eclectic. The second part presents the basic contours of a participatory model of integral transformative education using the organic metaphor of the four seasons. We also stress the importance of integrating "feminine" and "masculine" principles in whole-person learning and outline several basic features of integral transformative education (for caveats about the use of the terms *feminine* and *masculine*, see chapter 4, note 4). In the third part of the chapter, we discuss several challenges for the implementation of integral transformative education in modern academia and suggest that these challenges can be seen as precious opportunities to reconnect education with its transformative and spiritual roots. The chapter concludes with some reflections on the transpersonal nature of human participatory inquiry.

INTEGRAL EDUCATION:
ELEMENTS, DIMENSIONS, AND APPROACHES

In this section, we introduce the idea of an integral education through the identification of (1) the elements of an integral curriculum, (2) the horizontal and vertical dimensions of integral learning, and (3) three main types of integral pedagogical approaches.

Elements of the Integral Curriculum: Content, Training, and Inquiry

Before discussing integral education, we distinguish three basic elements of learning, or three types of pedagogical emphasis—content, training, and inquiry—and situate them in the context of an integral curriculum. The element of *content* refers to the presentation, explication, discussion, analysis, critique, comparison, and integration of information (e.g., facts, ideas, theories, models, approaches, traditions). Content-based learning has historically been the mark of mainstream Western education. It can be extremely creative as well as integral in the sense of working with or toward integrative frameworks, approaches, and understandings (e.g., synthetic thinking, multiperspectivism, interdisciplinarity, cross-cultural studies). The element of *training* focuses on the acquisition of specific skills and capabilities at all levels; for example, technical skills, research and writing skills, clinical skills, interpersonal and emotional skills (e.g., group dynamics), dialogical and argumentative skills, postformal and complex thinking skills, somatic/pranic skills (e.g., through yoga, sensory awareness, or tai chi chuan), and contemplative skills (e.g., meditation classes). The element of *inquiry* focuses on the facilitation of pedagogical spaces that foster individual and collective inquiry into focused topics, questions, or problems. This dimension can be accessed using (1) mental or verbal approaches such as dialogical inquiry, argumentation, or trans-disciplinarity, or (2) multidimensional approaches, such as supplementing mental or verbal approaches with others that engage the voices of the body, the vital, the heart, intuition, special states of consciousness, and so forth.

We begin by offering some general thoughts about these elements and clarifying their significance in a graduate-level integral curriculum.[2] First, these three categories are not mutually exclusive, and most traditional and alternative educational practices engage all three to some extent (except, in most cases, multidimensional inquiry approaches). Second, all three pedagogical forms are equally important elements of education and learning, and different courses can naturally stress one or several of them, depending on their aim and focus. Third, as learners move from school to college, from college to university, from undergraduate to graduate education, and from master to doctoral levels, there needs to be a gradual but increasing shift of emphasis from an educational praxis based mainly on content and training (arguably more appropriate for children and young adults requiring epistemic foundations) to one based mainly on inquiry and training (arguably more appropriate for adults who aspire to contribute new knowledge or practical service to the world). In the latter, many of the training programs may take the form of the acquisition of (1) practical skills (e.g., technical skills, organizational skills, clinical skills), (2) facilitation skills (e.g., interpersonal skills, emotional skills, leadership skills), and (3) skills that can be used as inquiry tools once learned (e.g., meditation practice, somatic techniques, complex thinking). Thus, a graduate-level integral curriculum might include a creative mix of a few foundational content-based courses (especially at the master's level), some training-based courses of the types appropriate to each program's focus, and many inquiry-based courses of both verbal/mental and multidimensional types. Different courses could combine these elements creatively in numerous ways.[3]

Horizontal and Vertical Dimensions of Integral Education

The simplest way to start exploring the idea of an integral education is in terms of the discipline's horizontal and vertical dimensions. As Wexler (2004) stated, the *horizontal* dimension refers to the integration of knowledge (i.e., content, training, and mental inquiry) and the *vertical* dimension refers to the integration of multiple ways of knowing (i.e., special trainings and multidimensional inquiry). These dimensions can cross-fertilize and shape each other in complex ways; for example, engaging in certain forms of transdisciplinary inquiry may call for multiple ways of knowing, and including multiple ways of knowing in the learning process may call for transdisciplinary approaches to inquiry.[4] In the following paragraphs, we explore each dimension in more detail.

The horizontal dimension is intimately connected to what Boyer (1990) called the "scholarship of integration" (p. 18; see also D. K. Scott, 2005). According to Boyer, the scholarship of integration emerged from the increasing need of many researchers to "move beyond traditional disciplinary boundaries, communicate with colleagues in other fields, and discover patterns that connect" (p. 20). "Interdisciplinary and integrative studies" (p. 21), Boyer added, "long on the edges of academic life, are moving to the center, responding both to new intellectual questions and to pressing human problems" (p. 21).

These are the four main types of horizontal integral scholarship:

- *Disciplinary* integral scholarship pursues the integration of models, theories, schools, and so forth within a single discipline of knowledge (e.g., integration of object-relation models in developmental psychology; integration of structuralism, feminism, and critical theory in sociology).

- *Multidisciplinary* integral scholarship is the study of a phenomenon from multiple disciplinary perspectives (e.g., the study of human consciousness from the perspectives of neuroscience, cognitive psychology, phenomenology, and mysticism; J. Klein, 1990, 1996).

- *Interdisciplinary* integral scholarship consists of the transfer of principles or methods from one discipline to another (e.g., methods of nuclear physics to medicine or somatic techniques to spiritual inquiry; Lattuca, 2001; Nicolescu, 2002). Repko (2008) used this term as other authors used multidisciplinary, that is, as the integration of insights from different disciplines with the aim of achieving an interdisciplinary understanding of a topic (e.g., insights from cognitive psychology, political science, and cultural anthropology in the comprehension of suicide terrorism).

- *Transdisciplinary* integral scholarship is a problem-centered or inquiry-driven integrative approach that creatively applies any relevant perspective across disciplines (i.e., transcending the disciplinary organization of knowledge) with an awareness of their underlying paradigmatic assumptions and the practice of complex thinking (Leavy, 2011; Montuori, 2005a; Nicolescu, 2002).

There are two important qualifications to this information. First, each horizontal approach potentially involves the integration of various research methodologies and techniques (e.g., qualitative and quantitative; phenomenology and electroencephalography), epistemic standpoints (e.g., emic and etic; first-, second-, and third-person), and epistemologies (e.g., Buddhist and Western science). Second, all types can have two chief orientations: (1) *basic*, aiming at the conceptual integration of two or more authors, approaches, theories, models, schools, or disciplines (e.g., the thought of Jung and Campbell; feminism and critical theory) into a more encompassing integrative framework, theory, or new discipline; and (2) *applied*, using of previously constructed integrative frameworks as a tool to study, situate, critique, interpret, understand, or develop transformative action regarding a phenomenon (e.g., using Wilber's [1996a] Four Quadrant Model as a lens to study the various theories of art interpretation).

Horizontal integrative scholarship can be motivated by the following nonexclusive regulative goals: *harmonization*, reconciling apparently contradictory data or conflicting views within a larger vision or integrative framework; *holism*, addressing the fragmentation of knowledge that is the fruit of the hyperspecialization of modern science and academia; *multiperspectivism*, deepening knowledge about a subject or phenomenon by applying different perspectives, models, and fields of knowledge; creation of *new fields of inquiry*, such as psychoneuroimmunology, ecofeminism, psychohistory, or neurophenomenology; and fostering the *cognitive and psychospiritual development* of researchers and readers (e.g., linking multiperspectivism and transdisciplinarity with postformal modes of cognition such as Gebser's [1986] integral consciousness, Morin's [2008] complex thinking, Kegan's [1998] fifth order consciousness, or Wilber's [1996b] vision logic, some of which are considered fundamental stepping stones toward transpersonal and contemplative ways of knowing).

Although methodological clarity about the horizontal dimension is yet to be achieved (Repko, 2008), the greatest challenge of integral education lies in the facilitation of the vertical dimension of learning: multidimensional inquiry or the integration of multiple ways of knowing. It is essential that contemporary holistic educators address the vertical dimension of education for three reasons. First, the presence of this dimension can facilitate not only an existentially meaningful integrative framework for students' academic pursuits, but also the ongoing integral transformation of students, faculty, and institutions. Second, the practice of multidimensional inquiry constitutes the cutting edge of integral education; horizontal integrative scholarship is already common practice in many mainstream educational programs, departments, and universities—as the *Report of the Carnegie Foundation* (Boyer, 1990) showed more than twenty-five years ago (cf. Repko, 2008; D. K. Scott, 2005). Third, as we elaborate in the following section, the incorporation of the vertical dimension can reconnect education with its transformative and spiritual potential. Therefore, although we do not underestimate the importance of horizontal integralism, in this chapter we focus on the vertical dimension and explore the challenges involved in its implementation.

Approaches to Integral Education: Mind-Centered, Bricolage, and Participatory

Although most holistic educators agree that all human dimensions should be incorporated into learning and inquiry (e.g., M. Anthony, 2008; B. Hocking, Haskell, & Linds, 2001; R. Miller, 1991; O'Sullivan, Morrel, & O'Connor, 2002; Rothberg, 1999), the practical efforts to materialize this vision tend to crystallize in three quite different approaches: mind-centered or intellectualist, bricolage or eclectic, and participatory. We examine each of them independently here, but in actual practice these approaches can be combined in diverse and productive ways.

THE MIND-CENTERED OR INTELLECTUALIST APPROACH

This approach is based on the intellectual study and elaboration of integral visions or understandings. It uses the intellectual tools of mainstream education (e.g., logical analysis, rational argumentation, synthesis of literature) to reach a more integrated understanding of the topic of study, and can include fundamental questions such as the nature of the human being, life, reality, or the cosmos. It is usually offered above in the context of a traditional pedagogical methodology (e.g., magisterial lectures, textual research, assessment of learning through written essays). The mind-centered approach to education is integral in its object of study but not in its pedagogy, methodology, or inquiry process. In terms of the conceptual distinctions offered, the mind-centered approach focuses on the horizontal dimension of integral education and neglects the vertical one.

Whereas the intellectual engagement of integral understandings is an important corrective to the usually fragmented nature of Western education, the reduction of integral education to merely intellectual activity generates a deep incoherence that can undermine its transformative and emancipatory potential. An exclusively or eminently intellectual approach perpetuates the cognicentrism of mainstream Western education in its assumption that the mind's cognitive capabilities are or should be the paramount masters and players of learning and inquiry.[5] A common consequence of this reduction is the confusion of an expanded intellectual understanding with genuine integral knowledge. Most phenomena studied in the human and social sciences, and arguably in the biological and physical sciences, partake of different nonmental dimensions (e.g., material, energetic, emotional, spiritual). Therefore, an eminently mental approach is likely to lead to partial understandings and even significant distortions.

This problem is heightened in the study of human spirituality. Most spiritual traditions posit the existence of an isomorphism or deep resonance among the human being, the cosmos, and the mystery out of which everything arises (as above so below, the embodied person as microcosm of the macrocosm; Chittick, 1994a; Overzee, 1992; Saso, 1997; Shokek, 2001). Therefore, the more dimensions of the person that are actively engaged in the study of the mystery, or of phenomena associated with it, the more complete the knowledge will be. This completion should not be understood quantitatively, but rather qualitatively. More human dimensions creatively participating in spiritual knowing leads to greater dynamic congruence between inquiry approach and studied phenomena, making knowledge more coherent with, or attuned to, the unfolding nature of the mystery.

THE BRICOLAGE OR ECLECTIC APPROACH

The bricolage approach—by far the most widespread in alternative educational institutions—incorporates experiential moments or practices (e.g., movement, meditation, ritual) into mind-centered education and offers eclectic curricular courses that engage other human attributes (e.g., tai chi for the vital/prana, somatic techniques or hatha yoga for the body, meditation for spiritual consciousness). Although some classes may engage and to some extent develop the nonmental dimensions, these dimensions are rarely part of the substance of the educational process (e.g., inquiry tools into subject matters, evaluators of inquiry outcomes), which is mainly planned, conducted, and assessed from the perspective of the mind. The bricolage approach can take place in the context of traditional education (not aiming at integral understandings) and mind-centered integral education (which studies or attempts to develop integral visions).

The bricolage approach engages the horizontal and vertical dimensions of integral education in an unintegrated and ultimately deceptive way. It is unintegrated because the intellect does not work in collaboration with other ways of knowing in the context of a creative cycle of integral learning and inquiry (see the next section for an illustration of what such a collaboration might look like). It is deceptive because it can create the false impression that students are engaged in integral learning simply because of the relative attention paid to other dimensions of the person, especially in contrast with traditional, mind-centered education.

Although the bricolage approach constitutes an important advance in relation to mainstream education, genuine integral learning cannot be accomplished by a training process regulated by mental parameters. It is crucial to distinguish between the eclectic engagement of nonmental human attributes as supplements of learning and their integrated creative participation at various stages of the inquiry and learning process. The bricolage approach, despite its advantages over a purely intellectualist education, remains fundamentally cognicentric.

THE PARTICIPATORY APPROACH

The participatory approach seeks to facilitate the cocreative participation of all human dimensions at all stages of the inquiry and learning processes. Body, vital, heart, mind, and consciousness are considered equal partners in the exploration and elaboration of knowledge. This approach invites the engagement of the whole person, ideally at all stages of the educational process, including construction of the curriculum, selection of research topics, inquiry process, and assessment of inquiry outcomes.[6] The novelty of the participatory proposal is essentially methodological—it stresses the need to explore practical approaches that combine the power of the mind and the cultivation of consciousness with the epistemic potential of human somatic, vital, and emotional worlds. The participatory approach aims for synergic integration of the horizontal and vertical dimensions of integral education, as well as coherent alignment of the verbal and multidimensional inquiry modalities.

We do not consider the participatory approach merely one more alternate perspective; instead, we firmly believe that, if skillfully implemented, it constitutes a richer, more natural, and more transformative integral pedagogy. Sri Aurobindo (the originator of integralism in India; Aurobindo, 1993) distinguished between the spiritual liberation of consciousness and an integral transformation that entails the spiritual alignment of all human dimensions. In the same way, we differentiate between an educational process regulated by the conscious mind and one organically orchestrated by all human attributes. We propose that a participatory approach is not only more satisfactory but also more natural and coherent with the multidimensional makeup of the human being. If it may not look "natural" at first, we suggest that this could be the result of dissociated dispositions embedded in the modern Western self. We return to this issue later in the chapter.

The fundamental question is how to implement participatory approaches in modern academia.[7] To begin exploring this question we use the metaphor of the four seasons to illustrate a way in which multiple human dimensions can participate in a complete cycle of creative academic inquiry. Our intention is not to offer a paradigmatic model for others to follow, but rather to provide a possible general orientation whose ultimate value should be assessed by teachers and students as they attempt to cultivate integral approaches to academic work.

A PARTICIPATORY MODEL OF INTEGRAL EDUCATION

This section outlines a model of integral education based on the image of nature's four seasons. Using this metaphor allows us to (1) highlight the importance of integrating "feminine" and "masculine" principles in educational practice, and (2) identify six basic features of integral education.

The Four Seasons of the Integral Creative Cycle

Whether in nature or in human reality, a creative process usually unfolds through several stages that correspond roughly with the seasonal cycle of nature: (1) *action* or autumn, preparing the terrain and planting the seeds (the body, studying what is already known about a subject matter), (2) *germination/gestation* or winter, rooting and nourishment of the seed inside the earth (the vital, the conception of novel developments in contact with unconscious transpersonal and archetypal sources), (3) *blooming* or spring, emerging toward the light of buds, leaves, and flowers (the heart, the first conscious feelings and rough ideas), and (4) *harvest* or summer, selecting mature fruits and sharing celebration (the mind, intellectual selection, elaboration, and offering of the fruits of the creative process).[8] Next, we briefly examine each season and how each can be supported in the context of academic work (see Figure 5.1, page 128).

AUTUMN: THE BODY, PLANTING, ACTION

In many lands across the globe, autumn is the time to prepare the soil for the new harvesting cycle. The soil is scrabbled, cleansed of old roots

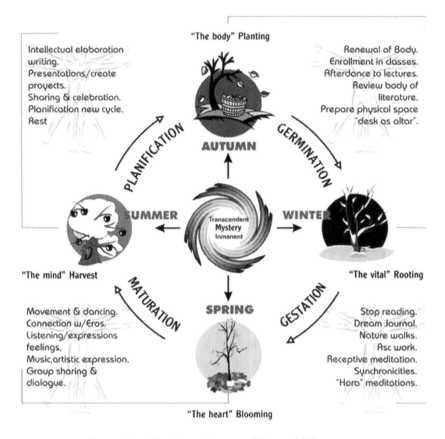

Figure 5.1. The Four Seasons of Integral Education.

and stones, and fertilized; then, new seeds are planted in the soil.

In the human creative cycle, autumn is the time for preparing the physical body to be a solid and porous receptacle for the germination of new vital seeds.[9] It is important to release accumulated tensions from the body to make it more open and permeable. It is also essential to relate to the body as a living organic reality, holding meaningful contents that cannot be intentionally accessed through the mind or consciousness.

Academically, autumn is the time to take actions such as enrolling in stimulating courses, attending lectures, and creatively reviewing the body of the literature—which can be approached as a set of potentially seminal works generated by "our ancestors" (Montuori, 2005b, p. 377) with the power to impregnate the vital seeds of many individuals. During lectures, dialogues, and readings it is crucial to cultivate an attitude of receptivity, as if one were planting seeds in one's inner soil. This is also the time to prepare the physical space in which the creative process will take place, for example, by cleaning and organizing the office space and, as Metzger (1992) wrote, preparing the desk as an altar as the bride chamber is prepared for the beloved (i.e., the muse, the *daimon*, or the creative wellspring within).

In autumn, the mind supports appropriate action by engaging in behaviors that create optimum conditions for listening to the body, actualizing physical structures, and searching for new resources. It is also a time for the mind to let go of old ways of thinking so it can support and recognize the fruits of the new creative cycle. During autumn, the mind can stagnate the creative process if it spends too much time wondering about the ultimate outcome of the inquiry, tries to predetermine its development, or arrives at its own answers before the stages of the creative process have the chance to unfold. Autumn is the season to trust the body, support the structural dimension of reality, and rely on the power of action.

WINTER: THE VITAL, ROOTING, GESTATION

Once seeds have been planted, the cultivator cannot do much else. Winter is a time of waiting, darkness, silence, and, most importantly, gestation. It is imperative to stop the activity of autumn so the planted seeds can do their own autonomous work: splitting open, rooting in the soil, and getting fed by the earth's essential nutrients.

In the same way that a germinated seed first grows toward the darkness of soil to be nourished and develop roots as the necessary base for the upward growth of the plant toward light, in the human being, an activated vital seed first plunges into the depths of the personal and collective unconscious. Like the roots of trees in a forest, human vital depths are interconnected in the unconscious, where they can be nurtured not only by the collective wisdom of human heritage, but also by the generative, immanent dimension of the mystery. This contact between the vital world and immanent mystery makes winter a sacred season that needs to be honored properly. As with the dormant appearance of nature in winter, it may appear to the conscious mind that nothing is happening at this juncture of the creative process, but it is important to remember that powerful and creative forces are at play in the darkness. During spring, these forces will catalyze not only the regeneration and blooming of life in nature, but also the emergence of creative impulses in the human soil.

In academia, winter is a time in which it may be important to stop reading or assimilating further information in any other way. The process of creative gestation requires its own inner space, which is facilitated by silence, interiorization, and stillness. Not knowing how to accompany this stage of gestation, too often students—especially at their dissertation stage—paralyze the creative process with their inability to stop reading. (This consideration has obvious implications for the sequence of readings required in academic courses.) The conscious mind, not able to see in the darkness of this stage, can believe that in order to move ahead, it has to continue incorporating new theories and ideas. There will always be articles or books to read, but in the same way that people need to stop eating to facilitate an effective and nourishing digestion, it is necessary to stop reading in winter for adequate gestation of the creative impulse. Appropriate activities during this season are not those seeking to find immediate answers but those that support the alignment of the mind or consciousness with the process of gestation. It is crucial to cultivate a sense of trust in the natural processes that take place within the creative matrix during winter, much as a pregnant woman must trust the gestation of a fetus. Examples of supporting activities include keeping a dream journal; taking nature walks; working with special states of consciousness; practicing receptive forms of meditation such as *vipassana* (mindfulness meditation), *wu-wei* (without doing), or *shinkan taza* (sitting-only); cultivating visionary imagination; doing symbolic work; paying attention to synchronicities in everyday life (including that book that fell from the shelf); and engaging practices that facilitate an embodied contact with the vital center or *hara* (Dürckheim, 1962) as the physical and energetic container of creative pregnancy.

In winter the mind needs to cultivate an attitude of patient receptivity, not knowing, and humble respect. It is important to develop patience and receptivity toward stages of the creative process whose rhythm and unfolding elude the mind's intentional control. Respect and not knowing naturally emerge from the mind's recognition that something is happening beyond what it can see directly. Humility is born out of the awareness that, although the mind can be present to the process, the creative dynamism does not need its powers at this stage. During winter, the mind can abort the creative cycle if—out of ignorance, impatience, or mistrust—it attempts to control the process or prematurely know the nature of the still embryonic creative drive. It is as if a farmer, not trusting the chthonic process of the seed, anxiously digs up the soil to see what is happening or actively help the seed grow. Winter is the season to cultivate patient receptivity toward the unknown and to trust in those aspects and stages of life that transcend the intentionality of the human mind and consciousness.

SPRING: THE HEART, BLOOMING, DIVERSITY

Spring is the season for the shameless blossoming of newly regenerated life. It is a time of spontaneity, contrasts, and celebration of diversity; a time for the sprouting of buds and the blooming of flowers; and a time of tremendous fragility and intensity. If the conditions are appropriate, spring is also a time of countless surprises.

In the creative process, spring is the season to open the heart, breathe deeply and widely, listen to one's affective world, and make room within so the raw sensations associated with the upwelling creative energy emerging out of the gestation process can be organically incorporated as emotions and feelings. This is the stage of first contact with—and embodiment of—the creative impulses gestated in winter. This can be a time of joyful exhilaration in the wake of the fresh contents emerging from within, and a time in which it is crucial to avoid the mental temptation to prematurely assess what is emerging. At the end of the season, it is important to let go of developments that, like spring flowers, were temporary manifestations of the creative process and to start contemplating those that remain and may become fruits in the summer.

In academic work, the first part of spring calls for activities that support the embodied magnification of the first creative energetic blossoms, including physical games that involve movement and dance (e.g., dancing one's research question) and sensual or sexual explorations to awaken and integrate the erotic power of life into the inquiry process. The importance of eros and sexuality in a genuinely creative process cannot be understated.[10] Eros is the creative power of life in its primordial, undifferentiated state, and sexuality is one of the first soils for the organization and creative development of such primary energy in human reality. It is thus important that sexuality is an open and porous soil based on natural evolutionary principles and not on fears, conflicts, or artificial impositions dictated by the mind, culture, or spiritual ideologies. The second part of spring calls for activities such as somatic expression, verbalization of feelings, embodied practices that facilitate listening to emotions and feelings, and artistic expression (e.g., music, painting, sculpture, plastic arts, poetry, singing). Peer-group work becomes central at this stage, as it provides a social context for nonjudgmental contrasts and cross-fertilization among incipient creative expressions.

Two qualities are essential for the mind to cultivate in spring. First is an attitude of genuine curiosity by which the mind looks at the emerging contents as if seeing them for the first time, avoiding their codification through previously learned conceptual schemes or theories. Second is an attitude of unconditional acceptance and support of the budding contents. At this stage, the creative process can be aborted if the mind projects its previously learned schemes or theories onto what is emerging, or if it prematurely judges their value. Spring is not the season of the mind; it is a time to trust the heart and unconditionally support its processes.

Summer: The Mind, Harvest, Celebration

During summer, some flowers mature into fruits and some of those fruits become ripe. It is the season of harvest, celebration, sharing, and gratitude. It is also a time to rest, peacefully contemplate the new seeds contained in the fruits, and plan another cycle for the following autumn.

In the creative process, the fruits represent the ideas or expressions selected for further elaboration and refinement. If the mind has accompanied the entire process with the appropriate stage-specific attitudes of a sensitive farmer, it will easily discern at this stage the mature fruits that deserve further consideration. Summer is the season of the mind—a time for the intellectual and aesthetic elaboration of ideas. It is also an auspicious time to open oneself to the transcendent sources of the mystery, which can now illuminate the mind with insights that may enrich the refinement of the creative fruits.

In the academic system, summer is the season to focus on the articulation of ideas with clarity, beauty, elegance, precision, and sophistication. It is also the time to dialog with others about ideas to polish them in substance and verbal or nonverbal expression. Putting those ideas into writing or other expressive means is a step further in the materialization of the creative process. The writing style should be coherent with the original creative impulse, so the words embody the message without distortions. This is the season to contrast one's fruits with already existing developments and ideas (i.e., with the fruits of the creative processes of others). In mainstream education, those contrasts occur long before the creative process has delivered mature fruits, and, although this can be helpful, it can also endanger the process, leaving students with a lack of confidence that can lead to a compensatory mental reformulation of already existent ideas. Summer is also the time for sharing refined ideas through class presentations, written papers, or other creative projects, and it may be important to explore different modalities to convey those ideas (e.g., visual, aesthetic, dramatic). A further stage in this process could be the publication of the fruits of the season in magazines or journals, or their presentation at professional conferences and public events. Last, summer is the time to raise new questions, plan a new research cycle, and explore avenues for further inquiry that may awaken new vital seeds.

If the mind has been in contact with the multidimensional nature of the creative process, the attitude it will naturally display in the presentations of the fruits of summer will be one of passionate humbleness. The mind will be passionate because the ideas will be grounded in somatic, vital, and emotional experience, and it will be humble out of recognition that the ultimate sources of the creative process transcend both mental structures and personal individuality—that is, they are both transcendent and transpersonal. Learners can feel that they have been both gardener and soil in the creative process, while being aware of the many participating elements that have collaborated in the unfolding of that process (e.g., body, vital, heart, mind and consciousness; the personal and the collective unconscious; immanent and transcendent mystery). Passion without humbleness can become arrogance, and arrogance may be a sign that the person is aware only of the personal dimension of the process. Humbleness without passion can become weak and even boring and may be a sign that the person is overlooking the personal grounding of the process. An attitude of passionate humbleness honors the personal and transpersonal dimensions of the creative process.

Before closing this section, we stress the general nature of this integral creative cycle. Although it can serve as an orientation for integral pedagogical practice, this cycle should not be made paradigmatic for all individuals. Many dispositions and associated dynamics exist in the unfolding of the creative process. A serious consideration of the diverse individual rhythms in the gestation and maturation of creative fruits may lead to the revision of standard academic practices, such as predetermined timeframes for academic accomplishment or collective deadlines for the delivery of inquiry outcomes. Furthermore, there can be an indefinite number of seasonal subcycles (autumn-winter-spring-summer) in the context of a larger creative project, and these subcycles can take place both sequentially and simultaneously. Last, and perhaps most important, the suggestion of a rough correspondence between creative stages and specific human attributes is simply a didactic orientation. A human being is a multidimensional unity; body, vital, heart, mind, and consciousness are petals of the human flower. All human attributes are present and operative at all stages of the creative cycle. However, this fact does not preclude that, as in the early stages of human development—from organic matter and vital impulse, to proto-emotions and differentiated feelings, to thoughts and formal cognition—certain attributes may have greater preeminence than others at certain stages. For these reasons, although we believe the sequence sketched here accurately reflects deep dynamics of the creative cycle, we also emphasize that it has an indefinite number of variations and should not be viewed in a strictly linear fashion.

Integration of "Feminine" and "Masculine" Principles

In this expanded educational context, one can acknowledge that both mainstream and alternative modern academia focus on the autumn and the summer phases of action and harvest (the more "masculine" aspects of the process), and tend to overlook the facilitation of spaces for the winter and the spring: germination, gestation, and giving birth (the more "feminine" aspects of the process).[11] Students spend most of their time inside and outside the classroom reading, studying, and discussing knowledge already elaborated by others (autumn), after which they are expected to produce original contributions in their final presentations and papers (summer). The deep structure of modern education tends to skip the more "feminine" and more deeply generative stages of the creative process (winter and spring). Seen in this context, the scarcity of genuinely creative developments in academia should not be surprising. There is much second-order creativity or smart mental permutation of already known ideas but little first-order creativity or organic, multidimensional emergence of genuinely innovative developments. Given the innumerable abortions of the creative process that these dynamics cause in the Western educational process, it is understandable and perhaps inevitable that so many students develop a lack of confidence in their own creative potential.

We suspect that this deeply masculinized pedagogical container may cause the intense and also masculinized reactivity of the "feminine" sensibility of both men and women, which faculty and students often witness in the classroom—even in courses in which the "feminine" is honored and included in content or more superficial process (e.g., inclusion of a "feminine" ritual in a masculinized pedagogical process). The deeply "feminine" is in a state of paralyzing despair that can easily burst into anger because it cannot understand why it still feels profoundly dishonored when it is apparently attended to or explicitly championed. This situation parallels the current despair of the African American community in the United States, which, as West (1999) pointed out, hoped for future genuine integration before its members gained civil rights but today faces an increasing nihilism in the wake of the unsatisfactory alternatives of either becoming like "the white folks" or remaining in the ghetto or the jail.

It is likely that integral transformative education will gradually restructure the pedagogical process in ways that truly and deeply integrate the "masculine" and "feminine" dimensions of the inquiry process. This restructuring may involve the facilitation of spaces not only for the intellectual discussion and production of knowledge, but also for the vital germination and gestation of the creative seeds of the individual.

Basic Features of Integral Transformative Education

To conclude this section, we summarize six basic features of integral education.

1. Integral education fosters the cocreative participation of all human dimensions in the learning and inquiry processes. A genuine process of integral learning cannot be directed exclusively by the mind, but needs to emerge from the collaborative epistemic participation of all human dimensions: body, instincts, heart, mind, and consciousness. All human dimensions need to be actively encouraged to participate creatively at appropriate stages of the inquiry and learning process (e.g., as inquiry tools into subject matter, as evaluators of inquiry outcomes).

2. Integral education aims at the study and elaboration of holistic understandings, frameworks, theories, or visions. Whether disciplinary, multidisciplinary, interdisciplinary,

or transdisciplinary, integral inquiry builds bridges across disciplines and searches for commonalities while honoring differences in its striving toward integrated understandings that counter the partial or fragmented current state of human knowledge.

3. Integral education fosters the activation of students' unique vital potentials and their creative development in the construction of knowledge. Each human being is a unique embodiment of the mystery potentially able to develop a unique perspective to contribute to the transformation of community or society. When learning and inquiry are grounded in one's unique vital potentials, academic life becomes existentially significant and more creative, exciting, and fun.

4. Integral education balances the "feminine" and the "masculine." It combines the more "masculine" elements of the training of skills and analysis of already constructed knowledge with the more "feminine" elements of gestating and engendering new knowledge from within. As in life, a dialectical relationship between these principles exists in the creative process, and integral education seeks practical ways to honor and actualize this relationship.

5. Integral education fosters inner and outer epistemic diversity. Taking into account the importance of multiple perspectives for the elaboration of valid, reliable, and complete knowledge about any object of study, integral education incorporates inner or intrapersonal epistemic diversity (i.e., vital, instinctive, somatic, empathic, intellectual, imaginal, contemplative ways of knowing) and outer or interpersonal epistemic diversity (i.e., knowledge from the various human collectives, ethnic groups, cultures, classes, genders, and sexual orientations, as well as from associated cross-cultural epistemological frameworks and emic standpoints). These two types of diversity are intimately connected.

6. Integral education promotes the integral development and transformation of students, faculty, and the larger educational container or institution. The inclusion of all human

dimensions in the learning process naturally enhances the transformative, healing, and spiritual power of education, as well as its potential to restructure academic policies and institutional practices.

CHALLENGES AND PROSPECTS OF INTEGRAL EDUCATION

In this section, we discuss three challenges faced by participatory integral pedagogies. We also suggest that they can be seen as precious opportunities to rescue the transformative and spiritual potentials of educational practice.

From Lopsided Development to Integral Transformation

Modern Western education focuses almost exclusively on development of the rational mind and its intellectual powers, with little attention given to the maturation of other dimensions of the person (M. Anthony, 2008; B. Hocking et al., 2001; R. Miller, 1991; O'Sullivan, 1999). As a result, most individuals in Western culture reach adulthood with a somewhat mature mental functioning but with poorly or irregularly developed somatic, vital, emotional, aesthetic, intuitive, and spiritual intelligences (Emmons, 1999; Gardner, 1983/1993).[12]

As I describe in chapter 4, given the extreme mind-centeredness of this way of life, a continued emphasis on mental learning and inquiry seems inevitable, which leads to the greatest tragedy of cognicentrism: it generates a vicious circle that justifies itself. Because modern education does not create spaces for the autonomous maturation of the body, instincts, and heart, these worlds cannot participate in an inquiry process unless they are mentally or externally guided. Yet, insofar as they are mentally or externally guided, these human dimensions cannot mature autonomously, and thus the need for their mental or external direction becomes permanently justified.

Complicating this situation further, after many generations of mind-centered life and education—often combined with the gross or subtle control and inhibition of the body, instincts, sexuality, and passions—these nondiscursive worlds are frequently wounded or distorted, and may even manifest regressive tendencies (and this arguable general condition is obviously exacerbated in cases of unhealed physical and sexual trauma or other biographical complications). Thus, when an individual seeks knowledge in these worlds, she typically first encounters a layer of conflicts, fears, or confusion, and such encounters perpetuate the belief that these worlds are epistemically barren (Romero & Albareda, 2001). Normally overlooked, however, is an essential primary intelligence beneath this layer that, if accessed, can heal the root of the conflict while fostering the maturation and epistemic competence of these worlds from within. Spaces must be created in which these human dimensions can achieve epistemic competence according to their own developmental principles and dynamics rather than those the mind thinks are most adequate (see chapter 4). When the body, instincts, sexuality, and heart are allowed to mature autonomously, they will become equal partners with the mind and be capable of cocreatively participating in a truly integral process of inquiry and learning.

Rescuing the healing and transformative dimensions of education should not be regarded as turning education into a therapeutic process. The main goal of integral education is not personal healing or group bonding (although these may naturally occur, and any genuine integral process should welcome and even foster these possibilities), but multi-dimensional inquiry and the collaborative construction of knowledge. For example, take a hypothetical situation in which access to nonmental worlds (e.g., through guided visualization, interactive meditation, or movement) activates personal material in need of healing that may interfere with the inquiry process in some students. In the context of a pedagogical (vs. therapeutic) container, this situation can be approached as a fruitful stage of the inquiry process. A skillful facilitator can use this situation to help learners become aware of personal dispositions that may color, shape, and perhaps distort their intellectual discernment. This stage can be seen as a kind of inner hermeneutics of suspicion that may lead to the critical identification of distorting epistemic blinders and standpoints—distinguishing between enabling and blinding prejudices and dispositions is one of the main tasks of hermeneutics (Gadamer, 1990). After this stage of awareness of personal dispositions and famil-iarization with experiential access to nonmental worlds, a genuine mul-tidimensional inquiry can gradually emerge.

In sum, the challenge raised by lopsided development is as a fertile opportunity to turn education into a process of integral transformation that can help learners achieve maturity at all levels, not only mentally. In the context of integral education, transformative healing opens the doors of human multidimensional cognition.

From Mental Pride to Spiritual Awakening

Our understanding of mental pride is not associated with what is conventionally regarded as a proud personality. By *mental pride* we mean the deep-seated disposition of the mind to consider itself the most important player or chief director of any process of knowledge and/or able to attain complete understanding without the collaboration of other human attributes. Given this definition, it is possible for a person to be psychologically humble (e.g., about personal talents or achievements) but maintain a strong mental bias in life direction and the search for knowledge, thus falling prey to mental pride.

In an academic context, mental pride manifests in a variety of ways, including (1) the confusion of global intellectual visions with genuine integral knowledge; (2) difficulties in acknowledging the partiality of all intellectual visions; (3) flagrant or subtle devaluation of the epistemic value of other human attributes, even in cases in which such value is intellectually accepted; (4) perpetuation of the mind's epistemic hegemony through insistence on the already developed condition of the nonmental worlds (in oneself or one's culture) as an unconscious defense mechanism against their development; (5) lack of patience with the usually slower rhythm that the nonmental worlds require to offer their contributions to an inquiry process; and (6) a compulsive need to control the inquiry process mentally (e.g., through premature conceptualization or application of intellectual constructs).

As the mind gradually lets go of its pride and opens itself to learn from the other human attributes and collaborate with them as equals in the elaboration of knowledge, it can be gradually released from the burden of doing most of the inquiry work. The mind becomes humble, recognizing its intrinsic limitations and realizing that it does not need to know everything because there are greater sources of knowledge to which it can be connected. Then the mind can rest and relax, attain inner peace and silence, and become porous to the immanent and transcendent energies of the mystery—energies that respectively vitalize and illuminate the mind with a knowing that the mind will never be able to encompass fully with its mental structures, but to which it can be attuned and by which it can be inspired and guided.

In sum, the pride of the mind can be seen as an opportunity to turn education into a process of genuine spiritual awakening in intimate contact with immanent and transcendent sources of the mystery.

Beyond Cognicentrism and Anti-Intellectualism in Integral Studies

The critique of cognicentrism and emphasis on the nondiscursive and spiritual elements of human inquiry can easily raise the specter of anti-intellectualism. The basic concern is that the incorporation of somatic, vital, and emotional experience into the educational container may jeopardize intellectual rigor and potentially debilitate the intellectual standards of rational criticism. Can teachers prevent the degeneration of educational practice into a fluffy, warm, but ultimately uncritical process that bypasses the meticulous elaboration and appraisal of knowledge?

Although including the nondiscursive human dimensions in teaching and learning process does not imply the rejection or devaluation of intellectual knowledge, this is a valid concern that deserves serious consideration. This worry is understandable, given the tendency in the West to polarize mind and body or reason and emotion (Bordo, 1987; Jaggar, 1990). From trends in the Romantic revolt against the Enlightenment's enthroned Reason, to the "turn off your mind" motto in certain trends of the 1960s counterculture (Lachman, 2001), to contemporary New Age's emotionalism and uneasiness with intellectual rigor, most historical challenges to cognicentrism flirt with or fall prey to anti-intellectualist tendencies. The abuses of the 1960s, as well as a plethora of unsuccessful alternative pedagogical experiments in recent decades, are still fresh in the minds of many academics, and it is thus natural that a proposal denouncing cognicentrism and advocating the incorporation of multidimensional knowing may create suspicion in some scholars.

However, anti-intellectualism reactively labors in the same deep structure of hierarchical, polarizing thinking as does cognicentrism. Anti-intellectualism is the equally problematic backside of cognicentrism. The pressing challenge today is to break away from dichotomizing tendencies, and to explore integrative approaches that allow intellectual knowing and conscious awareness to be grounded in and enriched by somatic, vital, emotional, aesthetic, intuitive, and spiritual knowing without losing their powers of clarity and discrimination. In other words, the contemporary task is to forge a middle path that avoids the pitfalls of both cognicentrism and anti-intellectualism.

Even with this recognition, the practical challenge remains. In our pedagogical practice, for example, we have repeatedly observed how difficult it is for a majority of students to flow between discursive reason and nondiscursive experience, and to engage in an integrated inquiry that incorporates both epistemic modes harmoniously. In practical terms, therefore, most students are at first incapable of elaborating intellectual knowledge from emotional or somatic experience, and unable to remain in mindful contact with their hearts and bodies while engaging in intellectual discussion. We interpret this difficulty as a sign of the prevalent state of dissociation between these worlds in the modern Western self (Bordo, 1987; Jaggar, 1990; Leder, 1990; Spiegel, 1994). (In some individuals, these worlds are not dissociated but undifferentiated, which creates a similar difficulty but may require a different pedagogical intervention.) This predicament calls for the exploration of methodological structures that systematically bridge those worlds, foster their collaborative epistemic competence, and lead to creative academic fruits and sound shared knowledge.[13]

Even considering this potential risk, what is the alternative? Is it sufficient to continue offering an educational practice that exclusively or essentially focuses on the supposedly "safer," less "messy" levels of the mind and consciousness and keeps the other worlds at bay or in a state of perpetual immaturity under parameters set by the mind? Can teachers say to themselves and to the world that they are offering integral or transformative education if they do not incorporate the body, vital world, and heart into the substance of learning and inquiry? We placed "safer" and "messy" in quotation marks because these nondiscursive worlds—now marginalized, often repressed, and given no or very little space in the classroom—tend to reappear in class dynamics under different guises (e.g., compensatory mental rigidity; attitudes of superiority; angry outbursts at the masculinized, patriarchal, or disembodied pedagogical container; diplomatic passive aggression; or a diffuse sense of sadness, frustration, or resentment). Using a gross analogy, imagine a house that has not been cleaned for years and whose furniture is covered by thick layers of dust. If the house is left alone, it will look less messy than when someone starts stirring the dust. However, this is obviously a case of erroneous perception, and there is no doubt that the neatness and freshness achieved by a thorough cleaning will be more real and satisfying than if the house is left untouched because of worries about temporary disarray.[14]

In sum, a participatory perspective denounces both extremes—anti-intellectualism and cognicentrism—as equally one-sided and problematic, and proposes that head and heart, intellect and emotion (along with body, instincts, and intuition) can be equal partners in the inquiry process and elaboration of more integral understandings. Because of the widely undeveloped, undifferentiated, or dissociated state of many of those worlds in the modern self, this process may involve temporary periods of chaos and confusion, but we regard these as fertile steps toward the achievement of genuinely integrated cognition and higher orders of complexity in the creative apprehension of life and the world.

CONCLUSION

It is likely that much of what is offered today in adult education under the rubrics of *alternative, holistic,* or *integral* is mind-centered or bricolage pedagogy (with participatory elements, in some cases), and that participatory approaches may constitute the horizon of integral education in the twenty-first century. In other words, we believe that integral education will gradually move toward participatory pedagogical approaches in which all human dimensions are actively encouraged to participate creatively at all stages of inquiry and learning. The explicit inclusion of all human attributes in the inquiry process will naturally reconnect education with its root meaning (*edu-care*: "bringing out the wholeness within"; R. Miller, 1991b, p. 6) and, therefore, with transformative healing and spiritual growth, both of which involve a movement toward human wholeness. This inner epistemic diversity will also promote a genuine integration of "feminine" and "masculine" principles in learning and creative inquiry. Multidimensional inquiry and masculine-feminine balance are pivotal for the creative vitality of integral studies and educational practice, and any institution that pioneers their systematic exploration will be remembered historically as epoch-making.

We conclude by highlighting the spiritual or transpersonal dimension of human participatory inquiry. As human beings gradually open themselves to the epistemic power of all human attributes, they can perhaps realize that through the exercise of their own creative capabilities they are fostering the unfolding of the mystery's infinite generativity in the world. Human multidimensional cognition channels the mystery's outpouring of new meanings onto this plane of physical reality more loyally and completely than does the isolated intellect, and these meanings can radically change both the perception of the world and the world itself. The world then stops being sensed as having an independently objective nature and becomes a relational and intersubjective reality enacted in a multiplicity of conceptual and transconceptual ways, partly depending on the human approaches and ways of knowing involved in the act of apprehension. The world is now recognized as a *hierophany* (Eliade, 1959)—a sacred process of spiritual unfolding, taking place in and through history, in which embodied human beings can creatively participate in intimate partnership with the mystery. This is the wider spiritual context in which the cultivation of participatory approaches to integral education gains the fullest import—and this is the context, we believe, that is crucial for the future of education in the new millennium.

SIX

TEACHING MYSTICISM FROM A
PARTICIPATORY PERSPECTIVE

How should teachers impart the graduate seminar in comparative mysticism? Is it enough to offer a survey of the field, training in comparative methodological skills, or a focus on a selected number of mystics, texts, or traditions? Or should we as teachers stress the primacy of inquiry in graduate education, supporting students' research on their own mystical interests while providing them with methodologically fruitful and personally significant inquiry tools? And should these inquiry tools be restricted to the mind's reflexive skills, or are we willing to create a more participatory learning environment in which students can incorporate other ways of knowing—such as somatic, emotional, and contemplative—in their investigations?

My main aim in this chapter is to describe a participatory integral pedagogy that engages multiple epistemic faculties in the teaching of an advanced doctoral seminar in comparative mysticism. First, I offer a brief account of the academic and curricular context, structure, and content of the seminar. Second, I introduce the seminar's participatory pedagogy, contrasting it with two other approaches to integral education: mind-centered and bricolage. Third, I discuss nine pedagogical strategies employed in the course: (1) invitation to participatory knowing; (2) guided contemplative inquiry; (3) unconditional acceptance and somatic grounding; (4) analogical inquiry and mandala drawing; (5) dialogical inquiry; (6) meditative reading; (7) empathic attunement through role play; (8) integral hermeneutics; and (9) spiritually informed scholarship. Fourth, I argue that this type of pedagogy paves a methodological middle way between engaged participation and critical distance in the teaching and study of mysticism. In conclusion, I stress the integrative thrust of participatory knowing and briefly reflect on the future of participatory approaches in the teaching of religion.

THE GRADUATE SEMINAR IN COMPARATIVE MYSTICISM

After introducing the institutional, academic, and curricular context of the seminar, this section offers a brief overview of its pedagogical structure and content.

Institutional and Academic Context

For the last fifteen years, I have taught "Comparative Mysticism" as a doctoral seminar offered by the department of East-West Psychology at California Institute of Integral Studies (CIIS), San Francisco. The alternative educational mission of the university makes it crucial to preface my discussion with some words about the seminar's larger academic context. CIIS was founded in 1968 by Haridas Chaudhuri, a leading exponent of the integral philosophy of the Indian mystic Sri Aurobindo (1872–1950). The university is not committed to any single philosophical or spiritual perspective, but some principles of integral philosophy have shaped its evolving educational mission. This mission includes the following principles: integration of body-mind-spirit, integral approaches to learning and research, spirituality in higher education, multiculturalism and diversity, sustainability and social justice, multiple ways of knowing, transdisciplinary inquiry, experiential and transformative learning, and integral and innovative governance.

Founded in 1976, East-West Psychology is a multidisciplinary department concerned with the meeting of Eastern, Western, and Indigenous psychological and spiritual traditions. The department seeks to ground academic excellence and the acquisition of professional skills in both students' personal transformation and a spiritually informed scholarship. As an academic field, East-West Psychology can be seen as a larger context for many disciplines that explore the interface between psychology and spirituality: for example, transpersonal and integral psychology, Consciousness Studies, depth psychology (Jungian, archetypal, and psychoanalytic), contemplative psychology, Shamanic and Indigenous studies, and ecopsychology. Pedagogically speaking, the department seeks to provide an integral transformative education that encourages students to engage in the twin tasks of the integration of knowledge and of multiple ways of knowing.

Curricular Context

Approaching the encounter among Eastern, Western, and Indigenous worldviews in the spirit of transformative dialogue and open inquiry, the department offers master's and doctoral East-West Psychology programs as well as two certificates: East-West Spiritual Counseling and Ecoresilience Leadership.[2] In this context, "Comparative Mysticism" is a one-semester advanced doctoral seminar, usually taken in the students' last years. Participants are thus prepared by prior course work in East-West psychological disciplines, world religions, and research methods in the human sciences. Advanced seminars have a cap of twelve students and are restricted to a doctoral level of instruction.

Structure and Content of the Seminar

The seminar has three main goals. The first is to provide a foundation through an examination of classic and contemporary approaches to the comparative study of mysticism. The second goal is to foster individualized inquiry by guiding students in the selection or development of a comparative approach appropriate to their research interests. To learn how to approach the study of mysticism in an empathic, participatory, and contemplative manner that integrates critical perspectives is the third pedagogical goal of the seminar.

"Comparative Mysticism" is usually structured as fifteen three-hour weekly sessions. After an introductory meeting, the seminar proceeds through three sections: "Methodological Foundations," "Interpretive Models in Comparative Mysticism," and "Contemporary Issues in the Study of Mysticism."

"Methodological Foundations" consists of three sessions. The first explores the various meanings of the term *mysticism* existing in both the literature and the classroom. The second discusses problems of definition, offers a historical overview of the field, and continues the exploration of students' preunderstandings of mysticism. The third presents methodological foundations and challenges of the field, critiques of the comparative method in religious studies, and the study of mysticism as a mystical-hermeneutical path.

"Interpretive Models in Comparative Mysticism" comprises five sessions surveying the main families of hermeneutic approaches in the field: traditionalist, perennialist, constructivist, feminist, neo-perennialist, postmodern, contextualist, pluralist, and participatory.

"Contemporary Issues in the Study of Mysticism" includes five topical sessions on areas of critical inquiry in the modern study of mysticism, including subjects such as intermonastic dialogue, psychedelics and mystical experience, and the ethics of mysticism. During this section, students offer oral presentations of their research projects.

At the final session, students complete their presentations, reflect on how their understanding of mysticism may have changed throughout the seminar, and assess collaboratively the collective inquiry process and research outcomes.

Many sessions employ case studies linked to specific readings. Case studies illustrate particular methodological issues (e.g., Jung and orientalism; J. J. Clarke, 1994), interpretive models (e.g., the construction of Buddhist mystical experience; Gimello, 1983), and contemporary topics in the study of mysticism (e.g., mysticism and African American women; Bostic, 2001). In addition, students critically analyze sample comparative papers in class using the integral hermeneutical method described herein.

For their final assignment, students select two or more mystical traditions, texts, authors, notions, or phenomena and compare them, applying one of the interpretive models studied or developing their own approach. Students are encouraged to incorporate accounts of their personal experience in support of their thesis. As mentioned, the assignment includes oral presentations of comparative projects in which students receive feedback from both instructor and peers.

The seminar differs from traditional courses on mysticism not only in its pedagogy but also in its contents. Most mysticism courses either offer a survey of mysticism in world religions or focus on the comparison of two or more mystics, texts, or traditions selected by the instructor. In contrast, "Comparative Mysticism" presents a rich array of hermeneutical models, methodological tools, and thematic explorations as the context in which students focus their comparativist efforts on mystical subjects of their choice—an approach that may not be suitable for undergraduate or graduate introductory courses. Such an increased political participation enhances students' personal involvement and empowers the extended epistemic participation sought by a participatory integral pedagogy.[3]

A PARTICIPATORY APPROACH TO INTEGRAL EDUCATION

Briefly, a participatory pedagogy seeks to incorporate as many human faculties as appropriate into learning and inquiry. A participatory pedagogy should be sharply distinguished from both mainstream education and a

mind-centered approach to integral education that is based on the intellectual study or elaboration of holistic frameworks or understandings.
Even though intellectual discernment is important, mystical phenomena partake of many nonmental dimensions; thus, an eminently mental
approach can arguably lead to partial understandings and even significant
distortions. To fully understand their knowledge claims, mystics insist on
the necessity of transcending purely intellectual knowledge and engaging
a fuller range of epistemic competences (Ferrer 2000b, 2008; Hollenback,
1996; Idel & McGinn, 1996). In addition, most mystical traditions posit
the existence of an isomorphism or deep resonance among the human
being, the cosmos, and the mystery out of which everything arises (e.g.,
Chittick, 1994a; Faivre, 1994; Jónsson, 1988; Lincoln, 1986; Saso, 1997;
Shokek, 2001). If one entertains the plausibility of these emic claims, it
can be argued that the more human dimensions participate in the study
of mysticism, the greater will be the dynamic congruence between the
inquiry approach and studied phenomena and the more coherent with
the nature of mysticism will be the resulting knowledge.

A participatory pedagogy should also be distinguished from a *bricolage approach* (the most widespread in alternative education), which
either incorporates experiential practices such as meditation or ritual
into an essentially mind-centered education or offers an eclectic curriculum engaging many human attributes (e.g., hatha yoga for the body,
contemplation for spiritual awareness). Although these practices engage
nonmental dimensions, these dimensions rarely, if ever, become part
of the substance of the educational process, which is entirely planned,
conducted, and assessed from the perspective of the mind.[4]

In contrast, by fostering access to multiple ways of knowing, a
participatory approach invites the engagement of the whole person, ideally
at all stages of the educational process.[5] The novelty of the participatory proposal is essentially methodological. It stresses the exploration
of practical approaches that combine the power of the mind and the
cultivation of consciousness with the epistemic potential of human
somatic, vital, and emotional worlds. "Comparative Mysticism" uses a
partial (vs. complete) participatory praxis. On the one hand, a fully
participatory approach requires more potent experiential practices than
those described herein to access and activate the (often deeply buried,
undeveloped, or repressed) epistemic powers of the nonmental worlds.[6]
On the other hand, although the inquiry process is facilitated by a wide
array of human attributes, the seminar places a strong emphasis on the
intellectual elaboration, discussion, and critical appraisal of knowledge.

This emphasis is perfectly legitimate in courses focused on methodological training, critical discussion of textual sources, or hermeneutic study. Whereas educators should strive toward the inclusion of as many ways of knowing as possible in the classroom, the extent and range of this epistemic participation needs to be determined case by case.

Although standard lectures have their place in participatory education, a graduate seminar should stress the *primacy of inquiry* and provide students with practical methods and tools to carry out individual and collective investigation. As learners move from undergraduate to graduate education and from master's to doctoral level, there needs to be a gradual but increasing shift of emphasis from an educational praxis based mostly on offering content (arguably more appropriate for young adults requiring epistemic foundations) to one that predominantly facilitates inquiry (arguably more appropriate for adults aspiring to make an original contribution to their discipline and the world).

PARTICIPATORY PEDAGOGICAL STRATEGIES

"Comparative Mysticism" is the fruit of a fifteen-year pedagogical experimentation exploring the incorporation of participatory knowing in a graduate seminar. A chief pedagogical assumption of the seminar is that a deeper and yet critical understanding of mysticism and its study can be gained by moving beyond eminently mind-centered approaches and accessing participatory ways of knowing. What follows is a description of nine pedagogical strategies used to this end in the seminar.

Invitation to Participatory Knowing

At the first meeting, I introduce the notion that a fuller understanding of mysticism and a more integral approach to its study may be optimized by accessing participatory ways of knowing—ways that can involve the intellectual discernment of the mind, somatic transfiguration, erotic communion, the awakening of the heart, visionary cocreation, and contemplative intuition. After some discussion, I stress the importance of cultivating an attitude of "critical subjectivity" during participatory knowing in order to discern the possible biases of one's situated experiential perspective and seek a balance between engaged participation and critical distance in the study of mysticism (see "Methodological Discussion").[7] Later in the seminar, students read scholarly essays that elaborate these points, such as Staal's (1975) early plea to avoid an "armchair" approach to the study of mysticism by combining rational analysis and spiritual practice, Kripal's (2001) account of the hermeneutical-mystical experiences of scholars of religion and articulation of the mystical dimension of hermeneutics, and contemporary proposals for a "participatory turn" in religious studies (Ferrer & Sherman, 2008a, 2008b).

The invitation to participatory knowing continues throughout the seminar. In this regard, it is especially helpful to begin many sessions with an *opening walk*, in which students are invited, for example, to explore mindfully the classroom space through different sensory modalities; stretch the body to make it more present and porous; move or dance at the tempo of background music; or become aware of the state of their bodies, vital energy, hearts, minds, and consciousness. I consider these opening walks to be healing rituals of remembrance; students are consciously and unconsciously reminded that they do not need to leave their nonmental attributes and associated ways of knowing outside the classroom, as they have implicitly learned to do during most of their adult education. The opening walks notify students that they do not need to begin the session as "disembodied heads" and invite them to remain as present as possible during class activities—mentally, somatically, vitally, emotionally, and so forth.

Guided Contemplative Inquiry

Some weeks the opening walks are followed by a guided contemplative inquiry into questions connected to the session's readings or topics. To this end, students find a place in the room to lie down or sit in a posture that invites a state of relaxed alertness and optionally cover their eyes with a bandana offered as an aid for inner recollection. (Here I might remind students about the etymological meaning of the Greek term *mūstikos*: "to close the eyes or the lips"). Meditative music plays in the background. After some simple relaxation instructions, I announce that I will read a set of open questions or guide an experiential inquiry connected to the week's topic. Examples include the ontological status of mystical knowledge, the question of the universality of mystical experience, the relationship between mysticism and postmodernism, and an experiential exploration of Forman's (1998a) "pure consciousness events" using Assagioli's (1971) disidentification exercise, among others.

Before I read the questions, I ask students to be receptive not only to my words, but also to the personal resonances (e.g., physical sensations, energy movements, emotional states, memories, visions) that my words may awaken in them. As the object of the contemplative inquiry, students can either focus on the question(s) that most influenced them (concentrative approach) or simply remain present, open, and receptive to the fullness of their multidimensional experience without trying to search for anything in particular (mindfulness approach). I encourage students to explore which approach may be most fertile for them and to optionally place their hands over specific parts of their bodies—such as their forehead, heart, or lower belly—in an attitude of deep listening to what these centers may have to say about the question(s). After spending some time in silence to develop the inquiry, students form dyads or small groups to share their experiences and insights in a fresh, unrehearsed way. To close the session, everybody stands up or sits in a circle and each student optionally shares a selected aspect of her experience using words, gestures, or movement.

Unconditional Acceptance and Somatic Grounding: Working with Hermeneutical Preunderstandings, Part 1

In the first week, I announce that the next session will start with a ritual sharing of students' hermeneutical preunderstandings of mysticism. The ritual has three aims: first, to raise awareness of students' presuppositions about mysticism; second, to become familiar with the diversity of understandings of the mystical coexisting in the classroom prior to the seminar's inquiry; and third, to foster the grounding of students' inquiry in their embodied reality. To help students get ready for the ritual, I request the following homework:

> Mindfully prepare a space at home to carry out the following three-step inquiry: (a) Articulate, as clearly and succinctly as you can, your current conceptual understanding of mysticism. (b) Identify any possible biographical roots of this understanding (e.g., personal experience, intuition, readings, teachers, a mix of the above). (c) If your conceptual understanding stems to some extent from personal experience, examine how such an experience may have been shaped, consciously or unconsciously, by adopted views about mysticism, presuppositions about reality, or religious beliefs. All these questions will eventually enter our discussion, but in the ritual space you will be asked to share *only* your current conceptual-experiential understanding of mysticism. Please limit your sharing to three minutes.

The ritual is a circle of sharing shaped by the practices of uncon-ditional acceptance and somatic grounding. This is its basic structure: (1) Participants sit in a circle and for a few minutes reconnect in silence with their conceptual-experiential understanding of mysticism. (2) A bell marks the time for the first sharing, during which the group is encouraged to practice active listening. (3) After sharing, the student lies down in the middle of the circle and the other participants respectfully place an open hand over various body parts, cultivating an attitude of unconditional acceptance. (4) The physical contact ends and everybody sits back in the circle. A moment of silence is observed before another bell indicates that it is time for the second student to go through the cycle. The ritual ends once all participants, including the instructor, have shared their understandings of the mystical.

Two features of this practice require commentary. First, the social codes regarding what constitutes safe and appropriate physical contact in contemporary North American culture make it fundamental to stress the optional nature of the somatic grounding. In addition, given that the body can unconsciously store traumatic memories, students should be advised to stop the practice if they experience any discomfort, anxiety, or bodily contraction unrelated to the inquiry process. Students who decide that somatic grounding is not for them—and I make sure that everybody feels that both options are equally valid—simply return to the circle after sharing and the group practices the unconditional acceptance of the sharing without physical contact. Second, as background for the practice, I explain that unconditional acceptance can be transmitted simply through an open presence and, crucially, that it is not equivalent to uncritical agreement. To accept the place from which others begin the inquiry does not mean one agrees with their views. "In subsequent sessions," I tell students, "there will be plenty of time to agree or disagree among ourselves; now it is the time to simply accept where everybody is coming from." This practice makes students more sensitive to the hori-zons of understanding shaping the starting point of the group's inquiry, minimizing the emergence of disagreements based on semantics versus actual discrepancies.

Analogical Inquiry and Mandala Drawing: Working with Hermeneutical Preunderstandings, Part 2

The next session extends the work with hermeneutic preunderstandings from the linguistic, the logical, the conceptual, and the propositional to the imaginal, the analogical, the symbolic, and the presentational.

Important for any inquiry, to engage analogical ways of knowing seems particularly relevant in the teaching and study of mysticism; mystics often stress the limitations of discursive language and resort to a rich variety of symbolic means—such as poetry (e.g., de Brujin, 1997), painting (Rhie & Thurman, 2000), or radical action (e.g., Loy, 1988)—to convey their insights.[8]

The analogical inquiry proceeds as follows: I first ask students to bring to class an object that evokes or captures symbolically their felt-sense of the mystical. Typical objects include depictions of holy men and women; religious symbols, statuettes, and relics; paintings and drawings; and nature's elements, such as feathers or stones. After an opening walk, students sit or lie down, optionally cover their eyes with a bandana, and are invited to let go of intellectual considerations. Then I ask them to invoke and hold in their awareness whatever felt-sense of the mystical they may have, inviting them to (re)enact an experiential state they associate with the mystical. Here I have found it helpful to remind students that mysticism is as much about knowing as it is about not-knowing, as much about unfolding vision as it is about what remains hidden. In this spirit, I suggest to the students that they let go of any goal to achieve or see anything extraordinary and simply remain unconditionally receptive to whatever vision, symbolic expression, or embodied enactment may come to them. If they find it useful, students can place their hands over different parts of their bodies in an attitude of humble but deep listening to what these human dimensions may have to say about mysticism.

Once the inquiry ends, I provide drawing materials (colored papers, crayons, and markers) and invite students to craft an image or symbol. Although emphasis is placed on spontaneous expressions emerging from their experiential felt-sense, students can also depict something they may have seen or felt during the inquiry,[9] write poetry, or prepare a brief embodied dramatization through movement and gesture. After completing their creations, students collaboratively craft a collective mandala. To do this, they one-by-one place their paintings, poetry, or symbolic objects in the center of the room. Then all the students sit in a circle and contemplate the mandala in order to become familiar with the group's analogical culture about the mystical and to honor analogical ways of knowing; participants may remain in silence or verbalize, Quaker style, or somatically enact anything they might feel while contemplating.

This practice admits many variations, such as the creation of another circle for poetry readings or storytelling about the objects brought to class. As optional homework, students can explore the connection between their conceptual and imaginal takes on the mystical.

Dialogical Inquiry

During the discussion of readings and thematic issues, students are encouraged to practice dialogical inquiry, which seeks to integrate the strengths of Bohmian dialogue (Bohm, 1996) and standard academic discussion so that argumentation and polemics may become penetrating tools to inquire into the possibilities and limitations of all views. Moreover, dialogical inquiry reframes class discussion as an opportunity to practice contemplative skills in the intersubjective world. Examples of these skills are mindfulness (i.e., a nonjudgmental awareness of one's thoughts, emotions, and sensations), active listening as an act of generosity, mindful speech (e.g., offering criticism without sarcasm, mockery, or condescension), service (e.g., to truth, truthfulness, or the generation of shared meaning), nonattachment to views, and openness to transformation.

To reinforce the dialogical competence of the group, I may begin some sessions by asking students to blindly pick up a card with the name of a particular skill (e.g., active listening) that becomes the focus of their practice. These sessions can end with a brief round of sharing in which students disclose the practiced skill, reflect on their performance, and receive feedback from the group. Pedagogically, I have found it more effective to break up the practice of dialogue into a number of concrete microskills than to simply ask students to try to "be dialogical" in an abstract way. The number of sessions in which I use the cards varies from group to group.

Meditative Reading: Interreligious Lectio Divina

After a short lecture on the contemplative status that reading sacred texts has in many traditions, I introduce an interreligious version of the Christian practice of lectio divina (meditative reading).[10] Throughout the semester I ask two to four volunteers to bring to the next session a brief mystical passage. At the opening of these sessions, students read the mystical passages, seeking to evoke the emotional tone they perceive in them (e.g., burning passion, unshakeable equanimity, or exhilarating joy). While the students listen to the passages, I invite them to empathically enter their meaning and use the power of their visionary imagination to experientially reconstruct the mystical event conveyed in the texts. Each reading is followed by one or two minutes of receptive contemplation in silence until a bell indicates the beginning of the next reading. The practice ends with a longer period of receptive contemplation.

Three remarks: First, I see this practice as an attempt to cultivate a hermeneutical-mystical union with the texts (Kripal, 2001) via the reenactment of both the semantic meaning (Sells, 1994) and the experiential qualities of the mystical event. Second, although potentially interreligious, the practice retains essential elements of the *lectio divina* tradition, such as the dialectic between an active movement of reading/listening to understand/apprehend (*lectio* and *meditatio*) and a more receptive movement of turning inward (*oratio*) and being open to the gifts of spirit (*contemplatio*). Third, the practice also admits many variations and can catalyze follow-up discussion. For example, students can read a single passage many times or form small groups to discuss the universality versus plurality of mystical states in light of their experiences during an interreligious *lectio divina*.

Empathic Attunement through Role Play

In the practice of role play, two or more students take the identities of scholars holding conflicting views on particular issues as a platform for subsequent group dialogue. For example, students might be requested to recreate in class the exchange between Seyyed H. Nasr and Sally B. King (S. B. King, 2001; Nasr, 1993, 2001) on the validity of traditionalist metaphysics to account for Mahayana Buddhism. The task here is to sum up the content of these essays and engage in a dialogue that gives voice to their authors' perspectives. I may even add a theatrical touch: I introduce the presenters as Dr. Nasr and Dr. King, speaking in a panel at an American Academy of Religion meeting, for example. As the dialogue opens to the group, presenters are free to "let go of their role" and express their own viewpoints (which at times may have changed through the role play).

I have found that the practice of role play not only enhances students' empathic attunement with the different interpretive models of mysticism surveyed in the seminar but also deepens the understanding of the views under discussion. In some cases, students might benefit from taking the role of authors whose perspectives they find questionable or even disturbing. Besides bolstering emotional intelligence, this practice fosters cognitive developmental competences, such as the ability to take the role of the other, and trains students in scholarly activities such as public speaking and debate. Finally, students love these engaging dramatizations, and I believe it would be an oversight to undervalue the role of fun in effective learning.

Integral Hermeneutics

As the seminar proceeds, students analyze sample papers that have been carefully selected to illustrate particular virtues or pitfalls of the comparative enterprise. Unknown to students, one sample may have been selected, for example, because of the biased nature of its comparative categories; another, for its elegant and comprehensive comparative framework. Students are encouraged to analyze the samples using an "integral hermeneutic approach"—or extended spiral of understanding—that comprises four hermeneutical moments.

1. *Hermeneutics of recovery.* Students first seek to discern, retrieve, and articulate the intended meaning of the text. The focus here is on what the author is saying, the text's main thesis or objectives, the main arguments offered, and the conclusion. At this stage, the task is to achieve the clearest comprehension possible of the text's meaning.

2. *Hermeneutics of the heart.* Here students pay attention to somatic, vital, and emotional reactions emerging while reading the paper (e.g., anger, joy, boredom) and take these reactions as a starting point for inquiry. By looking deeply into the roots of these embodied experiences, students often recognize previously unseen layers of meaning of the text and are able to articulate more clearly their appreciative and critical perspectives. Although the hermeneutics of the heart can lead to positive considerations, the emergence of "negative" responses leads to critical hermeneutics.

3. *Critical hermeneutics.* Students identify argumentative flaws, content inaccuracies, and possible biases in the comparative analysis, raising questions such as: Who benefits from the conclusions this article reached? Are the compared mystics or traditions fairly represented? Or is one tradition grossly or subtly distorted to show the superiority

of another? Has the author avoided the pitfalls of comparative hermeneutics surveyed in the course (e.g., "going
native" or naive universalism)? Students also look at the
design of the comparative framework, evaluate the neutrality and productive fit of its comparative categories, and
situate the author's methodological standpoint (e.g., along
the engagement/detachment continuum; see below).

4. *Mystical hermeneutics*. Adapting and combining Kripal's
(2001) and Sells's (1994) proposals, students explore the
degree of hermeneutical-mystical union achieved with the
text and the possible emergence of a "meaning event"
of semantic (as Sells proposed) and experiential dimensions. Here students may inquire into the spiritually transformative or challenging impact of their hermeneutical
engagement with the text, and the influence such personal
responses may have on their understanding.

Seeking to exhaust the meaning units of a text, students may go
through several cycles of this extended spiral of understanding. As they
gradually identify or develop their own hermeneutic style, they can
change the sequence of these hermeneutical moments or work through
all four simultaneously. I often insist on the value of starting with the
hermeneutics of recovery at the initial stages of students' work, because
I have noted that students who start with, or move too quickly to, the
critical stance usually have difficulties in describing the text's meaning
in its own terms or unfiltered by their critical lens.

Spiritually Informed Scholarship

A general feature of my participatory pedagogy is the integration of
spirituality into academic work. As discussed above, one way to pursue
this goal is by engaging a multiplicity of ways of knowing in the inquiry
process; another is by encouraging students to take all aspects of research
and writing as opportunities to practice spiritual values. In this regard, I
point out the likeness of many contemplative qualities and the traits of
the paradigmatic critical thinker, such as intellectual humility, courage,
or integrity.[11]

In this context, I identify five meeting points between spirituality
and scholarship: (1) The *nature of scholarship* is the understanding of

the hermeneutic production of meaning as potentially emerging from human participation in the creative power of life or the mystery. (2) *Content*, for example, considers the fairness in the selection of sources or the explicit discussion of spiritual questions. (3) *Form*, for example, encompasses considerations of elegance, grace, and beauty in writing; questions of tone such as avoiding condescension in criticism; or work with spiritually evocative scholarly styles such as storytelling, dialogue, visual materials, or poetry. (4) *Process*, for example, considers the commitment to truthfulness and truth in inquiry and writing. And (5), *impact* is the extent to which one's scholarship fosters the spiritual edification of both author and readers.

A full account of this approach to scholarship would require an entire paper, but, to offer a few examples, I might recommend to students that they change the root metaphor of scholarly work from "production" to a "pregnancy and birthing process" whose creative seed needs to be nourished; consider Metzger's (1992) advice to prepare their desk as an altar—or as the bridal chamber for the beloved (i.e., the creative wellspring within); or keep a dream journal and pay attention to synchronicities (for an extended discussion, see chapter 5).[12]

METHODOLOGICAL DISCUSSION:
THE WAY OF CRITICAL PARTICIPATION

The general point of this section is that a participatory pedagogy such as the one just outlined paves a middle way between the extremes of engaged participation and critical distance in the teaching and study of mysticism. Articulations of this (less-traveled) middle road have a long pedigree in religious studies. More than thirty years ago, Neville (1982) offered a vigorous defense of the value of combining the virtues of the *dao* (i.e., participatory engagement and existential access to religious phenomena) and the *daimon* (i.e., critical distance and vulnerability to correction) in the study of religion. Such a combination, argued Neville (2002), can prevent both the "blindness of uncritical participation" and "the projection of one's methodological, theoretical, and more broadly cultural assumptions onto the religious path being studied" (p. 109). Today, the fact that an increasing number of scholars of religion display both religious commitments *and* critical perspectives on traditional religious beliefs (Barnard, 1994; Cabezón, 2006) further problematizes this and other related modernist dichotomies such as insider/outsider, emic/etic, or confessional/academic.

In her discussion of insider/outsider perspectives, for example, Knott (2005) situated various degrees of detached observation and engaged participation along a continuum of possibilities, ranging from the "complete observer" to the "observer-as-participant" to the "participant-as-observer" to the "complete participant." Commenting on the work of scholars of religion who value participation and critical distance, Knott wrote:

> Such an insider-researcher acts as both insider and outsider, and the movement back and forth opens him or her up to a range of types of information: that which is available to outsiders, that which is only available to those within the researched community (insiders), and that which becomes available to the researcher through his or her reflexive participation in the research process. (p. 254)[13]

My position on this question is germane not only to Knott's observation but also to Kripal's (2001) "methodological nondualism," which intends to

> challenge the dichotomy between insider and outsider and not assume *either* that the historian, psychologist, or anthropologist who seems to be outside . . . does not also know and appreciate something of the shimmering truths of which the insider so passionately speaks *or* that the insider, however devoted to an ideal, cannot also see clearly and bravely something of the actual of which the scholar tries to speak. (p. 323)[14]

How may walking this middle path influence the teaching of mysticism? To begin, given that these standpoints can be combined in scholarly sound and fruitful ways, to present them as dichotomous not only is fallacious but also may constrain students' methodological choices. I have repeatedly witnessed how a participatory pedagogy naturally fosters the adoption of a perspective of "critical participation"—one that can potentially dance between insider and outsider positions.

It cannot be stressed enough that to embrace a participatory approach does not mean to eschew critical perspectives of mystical phenomena. On the contrary, going into the depths of one's emotions (and their fierce moral discrimination) via a hermeneutics of the heart, cultivating empathic attunement through role play, paying attention to one's bodily reactions while engaged in dialogical inquiry, and being receptive to visions or insights in contemplative exercises—all these strategies can offer potent resources for critical discernment in the teaching and study of mysticism.

Here are some examples: Looking deeply into her anger, one of my students discerned a subtle patriarchal bias in a paper's comparative categories; becoming aware of a constriction in the flow of her vital energy, another raised questions about a sexually dissociative account of spiritual realization presented in class; and a third student, paying attention to her body's experience of lifeless stagnation while reading, developed a critical account of certain types of mysticism as disembodied and even ecologically pernicious. Thus, a critical-participatory approach opens a vast methodological sea between the extremes of engaged participation and critical distance that, if skillfully navigated, can integrate the virtues of both standpoints while avoiding their shortcomings.[15]

As should be obvious, however, there is not a generic formula to integrate engaged and detached perspectives in the teaching and study of mysticism. Both teachers and students need to locate themselves at a point of the continuum described by Knott (2005), justify their methodological choice, and clearly state the specific manner in which they develop (or plan to develop) their scholarship. That said, students can legitimately reject the value of participatory engagement and choose to develop their scholarship from an entirely detached or critical perspective—an approach prevalent in the socioscientific study of religion and theoretically developed by authors such as Segal (1992), Wiebe (1999), Strenski (2006), Preus (1987), and McCutcheon (2001). Likewise, students can reject the value of detached observation and choose to work from a strictly engaged or participatory perspective, as in certain forms of theological and confessional scholarship. In both cases, however, students (and teachers) should not be allowed to remain nonresponsive to the many criticisms raised about these extreme standpoints. Strictly "detached" students will need to address the challenges to the value and very possibility of pure objectivity or metaphysical agnosticism issued by the postempiricist philosophies of science, feminism, social constructivism, poststructuralism, and religious emic epistemologies, among other disciplines. And strictly "engaged" students will need to respond to the charges of dogmatism, circularity, and epistemological blindness raised by modern critical thinkers. The bottom line is that in both cases students need to justify their positions in the wake of these critiques and display a high degree of self-reflexivity about their chosen methodological standpoint—both basic features of any robust scholarship.

CONCLUSION

In this chapter, I have described a participatory integral approach to the teaching of a doctoral seminar in comparative mysticism. I believe it is fair to say that this participatory pedagogy engages a fuller range of epistemic competences than those usually accessed in mainstream graduate education. Besides intellectual reason, the seminar's pedagogical strategies foster the development and participation of students' somatic, emotional, intuitive, imaginal, and spiritual intelligences. I have also argued that this pedagogical approach forges a methodological stance capable of integrating the strengths of engaged participation and critical distance.

My pedagogical experimentation is motivated by the conviction that the teaching and study of mysticism must be exclusively guided neither by a "participatory heart," which feels deeply but lacks critical rigor, nor by a "cognicentric mind," rightfully critical of religious dogma and ideology but usually out of touch with the person's intuitive powers and the world's mysteries. As Gold (2003) persuasively argued, what defines the work of the most successful interpretive writers of religion—from Mircea Eliade to Clifford Geertz to Georges Dumézil to Wendy Doniger—is *precisely* a synthesis of a "soft heart," characterized by empathic imagination and intuition, and a "hard mind" capable of penetrating analysis through the use of the critical intellect. From a participatory perspective, however, an integrated cognition is not exhausted by a fusion of head and heart; it also needs to incorporate the epistemic powers of the body, the erotic, and the mystical (Ferrer & Sherman, 2008a).[16]

As a final thought, I am mindful that the application of some of the participatory strategies described herein may be more fitting in alternative institutions such as CIIS than in standard universities. After all, most students come to the university seeking a more integral education that offers intellectual rigor, engages multiple ways of knowing, values personal experience, and takes seriously the potential cognitive value of spirituality. In addition, most students at the university are spiritual practitioners of various sorts, whose intellectual and spiritual paths are often intimately intertwined and who combine rational inquiry with experiential practice. In this context, the "cash value" of dancing between the engaged stance of the insider and the critical stance of the outsider is a "no brainer" for most CIIS students. That said, I feel confident that an increasing number of teachers and students of mysticism (and religion) in academia may recognize the value of exploring participatory approaches, and that in future years, mainstream education will embrace pedagogies that systematically engage multiple ways of knowing. The explicit inclusion of all human attributes in learning and inquiry goes a long way in reconnecting education with its root meaning (*edu-care*: "bringing out the wholeness within") and, therefore, with transformative healing and spiritual growth, both of which involve a movement toward human wholeness.

SEVEN

EMBODIED SPIRITUAL INQUIRY

A Radical Approach to Contemplative Education

Most spiritually informed approaches to education consist of the introduction of traditional contemplative practices—such as meditation, yoga, or Tai Chi—as independent courses in the curriculum or as components of class sessions. Typically, there is a period of mindfulness meditation before class begins, ritual closure, or contemplative "labs" (e.g., Hill, 2006; Miller, 1994; Simmer-Brown & Grace, 2011). These strategies are often understood as a preparation for—or enriching complement to—intellectual learning. For example, although Naropa University aims at the cultivation of a holistic human development, its official statement on contemplative education indicated, "the practice of sitting meditation and other contemplative practices . . . prepares the mind to process information in new and unexpected ways" (as cited in Gunnlaugson, 2009a, p. 19). Furthermore, as Gunnlaugson (2009a, 2009b) showed, most contemplative educators use first-person (i.e., individual subjective) or third-person (i.e., presumably objective) approaches with insufficient attention given to second-person or intersubjective approaches. According to Gunnlaugson (2009b), these overlooked "second-person approaches to contemplative education involve exploring contemplative experience from an intersubjective position that is represented spatially as *between* us, in contrast to *inside* us . . . or *outside* us" (p. 27).

Given this context, the main purpose of this chapter is to introduce Embodied Spiritual Inquiry as a novel, second-person approach to participatory learning and contemplative education.[1] While second-person contemplative approaches tend to be verbal or dialogical (e.g., Sarath,

2006), or to use presence or awareness exercises (e.g., Barbezat & Bush, 2013; Gunnlaugson, 2009b, 2011), Embodied Spiritual Inquiry systematically—and, I argue, radically—engages contemplative intersubjectivity through *mindful physical contact* among practitioners. This contact occurs at not only the verbal and awareness levels but also the somatic and energetic levels. Contemplation is thus not applied as a preparation for or enhancement of intellectual learning (valuable strategies in themselves), but as the very means of a multidimensional, participatory inquiry seeking to intersubjectively access the epistemic power of all human attributes (i.e., body, vital world, heart, mind, and consciousness; see chapter 5). Exploring the methodology and pedagogy of Embodied Spiritual Inquiry as a research approach in a graduate course, this chapter aims to expand the repertoire of approaches to catalyzing intersubjective knowledge in the context of contemplative education.[2]

AN INTRODUCTION TO EMBODIED SPIRITUAL INQUIRY

Embodied Spiritual Inquiry names both a second-person contemplative research method (ESI hereafter) and a graduate course ("Embodied Spiritual Inquiry" hereafter), which I developed over the last thirteen years with the feedback of my students at California Institute of Integral Studies (CIIS), San Francisco. As a *research method*, ESI seeks to facilitate access to different ways of knowing (e.g., somatic, vital, emotional, intuitive) through intersubjective contemplative practice, in order to provide new perspectives within psychological or spiritual discourse. ESI integrates essential elements of Heron's cooperative inquiry paradigm (Heron, 1996; Heron & Reason, 1997, 2001), Albareda and Romero's integral transformative practice (see chapter 4; Malkemus & Romero, 2012), and participatory spiritual approaches that understand spiritual knowing as embodied, relational, and enactive or inquiry-driven (e.g., Ferrer, 2008, 2011; Ferrer & Sherman, 2008a; Heron, 1992, 2006; Lahood, 2007c). Specifically, ESI applies Albareda and Romero's interactive embodied meditations as chief inquiry tools to investigate questions and topics belonging to the human condition. Through the mindful physical contact facilitated by these meditations, participants access a variety of ways of knowing in the context of a partial form of cooperative inquiry (see below), in which coresearchers go through cycles of experience and reflection focused on collaboratively decided questions (Heron, 1996).

As a *graduate course*, I have taught "Embodied Spiritual Inquiry" every other year at CIIS since 2003, and in Summer 2009 at Ritsumeikan

University, Kyoto, Japan (see Nakagawa & Matsuda, 2010). I also presented the course at the 2011 American Academy of Religion annual meeting (Ferrer, 2011). Osterhold et al. (2007) provided a helpful summary of the main pedagogical goal:

> To inquire individually and collectively into collaboratively formulated spiritual questions, using methods that encourage integral ways of knowing, that is, ways that involve all human dimensions contributing equally in the inquiry process, including the body, the vital world, the heart, the mind, and consciousness. (p. 3)

Based on the particular collective interests of each "Embodied Spiritual Inquiry" student group over the years, a variety of inquiry topics have been explored, including several directly focused on the intersubjective domain. For example, Osterhold et al. (2007) presented the results of an ESI conducted at CIIS in 2006 that addressed the nature of relational spirituality and participants' experiences of the spiritual presence reportedly emerging "in-between" persons (cf. Heron & Lahood, 2008). Also, a case study of an ESI carried out in 2013 elucidated the experiential differences between the states of dissociation, merging, and integration—contingent on boundary firmness and permeability—within both interpersonal and intrapersonal domains (Sohmer et al., forthcoming). Other ESI topics have included the identification of experiential markers distinguishing genuine from unreliable spiritual knowledge, the multidimensionality of the human condition, the "shadow" in its personal and collective manifestations, and the nature of the "masculine" and the "feminine" in relation to human embodied experience.[3] As presented in these case studies, "Embodied Spiritual Inquiry" as a graduate course fully incorporates the ESI research methodology, addressing students as coresearchers who not only participate in the inquiry for personal learning and development, but also can elaborate, analyze, and report the collaborative findings.

ESI can be used as a research method independent of a graduate course. However, as the majority of ESIs to date have been conducted in an academic setting, the following discussion addresses this context most directly. Thus, this chapter describes the methodology, epistemology, inquiry tools, and inquiry structure of the "Embodied Spiritual Inquiry" course. Since the ESI methodology has so far been intrinsic to the graduate course, I also discuss the validity of ESI as research method.

METHODOLOGY AND EPISTEMOLOGY

The methodological structure of "Embodied Spiritual Inquiry" is shaped by central elements of Heron's (1996) cooperative inquiry. Challenging the received research paradigm that asserts a separation between researcher(s) and the subject(s) of the research, "cooperative inquiry is a form of participative, person-centered inquiry which does research *with* people not *on* them or *about* them" (p. 19). Cooperative inquiry unfolds through cycles of reflection and action/experience focused on a collaboratively decided inquiry topic or question. The method is based on the inclusion of all the participants as fully involved coresearchers in all research decisions about the content and structure of the inquiry.

Heron (1996) differentiated between full and partial forms of cooperative inquiry. In the *full form*, all the participants (including the facilitator or initiating researcher) are equally involved as coresearchers and participate equally in all cycles of reflection and action. In the *partial form*, all participants act as coresearchers but the facilitator is only partially involved as subject because she does not partake in the action/experience phases. Although in both forms the facilitator typically has a greater role in "methodological know-how and facilitative guidance" (p. 23), cooperative inquiry works toward breaking down the differential role between facilitator and participants. Because of the academic context in which "Embodied Spiritual Inquiry" has been conducted to date, as well as the use of Albareda and Romero's interactive meditations (see chapter 4) as main inquiry tools, the course uses the partial form of cooperative inquiry: The instructor and teaching assistant launch the inquiry, provide the initial inquiry tools, and facilitate class activities. As the course progresses, however, the coresearchers move from engaging in clearly structured practices toward greater freedom in their use of the inquiry tools (e.g., selecting practices, choosing to work in dyads or triads, and even modifying the practices themselves). Since the coresearchers usually have no prior experience with participatory and cooperative inquiry methods, the instructor maintains a guiding role in the group and participates in the interactive meditations only as a facilitator. Furthermore, although at times the instructor and teaching assistant offer their personal impressions during group sharing, their experiences or insights are not used as research data.

A chief epistemological principle of Heron's (1996) cooperative inquiry is that *propositional knowing* (i.e., conceptual statements about the nature of reality) is interconnected with three other kinds of knowing:

experiential, presentational, and practical (see also Heron & Reason, 2008). *Experiential knowing* refers to the direct and personal experience of oneself, the world, and others within a particular inquiry domain. *Presentational knowing* is the nonverbal or nonconceptual expression (e.g., aesthetic, symbolic, embodied) of the felt meaning gained through direct experience of the inquiry domain (i.e., through experiential knowing). Finally, *practical knowing* refers to skills and abilities gained through the inquiry process that allow coresearchers to affect and transform the inquiry domain. According to Heron, one major problem of modern education is its privileging of propositional knowing over all else—other forms of knowing are often ignored or marginalized in the learning process, a predicament Ferrer, Romero, and Albareda (see chapter 5) and Ferrer and Sherman (2008a) termed *cognicentrism.*

"Embodied Spiritual Inquiry" adopts Heron's (1996) extended epistemology, explicitly seeks to avoid cognicentrism, and values equally the four aforementioned types of knowing. By systematically including opportunities for coresearchers to engage and express propositional, experiential, presentational, and practical knowing—as well as the knowledge that originates within the human body, heart, vital, and mind as unique yet interconnected centers of awareness—"Embodied Spiritual Inquiry" strives to facilitate the emergence of the full epistemic spectrum accessible through second-person contemplative practice.

INQUIRY TOOLS

Interactive embodied meditations constitute the course's main inquiry tools. These meditations stem from the integral transformative work cocreated by Albareda and Romero (see chapter 4), aspects of which Ferrer and Romero have applied to graduate educational settings (see chapters 5 and 6). The practices seek to foster participants' contemplative access to deep layers of human somatic, vital, emotional, and mental worlds and associated ways of knowing. More specifically, these interactive meditations aim to facilitate a deep listening to these essential human dimensions through mindful physical contact between two or more practitioners.

In each meditation session, one person plays a receptive role (i.e., receiving the physical contact) while the other plays an active role (i.e., giving the physical contact). Participants then exchange roles, or rotate if more than two people are involved in the same practice. Importantly, in both the receptive and active roles, participants are encouraged to focus on their own experience and avoid getting distracted by thoughts about their partners' experience.

In these interactive embodied meditations, access to five fundamental human dimensions (body, vital world, heart, mind, and consciousness) is sought through mindful physical contact with specific bodily parts: The mind is accessed through contact with the head and forehead; consciousness is accessed through the top of the head; the heart through contact with the center of the chest, arms, hands, and back; the vital world through contact with the lower abdomen; and the body through contact with the feet and legs. Based on several decades of lived inquiry with hundreds of individuals, Albareda and Romero hold that these physical areas are entryways into the depths of these human attributes and associated ways of knowing (see chapter 4).

To be more precise, Albareda and Romero do not claim that a strict correspondence exists between these bodily areas and the various human attributes (see Malkemus & Romero, 2012). A human being is a multidimensional unity, and any attribute can therefore potentially manifest throughout the entire organism. This fact does not preclude, however, that sustained contact with certain bodily areas tends to facilitate access to specific experiential worlds for most individuals; after all, it is generally easier to feel one's emotions when being touched in the heart center than in the toes or the nose. As Malkemus and Romero (2012) put it, "While being profoundly interwoven within the flow of full-bodied living, each center reflects specific experientially discernable characteristics of that area related to specific regions in the human form" (p. 34). This understanding has received support from the experiences and inquiry outcomes of past ESI coresearchers (e.g., Osterhold et al., 2007; Sohmer et al., forthcoming).

In sum, interactive embodied meditations are used as tools to (1) explore coresearchers' somatic, vital, emotional, and mental dispositions; (2) facilitate the emergence of potential inquiry topics and questions; (3) carry out the inquiry into the selected topic or question; and (4) generate inquiry data from the deep layers of somatic, vital, emotional, and mental worlds. To collect diverse data, the group also uses other inquiry tools including drawing, symbolic movement, journaling, critical discussion in dyads and small groups, whole-group sharing, and a final reflection paper written by each coresearcher. In the case of further data analysis for reporting, group sharing sessions are audio recorded and transcribed, and drawings are catalogued.

CYCLES OF THE INQUIRY PROCESS

Closely following the cyclical structure of cooperative inquiry (Heron, 1996), ESI proceeds through research cycles consisting of four stages: initial reflection, move to action, full experiential immersion, and final reflection. Typically, the group meets for an introductory three-hour class at CIIS, followed by three intensive weekend retreats meeting every other week at an off-campus studio.

The initial reflection stage corresponds to the planning stage of the research cycle, in which the initiator introduces the basic methodology, and coresearchers select an inquiry question and plan of action to investigate it. In the "Embodied Spiritual Inquiry" course, this stage corresponds to the introductory class, where the facilitator offers an overview of the ESI method, as well as the first weekend retreat, where coresearchers become familiar with the inquiry tools (i.e., interactive embodied meditations) and delimit an inquiry domain. The inquiry domain is then further discussed and synthesized into a focused inquiry question by e-mail before the second weekend retreat begins. In the context of ESI, this stage includes an important action/experiential component wherein coresearchers practice the interactive meditations, to prepare for the later stages of inquiry and engage different ways of knowing (e.g., mental, emotional, somatic) prior to the selection of the inquiry domain.

In ESI, the second and third stages are interconnected. The second stage is the first action phase, where coresearchers initiate the experiential, action-oriented exploration of the inquiry question, apply the chosen inquiry tools and skills, and begin to generate and record data. The third stage constitutes a deeper immersion into the second through "full engagement with the relevant experience or practice" (Heron, 1996, p. 54) and "great openness of encounter with the chosen domain" (p. 54).

In the "Embodied Spiritual Inquiry" course, the second and most of the third weekend retreats correspond to the second and third stages of the inquiry process, respectively. It is important to note, however, that there is a mini-reflection phase between weekends, in which the group decides whether to continue with the same inquiry question or to modify it after their experience during the second weekend. In both weekends, coresearchers gain experiential and practical knowledge through the interactive meditations, and generate a variety of presentational and propositional outcomes including visual art, poetry, symbols, embodied dramatizations, and conceptual statements. These inquiry outcomes constitute a substantial part of the data collected "in the field" to be analyzed and interpreted in the fourth stage of the research.

The fourth and last stage of the inquiry process corresponds to the final reflection stage, in which coresearchers consolidate, analyze, and interpret the data generated. In "Embodied Spiritual Inquiry," this stage includes a whole-group discussion at the end of the third weekend retreat, to reflect on the overall outcomes of the inquiry. In addition, each coresearcher further reflects on their experience by writing a final paper that can include the presentation of visual art and poetry. Finally, in those cases in which one or more coresearchers decide to generate a written report of the inquiry outcomes on behalf of the whole group, these authors carry out the data analysis and interpretation, inviting confirmation of the final draft from all of the participants.

BASIC STRUCTURE OF A TYPICAL SESSION

Each "Embodied Spiritual Inquiry" session consists of different activities and meditation practices aimed at fostering a state of contemplative awareness and receptivity. Each class usually begins with a mindful walk in the room or a game, both in the morning and afternoon. The interactive meditations are conducted twice a day in dyads or triads.

Each meditation follows a general structure. In a practice focused on the heart center, for example, the receiver lies down while the person in the active role initiates and maintains a contemplative physical contact by mindfully placing the hands, forehead, or chest over the uppermost part of the partner's chest, as agreed in advance. Before the meditation begins, partners are invited to agree upon any possible boundaries of the physical contact. During the meditation, both parties, regardless of role, are invited to stay focused on their own experience while immersed in the generated intersubjective field,[4] as the facilitator guides them into the contemplative exploration of the inquiry question. While coresearchers are encouraged to stay with their experience during the meditation, either partner can end or pause to modify the meditation as necessary at any time. Music is played that evokes or resonates with the particular attribute focused on during the practice (e.g., simple, slower drum beats for the body; more emotive music for the heart). Once coresearchers are immersed in the practice, the facilitator reads aloud the inquiry question and/or related statements seeking to evoke resonances and responses from those attributes. Coresearchers are encouraged to allow and pay attention to any images, feelings, thoughts, or other sensations that may emerge while they "listen" to a particular attribute in response to the inquiry question, as well as to let go of the need to immediately make intellectual sense of those responses.

After each meditation practice, coresearchers are invited to freely draw for a few minutes in order to facilitate the nonverbal integration and expression of their experience, in line with Heron's (1996) notion of presentational knowing. After completing the drawings, the two or three partners share relevant aspects of their experience, exploring both similar and different perceptions, images, and themes. Then, the entire group gathers in a circle to share individual findings through cognitive, descriptive statements about the quality of their experience, the imagery that emerged through drawing, or other nonverbal means such as movement or embodied dramatization. Thus, each individual inquiry session follows an epistemic cyclical structure, moving from experiential knowing (direct immersion in the inquiry domain), to presentational knowing (drawing, poetry, movement), to propositional and practical knowing (verbal sharing about conceptual and "know-how" insights).

INQUIRY QUESTION

The group delimits an inquiry domain through a dialogical exploration of potential inquiry questions emerging during or after the interactive meditation practices introduced in the first weekend. The exploration typically has three stages: small-group, whole-group, and e-mail discussion. Synthesizing the prevalent themes discussed, the group gradually agrees to focus on a particular inquiry question. Inquiry questions emerge from the particular interests of each group, and, as stated above, past ESIs have asked: "What are the experiential differences between dissociation, merging, and integration—contingent on boundary firmness and permeability—within both interpersonal and intrapersonal domains?" (Sohmer et al., forthcoming), and "What is the nature of relational spirituality and participants' experiences of the spiritual presence emerging 'in-between' persons?" (Osterhold et al., 2007).

VALIDITY: SOUNDNESS AND LIMITATIONS CONSIDERED

In this section, I consider the validity and limitations of ESI as a research method. The discussion is organized around five themes: (1) the strengths and limitations of ESI as cooperative inquiry, (2) generalizability and contextual validity, (3) issues around terminology, (4) transformational validity, and (5) subjectivity, objectivity, and participatory validity.

ESI as Cooperative Inquiry

Heron and Reason (1997, 2008) described cooperative inquiry as a research method that breaks down the roles of researcher and "subject," allowing data to organically emerge from both intra- and interpersonal interactions. In each ESI, participants are encouraged to engage subjective as well as intersubjective processes, and both are valued in the data collection process. In addition, the group cooperatively participates in the development of most stages of the inquiry process, including selection and refinement of the inquiry question, agreement on the inquiry tools, optional modification of the inquiry tools in the final weekend, dialogical elaboration of knowledge, and discussion of inquiry outcomes.

While the formulation of the inquiry question, as well as the data collected, emerges organically from the participants' process, there are two important limitations to be considered. First, although coresearchers can eventually modify them, the facilitator selects the initial inquiry tools (i.e., interactive embodied meditations), and the inquiry question emerges from coresearchers' experiences during this particular form of meditation practice. Although Romero and Albareda (2001) claimed that interactive meditations merely facilitate the direct perception of the deep energetic state of various human attributes (see chapter 4), some form of intentionality is arguably inevitable in all human activity. So, it is likely that these initial, facilitator-selected practices shape the coresearchers' experience in certain directions.

Second, the selection of the inquiry question is further influenced by group dynamics, including different levels of individual assertiveness as well as hierarchical roles inherent to the group. For example, even if collectively agreed upon, the inquiry question is influenced by those coresearchers who assert their interests more strongly, and by the facilitator who usually helps to craft its final articulation. Although perhaps inevitable in this specific academic context, these factors ultimately impact the direction of the research, arguably weakening the fully collaborative spirit that cooperative inquiry seeks to foster.

Generalizability and Contextual Validity

The findings of each ESI are based on the particular experiences of a specific group of individuals and the group's unique intersubjective field, making the nature of ESI validity strictly *contextual*. In other words, the outcomes of an ESI may differ (perhaps even significantly) depending on the group configuration, and cannot be extrapolated beyond each particular inquiry process. For example, variations in age, race, cultural background, class, sex, gender identity, and sexual orientation can impact both the wording of the inquiry question and the nature of the inquiry outcomes. While aspects of the ESI process acknowledge social identity and cultural influences, the research design and data analysis only address these variables when they are considered central to the inquiry question itself. The methodological and epistemological openness of ESI, however, makes it an optimal methodology for exploring the intersubjective terrain of social and cultural identities, providing fertile ground for future inquiries.

That said, in an ESI context it is hypothesized that shared, similar, or aligned inquiry outcomes from different coresearchers may reveal more collective aspects of the human condition. Likewise, conflicting or dissimilar inquiry outcomes from different coresearchers may reveal more individual or personally idiosyncratic aspects. Whereas shared outcomes suggest the possibility of their future generalizability, further investigations of the same question with different group constellations, as well as with the same and different inquiry method(s), would be needed before seriously entertaining such a consideration. In an ESI context, both shared and conflicting inquiry outcomes are equally valued, as they are regarded to open different windows—ranging from more individual to more collective—into the inquiry domain.

Terminological Issues

To support the authentic engagement of each coresearcher with the inquiry question, its key terms are left open for participants' interpretation throughout the ESI. In the spirit of open-ended inquiry (Almaas, 2002), the meanings of particular terms are not established in advance so that coresearchers can be open and curious about potential discoveries, following the natural unfolding of the thread of lived experience. For example, in the ESI into the experiential nature of interpersonal and intrapersonal boundaries, the terms *dissociation, merging,* and *integration* were not defined a priori; instead, their meaning gradually emerged throughout the inquiry process as coresearchers both experienced and conceptualized those states. Hence, typically, more delimited definitions of terms arise only after the inquiry outcomes are discussed at the end of the inquiry process.

There are, arguably, merits to this procedure. For example, it allows for the organic emergence of experiential meaning from within each participant, not constrained by a priori definitions. In addition, to keep the language used as close as possible to coresearchers' everyday experience, the collaborative process for developing the inquiry question relies upon colloquial (vs. academic) vernacular.

However, these strengths must be contextualized alongside inherent limitations. Since there may not be a shared preunderstanding of the terms used in an ESI, individual inquiry outcomes rely on how each participant interprets the terms. These individual preunderstandings can create fluctuations in the intended meaning reported by each coresearcher in both the expression and the interpretation of data.

Transformational Validity

According to Anderson and Braud's (2011) notion of *transformational validity,* the personal transformation of researchers and participants is an important validity standard that is especially central to transpersonal research methods (see also Braud & Anderson, 1998). In this regard, ESI coresearchers are not only carrying out a systematic collective inquiry into a focused question, but also accessing deeper aspects of themselves—some of which have been marginalized or repressed throughout the coresearchers' previous educational experience (see chapter 5). This access can be experienced as both profoundly liberating and personally meaningful, and participants often report significant personal insights during or after the interactive meditations. Through these meditations, coresearchers also acquire practical skills that can be used in their everyday relationships, and transform themselves in personal dimensions related to the selected inquiry domain. For example, many coresearchers of the ESI on the experiential nature of human boundaries reported both a heightened awareness of their own relational challenges (e.g., a tendency to merge with and lose themselves in the other) and an enhanced capability to self-regulate their own interpersonal boundaries (Sohmer et al., forthcoming). Thus, the ESI process not only brings forth a variety of propositional and presentational outcomes, but is also personally healing and transformative for many participants, which enhances the validity of findings in a transpersonal research context.

Subjectivity, Objectivity, and Participatory Validity

ESI data are generated and collected through various means, including contemplative, somatic, aesthetic, verbal, and written approaches. This procedure facilitates the expression and collection of a wide diversity of inquiry outcomes. Participants' expressions often transcend conceptual and written language, and include reports of direct experience through artistic creations or embodied dramatizations. In addition to enriching the inquiry's findings, this approach arguably empowers participants to express themselves more holistically, increasing the authenticity of their reports.

From the perspective of conventional research, however, collecting data this way can be seen as problematic. Due to the "subjective" nature of direct experience, it might be said that this form of data collection does not allow "objective" claims. The very subjective/objective dichotomy, however, is contingent of a Cartesian epistemology whose validity has been questioned even in the context of naturalistic science. As Malkemus (2012) pointed out, "A closer examination of experience reveals the fact that all so-called objectivity, and thus the objective claims of science, are in fact founded upon the subjectivities of the very people who are making objective claims" (p. 213; see also Wallace, 2000). When studying inquiry domains belonging to the human condition, the problems with objectivist standards of validity become exacerbated. In the context of transpersonal research, Braud (1998) stated: "Validity can be not only a measure of objective consistency and fidelity but also a feature that is able to convey a strong subjective impression of significance" (p. 224).

The participatory epistemologies upon which ESI is founded arguably overcome the Cartesian subjective/objective dichotomy through alternative paradigms of cognition that hold knowledge to be simultaneously subjective *and* objective, or, in a word, *participatory* (cf. Hartelius & Ferrer, 2013; Heron, 2006; Kripal, 2010; R. Tarnas, 1991). For example, my participatory approach (Ferrer, 2002, 2008) adopts Varela et al.'s (1991) enactive cognitive paradigm, according to which cognition is not the subjective representation of objective givens, but rather an embodied action through which an organism brings forth a domain of distinctions in interaction with its environment. In this context, alternate participatory standards of validity such as emancipatory and transformational power, among other pragmatic markers, gain greater relevance.[5]

To sum up this section, the type of validity coherent with the ESI approach is contextual, transformational, and participatory. Some of the apparent limitations of ESI as a research methodology can be seen as strengths when considered from alternative epistemological frameworks that value the generation of a more personally significant pool of data and inquiry outcomes. In the context of inquiries into the human condition, such an approach is likely to enhance the validity of the outcomes, fostering a research culture that is alive and imbued with human nature in alignment with the spirit of both contemplative education and participatory research.

CONCLUSION

To close this chapter, I argue that ESI constitutes a radicalizing of second-person contemplative education. If that claim seems too broad, I demonstrate its veracity regarding at least the following four pedagogical elements: (1) intrapersonal epistemic diversity, (2) embodiment and "bodyfulness"; (3) deep relationality, and (4) transpersonal morphic resonance.

First, ESI radically expands the range of epistemic resources usually available in prevalent forms of second-person contemplative approaches, which tend to remain at the verbal or awareness levels (e.g., Barbezat & Bush, 2013). The practice of interactive embodied meditation reportedly allows ESI coresearchers to access not only their minds and consciousness, but also the epistemic powers of the heart, the body, and the vital world (for some students' reports, see Nakagawa & Matsuda [2010]). This wider *intrapersonal epistemic diversity* arguably makes the resulting knowledge (i.e., inquiry outcomes) more holistic and complete. Through this diversity, ESI also extends contemplative practice itself beyond its historically customary parameters (e.g., mental concentration and pacification, heightened awareness of self and environment, expanded states of consciousness) and makes the inquiry process more personally meaningful for coresearchers (see Osterhold et al., 2007; Sohmer et al., forthcoming).

Second, ESI brings *embodiment* to the forefront of contemplative education. In contrast to contemplative techniques that focus on mindfulness of the body, the mindful physical contact among practitioners provided by Albareda and Romero's interactive meditations (see chapter 4) leads to states of being that are more accurately articulated in terms of *bodyfulness* (see chapter 3). In bodyfulness, the psychosomatic organism becomes calmly alert without the intentionality of the conscious mind. As Caldwell (2014) explained, "some of what could be considered as under the rubric of bodyfulness has been articulated in the name of mindfulness" (p. 76). However, she continued, "[although] mindfulness will sometimes involve body practices . . . and begins to approach aspects of bodily life . . . the body itself is capable of awakened states that go beyond these methods and practices" (p. 76). Thus, although the current research focus on mindfulness is important, I suggest that contemplative studies and education may also benefit from exploring states of bodyfulness.

Third, the engagement of various human attributes and associated ways of knowing, as well as the embodied approach used to provide such an access, drastically augments the depth of *relationality* achieved by ESI coresearchers. In particular, ESI's use of mindful physical contact as an inquiry tool represents a radical departure from the touch-aversive contemporary Western culture and educational practice. When applied in a mindful and respectful manner (i.e., with mutually defined boundaries and consent), physical touch is a chief foundation of not only safe personal intimacy and social bonding, but also psychosomatic healing and wholesome human development (Caplan, 2008; Linden, 2015; Montagu, 1971). Many ESI coresearchers have reported not only access to sources of knowledge beyond the mental or awareness levels, but also the emergence of a deep intimacy with other participants—a relationality that is normally restricted in Western culture to special friendships or romantic partnerships (see Osterhold et al., 2007; Sohmer et al., forthcoming).

Finally, in addition to facilitating epistemic diversity within individuals, ESI leads to the emergence of knowledge arising between participants, in the group as a whole, as well as within each ESI group in relation to those that preceded it. As Bache (2008) compellingly articulated, the transpersonal resonance that occurs within the classroom may allow individuals to participate in a shared group mind shaped by the facilitator, current students, and all of the students in previous classes. This *transpersonal morphic resonance* is visible in many ESI inquiry outcomes, including emergent shared experiences between meditation partners, the interconnection of themes arising within the group, and the body of knowledge growing out of different ESI courses as captured in case studies (see Osterhold et al., 2007; Sohmer et al., forthcoming).

PART THREE

SPIRITUALITY AND RELIGION

EIGHT

STANISLAV GROF'S CONSCIOUSNESS
RESEARCH AND THE
MODERN STUDY OF MYSTICISM

To discuss Stanislav Grof's fifty-year consciousness research and its profound implications for contemporary psychology, psychiatry, science,
philosophy, and society is beyond the scope of this chapter. It should
suffice to mention that Grof's research was pivotal for the development
of the field of transpersonal psychology (Grof, 1985, 2000, 2012), the
identification of the perinatal and transpersonal sources of psychopathol-
ogy and mental health (Grof, 1975, 1985), the understanding of spiritual
emergencies (Grof, 1988a; C. Grof & S. Grof, 1990; S. Grof & C. Grof,
1989), the challenge to the Cartesian-Newtonian scientific paradigm in
psychology (Grof, 1985, 2000, 2012, 2013), and the development of a
transpersonal approach to the critical analysis of social, cultural, and
global issues (Grof, 1988b, 2012), among other contributions.

   This chapter focuses on Grof's account of the spiritual states and
insights that occur during special states of consciousness facilitated by
entheogens and Holotropic Breathwork (i.e., sustained hyperventilation
combined with evocative music and bodywork; see Grof, 2012; S. Grof
& C. Grof, 2010).[1] Specifically, I show that (1) Grof's research provides crucial empirical evidence to potentially resolve one of the most
controversial issues in the modern study of mysticism—the question
of mediation in spiritual knowledge; (2) Grof interprets his findings as
supporting a neo-Advaitin, monistic, esotericist-perspective version of
the perennial philosophy; and (3) a more pluralist participatory vision
of human spirituality can harmoniously house Grof's experiential data

while avoiding certain shortcomings of perennialism. I conclude suggesting that a participatory account of Grof's data not only brings forth richer and more pluralistic spiritual landscapes, but also has emancipatory potential for spiritual growth and practice.

CURRENT TRENDS IN THE
MODERN STUDY OF MYSTICISM

Classical definitions of mysticism explain mystical knowledge in terms of an identification with, or direct experience of, the ultimate ground of Being, which is variously interpreted and described in terms such as God, the Transcendent, the Absolute, the Void, the Noumenal, Ultimate Reality, or, more simply, the Real (e.g., Hick, 1989; Huxley, 1945; Schuon, 1984; Underhill, 1955). These definitions are perennialist insofar as they assume the existence of a single, ready-made ultimate reality that is directly accessed, partially or totally, by mystics of all kinds and traditions. If mystical knowledge is direct and ultimate reality is One, so the reasoning goes, mystical experiences must either be phenomenologically identical, or, if different, corresponding to dimensions, perspectives, expressions, or levels of this singular spiritual ultimate. As Perovich (1985), a contemporary perennialist, put it: "The point [of the perennial philosophers] in insisting on the identity of mystical experiences was, after all, to bolster the claim that the most varied mystics have established contact with 'the one ultimate truth'" (p. 75).

Perhaps the most influential version of perennialism is the one developed by the traditionalist or esotericist school, whose main representatives are René Guénon, Ananda K. Coomaraswamy, Frithjof Schuon, Huston Smith, and Seyyed H. Nasr (Borella, 1995; Lings & Minaar, 2007; Oldmeadow, 2000; Quinn, 1997).[2] Although with different emphases, these authors claimed that while the exoteric beliefs of the religious traditions are assorted and at times incompatible, their esoteric or mystical core reveals an essential unity that transcends doctrinal pluralism (Quinn, 1997; Schuon, 1984; H. Smith, 1976). This is so, traditionalists argued, because mystics of all ages and places transcended the different conceptual schemes provided by their cultures, languages, and doctrines, and consequently accessed a direct, unmediated apprehension (*gnosis*) of reality. Most perennialists distinguished between mystical experience, which is universal and timeless, and its interpretation, which is culturally and historically determined (e.g., Smart, 1980). According to this view, the same mystical experience of the nondual Ground of Being would be interpreted as emptiness (*sunyata*) by a Mahayana Buddhist, as Brahman by an Advaita Vedantin, as the union with God by a Christian, or as an objectless absorption (*asamprajnata samadhi*) by a practitioner of Patanjali's yoga. In all cases, the experience is the same, the interpretation different.

This classical perennialist view was strongly challenged by Katz and other contextualist scholars, who argued that all mystical experiences—as any other human experience—are mediated, shaped, and constituted by the language, culture, doctrinal beliefs, and soteriological expectations of the traditions in which they occur (Gimello, 1983; Katz, 1978a, 1983b). There are two versions of this thesis of mediation: strong and weak. The *strong thesis of mediation* asserts that all mystical experiences are always entirely mediated—that is, the phenomenology of mysticism can be *fully* explained by resorting to formative variables such as the concepts, doctrines, and expectations that mystics bring to their experiences (e.g., Gimello, 1983). In contrast, the *weak thesis of mediation* asserts that most mystical experiences are heavily mediated by contextual variables, but that mystical phenomenology is the product of a complex interaction between formative variables, the creative participation of the mystic, and, in some cases, an encounter with actual ontological realities (e.g., Stoeber, 1994). In the first half of this chapter, I show that Grof's consciousness research renders the strong thesis of mediation implausible; in the second half, I introduce a participatory vision of human spirituality that embraces a radical version of the weak thesis of mediation.

Regarding Katz's (1978a, 1983) stance, although he has often been misunderstood (and, arguably, unfairly critiqued) as holding the strong version of the mediation thesis, his actual stance seems closer to the weaker version. When asked whether he believed that mystical experiences were entirely made up by mystics' prior beliefs and expectations, he responded: "That's not what I say. I say there is a dialectic between our environment and our experience" (as cited in Horgan, 2004, p. 46). However, Katz suggested that it is impossible to transcend cultural context, thereby falling into a mystical version of Popper's (1994) *myth of the framework*, which fallaciously holds that human beings are epistemic prisoners of their cultures, religions, and associated conceptual schemes (see chapter 9; Ferrer, 2002). In addition, Katz stated that the various mystical ultimates are incomplete glimpses of the same absolute reality: "All of us see only one aspect, only one attribute, only a partial vision. And ultimate reality, by its very nature, escapes us, because it is ultimate reality, and as human beings we are partial observers" (as cited in Horgan, 2004, p. 47). This statement brings Katz strikingly close to a perspectival perennialism (see Ferrer, 2002), as well as to a neo-Kantian metaphysical agnosticism regarding the possibility of human knowledge of ultimate reality.[3]

In any event, what contextual and conceptual factors influence, then, is not only the interpretation of mystical states (as most perennialists admit), but also their very phenomenological content: "The experience itself as well as the form in which it is reported is shaped by concepts which the mystic brings to, and which shape, his experience" (Katz, 1978b, p. 26). Therefore, for contextualists, there is not a variously interpreted universal mystical experience, but at least as many distinct types as contemplative traditions (Almond, 1982; Fenton, 1995; Hollenback, 1996). What is more, these types of mysticism do not necessarily correspond to different dimensions or levels of a single spiritual ultimate, but may be independent contemplative goals determined by particular practices, and whose meaning and soteriological power largely depend on their wider religious and metaphysical frameworks (Heim, 1995; Kaplan, 2002). Consequently, as Katz's (1978b) seminal essay concluded, " 'God' can be 'God,' 'Brahman' can be 'Brahman' and n can be n without any reductionistic attempt to equate the concept of 'God' with that of 'Brahman,' or 'Brahman' with n" (p. 66).

Needless to say, such a direct threat to the widely cherished idea of a common spiritual ground for humankind did not go unnoticed or unchallenged. On the contrary, the writings of Katz and his collaborators set the stage for two decades of lively, and often heated, debate between a plethora of perennialist- and contextualist-oriented scholars. Although this is not the place to review this debate (see Ferrer, 2000a, 2002), I should say here that, as the dialogue between these two camps evolved, their differences have gradually become more of emphasis than of radical disagreement. For example, most perennialist authors recognize today, although against a universalist background, some degree of contextuality in mysticism and a reciprocity between mystical experience and interpretation (e.g., Forman, 1990, 1998b, 1999).

ENTERS GROF

In the context of the modern study of mysticism, perhaps the most striking and revolutionary finding of Grof's consciousness research is that traditional spiritual experiences, symbolism, and even ultimate principles can allegedly become available during special states of consciousness, such as those facilitated by entheogens, breathwork, or other technologies of consciousness. What is more, according to Grof (1985, 1988a, 1998), subjects repeatedly report not only having access but also understanding spiritual insights, esoteric symbols, mythological motifs, and cosmologies belonging to specific religious worlds *even without previous exposure to them*. In Grof's (1988a) words:

> In nonordinary states of consciousness, visions of various universal symbols can play a significant role in experiences of individuals who previously had no interest in mysticism or were strongly opposed to anything esoteric. These visions tend to convey instant intuitive understanding of the various levels of meaning of these symbols.
>
> As a result of experiences of this kind, subjects can develop accurate understanding of various complex esoteric teachings. In some instances, persons unfamiliar with the Kabbalah had experiences described in the Zohar and Sepher Yetzirah and obtained surprising insights into Kabbalistic symbols. Others were able to describe the meaning and function of intricate mandalas used in the Tibetan Vajrayana and other tantric systems. (p. 139)

Similarly, Grof (1998) explained how Jungian archetypes—in both their primordial essence (e.g., the Great Mother Goddess) and their culturally specific manifestations (e.g., the Virgin Mary, the Greek Hera, the Egyptian Isis)—can be directly experienced during special states of consciousness. According to Grof, the identification with culturally bound archetypal motifs is often independent of cultural background and prior personal learning. For example, Buddhists and Hindus can experience the Western archetypal figure of Christ on the Cross, and Euro-Americans can identify themselves with the Buddha, Shiva, or the Sumerian Goddess Inanna. Commenting on this evidence, Grof (1998) wrote:

> The encounters with these archetypal figures were very impressive and often brought new and detailed information that was independent of the subject's racial, cultural, and educational background and previous intellectual knowledge of the respective mythologies. (pp. 23–24)

Grof (1998) explained this fascinating phenomenon by appealing to the collective unconscious hypothesized by C. G. Jung, which contains "mythological figures and themes from any culture in the entire history of humanity" (pp. 18–19).[4] During special states of consciousness, that is, individuals would draw from the collective unconscious both the archetypal symbols and the necessary hermeneutic keys to decode their meaning. To illustrate the genuinely transpersonal nature of these insights (i.e., that they bring accurate information of cultural and religious systems with which the individuals were personally unfamiliar), Grof (1998, 2006) described the case of Otto, one of his clients in Prague who suffered from a pathological fear of death. During an LSD session, Otto experienced the vision of a frightening pig-goddess guarding the entrance to the underworld, and then felt compulsively drawn to draft a variety of complex geometrical patterns, as if he was trying to find the correct one for a very specific purpose. The meaning of this imagery remained a mystery until, many years later, Grof discussed the details of the session with the mythologist Joseph Campbell.[5] According to Grof (1998), Campbell immediately identified the imagery of the pig-goddess and the geometrical patterns with a vision of "the Cosmic Mother Night of Death, the Devouring Mother Goddess of the Malekulans in New Guinea" (p. 20). Campbell added that the Malekulans not only believed that a terrifying female deity with distinct pig features "sat at the entrance into the underworld and guarded an intricate labyrinth design" (p. 20), but also practiced the art of labyrinth drawing as a preparation for a successful journey to the afterlife.

An intriguing question raised by these phenomena is why this transpersonal access to cross-cultural spiritual symbolism has not been reported before in the world's religious literature or pictorial history, even by traditions ritually using entheogens, breathing, or other technologies of consciousness modification, such as many shamanic cultures and certain schools of Sufism, Tantra, and Hinduism (Grof, 1988a; Jesse, 1996; Metzner, 1999). In other words, if transpersonal consciousness allows human beings to access transcultural religious symbolism, why cannot scholars find, for example, Buddhist or Christian motifs in Indigenous pictorial art? Or reports of Kabbalistic symbols and experiences in the Tantric or Sufi literature? Many of these traditions were very prone to describe—either pictorially or literarily—their spiritual visions in great detail; had their members encountered the powerful symbolic motifs that Grof's subjects report, it would be reasonable to expect finding some records of them, and to my knowledge scholars have found none.

In the wake of this situation, the modern mind may be tempted to explain away the phenomena reported by Grof in terms of *cryptoamnesia* (i.e., the subjects had forgotten their previous exposure to those symbols and the special state of consciousness simply brings the memories to consciousness; see Grof, 2006). This explanation needs to be ruled out, however, because Grof's subjects reportedly access not only the form of religious and mythological symbols, but also detailed experiential insights into their mystical or esoteric meaning that even ordinary practitioners of those religions do not usually know. Furthermore, although the crypto-amnesia hypothesis may account for some of the cases reported by Grof (e.g., self-identification of modern Japanese people with the figure of Christ on the Cross), it would be very difficult to explain in these terms reports of subjects (such as Otto) accessing detailed knowledge of mythological and religious motifs of barely known cultures such as the Malekulans in New Guinea. In these cases, the possibility of previous intellectual exposure to such detailed information is remote enough, I believe, to rule out the cryptoamnesia hypothesis as a plausible general explanation of these phenomena.[6]

In some of his lectures, Grof suggested an alternative explanation: contemporary transpersonal access to cross-cultural symbolism may reflect the emergence of a novel evolutionary potential of the human psyche consisting in the capability of accessing transcultural layers of the collective unconscious. The emergence of this potential, he continued, may mirror in the unconscious the greater interconnectedness of human consciousness in global times (e.g., through media, television, cinema, and especially the World Wide Web). Expanding this account, I conjecture that this transcultural access may have been facilitated by a combination of the following interrelated factors: (1) the lack, after the decline of Christianity, of an unequivocal religious matrix in the modern West that would provide a definite symbolic container for spiritual experiences; (2) the fact that the ritual space for Grof's (1975, 1988a) psychedelic and breathwork sessions is not usually structured according to any specific traditional religious symbolism or soteriological aim (as it was generally the case with the ritual use of entheogens in traditional settings); (3) the "seeking" impetus of the modern spiritual quest in Euro-America, arguably especially strong in individuals who feel drawn to experiment with psychedelics or breathwork (see Roof & Greer's [1993] characterization of modern American spirituality as a "quest culture" composed by a "generation of seekers"); and (4) the importation of modern Western values of open inquiry to spiritual matters. The combination of these factors may have paved the way for a more open-ended search for, and receptivity to, a larger variety of sacred forms and fostered access to spiritual visions cultivated by different religious traditions.

Whatever explanation results in being more cogent, the fact remains: Grof's (1988a, 1998) subjects were able to directly experience and understand spiritual insights and symbols of different religious traditions without previous knowledge of them. Although Grof's research awaits the more systematic replication necessary to achieve superior scientific status, his data suggest the limitations of the contextualist account of religious diversity and, if appropriately corroborated, constitute an empirical refutation of the strong thesis of mediation (i.e., the cultural-linguistic overdetermination of religious knowledge and experience). Remember that, for some contextualist theorists, religious phenomena are always entirely constructed by doctrinal beliefs, languages, practices, and expectations. As P. Moore (1978) put it, "the lack of doctrinal presuppositions might prevent the mystic not only from understanding and describing his mystical states but even from experiencing the fullness of these states in the first place" (p. 112). Whether or not Grof's subjects experience "the fullness" of mystical states and attain a complete understanding of traditional spiritual meanings is an open question. Even if this were not the case, the evidence provided by Grof's case studies is sufficient, I believe, to render the cultural-linguistic strong thesis of mediation questionable on empirical grounds. Grof's subjects report experiences that should *not* take place if the strong thesis of mediation is correct.

GROF'S PERENNIAL PHILOSOPHY

Grof's (1998) *The Cosmic Game* is an exploration of the metaphysical implications of his research into nonordinary (or *holotropic,* in his term, which means "moving toward wholeness") states of consciousness. In the introduction, Grof stated that the experiential data he gathered support the basic tenets of the perennial philosophy:

> This research . . . shows that, in its farther reaches, the psyche of each of us is essentially commensurate with all of existence and ultimately identical with the cosmic creative principle itself. This conclusion . . . is in far-reaching agreement with the image of reality found in the great spiritual and mystical traditions of the world, which the Anglo-American writer

and philosopher Aldous Huxley referred to as the "perennial philosophy." (p. 3)[7]

He added, "the claims of the various schools of perennial philosophy can now be supported by data from modern consciousness research" (p. 4). Later on, I argue that Grof's experiential data can be consistently explained without appealing to perennialist metaphysics, but first it may be helpful to identify Grof's specific brand of perennialism (for a typology of perennialisms, see Ferrer, 2002).

First, Grof (1998) shares with *esotericist* perennialists the belief that true spirituality needs to be sought in an esoteric core purportedly common to all religious traditions. In support of this idea, for example, he wrote: "Genuine religion is universal, all-inclusive, and all-encompassing. It has to transcend specific culture-bound archetypal images and focus on the ultimate source of all forms" (1998, p. 24). Grof's (1988a, 2000) distinction between spirituality and (exoteric) religion is also indicative of this stance: "The spirituality that emerges spontaneously at a certain stage of experiential self-exploration should not be confused with the mainstream religions and their beliefs, doctrines, dogmas, and rituals" (1988a, p. 269). Echoing the voice of esotericists such as Schuon (1984) or H. Smith (1976), he added: "The really important division in the world of spirituality is not the line that separates the individual mainstream religions from each other, but the one that separates all of them from their mystical branches" (p. 270).

Second, Grof's (1998) perennialism is *perspectival* in that he explains the diversity of spiritual ultimates (e.g., personal God, impersonal Brahman, emptiness, the Void, the Tao, pure consciousness) as different ways to experience the same supreme cosmic principle. As I explained elsewhere (Ferrer, 2002), perspectival perennialism understands the variety of experiences and accounts of ultimate reality as different perspectives, dimensions, or manifestations of a single supra-ultimate principle or pregiven Ground of Being.[8] In this spirit, Grof (1993) wrote, "The ultimate creative principle has been known by many names—Brahman in Hinduism, Dharmakaya in Mahayana Buddhism, the Tao in Taoism, Pneuma in Christian mysticism, Allah in Sufism, and Kether in Kabbalah" (p. 164). Or, as he put it more recently, "The name for this [ultimate] principle could thus be the Tao, Buddha, Shiva (of Kashmir Shaivism), Cosmic Christ, Pleroma, Allah, and many others" (2013, p. 93).

Third, Grof (1998) described this esoteric core, supreme cosmic principle, and ultimate source of all religious systems in terms of

Absolute Consciousness. This Absolute Consciousness is both the ultimate ground of all that exists (monism) and essentially identical to
the individual human soul (nondual). Talking about the nondual relationship between Absolute Consciousness and the individual soul, for
example, Grof (1998) stated:

> When we reach experiential identification with Absolute
> Consciousness, we realize that our own being is ultimately
> commensurate with the entire cosmic network. The recogni-
> tion of our own divine nature, our identity with the cosmic
> source, is the most important discovery we can make during
> the process of deep self-exploration. (p. 38)

For Grof (1998), this recognition confirms the truth of the essential message of the Hindu Upanishads: *"Tat twam asi"* or "Thou are that"—that
is, the essential unity between the individual soul and the divine.[9] In
his own words:

> Our deepest identity is with a divine spark in our innermost
> being (Atman) which is ultimately identical with the supreme
> universal principle that creates the universe (Brahman). This
> revelation—the identity of the individual with the divine—is
> the ultimate secret that lies at the mystical core of all great
> spiritual traditions. (Grof, 2013, p. 92)

Fourth, Grof (1998) read some of his experiential data as supporting Sri Aurobindo's (2001) notion of involution, according to which
the material world is the product of a process of restriction, partition, or
self-limitation of Absolute Consciousness. From a state of undifferentiated unity, Grof pointed out, Absolute Consciousness splits and forgets
itself to create infinite experiential realities. Although a variety of reasons for this self-forgetting are suggested, Grof (1998, 2000, 2013) usually
used Hindu terminology to explain it and repeatedly suggested that the
entire creation is *lila* or a cosmic drama ultimately played out by only
one actor: Absolute Consciousness. Talking about the dimensions of the
process of creation, for example, Grof (2000) wrote:

> These are elements that have best been described in ancient
> Hindu texts which talk about the universe and existence as
> *lila*, or Divine Play. According to this view, creation is an

intricate, infinitely complex cosmic game that the godhead, Brahman, creates himself and within himself. (p. 278)

Fifth, Grof (1998) supported Sri Aurobindo's (2001) view that evolution is not merely a return to the One, but "the gradual emergence of higher powers of consciousness in the material universe leading to an even greater manifestation of the divine Consciousness Force within its creation" (p. 79). However, Grof also stated that the ultimate goal and zenith of spiritual evolution is self-identification with Absolute Consciousness: "In its farthest reaches, this process [evolution] dissolves all the boundaries and brings about a reunion with Absolute Consciousness" (p. 79). Despite Grof's (1996, 2013) criticisms of Wilber's (1995, 1996b) work, the endorsement of this particular spiritual goal for all humankind brings Grof close to Wilber's hierarchical arrangement of spiritual insights and traditions (see chapter 9). In this regard, Grof (2013) wrote: "Despite the difference in the sources of data, it is not difficult to arrange transpersonal experiences in my classification in such a way that they closely parallel Wilber's description of the levels of spiritual evolution" (p. 101).

Finally, Grof's (1998) description of his cosmology included statements suggesting a subtle devaluation of the material world as illusory, imperfect, or even defiled. Summarizing the conclusions of his research, for example, he wrote:

In the light of these insights, the material world of our everyday life, including our own body, is an intricate tissue of misperceptions and misreadings. It is a playful and somewhat arbitrary product of the cosmic creative principle, and infinitely sophisticated "virtual reality," a divine play created by Absolute Consciousness and the Cosmic Void. (p. 39)

A similar tendency can be observed in his description of involution, which, for Grof (1998), implied an increasing loss of contact with the pristine nature of the original unity (p. 50). To illustrate this process, Grof appealed to Jain cosmology, according to which "the world of creation is an infinitely complex system of deluded units of consciousness . . . trapped in different aspects and stages of the cosmic process. Their pristine nature is contaminated by their entanglement in material reality and, particularly, in biological processes" (p. 52). Finally, Grof repeatedly suggested that his research supports the Hindu view that "the material reality as we perceive it in our everyday life is a product of a fundamental cosmic illusion called *maya*" (p. 66). Or, as he put it elsewhere in the book: "all boundaries in the material world are illusory and . . . the entire universe as we know it, in both its spatial and temporal aspects, is a unified web of events in consciousness" (p. 85).

To sum up, Grof (1998, 2013) interprets his findings as supporting a *neo-Advaitin, esotericist-perspectival version of the perennial philosophy*. The variety of spiritual ultimates is understood as different ways to experience the same universal ground, which can only be found, beyond all archetypal forms, in the esoteric universal heart of all religious traditions. This universal core is described as a monistic Absolute Consciousness, its relationship with human individual consciousness is understood in nondual terms, and the creation of an ultimately illusory material world is explained through the neo-Hindu notion of involution.

A PARTICIPATORY ACCOUNT OF
GROF'S CONSCIOUSNESS RESEARCH

In this section, I argue that Grof's commitment to a nondual perennialist metaphysics may have been both premature and problematic, and that a more pluralistic participatory account of human spirituality can consistently house his experiential data while avoiding the limitations of perennialism.

The many problems of perennialism have been extensively discussed elsewhere and do not need to be repeated here (e.g., Ferrer, 2000a, 2002; Griffiths, 1991; Hammer, 2001; Hanegraaff, 1998; Katz, 1978a; S. B. King, 2001). It should suffice to say that, despite their insistence on the ineffable and unqualifiable nature of a supposedly universal spiritual ultimate, perennialists consistently characterize it as nondual, the One, or Absolute Consciousness. The perennialist Ground of Being, that is, curiously resembles the Neo-Platonic Godhead or the Advaitin Brahman. Besides this reductionist, and often a priori, privileging of a nondual monistic metaphysics, perennialism is contingent upon questionable Cartesian presuppositions (e.g., about the pregiven nature of spiritual ultimate reality), leans toward faulty essentialisms that overlook fundamental spiritual differences among traditions (e.g., positing nonduality or pure consciousness as the ultimate or most fundamental referent for all genuine mysticism),[10] and raises important obstacles for interreligious dialogue and spiritual inquiry (e.g., traditions that do not accept the perennialist vision are regarded as inauthentic, lower, or merely "exoteric"; Ferrer, 2002). In addition to being textually unwarranted (Hollenback, 1996; Neville, 2001), esotericist universalism has been intersubjectively challenged (refuted?) in the contemporary inter-monastic dialogue. Buddhist and Christian monks, for example, acknowledge important differences on both their understandings *and* their experiences of what their respective traditions consider to be ultimate (Mitchell & Wiseman, 1997; S. Walker, 1987). What is more, even within a single tradition, strong disagreements about the nature of ultimate reality exist among monks, teachers, and contemplative practitioners.[11] In what follows, I outline a participatory understanding of spirituality that can explain Grof's experiential data while avoiding these problems.

Briefly, I understand spiritual knowing as a participatory activity (Ferrer, 2000b, 2002, 2008). Spiritual knowing is not objective, neutral, or merely cognitive, but rather engages human beings in a participatory, connected, and often passionate activity that can involve the opening not only of the mind, but also of the body, vital energies, the heart, and consciousness. Although particular spiritual events may only involve certain dimensions of human nature, all of them can potentially come into play in the act of participatory knowing—from somatic transfiguration to the awakening of the heart, from erotic communion to visionary cocreation, and from contemplative knowing to moral insight, to mention only a few. In this multidimensional human access to reality I call *participatory knowing,* the role that individual consciousness plays is not one of possession, appropriation, or passive representation of knowledge, but of *communion* and *cocreative participation.* This role is ontologically warranted by the fact that human beings are—whether they know it or not—always participating in the self-disclosure of the mystery of which they are part by virtue of their very existence.

Furthermore, following the groundbreaking work of Varela et al. (1991), my understanding of spiritual knowing embraces an enactive paradigm of cognition (see also Thompson, 2007). Spiritual knowing is not a mental representation of pregiven, independent spiritual objects, but an *enaction,* a "bringing forth" of a world or domain of distinctions cocreated by the different elements involved in the participatory event.[12] In other words, in the same way that Rorty (1979) debunked the myth of the human "mind as mirror of nature," I suggest that it is important to put to rest the equally problematic image of contemplative or visionary "consciousness as mirror of spirit" implicit in much classical and contemporary spiritual discourse. Some central elements of spiritual participatory events may include individual intentions and dispositions; the creative power of multidimensional human cognition; cultural, religious, and historical horizons; archetypal energies; encounters with subtle worlds and beings; and the apparently inexhaustible creativity of an undetermined mystery or generative power of life, the cosmos, or reality.

Although I concur with perennialism that most contemplative paths aim at overcoming self-centeredness and the emergence of transconceptual cognition,[13] I maintain that there is a *multiplicity of transconceptual disclosures of reality*. Because of their objectivist and universalist assumptions, perennialists erroneously assume that a transconceptual disclosure of reality must be necessarily "one," and, actually, *the* One metaphysically envisioned and pursued in certain traditional spiritual systems. The mystical evidence, however, strongly suggests that there is a variety of possible spiritual insights and ultimates (e.g., Tao, Brahman, *sunyata*, God, *kaivalyam*) whose transconceptual qualities, although sometimes overlapping, are irreducible and often incompatible (e.g., personal versus impersonal, impermanent versus eternal, dual versus nondual; Ferrer, 2002; Heim, 1995; Hollenback, 1996; Kaplan, 2002). The typical perennialist move to account for this conflicting evidence is to assume that these qualities correspond to different interpretations, perspectives, dimensions, or levels of a single ultimate reality. However, this move is not only unfounded, but also problematic in its covertly positing a pregiven spiritual ultimate that is then, explicitly or implicitly, situated hierarchically over the rest of spiritual ends. I submit that a more fertile way to approach the plurality of spiritual claims is to hold that the various traditions lead to the enactment—or "bringing forth"—of different subtle worlds, spiritual ultimates, and transconceptual disclosures of reality. Although these spiritual ultimates may apparently share some qualities (e.g., nonduality in *Brahmajñana* and *sunyata*; see Loy, 1988), they constitute independent religious aims whose conflation may prove to be a serious mistake (thus, e.g., the ontological nonduality of individual self and Brahman affirmed by Advaita Vedanta has little to do with the Mahayana Buddhist nondual insight into *sunyata* as the codependent arising or interpenetration of all phenomena). In other words, the ocean of emancipation has different shores.

This participatory account should not then be confused with the view that mystics of the various kinds and traditions simply access different dimensions or perspectives of a ready-made single ultimate reality. This view merely admits that this pregiven spiritual referent can be approached from different vantage points. In contrast, the view I am advancing here is that no pregiven ultimate reality exists, and that different spiritual ultimates can be enacted through intentional or spontaneous cocreative participation in an undetermined mystery or generative force of life or reality.[14]

In this context, what Grof's experiential data convincingly show is that, once a particular spiritual shore has been enacted, it becomes potentially accessible—at least to some degree and in special circumstances—to the entire human species. In other words, once enacted, spiritual shores become more easily accessible and, in a way, "given" to some extent for individual consciousness to participate in. In transpersonal cognition, spiritual forms that have been enacted so far are more readily available and tend more naturally to emerge (from *mudras* to visionary landscapes, from liberating insights to ecstatic types of consciousness). The fact that enacted shores become more available, however, does not mean that they are predetermined, limited in number, organized in a transcultural hierarchical fashion, universally sequential in their unfolding, or that no new shores can be enacted through cocreative participation. Like trails cleared in a dense forest, spiritual pathways traveled by others can be more easily crossed, but this does not mean that human beings cannot open new trails and encounter new wonders (and new pitfalls) in the seemingly inexhaustible mystery of being.

Grof's experiential data do not then need to be interpreted as supporting a perspectival account of the perennial philosophy. The various spiritual ultimates accessed during special states of consciousness, rather than being understood as different ways to experience the same Absolute Consciousness—which implicitly establishes a hierarchical ranking of spiritual traditions with monistic and nondual ones such as Advaita Vedanta at the top—can be seen as independently valid enactions of an undetermined mystery. Hierarchical arrangements of spiritual insights or traditions necessarily presuppose the existence of a pregiven spiritual ultimate relative to which such judgments can be made. Whenever objectivist prejudices in spiritual hermeneutics are dropped, however, the very idea of ranking traditions according to a paradigmatic standpoint becomes not only suspect but also fallacious and superfluous.[15]

This more pluralist account of Grof's findings is consistent with the synthesis of the psychedelic evidence offered by Merkur (1998). After indicating that most interpretations of the psychedelic evidence so far have been biased in favor of the idea of a universal mysticism, Merkur emphasized that empirical data have always pointed to a rich diversity of psychedelic spiritual states. Specifically, Merkur distinguished twenty-four types of psychedelic unitive states, suggesting that some of them may be more representative of certain religious traditions than others. What characterizes the psychedelic state, he wrote, is that it "provides access to all" (p. 155). Furthermore, although some of these states can be arranged in terms of increasing complexity, Merkur pointed out that "their development is not unilinear but instead branches outward like a tree of directories and subdirectories on a computer" (p. 98).[16]

CONCLUSION

In this chapter, I situated Grof's consciousness research in the context of the modern study of mysticism. On the one hand, Grof's findings hold the promise to settle one of the most controversial issues disputed by scholars of mysticism for the last four decades—the question of mediation in spiritual knowledge. Specifically, Grof's (1985, 1988a, 1998) research provides extensive evidence that individuals can not only access but also understand spiritual experiences, meanings, and symbols belonging to a variety of religious traditions even without previous exposure to them. This empirical finding, if appropriately corroborated, refutes the contextualist strong thesis of mediation, according to which spiritual experience and knowledge are always necessarily mediated by doctrinal beliefs, intentional practices, and soteriological expectations.

On the other hand, Grof (1998, 2013) suggested that the experiential data gathered during his fifty-year consciousness research support the idea of a perennial philosophy—more specifically, a neo-Advaitin, esotericist-perspectival type of perennialism. According to Grof (1998), all religious traditions, at their core, aim at the realization of an Absolute Consciousness that, being identical in essence to human individual consciousness, brings forth an ultimately illusory material world through a process of restriction or involution. The diverse spiritual ultimates espoused by the various religious traditions (e.g., *sunyata*, God, the Tao, *kaivalyam*, Brahman) are simply different ways to name and experience this Absolute Consciousness.

While I argued against this perennialist interpretation, I am not saying that the perennial philosophy cannot find support in Grof's data, or that Grof's research disconfirms perennialist metaphysics. As Grof (1998) showed, the psychedelic evidence can be interpreted in ways that are consistent with perennialism (although, I have argued, inconsistent with textual and phenomenological mystical evidence). This should not come as a surprise. In the same way that alternative or even logically incompatible theories can fit all possible evidence—as the Duhem-Quine principle of underdetermination of theory by evidence shows (Duhem,

1954/1991; Quine, 1953/1980)—it is very likely that alternative meta-physical systems could fit all possible experiences. What I suggest, in contrast, is that Grof's (1975, 1988a, 1998) empirical findings are also consistent with a more pluralist participatory vision of human spiritual-ity that is free from the limitations of perennialist thinking.[17] In other words, given the many problems afflicting perennialism, Grof's (1998, 2013) appeal to perennialism as the metaphysical framework to organize his experiential data may have been premature. In addition, I propose that a participatory account of Grof's data engenders a richer, more pluralistic, and arguably more spiritually emancipatory understanding of Grof's revolutionary findings.[18]

Once the dependence on objectivist and essentialist metaphysics is given up, the various spiritual paths can no longer be seen either as purely human constructions (as contextualism proposes) or as concurrently aimed at a single, pregiven spiritual reality (as perennialism holds). The vari-ous spiritual traditions, in contrast, can be better seen as vehicles for the participatory enaction of different subtle worlds, spiritual ultimates, and transconceptual disclosures of reality. In a participatory cosmos, human multidimensional cognition creatively channels and modulates the mys-tery's self-disclosing through the bringing forth of subtle worlds and spiritual realities—including transformative enactions of the physical or "natural" world. Spiritual inquiry then becomes a journey beyond any pregiven goal, an endless exploration and disclosure of the inexhaustible possibilities of an always undetermined mystery. Krishnamurti (1996) notwithstanding, spiritual truth is not a pathless land, but an infinitely creative adventure.

NINE

PARTICIPATION, METAPHYSICS,

AND ENLIGHTENMENT

Reflections on Ken Wilber's Integral Theory

This chapter critically examines Ken Wilber's (2006) latest theoretical work from a participatory perspective of human spirituality. For the sake of focus, I limit my discussion to the following four key issues: (1) the participatory critique of Wilber's work, (2) the cultural versus universal nature of Wilber's Kosmic habits, (3) the question of (post-) metaphysics in spiritual discourse, and (4) the nature of enlightenment. The chapter concludes with some concrete suggestions to move the dialogue forward.

THE PARTICIPATORY CRITIQUE OF WILBER'S WORK

The following summary of the participatory critique of Wilber's (2006) work is developed in response to the dialogue on Wilber's postmetaphysical approach between John Rowan and Michael M. Daniels, mediated by David Fontana and chaired by Malcolm Walley (Rowan, M. Daniels, Fontana, & Walley, 2009). In this dialogue, Rowan defended Wilber's model against critics who detected an Eastern bias in its allegedly universal spiritual map. To this end, Rowan offered a list of Western sources considered in Wilber's work; in addition, he endorsed Wilber's claim that Underhill's stages of the Christian mystical path conformed with Wilber's scheme.

This reply is unconvincing. With regard to Rowan's first defense, it should be obvious that the mere inclusion of Western sources does not warrant their *fair use*, so to speak. The issue is not that Wilber ignored Western (or Indigenous) traditions, but that he regarded their goals as lower spiritual expressions in a single developmental sequence culminating in a monistically based nondual realization. As I elaborated elsewhere (Ferrer, 2002), there is nothing new about this move. A legion of religious figures—from Ramanuja to Kukai, Vivekananda to Zaehner to the Dalai Lama—situated their favored (and remarkably different) spiritual choices at the zenith of a hierarchy of spiritual insights whose lower steps are linked to rival traditions or schools (Ferrer, 2002; Halbfass, 1988, 1991).[1] In any event, since the nondual realization of the ultimate identity between the self and the divine (or the cosmos) is the explicit goal of certain Eastern schools (e.g., Advaita Vedanta), it is understandable that scholars find an Eastern bias in Wilber's scheme.[2]

As for Rowan's second statement, although both Underhill (1955) and Wilber (1995, 2006) offered universal maps of spiritual development—a highly discredited notion in contemporary scholarship—their final stages are far from equivalent. Wilber erroneously equated Underhill's *divine mysticism* with his own *state of nondual union*. Underhill's unitive life, however, is characterized not by the nondual realization of one's deepest self as the divine, but by a process of deification (*theosis*) resulting from the ongoing spiritual marriage between God and the soul. In Christian mysticism, even for Pseudo-Dionysius, deification or "being as much as possible like and in union with God" (McGinn & McGinn, 2003, p. 186) is a gift bestowed by God based on the soul's participation in (vs. identity with) divine nature that should not be mistaken with monistic nondual claims (McGinn & McGinn, 2003). In fact, Underhill (1955) explicitly rejected monistic interpretations holding that "extreme mystics preach the annihilation of the self and regard themselves as co-equal with the Deity" (p. 419) and insisted that "the great mystics are anxious above all things to establish and force on us the truth that by deification they intend no arrogant claim to identification with God" (p. 420).[3] Even if a marginal number of Christian mystics might have reported states of nondual union with God—a view that Underhill did not support—those are arguably different from Wilber's nonduality.[4] Furthermore, not only nonduality but also mystical union fails to typify the dominant trends of the Christian mystical tradition, which are more adequately described as cultivating the "direct presence of God," as McGinn (1991, p. xvii) stated in the introduction to his authoritative multivolume history of Western Christian mysticism. Even if one cites the work of Marion (2000) or other modern Christian authors influenced by Wilber's model, doing so does not change two thousand years of documented history. In any event, since a variety of nondual states have been reported across traditions, I suggest that instead of an "Eastern bias," it may be more accurate to talk about a "monistic nondual bias" in Wilber's approach.

Rowan proceeded with a three-part defense of Wilber's work against my participatory critique (Ferrer, 2002). First, he claimed to be responding to my challenge of the perennialist idea that mystics are "all saying the same thing" (Rowan et al., 2009, p. 10) and, without providing supporting evidence, stated that "it turns out the more precisely the [mystical] experiences are described, the more similar they seem to be" (p. 10).[5] Without further explanation, he added that Wilber's version of the perennial philosophy is more sophisticated than the one I critiqued. However, among the varieties of perennialism discussed in my work— basic, esotericist, perspectival, typological, and structuralist—only the basic type holds that mystics are "all saying the same thing" (see Ferrer, 2002). I know of nobody today, including Wilber, who holds this view, so I am puzzled as to why Rowan brings it up in this context. As for Rowan's additional claim, contemporary scholarship reveals exactly the opposite picture: The more precisely mystical states are described, the more disparate they appear to be, such that features that may have initially appeared similar turn out, on closer inspection, to represent significant divergences. As Mommaers and van Bragt (1995) pointed out, "the mystics themselves would be the last ones to concede a single, common essence in mystical awareness" (p. 45). The supporting literature is too voluminous to cite here, but the reader can consult Hollenback's (1996) meticulous work, which showed the striking differences between the mystical states and understandings of Western, Eastern, and Indigenous figures. I am mindful that Wilber's model can explain these and other differences by appealing to his four mysticism types (psychic, subtle, causal, nondual), their enaction from the perspective of different structures of consciousness (archaic, magic, mythic, rational, pluralistic, integral, and super-integral), and the interpretive impact of each tradition's language and doctrines. I return to this hermeneutic strategy below, after discussing Rowan's second point.

Second, Rowan misconstrued my critique of experientialism— targeted at a subtly dualistic and individualist account of spirituality arguably associated with spiritual narcissism and integrative arrestment

(Ferrer, 2000b, 2002)—as suggesting the altogether different point that mystics are conformists. In any event, Rowan championed the view that the great mystics are spiritual revolutionaries, mentioning (as usual in these cases) Meister Eckhart as paradigmatic.[6] Unfortunately, Eckhart is so well known *precisely* because of his rather exceptional break with tradition and famous Inquisition trial (McGinn, 2001).[7] In other words, heretic mystics are actually the exception to the rule, and most mystics adhere to received doctrines and scriptures (Katz, 1983a, 1983b, 2000). As Harmless (2008) pointed out, "[t]he widespread intertwining of the doctrinal and the mystical is no accident. . . . Mystics often set forth their (or other's) experiences as the *experience of doctrine*" (p. 233). The romantic view of the mystic as revolutionary heretic is simply not supported by the textual and historical evidence.[8]

In addition, I am perplexed by Rowan's claim that the participatory approach renders mysticism dependent on cultural conditions, since my work explicitly critiqued this strong contextualist view and presented participatory spirituality as emerging from the interaction among human multidimensional cognition, historical-cultural background, and the mystery or generative power of life or the cosmos (Ferrer, 2002). Furthermore, whereas past mysticism may be largely conservative, participatory approaches (contra Rowan's depiction) invite scholars and practitioners to undertake not only the revision of traditional religious forms, but also the cocreation of novel spiritual understandings, practices, and even expanded states of freedom.

Third, Rowan claimed that my critique does not apply to Wilber's (1996) current views and that, as I indicated in *Revisioning Transpersonal Theory* (Ferrer, 2002), the majority of transpersonal writers "still do adhere to a more sophisticated view of the perennial philosophy" (Rowan et al., 2009, p. 10). I am not sure what to make of Rowan's last remark, but what I wrote at that time is no longer applicable in a transpersonal community that has mostly broken free from Wilber's stranglehold. It goes without saying that even if a majority would still support perennialism, this adherence has nothing to do with its validity. Turning to Rowan's more substantive point, it is true that in my early work, due to the vagaries of publishing that Rowan generously acknowledged,[9] I could not address Wilber-4 (2000c); however, I argue that the core of the critique holds for not only Wilber-4 but also Wilber-5 (2006).

Despite Wilber's (2006) significant revisions (e.g., letting go of "involutionary givens" in transpersonal stages), his current model holds that (1) spiritual development and evolution follow a sequence of (now evolutionarily laid down) states and stages (psychic/subtle/causal/non-dual); (2) this sequence is universal, paradigmatic, and mandatory for all human beings regardless of culture, tradition, or spiritual orientation; (3) nondual realization is the single ultimate summit of spiritual growth; and (4) spiritual traditions are geared to the cultivation of particular states and stages. To be sure, the Wilber-Combs lattice complicates this account by allowing that practitioners from any tradition and at any developmental stage can, in theory, access all transpersonal states (though the states would be interpreted from those corresponding perspectives; Wilber, 2006). Wilber's current formulation, however, retains a core problem and adds a new one. On the one hand, some traditions still rank lower than others since they aim at supposedly less advanced spiritual states and stages (e.g., theistic traditions rank lower than nondual ones, shamanic ones lower than theistic).[10] On the other hand, the new grace granted to rival traditions is a Faustian bargain: theistic and shamanic practitioners are told that they too can reach the most advanced spiritual stage, but only if they sacrifice the integrity of their own tradition's self-understanding by accepting Wilber's spiritual itinerary and nondual endpoint.[11] Although different traditions obviously focus on the enacting of particular mystical states and goals ("4" above), I strongly dispute the plausibility and legitimacy of Wilber's hierarchical rankings ("1–3" above).

Because the participatory approach has been pigeonholed as relativist and self-contradictory (Wilber, 2002), I should reiterate here that although my work does not privilege any tradition or type of spirituality over others on *objectivist or ontological grounds* (i.e., saying that theism, monism, or nondualism corresponds to the nature of ultimate reality or is intrinsically superior), it does offer criteria for making qualitative distinctions among spiritual systems on *pragmatic and transformational grounds*. Specifically, I have suggested three basic guidelines: the *egocentrism test*, which assesses the extent to which spiritual traditions, teachings, and practices free practitioners from gross and subtle forms of narcissism and self-centeredness; the *dissociation test*, which evaluates the extent to which spiritual traditions, teachings, and practices foster the integrated blossoming of all dimensions of the person; and the *eco-socio-political test*, which assesses the extent to which spiritual systems foster ecological balance, social and economic justice, religious and political freedom, class and gender equality, and other fundamental human rights (see chapters 1 and 10; Ferrer, 2002, 2008). To put it bluntly, I do not think it very important whether my friend's spiritual practice is Dzogchen meditation, entheogenic shamanism, or communion with nature—or whether she achieves nondual states, visions of God or the Goddess, or insight into the interrelatedness of all phenomena. What I really care about is whether she is becoming a more complete and liberated human being—that is, more selfless, more loving and compassionate, more capable of contributing to the spiritual transformation of the world, and so forth. In any event, since it is likely that most religious traditions would not rank too highly in these tests (see chapters 1 and 3), it should be obvious that the participatory approach also leads to a strong ranking of spiritual orientations.

The crucial difference is that the participatory rankings are not ideologically based on a priori ontological doctrines or putative correspondence to a single nondual Spiritual Reality (see Hartelius, 2015a; Hartelius & Ferrer, 2013), but instead ground critical discernment in the practical values of integrated selflessness and eco-socio-political justice. I stand by these values, not because I think they are universal (they are not), but because I firmly believe their cultivation can effectively reduce personal, relational, social, and planetary suffering. To be sure, this distinction can be problematized since the specificities of the various spiritual transformational goals often derive from descriptive or normative ontological views about the nature of reality or the divine. As I elaborate below, however, the participatory ranking is not itself precipitated by the privileging of a single spiritual goal, but rather explodes into a plurality of potentially holistic spiritual realizations that can take place within and outside traditions. Furthermore, most traditions are today reconstructing themselves in precisely these embodied and holistic directions (see chapters 3 and 10).

To summarize, even after Wilber's (2006) ad hoc modifications, his model still privileges nondual, monistic, and formless spiritualities over theistic and visionary ones,[12] even as it seeks to confine the multiplicity of spiritual expressions to a single, unilinear sequence of spiritual development (cf. Dale, 2014; Schlamm, 2001). Insofar as Wilber's model retains this sequence and associated doctrinal rankings of spiritual states, stages, and traditions, the essence of the participatory critique is both applicable and effective. While I do consider the critique justifiable, I do not think of it as a definitive refutation of Wilber's model (though its claimed universality is refutable by evidence). My sense is that both the participatory and Wilberian visions can accommodate spiritual diversity in different ways. As I discuss in chapter 8, in the same way that alternative and even logically incompatible theories can fit all possible evidence (Duhem, 1954/1991; Quine, 1953/1980), alternative, integral metatheories may be able to fit all possible spiritual data. In contrast to Wilber's theory, however, I submit that participatory integralism meets this challenge (1) by engendering more harmonious interreligious relations (see chapter 10); (2) by emancipating individual spiritual inquiry and growth from the constraints of an evolutionarily laid-down, pregiven sequence of transpersonal stages (Ferrer, 2002; Heron, 1998); and (3) without distorting traditions' self-understanding.

To elaborate on that last point, as the participatory approach makes a normative challenge to traditions, one can reasonably say that it does not fully honor some traditions' self-understanding. True enough. However, on the one hand it can be argued that the world traditions—from Christianity to Yoga, and Tantra to Buddhism to Judaism—are nowadays reconstructing themselves precisely in more holistic and embodied directions (e.g., Fox, 1988; Horton & Harvey, 2012; Lerner, 1994; Ray, 2008; Singleton, 2010; Urban, 2003); therefore, the participatory call can be seen as giving voice to and strengthening a preexisting trend within most traditions. On the other hand, and perhaps more crucially, the participatory approach does not require traditions to sacrifice their doctrinal integrity and embrace others' spiritual ultimate, because its equiplurality principle holds that all traditions can potentially become more embodied, holistic, and eco-socio-politically responsible *in their own terms* (e.g., contemplative categories, enacted ultimate realities). If Samkhya Yoga—arguably one of the most explicitly dissociative spiritual traditions of all—can be conceptually and practically reconstructed in embodied and integrative ways (see Horton, 2010; Singleton, 2010; Whicher, 1998), others can do the same. Whether or not this outcome is ultimately attainable, I firmly believe in the value of approaching this dialogue open to such possibilities.

In addition, I contend that the participatory approach is more aligned with the seemingly inexhaustible creativity of the mystery and more parsimonious in its accounting for the same spiritual evidence. Notably, it is unclear whether the ever-increasing conceptual proliferation of Wilber's integral theory is truly necessary, or whether it may suggest the exhaustion of the model's explanatory effectiveness and the possible degeneration of his research program. Similarly, Dale (2014) indicated regarding Wilber's (2000, 2006) work, "Whenever attempts are made to fit nonlinear patterns into linear frameworks, the resulting picture becomes overcomplicated and fragmented" (p. 135).

KOSMIC HABITS: CULTURAL OR UNIVERSAL?

In dialogue with M. Daniels, in this section I clarify my view of participatory cocreation and reflect on the related question of the cultural versus universal nature of Wilber's (2006) Kosmic habits. As a preliminary aside, I was relieved to finally see in print what has been in the mind of so many in transpersonal and integral circles for years: Wilber-5 is, in part, "a participatory revision of Wilber-4."[13] As M. Daniels noted, the cocreated nature of the spiritual path, the language of participation, and the use of the myth of the given in spiritual critical discourse are central features of the participatory approach introduced in my early work (e.g., Ferrer, 2000a, 2000b, 2002). This participatory reform is startling, especially given Wilber's (2002) dismissive account of *Revisioning* as expressing "a green-meme approach to spirituality, a kind of participatory samsara equated with nirvana" (p. 12).[14] As M. Daniels pointed out, Wilber often displays the disturbing scholarly habit of incorporating into his theorizing critical points made by others about his work—at times, points he previously dismissed as misinformed or conveying less evolved levels of spiritual discernment—and presenting them as autonomous developments of his thinking. In this case, Wilber (2006) assimilated aspects of the participatory approach into his integral vision; from a participatory perspective, however, many problems remain.

M. Daniels wrote that, whereas in my view the different "cocreated [spiritual] realities are cultural constructions" (Rowan et al., 2009, p. 21), for Wilber "these cocreated structures . . . become parts of the Kosmos . . . ontological realities that everybody has to negotiate" (p. 21). Stated this way, however, M. Daniels's account might mislead readers to associate the participatory approach with cultural constructivism (or contextualism; e.g., Gimello, 1983; Katz, 1978a), which I explicitly critiqued as operating under the spell of what Popper (1994) called the *myth of the framework* (Ferrer, 2000a, 2002). In the present context, this myth suggests that mystics and religious practitioners are prisoners of their cultures and conceptual frameworks, and that spiritual knowledge must always be shaped by or screened through such frameworks. In contrast, participatory approaches conceive mystical phenomena as cocreated events emerging not only from culture, but also from the interaction of human multidimensional cognition, subtle worlds and entities, and an undetermined mystery or creative power of life, the cosmos, or reality (Ferrer, 2002, 2008). In other words, participatory spirituality embraces the role of language and culture in religious phenomena while simultaneously recognizing the importance, and at times the central-ity, of nonlinguistic (e.g., somatic, energetic, imaginal, archetypal) and transcultural factors (e.g., subtle worlds; the creative power of life or the spirit) in shaping religious experiences. As we put it in the introduction to *The Participatory Turn*:

> The adoption of an enactive paradigm of cognition in the study of religion, however, frees us from the myth of the frame-work . . . by holding that human multidimensional cognition cocreatively participates in the emergence of a number of plausible enactions of reality. Participatory enaction, in other words, is epistemologically constructivist *and* metaphysically realist. (Ferrer & Sherman, 2008a, p. 35)

As Gleig and Boeving (2009) wrote in their essay review of the book: "Ontological veracity . . . is not inherently at odds with a contextualist sensibility. To acknowledge that humans do not only discover but also shape and cocreate spiritual landscapes does not annul the metaphysi-cal reality of such mystical worlds" (p. 66).[15] Similarly, Hartelius (2016) stated in relation to the participatory approach, "culturally-situated ulti-mates actually exist and are ontologically real within particular relational fields; they will necessarily differ between communities that participate in different fields" (p. v).

I suspect that the source of M. Daniels's apparent misapprehension of my view is largely semantic. In particular, I wonder whether it emerges from the implicit equation of *Kosmic* (or *ontological*) with *universal* in the dialogue. After all, M. Daniels wrote:

> I don't deny that groups of people can cocreate . . . mor-phogenetic fields—or habits of working, or patterns of work-ing. . . . What I am denying is that they become Kosmic habits—that they become realities that are given in the Kosmos, and are fixed, and everyone has to go through them. (Rowan et al., 2009, p. 35)

I concur. M. Daniels immediately added, however, that I view cocreated spiritual realities as "cultural habits . . . not Kosmic habits" (p. 36). To which I respond, yes, they are cultural but not *merely* cultural; they are also morphogenetic fields of energy and consciousness, which, although not universal or mandatory, can become more available as new shores of the Kosmos are enacted and explored. The key point is that *there is no need to conflate Kosmic and universal if the Kosmos is considered a plural cornucopia creatively advancing in multiple ontological directions.* Wilber (2006) sought to confine such an ontological multiplicity to his unilinear evolutionary sequence, but I believe it is both more accurate and more generous to envision cosmic and spiritual evolution as branching out in many different but potentially intermingled directions (or as an omnicentered rhizome propagating through offshoots and thickenings of its nodes; Deleuze & Guattari, 1987). Dale's (2014) nonlinear transpersonal paradigm also supports the existence of multiple developmental and evolutionary pathways that branch claidogenetically, that is, via collateral modules moving toward "specializing diversification" (p. 219); for Dale, Wilber's (2000, 2006) works are "the epitome of the [linear] statistical averaging approach" (p. 135). In the context of this pluralistic account, the ontological nature of a multiplicity of Kosmic habits can be affirmed free from Wilberian dogmatic constraints.

There may also be deeper philosophical issues behind M. Daniels's reluctance to grant an ontological status to Wilber's (2006) Kosmic habits. Following Jung, M. M. Daniels (2001) proposed that transpersonal psychology should remain metaphysically agnostic toward any ontological reality beyond the physical and psychological (cf. Friedman, 2002, 2013a) and should focus on the phenomenological study of human experience. As I discuss in chapter 2, however, this apparently cautious stance is rooted in an implicit allegiance to neo-Kantian frameworks that either bracket or deny the existence of supernatural and metaphysical realities. At its heart rests the Kantian belief that innate or deeply seated epistemic constraints in human cognition render impossible or illicit any knowledge claim about such metaphysical realities. In other words, metaphysical realities *may* exist, but the only thing human beings can access is a situated phenomenal awareness of them. The legitimacy of metaphysical agnosticism is thus contingent on the validity of a neo-Kantian dualistic metaphysics, which, although not necessarily wrong (based on its metaphysical status, that is), nonetheless undermines the professed neutrality of metaphysical agnosticism (cf. R. King, 1999; Lancaster, 2002). Indeed, as Northcote (2004) argued, the methodological suspension of the validity of supernormal claims (e.g., about metaphysical entities or levels of reality), far from warranting objectivism or scholarly neutrality in the study of religion, may actually constitute a bias against "the possibility that people's thinking and behaviour are indeed based on various supernormal forces . . . a bracketing approach will falsely attribute mundane sociological explanations to behaviour that is in actuality shaped by supernatural forces" (p. 89).

As I elaborate in chapter 2, the point here is that unless one subscribes ideologically to a naturalistic metaphysics,[16] it may be prudent—and heuristically fertile—not to reject a priori the possibility of effective causation from the various metaphysical sources described in religious utterances. In addition, Western epistemologies (such as the neo-Kantianism prevalent in modern academia) may not be the last arbiters in the assessment of religious knowledge claims, and in particular of those emerging from long-term contemplative practice.[17]

Why do I insist on the ontological (vs. merely cultural) nature of Kosmic habits? As I see it, this account is the most plausible explanation for the well-documented transcultural access to apparently given spiritual motives and realities (see chapter 8; Grof, 1988a, 1998; Shanon, 2002). The other alternative is to appeal to Jung's notions of the collective unconscious and universal archetypes, but as Shanon (2002) explained, Jungian explanations fall short. On the one hand, many psychedelic visions are very different from those connected with the Jungian archetypes (e.g., the Hero, the Trickster, the Great Mother); on the other hand, many visions are culture-specific and do not have the universal status of the archetypes, which Jung posited as "associated with the common heritage that is shared by all human beings and which may well have evolved throughout the history of the species" (p. 391). After a lucid discussion of biological, depth psychological, cognitive, and supernatural interpretations of the related phenomenon of cross-cultural commonalities in ayahuasca visions, Shanon rejected supernatural accounts and leaned toward cognitive considerations. His final conclusion, however, was highly attuned to the participatory view of spiritual cocreation:

> The cross-personal commonalities exhibited in Ayahuasca visions, the wondrous scenarios revealed by them, and the insights gained through them are perhaps neither just psychological, nor just reflective of other realms, nor are they "merely" a creation of the human mind. Rather, they might be psychological *and* creative *and* real. (p. 401)

In any event, as M. Daniels pointed out, Wilber's (2006) attempt to make the transcultural accessibility to spiritual states and referents mandatory for the entire human species is misleading. Once enacted, spiritual realities become more easily accessible, but this does not mean that they are mandatory, predetermined, organized in a transcultural hierarchical fashion, universally sequential in their unfolding, or limited in number, or that new pathways cannot be enacted through cocreative participation.

In my view, then, cocreated spiritual realities (1) can become ontologically given in the cosmos, (2) are not fixed but are dynamic and open to human participatory endeavors, (3) are not mandatory, and (4) are always options among other new pathways that can be potentially enacted. Thus, when Fontana cautiously left open "for general debate as to whether these Kosmic habits are cultural, or whether they are indeed Kosmic" (Rowan et al., p. 37), participatory scholars might have responded that they are *both* cultural *and* Kosmic, but in the open and pluralistic fashion outlined above.

POSTMETAPHYSICAL VERSUS PARTICIPATORY SPIRITUALITY

In *Integral Spirituality*, Wilber (2006) introduced an allegedly postmetaphysical approach that conceived spiritual worlds not as preexisting ontological levels but as cocreated structures of human consciousness.[18] As discussed above, once evolutionarily laid down, Wilber believes that these structures become Kosmic habits or "*actually existing structures* in the Kosmos" (p. 247), although by this he meant that they exist within the inner realms of the individual. In his own words:

> The claim of Integral Post-Metaphysics is that the invaluable and profound truths of the premodern traditions can be salvaged by realizing that what they are saying and showing applies basically to the Upper-Left quadrant [i.e., the interior of the individual]. (p. 46)

I have often been asked what I think about Wilber's postmetaphysical spirituality. My answer: It is not only unoriginal, but also arguably reductionist. I fail to see novelty in it because many contemplative traditions—such as Yogacara (Mind-Only) Buddhism or most Tibetan Buddhist schools—explicitly accounted for spiritual realms in terms of subtle dimensions of consciousness, not as external metaphysical levels of reality. Wilber seems to be reacting against a special brand of Neo-Platonic metaphysics (the Great Chain of Being), but his postmetaphysical formulation does not add anything to the way some other traditions have understood spiritual realities for centuries. I am somehow surprised each time Wilber borrows age-old notions and presents them as not only the newest spiritual vision, but one that supersedes all previous visions.[19]

Before explaining why Wilber's postmetaphysics may be reductionist, it is important to distinguish between two related but independent meanings of the term *metaphysics*. On the one hand, the notion of metaphysics in Western philosophy is generally based on the distinction between appearance and reality, with a metaphysical statement being one claiming to portray that reality presumably lying behind the realm of appearances (Schilbrack, 2014; van Inwagen, 1998). In addition to this use, on the other hand, many religious traditions also use the term *metaphysical worlds* to refer to levels or dimensions of reality existing beyond the sensible world or within the subtle ontological depths of human consciousness. The first usage is the main target of Derrida's (1976) attack on the metaphysics of presence. On a strong reading, this critique leads to the a priori denial of the ontological status of any "supernatural" or metaphysical reality; the weaker reading simply requires a declaration of metaphysical agnosticism.[20]

Several years before Wilber articulated his integral postmetaphysics, the participatory approach eschewed the dualism of appearance and reality, as well as endorsed modern and postmodern critiques of traditional metaphysics of presence (Ferrer, 2002). In contrast to Wilber, however, I believe it is entirely possible to consistently drop the mentalist dualism of appearance and reality, and simultaneously entertain the plausibility of a deep and ample multidimensional cosmos in which the sensible world does not exhaust the possibilities of the Real (see chapter 2 and Postscript).

In this light, a major problem with Wilber's (1996) formulation becomes apparent: It created a *false dichotomy between pregiven ontological levels and his postmetaphysical account of spiritual worlds within the interior realms of the individual.* This dichotomy is fallacious because, among other possibilities, it overlooks the possible existence of subtle worlds or dimensions of reality coexisting with the physical realm that potentially house indwelling nonphysical entities. As anyone who has engaged systematically in entheogenic inquiry knows, for example, subtle worlds and ostensibly autonomous spiritual entities can be encountered not only within one's inner visionary landscapes (e.g., Strassman, 2001), but also in front of one's open eyes in the world "out there" (Shanon, 2002)—and these external visions can sometimes be intersubjectively corroborated (see chapter 2).[21]

This discussion raises the thorny issue of the ontological nature of subtle or nonphysical entities. Are they constructed, cocreated, or fully independent? I do not have a definitive answer to this question, but I offer three remarks. First, I see no conflict between maintaining that entities such as angels or *dakinis* may have been historically cocreated and that they can also have autonomy and agency independent from human experience. In my view, some of these beings are not reducible to culturally constructed psychological visions, but may rather be endowed with an extrapsychological ontological status emerging from collectively maintained enactive interactions between human multidimensional cognition, cultural-religious memes, and the creative power of life, reality, or the cosmos. Second, if one accepts the possibility of an afterlife scenario in which personal identity is somehow maintained, it becomes possible to contemplate the feasibility of human encounters with non-cocreated entities such as deceased saints, *bodhisattvas*, ascended masters, and the like.[22] (I leave open the possibility that so-called angels or *dakinis* may be evolved incarnations of these deceased personhoods in other dimensions of the cosmos). Finally, as many traditions maintain, it might be conceivable to entertain the possibility of parallel realms or dimensions of reality inhabited by fully autonomous entities endowed with self-awareness and volition. In the case of angels, *dakinis*, and the like, however, I confess that their cultural specificity (forms, qualities, etc.) makes me wonder about their cocreated nature.[23]

In any event, if the plausibility of a multiverse or multidimensional cosmos is accepted—as many shamanic, esoteric, and contemplative traditions affirm—*Wilber's integral postmetaphysics is reductionist in its relegation of all spiritual realities to the inner depths of the individual* (see also Hartelius, 2015a; Hartelius & Ferrer, 2013). If Wilber is also suggesting that *all* spiritual realities and entities are human cocreations, his proposal could have also been charged with anthropocentrism.

A participatory understanding, in contrast, allows a bold affirmation of spiritual realities without falling into a reified metaphysics of presence, nor into any of today's fashionable postmetaphysical reductionisms (whether biological, cultural, or Wilberian-integral). On the one hand, a participatory account of religious worlds overcomes the static and purportedly universal metaphysical structures of the past because it holds that culturally mediated human variables have a formative role in the constitution of such worlds. Whereas the openness of religious worlds to the ongoing visionary creativity of humankind entails their necessary dynamism, the contextual and embodied character of such creative urges requires their plurality. On the other hand, the participatory embrace of the human's constitutive role in religious matters need not force the reduction of all spiritual realities to mere products of a culturally shaped human subjectivity, nor their necessary confinement to the interior worlds of the individual.

THE QUESTION OF ENLIGHTENMENT

I close this chapter with some reflections on the nature of enlightenment (see also Ferrer, 2002). Although M. Daniels suggested more pluralistic possibilities, I was struck by the generalized assumption in the dialogue regarding the unity of enlightenment or the belief that there is a single kind of ultimate spiritual realization. In what follows, I question such an assumption and provide a participatory account of spiritual individuation that allows and supports multiple forms of more holistic spiritual awakenings, which nonetheless can share qualities such as selflessness and embodied integration.

Let me begin by considering Wilber's (2006) definition: "Enlightenment is the realization of oneness with all states and structures that are in existence at any given time" (p. 95). To clarify what he meant, Wilber proposed a "sliding scale of Enlightenment" (p. 235) according to its *Emptiness* and *Form* aspects. Since the structures of consciousness unfold evolutionarily in the world of Form, one can realize the same Emptiness at any point of history, but later practitioners can embrace Form in fuller ways: "A person's realization today is not Freer than Buddha's (Emptiness is Emptiness), but it is Fuller than Buddha's (and will be even fuller down the road)" (p. 248).

Wilber's (2006) approach has three important shortcomings. First, it reduces the rich diversity of spiritual soteriologies and goals (e.g., deification, *kaivalyam*, *devekut*, *nirvana*, *fana*, visionary service, *unio mystica*) to a rather peculiar hybrid of Buddhist emptiness and Advaita/Zen nondual embrace of the phenomenal world. I critiqued this reductionism elsewhere (Ferrer, 2002) so I will not press the issue again here, but readers can consult the works by Heim (1995), Hollenback (1996), and Kaplan (2002), among many others, for detailed accounts of a variety of remarkably different spiritual goals and realizations. Even a single tradition usually houses different goals and corresponding liberated states. Consider Buddhism, in the words of the Dalai Lama (Tenzin Gyatso, 1988):

Questioner: So, if one is a follower of Vedanta, and one reaches the state of *satcitananda*, would this not be considered ultimate liberation?

His Holiness: Again, it depends upon how you interpret the words, "ultimate liberation." The moksa which is described in the Buddhist religion is achieved only through the practice of emptiness. And this kind of nirvana or liberation, as I have defined it above, cannot be achieved even by Svatantrika Madhyamikas, by Cittamatras, Sautrantikas or Vaibhasikas. The follower of these schools, *though Buddhists*, do not understand the actual doctrine of emptiness. Because they cannot realize emptiness, or reality, they cannot accomplish the kind of liberation I defined previously. (pp. 23–24)

Like the Dalai Lama, Wilber may retort that many traditions are not aimed at (what he considers to be) ultimate liberation.[24] Such a response, however, begs the question by assuming the validity of the very framework being challenged: Wilber's (2006) ranking of spiritual states/stages and account of final liberation.

Second, serious questions can be raised about Wilber's (2006) claim that the Buddha achieved complete freedom. In contrast to later articulations of emptiness (*sunyata*), the Buddha's *nirvana* is described in the Buddhist canon as an utterly disembodied state of blissful consciousness in which all personality factors—including sensations, desires, feelings, and thoughts—have been totally extinguished (P. Harvey, 1995). This should not come as a surprise: Most traditions spawned in India regarded embodied life as illusory or a source of suffering, thus seeking liberation in its transcendence. The dominant view in the Indian tradition is to consider spiritual freedom (*moksa, mukti*) as the release from the cycle of transmigratory experience (*samsara*), the body as bound and even created by karma and ignorance, and bodiless liberation (at death) as superior to living embodied liberation (Fort, 1998). Immersed in this cultural-religious matrix, the Buddha also believed that the body and sexuality (and aspects of the heart, such as certain passions) were hindrances to spiritual flourishing (Faure, 1998), and early Buddhism pictured the body as a repulsive source of suffering, *nirvana* as extinction of bodily senses and desires, and "final *nirvana*" (*parinirvana*) as attainable only after death (S. Collins, 1998). Although some exceptions may be found, this trend generally led the various Buddhist schools and vehicles to the repression, regulation, or transmutation of body and sexuality at the service of the higher goal of the liberation of consciousness (see chapter 3).

So, was the historical Buddha entirely *Free*, as Wilber believes? My answer: Only if you understand spiritual freedom in the disembodied, and arguably dissociative, way pursued by early Buddhism.[25] Despite his downplaying the spiritual import of sexuality and the vital world, Sri Aurobindo (2001) was correct when he pointed out that the liberation of consciousness should not be confused with an integral transformation that entails the spiritual alignment of all human dimensions (pp. 942ff). With this in mind, I have proposed an integral *bodhisattva* vow in which the conscious mind renounces its own full liberation until the body, the heart, and the primary world can be free as well from the alienating tendencies that prevent them from sharing freely in the unfolding life of the mystery here on Earth (see chapters 1 and 3).

Third, despite Wilber's (1995) plea for the integration of ascending and descending spiritual trends, his account of spiritual freedom in terms of Buddhist emptiness revealed an ascending and monopolar bias. Since the ascending bias has been already discussed (M. M. Daniels, 2005, 2009), I focus here on the monopolar charge. As Heron (1998, 2006) explained, in addition to spiritualities that blatantly devalue body and world, monopolar spirituality is a more subtle type of disembodied orientation that sees spiritual life as emerging from the interaction of human beings' immediate present experience with transcendent fields or states of consciousness (cf. Ferrer et al., 2004).[26] The shortcoming of this monopolar understanding is that it ignores the existence of a second spiritual pole—immanent spiritual life or energy—that is intimately connected to the vital world and, arguably, stores the most generative power of the mystery (see chapter 3). Wilber's account is monopolar insofar as it conceived enlightenment in terms of a realization in consciousness that overlooks the crucial role of immanent life for genuinely integral spiritual growth and creative spiritual breakthroughs.

Wilber's (1995, 1996b) proposed logic of "transcend and include" as *the* formula of spiritual development gives the game away. When the mind emerges, it is said to transcend and include the body, vital energy, and emotions; when the witness consciousness emerges, it is said to transcend and include the mind; when higher structures of consciousness emerge, they are said to transcend and include the witness, and so forth.[27] Wilber (1995) regarded the body and sexuality as sacred in the sense of having spiritual "ground value" (i.e., they are expressions of absolute Spirit, emptiness, or God) and in that they can be sacralized in the nondual embrace; however, this account is very different from recognizing the centrality of intrinsically spiritual, immanent sources for integral transpersonal development. When both consciousness and energy (and matter) are understood as equally fundamental spiritual players, *integral spiritual development unfolds in a dialectical interaction with both transcendent and immanent spiritual sources that the linear logic of "transcend and include" fails to capture* (see chapter 4; Dale, 2014; Heron, 1998, 2006). A fully embodied spirituality, I suggest, emerges from the creative interplay of both immanent and transcendent spiritual energies in individuals who embrace the fullness of human experience while remaining firmly grounded in body and earth. Openness to immanent spiritual life naturally engenders a richer plurality of creative spiritual realizations—often connected with transformative personal life choices—that cannot be reduced to the homogenous "one taste" of Wilber's (1999) nondual realization.

I strongly suspect that this one-sidedness is behind Wilber's (2006) elevation of meditation as the royal path to spiritual growth. He wrote:

> No other single practice or technique—no therapy, not breathwork, not transformative workshops, not role-taking, not hatha yoga—has been empirically demonstrated to do this . . . the reason meditation does so is simple enough. When you meditate, you are in effect witnessing the mind, thus turning subject into object—which is exactly the core mechanism of development. (p. 198)

As M. M. Daniels (2009) indicated, however, meditation is, at least historically, an ascending spiritual practice.[28] Furthermore, remember that the particular meditative techniques favored by Wilber originated in religious systems seeking to liberate human beings from the suffering or illusory nature of both body and world through identification with the Self, the achievement of *nirvana*, and so forth. It may be countered that all contemplative traditions privilege one or another type of ascending meditation practice, to which I would respond that this is likely to be so because most past religious traditions were strongly patriarchal and leaned toward disembodiment and dissociation (see chapter 3). Consistent with his spiritual rankings, Wilber's enthroning of meditation as the spiritual practice par excellence privileges contemplative traditions over alternative visionary, wisdom, devotional, and socially engaged ones. In his concluding comment, Fontana got to the heart of the matter when, in light of the four yogas of Hinduism—*karma* (yoga of action), *bhakti* (yoga of devotion), *jnana* (yoga of wisdom), and *raja* (yoga of meditation)—he suggested meditation may be *the* path only for *raja* yogis (Rowan et al., 2009, pp. 58–59).

I am not questioning the value of meditation. I practiced Buddhist meditation (Zen and *vipassana*) regularly for about fifteen years, studied with meditation teachers, and attended many meditation retreats. Although I no longer practice daily, I sit sometimes and many features of meditation (e.g., mindfulness, inquiry) are central to the way I relate to my life and the world. In my experience, Buddhist meditation is extremely helpful to (1) become clearly aware of, learn to relate more adequately to, and free oneself from conditioning habits and plainly neurotic loops of the mind; (2) become more accepting, peaceful, and equanimous with one's own and others' experiences and reactions; and (3) enact and participate in a Buddhist engagement of the world marked by an awareness of impermanence, no-self, emptiness, and the interrelatedness of all phenomena that can lead to the emergence of beautiful spiritual qualities such as compassion and sympathetic joy. Although potentially deeply beneficial and transformative, traditional Buddhist meditation training has obvious limitations in fostering a truly integral spiritual development. This is evident, for example, in the control of body posture and potential repression of somatic intelligence (cf. Ray, 2008), the strict regulation of sexual behavior and prohibition of the creative exploration of sensual desire (Faure, 1998; Loy, 2008), the individualist focus and lack of relational and collective practices (Rothberg, 2008), the aversion toward the expression of strong emotions such as anger (Masters, 2000), and the overall lack of discrimination between attachment and passions.[29]

A last point about Wilber's (2006) view of meditation: As the above reflects, I wholeheartedly agree with Fontana that meditation may not be *the* most effective or appropriate spiritual practice for everybody (for some it can be even counterindicated; see D. H. Shapiro, 1992; Treleaven, 2010, 2018; Walsh & Roche, 1979). I want to add here that to elevate one's own spiritual choice as the universally superior one is a symptom of what I have called *spiritual narcissism*, which is unfortunately pandemic in the human approach to religious diversity (see chapter 10). From a participatory perspective, however, it is no longer a contested issue whether practitioners endorse a theistic, nondual, or naturalistic account of the mystery, or whether their chosen path of spiritual cultivation is meditation, social engagement, conscious parenting, entheogenic shamanism, sacred sexuality, or communion with nature. (Of course, it may be desirable to complement each pathway with practices that cultivate other human potentials—hence the importance of nonmentally guided integral practice; see chapter 4). The new spiritual bottom line, in contrast, is the degree to which each spiritual path fosters a fully embodied, integrated selflessness that makes individuals not only more empathic to the needs of others, nature, and the world, but also more effective cultural and planetary transformative agents in whatever contexts and measure life or the mystery calls them to be.

This account of spiritual individuation is, I believe, consistent with M. Daniels's intuition that spiritual realization will be different for different people. If human beings are considered *unique* embodiments of the mystery, would it not be natural that as they spiritually individuate, their spiritual realizations might be distinct even if they could be aligned with each other and potentially overlap in different regards?[30] After affirming a participatory account of spirituality that welcomes a multiplicity of paths, Hollick (2006) wrote:

> It is tempting to suggest that "balanced" spiritual growth would see each of us develop more or less equally along each path. . . . But I don't think that's how it works. We are all unique, and carve out our unique combinations of paths toward our unique revelation of Spirit. (p. 354)

To conclude, from a participatory perspective, Wilber's nondual realization can be seen as one among many other spiritual enactions—one that is not entirely holistic from any contemporary perspective recognizing the equal spiritual import of both consciousness and energy, both transcendent and immanent spiritual sources. I suggest that the cultivation of spiritual individuation—possibly regulated by something like the integral *bodhisattva* vow to minimize the pitfalls of past spiritualities—may be more effective than traditional paths to enlightenment in promoting not only the fully harmonious development of the person but also holistic spiritual realizations. This may be so because most traditional contemplative paths cultivate a disembodied, and potentially dissociative, spirituality even while providing access to such spiritual heights as classical mystical visions, ecstatic unions, and absorptions. Reasonably, one might ask whether the path of spiritual individuation may render such spiritual heights less likely—perhaps—but I wonder aloud whether the current individual, relational, social, and ecological predicament calls to sacrifice some height for breadth (and arguably depth). Put bluntly, in general it may be preferable today to shift the focus from those spiritual heights in order to "horizontalize," or pursue spiritual depths in the nitty-gritty of embodied existence. Even if slowly and making mistakes, I personally choose to walk toward such uncharted integral horizons rather than the road more traveled of disembodied spirituality.

CONCLUSION

In closing, three directions may be particularly productive in moving this dialogue forward. First, it may be important for Wilber to unpack more explicitly the ontological implications of his integral postmetaphysics. In particular, I wonder whether he truly meant to relegate spiritual realities to the individual's interiors, or whether this is an unintended upshot of his seeking to avoid the pitfalls of classical metaphysical systems. In addition, it is not clear whether he believes that all spiritual realities and entities are human cocreations or whether he is leaving room for the possibility that some may (co-)exist autonomously.

Second, transpersonal scholars may want to scrutinize the neo-Kantian assumptions lying beneath agnosticism toward the extraphysical and extrapsychological ontological status of spiritual realities (see chapter 2). I believe it is fundamental to be aware that such a stance, far from warranting neutrality or impartiality, is the fruit of a modern, Western, and dualistic epistemological ethos that automatically renders suspect mystical claims about the nature of knowledge and reality. In their noble attempts to promote the scientific legitimacy of the field, some transpersonal psychologists—from Washburn (1995) to Friedman (2002, 2013a) to M. M. Daniels (2001, 2005)—may have prematurely committed to a neo-Kantian dualistic epistemology that is in fact ideologically tied to a naturalistic, and often materialistic, metaphysics. Whether such a naturalistic worldview will ultimately be cogent is unknown (I strongly suspect it will not), but transpersonal scholars should be able to recognize and make explicit the metaphysical presuppositions implicit in such methodological agnosticism; in this way, they can avoid assuming or defending its purportedly scientific, metaphysically neutral status and thereby falling prey to one of science's most prevalent ideologies (van Fraassen, 2002).

Finally, I firmly believe that both the scholarly credibility and future relevance of transpersonal psychology will be enhanced by a more thorough discernment of the merits and shortcomings of past spiritual endeavors, a discontinuation of the common transpersonal practice of mystifying the mystics, and the undertaking of a critical exploration of the types of spiritual understandings and practices that may be most appropriate for the contemporary global situation.

TEN

RELIGIOUS PLURALISM AND THE

FUTURE OF RELIGION

Religious globalization, new religious movements, transnational religions, global proselytism, old and new fundamentalisms, religious violence, multiple religious identities, ecumenical services, religious syncretism, secular and postsecular spiritualities—all these are among the many remarkable trends that shape the religious landscape of the beginning of the twenty-first century. Despite the rampant materialism still dominant in an increasingly technocratic world, it is clear that these are times of rich spiritual diversity, proliferation, and innovation. For instance, when David B. Barrett, the main editor of the massive *World Christian Encyclopedia* (Barrett, Kurian, & Johnson, 2001), was asked what he had learnt about religious change in the world after several decades of research, he responded with the following: "We have identified nine thousand and nine hundred distinct and separate religions in the world, increasing by two or three religions every day" (as cited in Lester, 2002, p. 28). Although there may be something to celebrate in this spiritual cornucopia, it is also clear that the many conflicting religious visions of reality and human nature are a major cause of the prevailing skepticism toward religious and spiritual truth claims. Against the background of modernist assumptions about a singular objective reality, it is under-standable that the presence of a plurality of mutually exclusive accounts leads to the confident dismissal of religious explanations. It is as if con-temporary culture has succumbed to the Cartesian anxiety behind what W. E. Hocking (1956) called the "scandal of plurality," the worry that "if there are so many divergent claims to ultimate truth, then perhaps none is right" (J. J. Clarke, 1997, p. 134).[1]

This competitive predicament among religious beliefs is not only a philosophical or existential problem; it has also has profoundly affected how people from different credos engage one another and, even today, plays an important role in many interreligious conflicts, quarrels, and even holy wars. Although it would be naive to claim that these conflicts are mostly driven by competitive religious sentiments (economic, political, ethnic, and social issues are often primary), the rhetoric of religious exclusivism or superiority is widely used to fuel fundamentalist attitudes and justify interreligious violence across the globe. As Sen (2006) compellingly argued, exclusive religious identities are often exploited to perpetuate violence and religion-based terrorism—after all, it is much easier to kill your neighbor when you believe that God is on your side. The theologian Küng (1988) famously said that there can be "no world peace without peace among religions" (p. 194), to which I would add, "There might not be complete peace among religions without ending the competition among religions."

Typical responses to the scandal of religious plurality tend to fall along a continuum between two drastically opposite positions. At one end of the spectrum, materialistic, scientifically minded, and "nonreligionist" scholars retort to the plurality of religious world views to downplay or dismiss altogether the cognitive value of religious knowledge claims, regarding religions as cultural fabrications that, like art pieces or culinary dishes, can be extremely diverse and even personally edifying but never the bearers of any "objective" truth whatsoever (e.g., Rorty, 1998). At the other end, spiritual practitioners, theologians, and "religionist" scholars vigorously defend the cognitive value of religion, addressing the problem of religious pluralism by either endorsing the exclusive (or ultimately superior) truth of their preferred tradition or developing universalist understandings that seek to reconcile the conflicting spiritual truths within one or another encompassing system. Despite their professed integrative stance, most universalist visions of human spirituality tend to distort the essential message of the various religious traditions, hierarchically favoring certain spiritual truths over others and raising serious obstacles for interreligious relations, open-ended spiritual inquiry, and social harmony (Ferrer, 2002).

My intention in this chapter is to first uncover the spiritual narcissism characteristic of the prevalent historical approach to religious diversity, as well as briefly discuss the shortcomings of the main forms of religious pluralism that have been proposed as its antidote. Then I introduce a participatory pluralistic approach to the understanding of religion,[2] showing how it can provide a fresh appreciation of religious diversity that avoids the dogmatism and competitiveness involved in privileging any particular tradition over the rest without falling into cultural-linguistic or naturalistic reductionisms. In addition, I offer some practical orientations to assess the validity of spiritual truths and outline the contours of a participatory critical theory of religion. In the second part of the chapter, I explore different scenarios for the future or religion and suggest that a participatory approach to religion not only fosters spiritual individuation in the context of a common human spiritual family, but also turns the problem of religious plurality into a critical celebration of the spirit of pluralism.[3]

UNCOVERING SPIRITUAL NARCISSISM

A few marginal voices notwithstanding (Lings & Minnaar, 2007; Oldmeadow, 2004; Stoddart, 2008), the search for a common core, universal essence, or single metaphysical world behind the multiplicity of religious experiences and cosmologies can be regarded as over. Whether guided by the exclusivist intuitionism of traditionalism or the fideism of theological agendas, the outcome—and too often the intended goal—of such universalist projects was unambiguous: the privileging of one particular spiritual or religious system over all others. In addition to universalism, the other attempts to explain religious divergences have typically taken one of the three following routes: exclusivism ("my religion is the only true one, the rest are false"), inclusivism ("my religion is the most accurate or complete, the rest are lower or partial"), and ecumenical pluralism ("there may be real differences between our religions, but all lead ultimately to the same end").

The many problems of religious exclusivism are well known. It easily fosters religious intolerance, fundamentalist tendencies, and prevents a reciprocal and symmetrical encounter with the other where divergent spiritual viewpoints may be regarded as enriching options or genuine alternatives. In the wake of the scope of contemporary religious diversity, the defense of the absolute cognitive superiority of one single tradition over all others is more dubious than ever. Inclusivist and ecumenically pluralist approaches suffer from similar difficulties in that they tend to conceal claims for the supremacy of one or another religious tradition, ultimately collapsing into the dogmatism of exclusivist stances (Ferrer, 2002; Halbfass, 1998). Consider, for example, the Dalai Lama's defense of the need of a plurality of religions. While celebrating the existence of different religions to accommodate the diversity of human karmic dispositions, he contends that final spiritual liberation can only be achieved through the emptiness practices of his own Gelukpa school of Tibetan Buddhism, implicitly situating all other spiritual choices as lower—a view that he believes all other Buddhists and religious people will eventually accept (D'Costa, 2000). Other examples of inclusivist approaches include such diverse proposals as Kukai's ranking of Confucian, Taoist, and Buddhist systems as progressive stages toward his own Shingon Buddhism (Hakeda, 1972); Swami Vivekananda's proclamation of (neo-)Vedanta as the universal "eternal religion" (*sanatana dharma*) that uniquely encompasses all others (Halbfass, 1988); the Baha'i belief in its representing the last and highest, although not final, revelation of a succession of religions (Coward, 2000);[4] and Wilber's (1995) arrangement of all religious goals as hierarchical stages of spiritual development culminating in his own articulation of a nondual realization (see chapter 9).

I propose the various approaches to religious diversity—exclusivism, inclusivism, and ecumenical pluralism (more about the latter in a moment)—can be situated along a continuum ranging from more gross to more subtle forms of *spiritual narcissism*, which ultimately elevate one's favored tradition or spiritual choice as superior. That the Dalai Lama himself, arguably a paragon of spiritual humility and openmindedness, holds this view strongly suggests that spiritual narcissism is not necessarily associated with a narcissistic personality but rather a deeply seated tendency buried in the collective realms of the human unconscious. Commenting on this point, Lahood (2015) observed, "it is highly likely that ethnocentricity—the culturally inculcated or indoctrinated belief in religious superiority—contributes to this pervasive tendency" (p. 25).

In any event, the bottom line is that, explicitly or implicitly, religious traditions and schools have persistently looked down upon one another, each believing that their truth is more complete or final, and that their path is the only or most effective one to achieve full salvation or enlightenment. The next section examines several types of religious pluralism that have been proposed in response to this disconcerting situation.

THE VARIETIES OF RELIGIOUS PLURALISM

Religious pluralism comes in many guises and fashions. Before suggesting a participatory remedy to the prevalent spiritual narcissism in dealing with religious difference, I critically review here four major types of religious pluralism: ecumenical, soteriological, postmodern, and metaphysical.[5]

Ecumenical pluralism admits genuine differences among religious beliefs and practices, but maintains that they all ultimately lead to the same end (e.g., Hick, 1989; Hick & Knitter, 1987). The problem with this apparently tolerant stance is that, whenever its proponents describe such a religious goal, they invariably do it in terms that favor one or another specific tradition (e.g., God, the transcendently Real, emptiness). This is why ecumenical pluralism not only degenerates into exclusivist or inclusivist stances, but also trivializes the encounter with "the other" (cf. McGrane, 1989)—after all, what is really the point of engaging in interfaith exchange if practitioners already know that they are all heading toward the same goal? A classical example of this stance is Rahner's (2001) famous proposal that devoted practitioners of other religions could attain salvation by walking different paths because, although unknown to them, they are "anonymous Christians" who are delivered through God's grace. Students of religion have pointed out the contradictions of pluralistic approaches that postulate an equivalent end point for all traditions for decades (Cobb, 1975, 1999; D'Costa, 1990; Nah, 2013; Panikkar, 1987, 1995). A genuine religious pluralism, it is today widely accepted, needs to acknowledge the existence of alternative religious aims, and putting all religions on a single scale will not do it.[6]

In response to these concerns, some scholars have proposed a *soteriological pluralism* that envisions a multiplicity of irreducible transformative or experiential goals associated with the various religious traditions (e.g., Heim, 1995; LaFargue, 1992). Due to their diverse ultimate visions of reality and personhood, religious traditions stress the cultivation of particular human potentials or competences (e.g., access to visionary worlds, mind/body integration, expansion of consciousness, overcoming of suffering), which naturally leads to distinct human transformations and states of freedom or fulfillment. A variant of this approach is the postulation of a limited number of independent but equiprimordial religious goals and conceptually possible ultimate realities, for example, theism (in its various forms), monistic nondualism (à la Advaita Vedanta), and process nondualism (as in Yogacara Buddhism; Kaplan, 2002).

The soteriological approach to religious difference, however, remains agnostic about the ontological status of spiritual realities, being therefore pluralistic only at a phenomenological level (i.e., admitting different human spiritual fulfillments), but not at an ontological or metaphysical one (i.e., at the level of spiritual realities). For example, although discussing several possibilities, Heim (1995) is uncertain about the metaphysical vision behind his "more pluralistic hypothesis" (p. 146) and ultimately slipped back to an objectivist and representational account of spiritual truth as universal and pregiven: "Among the various religions," he stated, "one or several or none may provide the best approximate representation of the character of that cosmos, explaining and ordering these various human possibilities within it" (p. 215). This relapse is also evident when, after comparing the different religious ends to different cities, he wrote, "I regard these cities as sites within a single world, whose global mapping has a determinate character" (p. 220).

The combination of pluralism and metaphysical agnosticism is also a chief feature of the *postmodern* solution to the problem of conflicting truth claims in religion. The translation of religious realities into cultural-linguistic fabrications allows postmodern scholars to explain interreligious differences as the predictable upshot of the world's various religious beliefs, practices, and language games (Cupitt, 1998; Flood, 1999). In other words, the various gods and goddesses, spirits and ancestors, archetypes and visionary worlds, are nothing but discursive entities (Braun, 2000). Postmodern pluralism denies or brackets the ontological status of the referents of religious language, which are usually seen as meaningless, obscure, or parasitic upon the despotic dogmatism of traditional religious metaphysics. Further, even if such spiritual realities were to exist, the human cognitive apparatus would only allow knowing the culturally and linguistically mediated experience of them (e.g., Katz, 1988). Postmodern pluralism recognizes a genuine plurality of religious goals, but at the cost of either stripping religious claims of any extralinguistic veridicality or denying that such truths can be known even if they exist.

A notable exception to this trend is the *metaphysical* or *deep pluralism* advocated by a number of process theologians (Cobb, 1999; Griffin, 2005). Relying on Whitehead's distinction between "God's unchanging Being" and "God's changing Becoming," this proposal defends the existence of two ontological or metaphysical religious ultimates to which the various traditions are geared: God, which corresponds to the Biblical Yaveh, the Buddhist Sambhogakaya, and Advaita Vedanta's Saguna Brahman; and Creativity, which corresponds to Meister Eckhart's Godhead, the Buddhist emptiness and Dharmakaya, and Advaita Vedanta's Nirguna Brahman. A third possible ultimate, the cosmos itself, is at times added in connection to Taoism and Indigenous spiritualities that venerate the sacredness of the natural world. In addition to operating within a theistic framework adverse to many traditions, however, deep pluralism not only establishes highly dubious equivalencies among religious goals (e.g., Buddhist emptiness and Advaita's Nirguna Brahman), but also forces the rich diversity of religious ultimates into the arguably Procrustean theistic molds of God's "unchanging Being" and "changing Becoming."

PARTICIPATORY RELIGIOUS PLURALISM

Can the plurality of religions be taken seriously today without reducing them to either cultural-linguistic byproducts or incomplete facets of a single spiritual truth or universe? Is it really possible to avoid both spiritual narcissism (i.e., sectarianism) and relativism when asserting anything minimally generic about human spirituality? Can one even make such assertions beyond the confines of a specific local religious community or group? Can sectarianism be avoided without resorting to either (1) an ideological neo-perennialism that hides exclusivist claims or (2) an individualistic or cultural relativism that not only banalizes real differences, but also offers no grounds for the critique of oppressive, patriarchal, or eco-pernicious spiritualities? I believe that the above aspirations are (largely) achievable and, together with a number of scholars in the field of religious studies, I have called this third way possible the "participatory turn" in the study of religion and spirituality (Ferrer & Sherman, 2008a, 2008b).

The participatory turn argues for an understanding of the sacred that approaches religious phenomena, experiences, and insights as *cocreated* events. Such events can engage the entire range of human faculties (e.g., rational, imaginal, somatic, aesthetic, contemplative) with the creative unfolding of reality or the mystery in the enactment—or "bringing forth"—of ontologically rich religious worlds. Put somewhat differently, I suggest that religious and spiritual phenomena are participatory in the sense that they can emerge from the interaction of all human attributes and an undetermined mystery or creative dynamism of life or the cosmos. More specifically, I propose that religious worlds and phenomena—such as the Kabbalistic four realms, the various Buddhist cosmologies, or Teresa's seven mansions—come into existence out of a process of *participatory cocreation* between human multidimensional cognition, the possible agency of subtle entities or energies, and the generative force of life, reality, or the cosmos.

But, how far is it feasible to go in affirming the cocreative role of the human in spiritual matters? To be sure, today most scholars may be ready to allow that particular spiritual states (e.g., the Buddhist *jhanas,*

Teresa's mansions, or the various yogi *samadhis*), spiritual visions (e.g., Ezekiel's Divine Chariot, Hildegard's visionary experience of the Trinity, or Black Elk's Great Vision), and spiritual landscapes or cosmologies (e.g., the Buddhist Pure Lands, the Heavenly Halls of Merkavah mysticism, or the diverse astral domains posited by Western esoteric schools) are largely or entirely constructed. Nevertheless, I suspect that many religious scholars and practitioners may feel more reticent in the case of spiritual entities (such as the Tibetan *dakinis*, the Christian angels, or the various Gods and Goddesses of the Hindu pantheon) and, in particular, in the case of ultimate principles and personae (such as the Biblical Yaveh, the Buddhist *sunyata*, or the Hindu Brahman). Would not accepting their cocreated nature undermine not only the claims of most traditions, but also the very ontological autonomy and integrity of the mystery itself? Response: Given the rich variety of incompatible spiritual ultimates and the aporias involved in any conciliatory strategy, I submit that it is only by promoting the cocreative role of human cognition to the very heart and summit of each spiritual universe that the ultimate unity of the mystery can be preserved—otherwise, an arguably equally unsatisfactory alternative emerges, forcing one to either reduce spiritual universes to fabrications of the human imagination or posit an indefinite number of isolated spiritual universes. By conceiving spiritual worlds *and* ultimates as the outcome of a process of participatory cocreation between human multidimensional cognition and an undetermined creative power, however, one rescues the ultimate unity of the mystery while simultaneously affirming its ontological richness and overcoming the reductionisms of cultural-linguistic, psychological, and biologically naturalistic explanations of religion.

As I discuss in chapter 9, however, this account is not equivalent to saying that all subtle worlds and entities are the byproducts of bio-psycho-socially shaped human subjectivities. On the one hand, the participatory approach regards human beings as a nexus for the creative encounter of the transcendent and immanent sources of the mystery, turning human embodied subjectivity into a potential channel for the mystery's ontological urges (see chapters 3 and 5). On the other hand, autonomous nonhuman entities composed of energy and consciousness may exist, as well as participate in the cocreation of subtle worlds, both independently and through interaction with human enactive powers (see chapters 2 and 9). The participatory approach thus travels a precisely delineated path that avoids both reductionism and anthropomorphism.

As for the various spiritual ultimates described by the world's religious traditions, I contend that they can be cocreated through intentional or spontaneous participation in an undetermined mystery or generative force of life or reality. This participatory perspective does not contend that there are two, three, or any limited quantity of pregiven spiritual ultimates, but rather that the radical openness, interrelatedness, and creativity of the mystery or the cosmos allows for the participatory cocreation of an indefinite number of self-disclosures of reality, spiritual ultimates, and subtle worlds. These worlds are not statically closed; rather, they are fundamentally dynamic and open to the continued transformation resulting (at least in part) from the creative impact of human visionary imagination and religious endeavors.

In the context of the dilemmas posed by religious pluralism, one of the advantages of a participatory account of spiritual knowing is that it frees religious thinking from the presupposition of a single, predetermined ultimate reality that binds it to reductionistic, exclusivist, or dogmatic formulations (Ferrer, 2002, 2008). Once this assumption is dropped, on the one hand, and the ontologically creative role of spiritual cognition is recognized, on the other, the multiplicity of religious truth claims stops being a source of metaphysical skepticism and becomes entirely natural, perhaps even essential. If the various spiritual ultimates are conceived not as competing to match a pregiven spiritual referent but as creative transformations of an undetermined mystery, then the conflict over claims of alternative religious truths vanishes like a mirage. As Ogilvy (2013) stated in relation to my early work (Ferrer, 2002), this "newer, stronger pluralism . . . gives to the gods their sacred due, even as it widens the field for possible reverence" (p. 45).[7] Indeed, rather than being a source of conflict or a cause for considerate tolerance, the diversity of spiritual truths and cosmologies becomes here a reason for wonder and celebration—wonder inspired by the inexhaustible creative power of the mystery and celebration of the human participatory role in such creativity, as well as of the emerging possibilities for mutual enrichment that arise out of the encounter of traditions. Discussing participatory pluralism as an alternative to Tibetan Buddhist inclusivism, Duckworth (2014a) concluded:

> His [Ferrer's] most significant contribution may be in illustrating what a "nonsectarian" stance might look like in a contemporary, religiously diverse world. While doing so, he shows us what is lost, and what is gained, if we adopt such a truly "nonsectarian" or pluralist stance: what we stand to lose is our particular version of a determinate ultimate truth and a fixed referent of what the end religious goal looks like;

what we stand to gain is the real possibility of a transformative dialogue with different traditions, and a new, open relation to the world, ourselves, and each other. (p. 347)

In short, a participatory approach to religion seeks to enact with body, mind, heart, and consciousness a creative spirituality that lets a thousand spiritual flowers bloom.

Although this inclusiveness may at first sound like a rather "anything goes" approach to religious claims, I hold to the contrary that recognizing a diversity of cocreated religious worlds in fact asks both scholars and practitioners to be more perspicuous in discerning their differences and merits. Because such worlds are not simply given but involve human beings as agents and cocreators, individuals are not off the ethical hook where religion is concerned but instead inevitably make cosmo-political and moral choices in all their religious actions. As I discuss in chapter 1, ethical considerations are crucial, especially in light of the demonstrably pernicious ecological, political, and social impact many religions have historically had—and continue to have today (e.g., Ghanea-Hercock, 2010; Juergensmeyer, 2000; L. E. Nelson, 1998a).[8]

It cannot be stressed strongly enough that rejecting a pregiven spiritual ultimate referent does not prevent one from making qualitative distinctions in spiritual matters. To be sure, like beautiful porcelains made out of amorphous clay, traditions cannot be qualitatively ranked according to their accuracy in representing some imagined (accessible or inaccessible) original template. However, this account does not mean discernment cannot be cultivated regarding more (or less) evocative, skillful, or sophisticated artifacts.

Qualitative distinctions are fundamental, both intra- and inter-religiously. At their mystical core, most traditions teach a path going from an initial state of suffering, alienation, or delusion to one of happiness, salvation, or enlightenment. In an *intrareligious context*, qualitative distinctions (e.g., among various stages or states of the path) can offer valuable signposts for practitioners insofar as they confirm being on the right track, alert regarding stage-specific pitfalls, and so forth. Therefore, although a strict allegiance to stage models can potentially constrain the organic unfolding of one's unique spiritual potentials (Ferrer, 2002, 2014b, 2015; Rothberg, 1996), I do not see any major problem with such models in the context of specific traditions that aim at the gradual attainment of a particular spiritual goal.[9] Rather, problems emerge when one seeks to make the stages of a particular spiritual tradition (say,

Tibetan Buddhism or Christianity) or spiritual orientation (e.g., theistic, nondual, monist) paradigmatic for all. Whether naively or intentionally carried out, the consistent upshot of this move is the privileging of one's preferred spiritual tradition or orientation above all others (e.g., Stoeber, 1994; Wilber, 1995, 2006; Zaehner, 1957/1980)—an attitude I discussed above in terms of *spiritual narcissism*. In any event, generally speaking, it seems important (and common sense) to acknowledge that a novice Buddhist monk's understanding of emptiness (*sunyata*) is most likely not as complete or sophisticated as the Dalai Lama's (although one must remember Suzuki's [1970] famous claim, in the context of Soto Zen, that the beginner's mind is closer to enlightenment than that of a seasoned practitioner).

In an *interreligious context*, qualitative differences among traditions can also be observed, and this is important—from both "positive" and "negative" angles. In a "positive" light, for example, some traditions may have developed contemplative awareness more than others; the same could be said about psychophysical integration, emotional intelligence, social service, or eco-spiritual understandings and practices fostering a harmonious relationship with nature. In a "negative" light, some traditions may be more prey than others to somatic dissociation, sexual repression, class and gender oppression, religious fanaticism and violence, or ecological blindness, among others. The fact that different traditions have cultivated different human potentials is part of what makes interreligious cross-fertilization fruitful and, arguably, crucial for the development of more integral spiritual understandings and practices.

Whereas the participatory turn renders meaningless the postulation of qualitative distinctions among traditions according to a priori doctrines or a prearranged hierarchy of spiritual insights, these comparative grounds can be sought in a variety of practical fruits anchored around the three basic tests introduced in chapter 1 of this book: the *egocentrism test* (i.e., to what extent does a spiritual path, insight, or practice free its practitioners from gross and subtle forms of narcissism and self-centeredness?), the *dissociation test* (i.e., to what extent does a spiritual path, insight, or practice foster the integrated blossoming of all dimensions of the person?), and the *eco-socio-political test* (i.e., to what extent do spiritual systems foster ecological balance, social and economic justice, religious and political freedom, class and gender equality, and other fundamental human rights?). As I see it, this approach invites a more nuanced, contextual, and complex evaluation of religious claims based on the recognition that traditions, like human beings, are likely to be both "higher" and "lower" in relation to one another, but *in different regards* (e.g., fostering contemplative competences, ecological sustainability, mind/body integration). It is important then not to understand the ideal of a reciprocal and symmetrical encounter among traditions in terms of a trivializing or relativistic egalitarianism (McGrane, 1989). By contrast, a truly symmetrical encounter can only take place when practitioners and traditions open themselves to teach and be taught, fertilize and be fertilized, transform and be transformed.

It is probably sensible to supplement these orientations with not only a sharp cultural and contextual sensitivity, but also with a *retrospective test*, which alludes to the likely need—at least in certain cases—of allowing the passage of time before assessing the actual fruits of specific spiritual paths and insights. This consideration seems crucial, especially in light of certain dynamics of psychospiritual development, for example, cases in which (due to either biographical factors or intrinsic features of particular processes of spiritual opening) states or stages of self-inflation or even extreme dissociation may be a necessary step in the path toward overcoming narcissism and achieving a genuinely integrated selflessness (see Almaas, 1996; D. Anthony, Naranjo, Deikman, Fireman, Hastings, & Reisman, 1987; Rosenthal, 1987).[10]

In any event, the embodied and eco-socio-politically engaged impetus of the participatory turn is foundational for the development of a participatory critical theory of religion (see chapters 1 and 3). The participatory approach does not seek to chastise past spiritualities, which may have been at times—though by no means always—legitimate and perhaps even necessary in their particular times and contexts. Leaving history to itself, I propose that any ethically responsible contemporary approach to spirituality and religion needs to be critical of oppressive, repressive, and dissociative religious beliefs, attitudes, practices, and institutional dynamics.

THE FUTURE OF RELIGION: FOUR SCENARIOS

In light of the previous discussion, I ponder now on the future of world religion and spirituality. Where is the world heading religiously speaking? Will humanity ultimately converge into one single religious credo? Or will it, rather, continue to diversify into countless forms of spiritual expression often at odds with one another? Alternatively, can a middle path be envisioned capable of reconciling the human longing for spiritual unity, on the one hand, and the developmental and evolutionary pulls toward spiritual individuation and differentiation, on the other? I believe that it can, and in the second part of this chapter I offer the contours of such a vision after considering four other scenarios for the future of world religion.

A Global Religion

The first scenario portrays the emergence of a single world faith for humankind.[11] This global religion may stem from either (1) the triumph of one spiritual tradition over the rest (e.g., Catholic Christianity or the Dalai Lama's school of Tibetan Buddhism) or (2) some kind of synthesis of many or most traditions (e.g., New Age spiritual universalism). The former possibility, historically the ambition of most religions, entails the unlikely prospect that religious practitioners—except those from the "winning" tradition—would recognize the erroneous or partial nature of their beliefs and embrace the superior truth of an already existent tradition. Intrareligious diversity problematizes this scenario further: since the various Buddhist schools (for example) diverge on central questions of both doctrine and practice (e.g., Chen, 1972; Faure, 2009; Tenzin Gyatso, 1988), the real candidate here would not be Buddhism per se, but a particular Buddhist branch. The latter possibility means that most or all traditions would ultimately come together or be integrated—whether in an evolutionary, hierarchical, systemic, or perspectival fashion—into one world faith embraced by all religious people, perhaps as the ultimate upshot of increased interreligious interaction (e.g., Braybrooke, 1998). The dream of a global spirituality, however ecumenically or ideologically conceived, inspires spiritual sensibilities at work in such diverse spheres as interfaith dialogue, transpersonal psychology and integral theory, and many new religious movements.

Mutual Transformation of Religions

In this scenario, the various religious traditions conserve their identity, but are deeply and endlessly transformed through a variety of inter-religious exchanges and interactions (Cobb, 1996; Streng, 1993). The distinctive feature here is that, as the Jesuit thinker Teilhard de Chardin believed, religious cross-pollination will lead to spiritual "creative unions in which diversity is not erased but rather intensified" (Cousins, 1992, p. 8). This vision is consistent with not only the adoption of practices from other traditions by members of different faith communities (e.g.,

Gross & Muck, 2003), but also the deepening or reenvisioning of one's own tradition in light of other religious perspectives (e.g., Ingram & Streng, 2007)—a phenomenon that, when mutual, was aptly described by Sharma (2005) in terms of reciprocal illumination. A historical precursor of this possibility can be found in religious syncretism (i.e., the mixture or two or more traditions), such as the Haitian Vodou's blending of Christianity and African traditions (Bellegarde-Smith & Michel, 2006) or the Brazilian Santo Daime Church's incorporation of the Indigenous use of ayahuasca into a Christian container (Dawson, 2013). Today this religious cross-fertilization is visibly taking place in the interfaith dialogue, the New Age movement, and a legion of eclectic and integrative spiritual groups.

Within this scenario I also locate the growing phenomenon of multiple religious participation (Berthrong, 1999), in which an individual partakes in the practices and belief systems of more than one tradition, leading to a "multiple" or "hyphenated religious identity," such as Jewish-Buddhist, Hindu-Christian, Buddhist-Taoist, and so forth (for a participatory account of this phenomenon, see Bidwell, 2015). Also related to this picture is the ongoing renewal of many religious traditions through cross-cultural encounters, a trend that can be discerned in contemporary American Buddhism, neo-Hindu applied spiritualities, and the novel social understandings of salvation in Asia influenced by Western values (P. B. Clarke, 2006). What is more, some sociologists claim that this phenomenon may also be impacting secular culture. This is the gist of Campbell's (1999) Easternization thesis, according to which the West is changing its ethos via the importation of Eastern religions and adopting Eastern ideas and practices such as interconnectedness, reincarnation, or meditation (see also Bruce, 2002; Hamilton, 2002). An increasingly fashionable way to speak of all these richly transformative interactions, taken today by many to be historically normative, is in terms of a *cosmological hybridization* (Lahood, 2008) that is not only doctrinal (of spiritual teaching and beliefs), but also sometimes practical (of spiritual techniques) and even visionary (of spiritual ontologies and cosmologies). "We are all hybrids," is the new motto of this emerging spiritual ethos.

Interspiritual Wisdom

A third scenario stems from the affirmation or emergence of a number of spiritual principles, teachings, or values endorsed by all religious groups and traditions. Küng's (1991) proposal for a global ethics heralded this possibility, but it was the late Christian author Teasdale (1999) who offered its most compelling articulation in terms of a universal mysticism grounded in the practice of "interspirituality" or "the sharing of ultimate experiences across traditions" (p. 26). Specifically, Teasdale identified nine elements of such interspiritual wisdom: moral capacity, solidarity with all living beings, deep nonviolence, spiritual practice, humility, mature self-knowledge, simplicity of life, selfless service and compassionate action, and prophetic voice. Although seeking to avoid the homogenization of traditions into one single global religion, Teasdale used the traditional metaphor of the blind men and the elephant to convey his perspectival account of a given ultimate reality of which all religions have partial perceptions that nonetheless constitute paths leading to the same summit. Developing a similar intuition but eschewing Teasdale's objectivist assumptions is Lanzetta's (2007) recent proposal for an "intercontemplative" global spirituality that affirms the interdependence of spiritual principles and can "give birth to new traditions and spiritual paths in the crucible of dialogue" (p. 118). Also related is Forman's (2004) articulation of a trans-traditional spirituality that feeds on the teachings of all religious traditions but is not restricted by the confines of any particular credo.

Spirituality without Religion

This scenario comprises an impressive number of contemporary developments—from secular to postmodern and from naturalistic to New Age spiritualities—that advocate for the cultivation of a spiritual life free from traditional religious dogmas or supernatural beliefs (e.g., Caputo, 2001; Cupitt, 1997; Elkins, 1998; Heelas & Woodhead, 2005; Van Ness, 1996). In a way, this scenario is the predictable outcome of the confluence of two different sociocultural processes in the (post-)modern West: the *secularization* of traditional religious authority on the one hand, and the *re-sacralization* of self, nature, and the cosmos, on the other. In this postsecular context, adhesion to one or another form or "spirituality without religion" becomes an essential self-identification strategy—conscious, semiconscious, or unconscious—to minimize the cognitive dissonance (Cooper, 2007) stemming from (1) re-enchanting subjective life and world, while simultaneously (2) feeling that one may be regressing to problematically perceived, past religious attitudes (e.g., dogmatic faith, religious exclusivism, patriarchal authoritarianism).

Two prominent trends here are postmodern spiritualities and the New Age movement. Although the former rejects or remains agnostic about supernatural or metaphysical sources of religion and the latter tends to uncritically accept them, both join hands in their affirmation of the primacy of individual choice and experience, as well as in their criticism of many received religious dogmas and authoritarian institutions. Calls for a democratization of spirituality (Tacey, 2004), a direct path to the divine (A. Harvey, 2002), or the reclaiming of individual, inner spiritual authority (Heron, 2006) are intimately linked with these developments. I also locate here scholarly spiritualities that combine experiential participation and critical reason (e.g., Ferrer & Sherman, 2008b; Kripal, 2001; Neville, 2002), most forms of religious naturalism (e.g., Kauffman, 2008), modern religious quests (Roof, 2001), secular surrogates for religion (Ziolkowski, 2007), postsecular spiritualities (e.g., M. King, 2009), and proposals for a humanizing spirituality (Lesser, 1999). Expressions such as "spiritual but not religious" (Fuller, 2001; Mercadante, 2014), "religion without religion" (Caputo, 1997), "religion of no religion" (Kripal, 2007), and "believing without belonging" (C. Taylor, 2007) capture well the essential character of this orientation. The works of Harris (2014) and T. Moore (2014) offer two recent accounts of this increasingly prevalent approach.[12]

A PARTICIPATORY VISION OF THE
FUTURE OF RELIGION

As should be obvious, with the possible exception of a hegemonic global religion, the above scenarios are not mutually exclusive, and it is likely that they will all become key players in shaping the future of world religion in the next millennium. And yet, there is something intuitively appealing in the search for spiritual unity, and here I would like to outline how a participatory perspective addresses this concern while avoiding spiritual narcissism and without hampering the arguably wholesome impulses toward religious diversification and spiritual individuation at play in contemporary times.

To embrace human beings' participatory role in spiritual knowing may lead to a shift from searching for spiritual unity in a global religion organized around a single vision to recognizing an already existent spiritual human family that branches out in numerous directions from the same creative source. If spiritual diversification is taken as a positive, then the whole dream of a global religion becomes both illusory and misleading. Religious people may instead be able to find their longed-for unity not so much in an all-encompassing megasystem or super-religion, but in their common roots—that is, in that deep bond constituted by the undetermined creative power of spirit, life, or the cosmos in which all traditions participate in the bringing forth of their spiritual insights and cosmologies. The recognition of these shared roots naturally paves the way for a global approach to religious diversity that preserves a deep sense of communion across differences.[13]

An important practical consequence of this approach is that, if religious people were to adopt it, they could then, like members of a healthy family, stop attempting to impose their particular beliefs on others and might instead become a supportive force for practitioners' spiritual individuation both within and outside their traditions. This mutual empowerment of spiritual creativity may lead to the emergence not only of a human community formed by fully differentiated spiritual individuals, but also of a rich variety of coherent spiritual perspectives that can be potentially equally aligned or attuned to the mystery (for discussions of this equiplurality principle, see chapters 1 and 9).

In a significant work, Dale (2014) recently illuminated this pluralistic-participatory vision of the future of religion. After considering the possible convergence of religions, Dale presented an alternative view "in which religions achieve shared knowledge of the nature of spiritual reality through the diversification of dogmas, practices, and experiences rather than through their convergence" (p. 258). In this scenario, spiritual convergence will not be achieved through any kind of perennialist synthesis or underlying spiritual meta-ultimate, but rather through "the coordination of the knowledge that arises from multiple viewpoints" (p. 262). Paradoxically, spiritual diversification might lead to shared spiritual knowledge, because "it is through the coordination of divergent viewpoints that the fullest overall picture of spiritual reality or spiritual realities is possible" (p. 281). Whereas I feel enthusiastic about the implications of Dale's coordination approach for interreligious relations, I worry that holding the "superior" tradition as the one able to include all others brings back a problematic perennialist inclusivism, in which a single tradition (with its favored spiritual ultimate) claims to encompass all others, but not vice versa (cf. Duckworth, 2014a; Ferrer, 2002; Halbfass, 1991).[14] Perhaps an emerging, plural, global spirituality might be in the future capable of coordinating all spiritual viewpoints without falling into such ideological traps, but I take this ideal to be more regulative than practically reachable.

In this context, different spiritual perspectives can mutually illuminate and transform one another through unlimited doctrinal, practical,
existential, and visionary hybridizations. Doctrinally, teachings from different religious traditions can not only complement each other, but also
provide rich resources for the deepening of traditions' self-understanding
(e.g., Barnhart & Wong, 2001; Sharma, 2005). On a practical level,
traditions may eventually move from simple exchange among existing
spiritual practices (e.g., Buddhists practicing prayer, Christians practicing meditation) to the cocreation of novel ones (see Arévalo, 2012).
Existentially, practitioners can enact multiple spiritual identities that
simultaneously embrace both the truths and the practices of different traditions, as they cocreatively participate in their respective subtle worlds
and ultimate realities (see Bidwell, 2015). The most fascinating type of
hybridization, however, is the one taking place at the visionary or ontological level. In some contemporary ayahuasca ceremonies, for example,
people access visionary worlds that combine Indigenous and Christian
motifs (Dawson, 2013). In years to come, I believe, the world will witness an increased number of all these forms of religious hybridization,
leading to greater spiritual diversity and innovation.

In addition, this access to an increased number of spiritual insights,
practices, and visionary worlds may in turn foster further human spiritual
individuation as it expands the range of choices available for individuals
in the cocreation of their spiritual paths (cf. Heron, 2006). As Tacey
(2004) stated, contemporary spiritual culture is already moving in this
direction: "Spirituality has become plural, diverse, manifold, and seems
to have countless forms of expression, many of which are highly individualistic and personal" (p. 38).

In this scenario, it will no longer be a contested issue whether
practitioners endorse a theistic, nondual, or naturalistic account of the
mystery, or whether their chosen path of spiritual cultivation is meditation, social engagement, conscious parenting, enteogenic shamanism, or communion with nature.[15] The new spiritual bottom line, in
contrast, will be the degree to which each spiritual path fosters both
an overcoming of self-centeredness and a fully embodied integration to
make individuals not only more sensitive to the needs of others, nature,
and the world, but also more effective agents of cultural and planetary
transformation in their own unique ways.

The affirmation of a shared spiritual family calls for the articulation
of a common—nonabsolutist and contextually sensitive—global ethics
(Küng, 1991; Küng & Kuschel, 1993). This global ethics, however, cannot arise exclusively out of humanity's highly ambiguous moral, religious,

or even mystical past (see Barnard & Kripal, 2002; Juergensmeyer, 2000; Juergensmeyer, Kitts, & Jerryson, 2012), but needs to be crafted in the tapestry of contemporary interfaith interactions, comparative religious ethics, cross-cultural dialogue on global human rights, and cooperative spiritual inquiry. In other words, it is likely that any viable future global ethics will be grounded not only in human spiritual history, but also in the critical reflection on such a history in the context of present-day moral intuitions (e.g., about the pitfalls of religious dogmatism, fanaticism, narcissism, and dissociation). As Smart (2003) pointed out, however, it may be more sensible to search for a global pattern of civility that "does not lay down who is right and who is wrong but rather determines how peacefully the differing groups and beliefs can live together" (pp. 130-131).[16] In any case, besides its obvious relevance for regulating cross-cultural and interreligious conflicts, the adoption of global guidelines—including guidelines for dealing with disagreement—seems crucial to address some of the most challenging issues of the "global village," such as the exploitation of women and children, the increasing polarization of rich and poor, the environmental crisis, xenophobic responses to cultural and ethnic diversity, religion-based terrorism, and unfairness in international business.

To close this section on a more hopeful note, I propose that, situated at the creative nexus between the mystery's generative power and assorted psycho-cultural dispositions, spiritually individuated persons might become unique embodiments of the mystery, capable of cocreating novel spiritual understandings, practices, and even expanded states of freedom. Hence, the world's religious future may bear witness to a greater-than-ever plurality of visionary and existential developments grounded in a deeply felt sense of spiritual unity. This account is consistent with a view of the mystery or the cosmos as moving from a primordial state of undifferentiated unity toward one of infinite differentiation-in-communion. To wear my optimistic visionary hat just a bit longer, I would say that *the future of world religion will be shaped by spiritually individuated persons engaged in processes of cosmological hybridization in the context of a common spiritual family that honors a global order of respect and civility.* This is the scenario I would personally like to see emerging in the world and that I am committed to help actualize.

CONCLUSION

In sum, I propose that the question of religious pluralism can be satisfactorily answered by affirming the undetermined, generative power of life or the mystery, as well as the human participatory role in its creative unfolding. It is time to overcome spiritual narcissism and hold spiritual convictions in a more humble, discriminating, and perhaps spiritually seasoned manner—one that recognizes the plausibility of a multiplicity of spiritual truths and religious worlds while offering grounds for the critical appraisal of dissociative, repressive, and oppressive religious expressions, beliefs, and practices. To envision religious manifestations as the outcome of human cocreative communion with an undetermined mystery—or creative power of life or reality—allows affirming a plurality of ontologically rich religious worlds without falling into any of today's fashionable reductionisms. The many challenges raised by the plurality of religions can only be met by embracing critically the spirit of pluralism.

In addition, a participatory approach envisions the long-searched-for spiritual unity of humankind, not in any global spiritual megasystem or integrative conceptual framework, but in the shared lived experience of communion with the generative dimension of the mystery. In other words, the spiritual unity of humankind may not be found in the heavens (i.e., in mental, visionary, or even mystical visions) but deep down into the earth (i.e., in the embodied connection with a common creative root). As the saying attributed to the thirteenth-century Persian poet and mystic Rumi describes, "May be you are searching among the branches for what only appears in the roots." The recognition of such creative roots may allow for firmly growing by branching out in countless creative directions without losing a sense of deep communion across differences. Such a recognition may also engender a sense of belonging to a common spiritual family committed to fostering the spiritual individuation of its members and the eco-socio-politically responsible transformation of the world.

POSTSCRIPT

Reviewing and updating essays written during more than a decade inevitably leads to recognizing the evolution of one's thinking. Although I have sought to minimize inconsistencies between chapters, this book would not be complete without a final exposition of these conceptual changes, at least regarding three crucial themes. I refer to (1) the question of the undetermined nature of the mystery; (2) the naturalistic versus supernaturalistic character of participatory spirituality; and (3) the relationship between transcendence, immanence, and what I call in this book "subtle worlds."

THE UNDETERMINED NATURE OF THE MYSTERY

In my twofold attempt to both move beyond naive objectivism and minimize sectarian biases in spiritual discourse, I originally held the ultimate nature of the mystery to be *indeterminate*—that is, not susceptible to being adequately depicted through any positive attribute (e.g., dual, nondual, personal, impersonal; Ferrer, 2002). An obvious problem with this strategy is that some traditions favored just such a negative or apophatic account of spiritual or ultimate reality.[1] As I wrote in *Revisioning Transpersonal Theory* (Ferrer, 2002),

> [M]y account of the indeterminate nature of ultimate reality may be seen to be, legitimately I believe, more in alignment with some spiritual traditions than others. It can be said, for example, that to suggest that the Mystery of Being has no pre-given essence is more consistent with certain Buddhist understandings of emptiness (*sunyata*) than with traditional accounts of the Christian God or the Advaitin Brahman. (p. 179)

Anticipating this objection and in alignment with many Western and Eastern apophatic mystics (see Carlson, 1999; Sells, 1994; D. Turner, 1995), I argued that this denial of pregiven attributes was not equivalent to constructing a positive theory about the mystery (which could then be hierarchically posited as superior to other views).[2] Despite the apophatic mystics' insistence that such an account is more effective and appropriate to convey the ultimate nature of the mystery than any positive state-ment of its qualities, sectarianism was not entirely avoided. In other words, although this account does not necessarily privilege any specific religious tradition (e.g., Advaita Vedanta or Judaism) or mysticism type (e.g., theistic, monistic, nondual), it nevertheless favors apophatic (*via negativa*) over kataphatic (*via positiva*) spiritual orientations and associ-ated discourses.

It is important to reiterate here that no conceptual framework (participatory or otherwise) can successfully avoid privileging one or another perspective. As Derrida (1981) underlined, hierarchy is intrinsic to Western thinking and language. To affirm or deny one thing implicitly denies or affirms, respectively, its opposite, polar, or alternate reality. In the present context, determinate accounts of the mystery (e.g., personal God, Sat Chi Ananda, nonduality) challenge the legitimacy or ultimate veracity of apophatic accounts, while indeterminate accounts (e.g., *neti neti*, the "cloud of unknowing," nothingness) question the legitimacy or ultimate veracity of kataphatic accounts. Although I would argue that this hierarchical ethos can be radically overcome in human experience through transformed modes of being-in-the-world (cf. Loy, 1987; see also Park, 2006), the linguistic privileging of one or another standpoint seems inescapable, at least in modern Western discourse.

Hence, to qualify the nature of the mystery, I eventually opted to use the word *undetermined* over *indeterminate* (Ferrer, 2008).[3] Rather than affirming negatively (as the term *indeterminate* does), *undetermined* leaves open the possibility of both determinacy and indeterminacy within the mystery, as well as the paradoxical confluence or even identity of these two apparently polar accounts. This formulation, I think, provides an effective response to the understandable criticism that my account of the mystery as not pregiven and utterly indeterminate clashed with my also qualifying it as "dynamic" and "creative" (e.g., Stoeber, 2015). Indeed, in my attempt to neutralize objectifying and reifying tendencies in spiritual discourse, I described the mystery—perhaps paradoxically or somewhat contradictorily—as an indeterminate creative dynamism of life, the cos-mos, or reality. Although this earlier formulation can be legitimately seen as taking with one hand what it gives with the other, my hope is that the openness to both determinacy and indeterminacy allowed by the phrase *undetermined mystery* relaxes this possible tension.[4]

Mindful, however, that even this account does not entirely settle the issue (e.g., it questions the legitimacy of exclusively positive or negative metaphysical accounts of the mystery), I stress that my use of the term is mostly *performative*—that is, seeking to evoke the sense of not-knowing and intellectual humility I find most fruitful and suitable in approaching the creative power of life and reality that is the source of our being. In this regard, Duckworth (forthcoming) argued that whereas to claim the determinacy or indeterminacy of the mystery bounds one to a closed model of truth, the undetermined fosters an open-ended approach to such a mystery.[5] In his own words:

> In contrast to a certain claim of indeterminacy, the undetermined is not enframed by a determinate judgment. Rather, the undetermined involves a participatory attitude of openness, and a healthy suspicion of preconceptions that determine and delimit the ultimate truth. Thus, the *undetermined* refers not so much to a descriptive truth claim but rather to a comportment to the world—one of humility and openness. ("Introduction," para. 1)

As Duckworth noted, this approach is consistent with Vélez de Cea's (2013) important distinction between *claims* (which entail exclusive stances that deny their counter positions) and *attitudes* (which can be potentially open to a diversity of—even polar or apparently conflicting—stances). In a similar vein, regarding the nonabsolutist nature of participatory pluralism and germane approaches, I wrote:

> [R]ather than philosophical positions to be logically defended in an absolutist domain of discourse, they are attitudes toward life and other human beings characterized by both an openness to understand and be enriched by what is different, and a surrendering to the Mystery that can never be fully apprehended by the mind. As attitudes towards life rather than as philosophical positions, these approaches can be criticized, but not refuted. (Ferrer, 2002, p, 189; see also Ferrer, 1998a)

To further minimize the problem of sectarianism in the context of participatory pluralism, I also emphasize the importance of avoiding the neo-Kantian *dualism of the mystery and its enactions*.[6] Building on both the enactive paradigm's account of cognition as embodied action and its rejection of representational theories of knowledge (e.g., Chemero, 2009; Thompson, 2007; Varela et al., 1991), I maintain that in the same way an individual is her actions (whether perceptual, cognitive, emotional, or subtle), the mystery is its enactions. In this understanding, emptiness (*sunyata*), the Tao, and the Christian God (in their many inflexions) can be seen as creative gestures of the mystery enacted through participating human (and perhaps nonhuman) individuals and collectives.

Not positing a supra-ultimate spiritual referent beyond its specific enactions has two very important consequences. First, it preserves the ontological ultimacy of those enactions (e.g., God, emptiness, Tao, Brahman) in their respective spiritual universes, avoiding the traditionalist and neo-Kantian demotion of those ultimates to penultimate stations (see S. B. King, 2001; Nah, 2013). Second, it short-circuits the feasibility of promoting one tradition as objectively superior (i.e., holding the most accurate picture of the mystery), excising ontological competitiveness at its root and arguably settling one of the main challenges of religious pluralism (see chapter 10; Ferrer, 2008).

The problem of doctrinal ranking is further minimized by both the participatory grounding of qualitative distinctions on pragmatic values (e.g., integrated selflessness, embodiment, eco-socio-political justice), and its equiplurality principle, according to which there can potentially be multiple spiritual enactions that are nonetheless equally holistic, emancipatory, and ethically just (see chapters 1 and 10). I stand by these values—not because I think they are universal, objective, or ahistorical (they are not), but because I firmly believe that their cultivation can effectively reduce today's personal, relational, social, and planetary suffering.

To be sure, the specificities of the various spiritual, transformational goals often derive from ontological views about the nature of reality or the divine. Likewise—and even more so in participatory, enactive context—transformational goals impact ontological matters, thus possibly slipping back into doctrinal rankings (e.g., the goal of the embodied integration of consciousness arguably demotes traditional Samkhya-Yoga's dualistic metaphysics and its attendant spiritual aspiration of isolation—*kaivalyam*). As the equiplurality principle maintains, however, the participatory ranking is not itself precipitated by the privileging of a single spiritual goal, but rather explodes into a plurality of potentially holistic spiritual realizations that can occur within and outside traditions. This principle is founded on the double rejection of an objectivist account of the mystery and the representational paradigm of cognition, according to which there can be only one most accurate representation of an original template with supposedly pregiven features (for nonrepresentational epistemologies, see Frisina, 2002). Taken together, these features release participatory spirituality from the dogmatic commitment to any single spiritual system and pave the way for an ontologically and pragmatically grounded spiritual pluralism.

In summary, the participatory approach provides a framework that minimizes problematic hierarchies based on doctrinal ontological beliefs about the mystery (e.g., as being ultimately personal, impersonal, monistic, dual, or nondual), while conserving grounds for the criticism of dissociated, disembodied, narcissistic, and oppressive visions and practices (see chapters 3 and 10). This proposal does not seek to eschew the making of qualitative distinctions among spiritual insights, teachings, or practices. In contrast, it offers pragmatic standards to establish such distinctions while avoiding the "holistic fallacy"—that is, the spurious belief that cultures (or religious traditions) can be assessed to be superior or inferior to each other as wholes, ignoring how internally multilayered and diverse they actually are (Benhabib, 2002).[7]

While the participatory proposal might not entirely settle the question of ontological ranking, I maintain that the question is significantly relaxed through the qualification of the mystery as undetermined, the affirmation of a potential plurality of equally holistic visions unfolding through different enactions of the mystery, and the focus on transformational outcomes to make spiritual qualitative distinctions. Sectarianism cannot be fully overcome conceptually (i.e., through any theoretical framework, whether participatory or not), but I propose that it can be transcended in the realm of human experience. This transcendence comes through an attitude of intellectual humility and genuine openness to the other, as well as to the world's mysteries—particularly those mysteries that surpass the conceptual mind and can paradoxically (for the human mind, that is) house incompatible spiritual enactions, orientations, and values.

NATURALISM, SUPERNATURALISM, AND OPEN NATURALISM

The second area of conceptual change in my thinking also concerns the nature of the mystery—this time its naturalistic versus supernaturalistic nature. Although I originally used the terms *spirit* and *mystery* rather interchangeably (Ferrer, 2002), I gradually favored the arguably less metaphysically loaded and more open-ended term *mystery* when describing that creative power with which human and nonhuman beings interact in the enaction of spiritual phenomena, worlds, and ultimates:

> The term *mystery* does not entail any kind of essentialist reification of an ontologically given ground of being, as expressions such as "the sacred," "the divine," or "the eternal" often conveyed in classic scholarship in religion. . . . In contrast, we deliberately use this conceptually vague, open-ended, and ambiguous term to refer to the nondetermined creative energy or source of reality, the cosmos, life, and consciousness. Thus understood, the term *mystery* obstructs claims or insinuations of dogmatic certainty and associated religious exclusivisms; more positively, it invites an attitude of intellectual and existential humility and receptivity to the Great Unknown that is the fountain of our being. (Ferrer & Sherman, 2008a, p. 64)

Furthermore, Sherman and I stressed, such an account of the mystery (or spirit) could be equally understood in both naturalistic and supernaturalistic ways:

> It is important to emphasize, however, that to embrace a participatory understanding of religious knowledge is not *necessarily* linked to confessional, religionist, or supernaturalist premises or standpoints. . . . [V]irtually all the same participatory implications for the study of religion can be practically drawn if we were to conceive, or translate the term, *spirit* in a naturalistic fashion as an emergent creative potential of life, nature, or reality. (p. 72)

Leaving the door open to both naturalistic and supernaturalistic accounts of the mystery seemed cautious enough at that time, but I later came to recognize that the very postulating of a naturalistic/ supernaturalistic dichotomy is problematic. First of all, this dichotomy is contingent of Christian medieval theological considerations of dubious contemporary relevance (Bartlett, 2008; de Lubac, 1967; Sherman, 2014b). Second, it is also contingent on modern science's ideological endorsement of a narrow naturalism that is both linked to a disenchanted post/modern worldview and militant against so-called supernatural agents or principles (e.g., nonphysical entities, archetypal forces, or spiritual ultimates; see chapter 2). Third, since the natural/supernatural distinction is meaningless for most Eastern and Indigenous peoples (Kripal,

2014), its uncritical use perpetuates the Western cognitive colonialism and imperialism denounced in this book and by other scholars (e.g., R. King, 1999; Roth, 2008). Although in the context of the Western intellectual and religious trajectory, openness to what has been historically understood as "natural" and "supernatural" can be heuristically fertile, I have proposed that this artificial dichotomy is ripe to be abandoned.

In this light, I currently recommend following Stroud's (2004) plea for an "open naturalism" that is not committed a priori to any worldview such as scientific naturalism or any particular religious cosmology (see chapter 2). In the context of transpersonal studies and participatory spirituality, such an open naturalism, free from the materialism and reductionism constraining modern scientific naturalism, can seriously contemplate both the ontological integrity of spiritual referents and the plausibility of subtle dimensions of reality. This understanding takes me to my final consideration.

TRANSCENDENCE, IMMANENCE, AND THE SUBTLE

Overcoming the natural/supernatural dichotomy has important implications for how spirituality is usually conceptualized in the West. One major consequence concerns the category of transcendence, which has been traditionally contrasted to immanence and associated to a "supernatural" realm or ultimate principle existing beyond or outside the "natural" world (e.g., Olson & Rouner, 1981; Shah-Kazemi, 2006).[8] Open naturalism questions the traditional transcendent/immanence opposition by bridging the gulf between the "natural" and the "supernatural." In addition, open naturalism critiques this opposition: once it is acknowledged that modern scientific naturalism may not necessarily exhaust the possibilities of the real, envisioning a multiverse or multidimensional cosmos inclusive of a rich variety of subtle worlds or realms becomes increasingly plausible.[9]

Thus, although in my earlier work I wrote about *transcendent* spiritual realities (e.g., Ferrer, 2006), in this book I opted for the term *subtle* to refer to any possible coexisting or enacted worlds of energy and consciousness, as well as phenomena or entities associated with these worlds.[10] While I retained the term *immanent* to describe spiritual/creative sources located within—or emerging from—physical matter, body, sexuality, life, and nature (see chapter 3), I postulate no ontological gap or dualism between the immanent and the subtle. In contrast, I suggest that the relationship between subtle worlds and the physical world enacted by conventional perception and cognition is likely to be one of interconnected coexistence (cf. Irwin, 1996), even if all these worlds might be perfectly capable of operating independently from one another.

It is important to stress here that, from a participatory perspective, the physical world itself does not have a single pregiven nature perceived and represented differently by the various species and human cultures; rather, this world should be conceived as a richly open "multi-nature" (Viveiros de Castro, 2014, 2015) amenable to a multiplicity of embodied enactions and their resulting ontologically distinct worlds. In other words, not only may there be a multiplicity of subtle worlds, but also the physical world—or the world of nature—can be enacted in a multiplicity of ways.[11]

Assuming for a moment the ontological richness of subtle worlds, one might reasonably ask: Did the Buddhist worlds (e.g., Pure Lands) exist before Buddhists walked on earth? A positive answer would entail not only that such subtle worlds predate human existence, but also that the various religions somehow "descended" from them. One major problem with this proposal is that there are several thousands of religions in the world today (Barrett et al., 2001), many of which postulate different—and often incompatible—subtle worlds and associated postmortem realms. This positive answer must suggest that every time a human collective generates new beliefs about spiritual realms and claims to directly experience them, its practitioners are accessing preexisting subtle worlds, which seems unlikely. Some may respond that only the so-called world religions (e.g., Christianity, Judaism, Buddhism, Taoism) are "descended" traditions, while the rest are figments of human fantasy and wishful thinking. If so, however, where to draw the line? Perhaps most importantly, who can legitimately draw this line? Alternatively, a negative response to the question might take the following form: those religious worlds did not descend upon humans, but somehow "ascended" from or were shaped by sustained religious practice, long standing collective experience, and, perhaps, the cumulative impact of practitioners' postmortem existence. This explanation, although perhaps more plausible, can be charged with anthropomorphism due to its unwarranted assumption that all those worlds are entirely human constructions.

More nuanced responses, I think, are likely to be more complex than the white-or-black scenario painted above. Specifically, I propose that more effective responses should simultaneously entertain three possibilities. First, the physical world may be one among other possible worlds coexisting in a multidimensional cosmos (see chapter 2; Combs, Arcari, & Krippner, 2006). In addition, some of those subtle worlds and their corresponding inhabitants may exist independently from human enaction, and their existence may predate human history (see chapter 9). Finally, other subtle worlds—and associated postmortem realms (Barnard, 2007, 2011; Loy, 2010)—may have been historically cocreated by sustained collective religious practice and experience, in interaction with the mystery's generative powers and perhaps with nonhuman beings having enactive capabilities. Although these considerations are wildly speculative, I believe that this picture may begin to do better justice to the rich diversity of humanity's experiences of subtle worlds and beings.

In any event, I should clarify that my use of the term *subtle* is not necessarily related to the previous meanings it has received in the spiritual literature. Although my account of subtle worlds can include the various astral or etheric realms described in classical Western esotericism (e.g., Leadbeater, 1895/2005) or by contemporary New Age inquirers (e.g., Spangler, 2010), it is not reducible to them. The subtle worlds referenced in this book also encompass Indigenous and contemplative cosmologies not usually recognized in these discursive sites. My use of the term is also not equivalent to its meaning in traditionalist models and transpersonal theories that situate the subtle realm in-between: either between terrestrial and celestial planes (H. Smith, 1976) or between psychic and causal levels (Wilber, 1996).[12] In contrast, I use the term *subtle* in a more generic fashion to refer to any possible world or being shaped by the interaction of consciousness and energy, including coexisting and enacted spiritual realms and associated ultimate principles.

Understood this way, the subtle worlds include consciousness and energy, while the world of nature and society (i.e., the one accessed by the prevailing ordinary state of consciousness) includes consciousness and energy but is also made of *matter*. After Einstein's revolution in physics, however, mass and energy are regarded as fully interconvertible (Bodanis, 2000). This account suggests that the physical and the subtle worlds are ultimately united, possibly interacting in complex ways in the context of a seamless multiverse modulated by different degrees, frequencies, concentrations, or density states of consciousness and energy.[13]

I have no doubt that future researchers will find more appropriate and accurate ways to refer to these distinctions (perhaps in terms of precise understandings of energetic density or frequency). However, this task, like many other questions hopefully raised by this book, is a song for another day—one that I invite others to cocreate with me in that collaborative effort so essential for the unfolding of a truly participatory spirituality.

CODA

A SECRET POEM FOR YOU

I close this book on a more personal note by sharing a poem with you, the reader—a poem that evocatively conveys central elements of the shared, participatory relationship humans have with nature and its human and nonhuman worlds. I call this poem "secret" not because of its hermetic or esoteric meaning, but simply because it secretly held me for years, giving me strength and hope in times of crisis and difficulty. My father, its author, was born and raised in the orchards of Murcia, that fertile region of the south of Spain that prides itself—in that charmingly exaggerated way so defining of the Murcian spirit—on providing fruits and vegetables for the rest of the European continent. As my father moved to the culturally vibrant but highly industrialized city of Barcelona to work and start his new married life, essential seeds of his soul apparently decided to stay at the orchards. Then, as so often happens within the poet's heart, versed beauty began to sprout from the pain and isolation of a dismembered soul.

This is why the poem you are about to read was originally called "Solitude." Some years ago, with the author's consent, I changed its title from "Solitude" to "Plenitude," for a poem—as is true of anything that carries meaning for what matters—is never an indifferent or static object, but rather a living presence whose inner nature metamorphoses as it encounters a receptive heart. As I rescued those essential seeds that my father's soul left in Murcian soil, it became obvious that a change of title was not only justified, but actually called for, by the poem itself. In these times of rampant uprootedness from ancestry and tradition, we often forget that it is in the unfulfilled dreams of our parents where we can at times find the pearls that offer our souls the guidance they are longing for. What a magnificent miracle it is to discover that, as we walk that path, not only the dreams, but also the dreamer, can, at a deep level, begin to be realized.

Although containing many layers of meaning, this is a very simple poem. My father, as Charles Bukowski once said of himself, does not have grandiose thoughts, or thoughts of a philosophical nature, and so his poems tell us about very ordinary things. As do many visionary texts, however, this poem lures us into a journey. But this is not an invitation to the hero's journey, where a masculinized self leaves its motherland, encounters pitfalls and battles monsters, and triumphantly returns with a renewed sense of empowered solar identity. I believe that this poem tells us about a much lesser known kind of initiation, where the soul leaves her social, psychological, and even spiritual routines to delve anew and without struggle into the deeper sources of life, of nature, and of the mystery, so that we can return "in peace, with the flavor of the winds, between our hands . . ."

Before I leave you to enjoy the poem, however, let me tell you another secret. For its "magical" power to be conjured, this poem needs to be read out loud, and with both tenderness and passion. Hence, I invite you to take a deep breath, drop deep into your heart, and allow these words to perhaps narrow the gap between you and your own boundless potential.

Plenitud	Plenitude
Si un día no me encuentras	If one day you cannot find me
no pienses que me he vuelto loco	do not think that I have gone crazy,
sino cuerdo.	but sane.
Búscame lejos . . .	Look for me far away . . .
donde las gentes vuelan como pájaros	where people fly like birds
sobre los valles inmensos,	over immense valleys,
donde los tristes escarabajos	where the sad beetles
bañan su cuerpo de rocío	bathe their bodies in dew
y se visten de terciopelo negro.	and clothe themselves in black velvet.
Búscame lejos . . .	Look for me far away . . .
donde las vacas dan leche a cantaros	where the cows give milk in abundance
y lánguidas ovejas se agrupan	and the languid sheep gather
como nubes blancas,	like white clouds,
donde los bueyes te miran con ternura	where the oxen gaze with gentleness,
y los caballos de cola pacifica	and the horses with peaceful tails

sienten la caricia del viento,
donde mi frente descanse
sin reloj que mida el tiempo
—montaña arriba—
hacia la luz y el silencio.

Allí me encontrarás . . .
tendido en la yerba
con la flor de tomillo entre labios,
mirando al cóndor
y a las águilas reales volar . . .
y volar . . .

Allí me encontrarás . . .
aprendiendo a vivir de los insectos
y de las aves silvestres,
de los animales domésticos,
aprendiendo de los pájaros . . .

(¡No me da vergüenza . . . !)

Y puede que hasta aprenda
el vuelo de las abejas,
a dormir con las gallinas
y a conversar con lagartos . . .
y respiraré libre, al viento,
por los picos mas altos.

Oiré la voz que viene de lejos
del campesino que canta
coplas de amor a su amada,
y las campanas de bronce
que suenan en el lejano pueblo,
oiré la voz de los árboles,
de la brisa y del agua . . .

Estrenaré ojos nuevos
para mirar a mis anchas
donde cantan los grillos,
donde duermen las cigarras . . .

. . . Y cuando tú me encuentres,
besaré tu aliento
con más calor humano,

feel the caressing of the wind,
where I lay my head down
without a watch measuring the time
—up the mountain—
toward the light, and the silence.

There you will find me . . .
lying in the grass
with thyme blossoms between my lips,
gazing at the condor
and at the golden eagles flying . . .
and flying . . .

There you will find me . . .
learning to live from the insects
and from the wild birds,
from the domestic animals,
learning from the birds . . .

(I do not feel ashamed . . . !)

And it may be that I even learn
to fly like the bees,
to sleep with the hens
and to converse with the lizards . . .
and I will breathe freely, against the wind,
through the highest peaks.

I will listen for the voice from afar
of the countryman who sings
love songs to his beloved,
and the bronze bells
sounding in the far village,
I will listen to the voice of the trees,
of the breeze, and of the water.

I will use my new eyes for the first time
to look as far as my gaze roams
where the crickets sing,
where the cicadas sleep . . .

. . . And when you find me,
I will kiss your breath
with human warmth,

y te contaré lo que me ha enseñado,
el viento, el día, la noche,
la luz y las estrellas . . . ,
y aprenderemos juntos de una vez para siempre
a vivir en paz
con el sabor de los aires
entre nuestras manos . . .

and I will tell you what they have taught me,
the wind, the day, the night,
the light, and the stars . . . ,
and we will learn together for all time
to live in peace
with the flavor of the winds
between our hands . . .

José Antonio Noguera Giménez

APPENDIX ONE

PARTICIPATORY SPIRITUALITY AND

A. H. ALMAAS'S NEW DIAMOND APPROACH

In his book, *Runaway Realization*, Almaas (2014) presented a "new teaching" (p. 1) or "fourth turning" (p. 7) of his Diamond Approach that seems to move him much closer to a participatory approach. In this Appendix, I review the tenets of his new Diamond Approach in light of the present and future of participatory theory presented in this book.

In contrast to its past emphasis on oneness and nonduality, Almaas's (2014) new Diamond Approach conceives ultimate reality to be utterly indeterminate. This "entirely different paradigm" (p. 3) or "view of totality" (p. 3), Almaas stressed, resituates all past Diamond Approach teachings as "one kind of realization" (p. 2). In a strikingly similar move to the one made in *Revisioning Transpersonal Theory* (Ferrer, 2002), by affirming such an indeterminacy Almaas sought to articulate a "nonhierarchical view" (p. 2) that (1) overcomes the conflicting relationship between duality and nonduality, (2) embraces a diversity of enlightenment experiences and types of spiritual freedom, and (3) frees spiritual inquiry from having to lead to any particular end.

Readers familiar with my work will recognize these three theses of Almaas's (2014) new Diamond Approach as central to the initial articulation of the participatory approach (Ferrer, 2001, 2002). First, on positing how an indeterminate mystery nonhierarchically settles the conflict between duality, nonduality, and other spiritual ultimates:

Reality is far more indeterminate, far more mysterious that anything we can conceive of. No single view—whether dual, nondual, unilocal, or something entirely different—can capture the dynamism of reality. . . . Fundamental to this view

255

is that no perspective or orientation is negated. (Almaas, 2014, p. 9, 215)

> The *dynamic and indeterminate nature of Spirit* cannot be adequately depicted through any positive attribute, such as non-dual, dual, impersonal, personal, and so forth . . .
> The participatory vision, then, does not establish any hierarchy of positive attributes of the divine: Nondual insights are not higher than dual, nor are dual higher than nondual. Personal enactions are not higher than impersonal, nor are impersonal higher than personal. And so forth. Since the Mystery is intrinsically indeterminate, spiritual qualitative distinctions cannot be made by matching our insights and conceptualizations with any pre-given features. (Ferrer, 2002, p. 190)

Second, on the resulting nature of spiritual inquiry as being beyond any pregiven goal:

> One of the advantages of the view of totality is that it liberates us from having to choose what to experience, which frees inquiry from having to go toward any particular end. (Almaas, 2014, p. 215)

> Spiritual inquiry . . . becomes a journey, an endless exploration and disclosure of the inexhaustible possibilities of an always dynamic and indeterminate being. (Ferrer, 2002, p. 157)

And third, on the implications of these views to overcome exclusivist (or closed) accounts of the spiritual freedom:

> As long as we feel that there is an ultimate way of experiencing reality, it will be difficult for our inquiry to be truly open. (Almaas, 2014, p. 215)

> Most traditions equate spiritual liberation with boundless freedom. But if we rigidly maintain the exclusive Truth of our tradition, are we not bonding ourselves to a particular, limited disclosure of reality? And if we tie our very being to a singular, even if transconceptual, disclosure of reality, then,

we can rightfully wonder, how truly boundless is our spiritual
freedom? Is this freedom truly boundless or just a subtle form
of spiritual bondage? (Ferrer, 2002, p. 176)

Although the convergence of viewpoints is a cause for celebration—and even more so in relation to the ideas of such as a sophisticated spiritual writer as Almaas (1996, 2002, 2014)—two things give me
pause. First of all, it is puzzling that Almaas (2014) made no mention
of the substantial parallels between his new views and the participatory
approach—and yet, he has been exposed to my work. In 2007, I had a
private written exchange with Almaas mediated by a student of both
our work who was concerned with Almaas's presentation of spiritual
truths in an outdated objectivist fashion (e.g., pregiven truths, essential
qualities). During this time, Almaas reportedly spent part of one of his
personal retreats studying *Revisioning* (Ferrer, 2002). It is certainly possible that Almaas gradually incorporated participatory proposals into the
unfolding of his own spiritual realization, and that as a spiritual teacher
(vs. scholar) he has less imperative to credit the sources of his teaching.
While the omission is perhaps understandable, Almaas was actively critical of what he described in passing as "participation [*sic*] spirituality" (p.
118), without mention of any connection or similarity to his new views.

Second, a closer reading of *Runaway Realization* (2014) reveals
that perennialist thinking and exclusivism underlie Almaas's otherwise
well-intentioned thinking. Although one can find some seeds of Almaas's
new teaching in prior works (e.g., 2002, 2004), it is noteworthy that,
up to *Runaway Realization*, Almaas's Diamond Approach was arguably
constrained by both perennialist formulations and the myth of the given
(cf. Wilber, 2006). In his most important essay on spiritual diversity,
for example, Almaas (2004) held that while the various spiritual paths
lead to different truths and realizations, they all ultimately converge in
"the same destination" (p. 569)—even if such a destination is reached
through different routes. Although noting its limitations, Almaas used
the metaphor of "travelling to a faraway country from different directions" (p. 569), which conveyed his belief in a shared spiritual endpoint
and single territory. He did reject naive perennialist equivalences among
the various spiritual paths and truths, as well as the feasibility of an
unifying or synthetic vision, but Almaas's professed metaphor ultimately
rendered his account a perspectival perennialism, contingent on the
myth of the given (for a discussion of different types of perennialism,
see Ferrer, 2002). In addition, Almaas supported, first, the perennialist

notion that differences in truths and realizations amount to "different ways of conceptualizing [the same] spiritual dimensions and qualities" (p. 569); and second, the traditionalist account of the various spiritual ultimates as relative absolutes reliant on the dualism of the mystery and its enactions (see Postscript, note 6).

In sum, Almaas's writings on spiritual diversity and universalism prior to *Runaway Realization* (2014) not only were perennialist, but also adhered to several pernicious myths and dualisms of spiritual discourse. A way out of these problems—and their constraining implications for spiritual understanding, inquiry, and liberation—is to uphold the indeterminate (vs. determinate or objective) nature of the mystery as grounds to reconcile conflicting accounts of ultimate reality, emancipate spiritual inquiry beyond any pregiven goal, and expand spiritual liberation beyond univocal and exclusivist stances. This move, as discussed above, was precisely one of *Revisioning*'s core arguments and has now become the heart of Almaas's (2014) new Diamond Approach.

While Almaas's (2014) new teaching indeed incorporates central aspects of my early work, there are four important ways the Diamond Approach diverges from the participatory approach. First, whereas Almaas articulated a nonhierarchical account of the various spiritual ultimates, he also posited a "view of totality" (p. 237) that allegedly encompasses all of them and is thus implicitly superior (e.g., less attached to any particular view, spiritually freer). In this vein, he wrote about a "total freedom" (p. 227) or "freedom of realization" (p. 238) that is open to all forms of realization without being bound by them. Although Almaas rejected both pregiven and final goals in spiritual inquiry, one wonders how this "total/totality" (however open and dynamic it might be) does not ultimately function in the Diamond Approach—and will be taken by his students—as *the* final spiritual endpoint or highest goal for spiritual aspiration. In any event, Almaas's total/totality catapults the Diamond Approach back to perennialist, inclusivist stances (which posit a supra-ultimate that can include all other ultimates, but not vice versa; see Postscript), in tension with the participatory equiplurality principle (which grants all spiritual traditions the power to achieve the fullest spiritual freedom and integration in their own terms). For critiques of a very similar proposal in the work of Dale (2014), see chapter 10 and Ferrer (2015).

Second, despite Almaas's (2014) explicit attempt to articulate a nonprogressive, nonhierarchical account of spiritual inquiry, the last chapter of his book offers a gradual, sequential account of spiritual under-

standing that (most likely unintentionally) arranges insights from different spiritual traditions in a hierarchical fashion. In the way toward the
totality view and attendant total freedom, Almaas explained, individuals first experience their true nature, then discover pure awareness and
emptiness, and afterward the view of nonduality (cf. Almaas, 2004). The
participatory approach, in contrast, rejects any universal, paradigmatic
sequence of spiritual insights while defending the validity of gradual,
stage-like paths leading to specific goals in the context of certain spiritual traditions (i.e., those following gradual—vs. sudden—approaches to
achieve their goals; see chapter 10; Ferrer, 2015; Ferrer & Puente, 2013).
The problem with Almaas's account is that while his own personal spiritual trajectory may have followed that sequence, others may arrive—and
indeed, many have arrived—at similar (or different) spiritual zeniths
through radically different pathways of experience and understanding.
This point takes me to the next consideration.

Third, even in the new Diamond Approach turning, Almaas (2014)
has continued to display the problematic tendency to overlook the enactive (i.e., cocreative) nature of his own spiritual inquiry and realizations,
thus downplaying the personally situated nature of his proposed sequence
of spiritual insights—and presenting it as universal or paradigmatic. This
arguably blind spot, I think, is connected with Almaas's views on the
ultimately illusory nature of historically embodied individuality and his
related critique of the participatory account of spiritual cocreation (A.
H. Almaas, personal communication, March 4, 2007). At the time of
our exchange in 2007, for Almaas only Being—and never the embodied
individual—created its own forms and thus transpersonal cocreation was
taken to be an inflated case of spiritual titanism (in which human beings
are believed to display divine powers; see Gier, 2008).

To be sure, Almaas (1988) has differentiated between the historically conditioned, subjective egoic personality and the objective individual soul, considering the former a distortion of the latter (see Gleig,
2009); however, there is a crucial difference between our accounts.
Although in my work I have similarly distinguished between the
hyper-individualistic mental ego and the participatory selfhood forged
through the process of spiritual individuation (see chapter 1), I not
only consider the spiritually individuated self (and associated spiritual
trajectories) inevitably shaped by historical, contextual, and embodied
factors, but also do not take those factors to be necessarily distorting
or a pale reflection of either the world or supposedly pregiven essential or objective qualities of Being. Rather, these factors may be crucial

vehicles for the unfolding of the inexhaustible creativity of the mystery, as manifesting through participating individuals and collectives (for discussions of mediation in spiritual knowing, see Ferrer, 2002, 2008). As Gleig pointed out in 2009, the Diamond Approach did not pay enough "attention to the internalization of socio-cultural categories such as race, gender, sexuality, and class" (p. 84).

In his new book, Almaas (2014) has reframed his take on individuality in an even more positive light, positing it as both the organ of realization and an essential part of a dialectical relationship with Being that "has intrinsic significance and is fundamentally mysterious" (p. 111). Since this account parallels the dialectical view between the spiritually individuated person and the mystery put forward by the notion of transpersonal cocreation, I suspect that semantic confusion may lurk behind Almaas's criticism of this aspect of the participatory approach. In particular, Almaas wrote that transpersonal cocreation or coparticipation is improper because it "assumes that there actually are two things [i.e., the individual and Being]" (p. 118). "From the view of totality" (p. 118), Almaas continued, "there are not really two things, but there is not exactly one either. The mystery is more interesting and subtle than the two possibilities" (p. 118). My sense is that the participatory openness to different enactions of "self-and-the-world" and "self-and-the-mystery" largely accounts for, and may actually help to explain, Almaas's paradoxical understanding of the mysterious identity/difference of the individual and Being (or the mystery).

Fourth, whereas using the term *indeterminate* to qualify the mystery frees one from having to decide between duality and nonduality as spiritually or ontologically superior, Almaas (2014) overlooked that neither hierarchy nor sectarianism are fully avoided—affirming such an indeterminacy inevitably biases one's perspective in favor of apophatic (negative) spiritual orientations and against kataphatic (positive) ones. A partial way out of this conceptual and terminological dilemma, I have proposed, is to opt for the terms *undetermined* (Ferrer, 2008) or *nondetermined* (Ferrer & Sherman, 2008a), whose meaning and implications I discuss in this volume's Postscript (see also Duckworth, 2014a, forthcoming).

To conclude, Almaas (2014) has offered a highly participatory recasting of the Diamond Approach that nonetheless suffers from certain tensions and arguable inconsistencies. My sense is that many of these tensions stem from Almaas's lack of engagement with the enactive paradigm in the context of spiritual knowing and realization, and that a full incorporation of the notion of *participatory enaction* (Ferrer, 2008) would free the Diamond Approach from these limitations. In any event, participatory thinkers owe an immense debt of gratitude to Almaas for offering an experientially grounded and spiritually profound account of some central aspects of a participatory spirituality.

APPENDIX TWO

THE SOFT PERENNIALISM OF S. TAYLOR

The most recent attempt to bridge perennialist and participatory approaches is S. Taylor's (2017) proposal for a soft perennialism. After an overview of S. Taylor's project, this Appendix discusses its merits and shortcomings from the perspective of the participatory approach.

Briefly, S. Taylor (2017) has articulated a "soft" perennialism as a corrective to "hard" forms of the perennial philosophy that make transcendental and metaphysical claims about the nature of reality or the creative mystery. The crux of soft perennialism is a shift from metaphysics to phenomenology—or, as S. Taylor put it, from the perennial philosophy to a "perennial *phenomenology*" ("Soft" Perennialism section, para. 13). In a way, his proposal could have been named *participatory perennialism*, since it admittedly incorporates many participatory insights and is explicitly presented as a reconciling alternative to both perennialism and participatory spirituality. In alignment with the participatory approach, for example, S. Taylor rejected hierarchical relationships among spiritual traditions and states, as well as the existence of both paradigmatic stages of spiritual development and a single or final destination for spiritual aspiration. With perennialism, however, he maintained that both a universal spiritual energy and pregiven landscape are necessary to account for the strong phenomenological similarities in processes of awakening he detected both between and outside traditions. Specifically, S. Taylor identified seven of these similarities: heightened awareness; a movement beyond separateness toward connection and union; the cultivation of inner stillness and emptiness; increased inner stability and equanimity; increased empathy, compassion, and altruism; the relinquishing of personal agency; and enhanced well-being.

In contrast to the metaphysical claims of the perennial philosophy, soft perennialism regards the universal spiritual force as strictly immanent to the world, and the shared landscape as a psychological realm made up of experiential trends and tendencies. After discussing the aforementioned spiritual trends as they manifest in religious traditions and nonreligious individuals, S. Taylor (2017) concluded by urging transpersonal psychologists to move from metaphysical speculation to phenomenological research, and to pay greater attention to the spiritual transformative processes taking place outside religious traditions. In the remainder of this Appendix, I continue unpacking S. Taylor's soft perennialism as I discuss its merits and arguable shortcomings.

THE MERITS OF SOFT PERENNIALISM

Essentially, I find much of value in S. Taylor's (2017) proposal even beyond its fundamental points of convergence with the participatory approach. First, I strongly agree that transpersonal psychology would benefit from more phenomenological studies; as S. Taylor suggested, phenomenological research could help to ground, enrich, and even revise traditional accounts of both spiritual transformative processes and the creative mystery. Second, I also concur with S. Taylor that the inclusion of spiritual perspectives from outside religious traditions in transpersonal scholarship can illuminate, and perhaps offer crucial evidence for, contemporary transpersonal debates. Although I hope that S. Taylor's plea is seriously considered by transpersonal researchers, I do not perceive the absence of nonreligious perspectives in the transpersonal literature as severely as he does; after all, most of Grof's (1975, 1985, 1988a) experiential data are not derived from religious practitioners (see also Wade, 2004). Third, I find S. Taylor's discussion of seven spiritual trends shared across traditions stimulating and significant, especially as he cautiously acknowledged that those trends "are certainly emphasized to different degrees in certain traditions" (Common Themes section, para. 18) and that "there is clearly room for a great deal of variation amongst the traditions" (Common Themes section, para. 18).

While some of the spiritual trends identified by S. Taylor (2017) may better fit traditional contemplative paths than esoteric, visionary, or shamanic ones, his overall approach is consistent with both the multicentered account of religions (Vroom, 1989) and the related view of religion and mysticism as family resemblance concepts (e.g., Dupré, 1987; Fitzgerald, 1996; Harrison, 2006) embraced by the participatory approach (see Ferrer, 2002). From these views it follows that, although there is not a singular essence in religion, mysticism, or spirituality, there can be many overlaps among traditions because each tradition is similar in important respects to some others in the family, even if not in all respects to any, or in any respect to all. In this light, I have suggested several types of equivalencies among traditions (see Ferrer, 2002), which I update here:

1. *Cognitive*: common beliefs, doctrines, or ethical guidelines (e.g., belief in reincarnation [Moregan, 2008]; the notion of revelation as a linguistically mediated transformative process culminating in spiritual vision in Bhatrhari and Bonaventure [Carpenter, 1995]).

2. *Practical*: similar contemplative or spiritual attitudes, techniques, practices, rituals, or skills (e.g., Buddhist concentrative meditation and Christian contemplative prayer; see Gross & Muck [2003]).

3. *Functional*: spiritual doctrines, notions, symbols, or practices that, while having different meanings, play an analogous role in two or more religious traditions. (e.g., the symbols of Christ and Isvhara as mediating between world and God; see Panikkar [1981])—Panikkar (1996) termed these similarities *homeomorphic equivalents*.

4. *Structural*: similarities in the organization of religious groups, processes, or symbolic systems (e.g., Veda and Torah as representing, through divine language, the totality of ultimate reality and a blueprint for creation; see Holdrege [1996]).

5. *Phenomenological*: similar or identical experiential qualities or features between two or more traditions (e.g., the experience of pure consciousness; see Forman [1990]).

6. *Homoversal*: human invariants or universal truths for the human species (e.g., in relation to awake, dream, and dreamless sleep states of consciousness; see Paranjpe [1998]); the term *homoversal* was coined by Rosemont (1988) in a different context.

7. *Ontological*: overlapping elements in different participatory enactions of spiritual worlds or ultimate realities (e.g., ontological union with a personal God in Judaism, Christianity, and Islam; see Idel & McGinn [1996]).

While recognizing the value of S. Taylor's (2017) spiritual trends, I must offer some cautionary clarification. As S. Taylor noted, the participatory approach not only embraces many overlapping similarities among traditions, but also isolates three spiritual trends as regulative yardsticks for a wholesome and integral spiritual development (i.e., movement away from self-centeredness, embodied integration, and eco-socio-political ethics). However, S. Taylor stated, a soft perennialism is needed to account for the strong similarities he identified among traditions because the participatory approach is "too relativistic" ("Soft" Perennialism section, para. 1). Since he did not explain what he meant by *relativistic* or how the participatory approach falls into it, I have no grounds to respond to this charge. In any event, an important difference between S. Taylor's project and my approach is that, while he characterized the common trends as *descriptive* of collective spiritual processes, I have opted to offer the above standards in a *normative* fashion—that is, as principles grounded on the regulative ideal of a "socially responsible integrated selflessness" that can provide practical orientations for critical discernment in spiritual matters (see chapters 1 and 9; Ferrer, 2002, 2008). Although I am not denying the descriptive import of Taylor's categories, I proceed this way to avoid an idealized (and mostly ahistorical) *moral perennialism* that overlooks or underestimates the many ethical ambiguities, antinomies, and failures of both past and present spiritual adepts (see Barnard & Kripal, 2002; Kripal, 2003). I also believe that extreme caution should be employed when offering generalizations based on conceptual (i.e., interpreted) equivalences among traditions and the phenomenological study of fifty-seven modern Western individuals whose views of spirituality, as S. Taylor partially accepted, have been most likely shaped by widespread popular beliefs. That said, I consider S. Taylor's list of spiritual trends to be a solid platform for interreligious dialogue, hermeneutic inquiry, and phenomenological studies of cross-cultural contemplative development.

POSSIBLE SHORTCOMINGS

Having considered the merits of S. Taylor's (2017) soft perennialism, I move now to the discussion of three concerns about his account of human spirituality. In particular, I believe that Taylor's perennialism (1) is intrasubjectively reductionist; (2) contradictorily privileges immanent, monistic, and apophatic traditions; and (3) unnecessarily reifies an experiential realm or landscape that might resurrect the myth of the given in spiritual discourse.

Intrasubjective Reductionism

S. Taylor's (2017) soft perennialism is intrasubjectively reductionist because, à la Schleiermacher (1988), he confined spirituality to phenomenology and thus to individual inner experience. In his words, "my approach is primarily phenomenological—that is, it is based on the study of experience from the perspective of the individual" ("Soft" Perennialism section, para. 1). This phenomenological emphasis is largely motivated by S. Taylor's admitted desire to free transpersonal discourse from metaphysical (and, to a lesser degree, ontological) concerns.

As I elaborated elsewhere (Ferrer, 2002), however, the translation of spiritual phenomena into individual inner experience perpetuates the modernist marginalization of spirituality to the realm of the private and the subjective (see also Rothberg, 1993; Sharf, 1995, 1998). From a participatory perspective, this move is problematic because, for example, the transfiguration of the natural world taking place in nature mysticism (e.g., Marshall, 2005) or entheogenic shamanism (e.g., Winkelman, 2013) is not just a change in the human experience of a pregiven world. Once the Cartesian subject-object dualism is fully overcome, this transfiguration of the natural world can be recognized as the emergence of an ontological event in reality—one in which human consciousness creatively participates, and through which both human experience *and* world undergo a mutually codetermined transformation. Thus, a strictly phenomenological approach such as S. Taylor's (2017) only accounts for half of the equation—and arguably retains the Cartesian split.

As virtually all spiritual traditions maintain, spiritual phenomena are often not to be understood merely in phenomenological terms, but rather as emerging from human participation in spheres of being and awareness (e.g., subtle worlds) that transcend the merely human. S. Taylor's (2017) intrasubjective account of spiritual phenomena effectively voids spiritual knowing from cognitive or epistemic power—whether about the world, the cosmos, or reality. In this book, I have argued that the adoption of agnostic and bracketing stances toward spiritual knowing not only stands (arguably ethnocentrically) against the claims of most spiritual traditions, but is also metaphysically biased (e.g., in favor of scientific-naturalistic or neo-Kantian metaphysical frameworks), even when it is often presented as a way to minimize or avoid metaphysics (see chapters 2 and 9). Mindful that phenomenology entails ontology, however, S. Taylor offered his own ontological musings on the nature of his universal spiritual force, to which I now turn.

"Soft" Hierarchies

Unfortunately, S. Taylor's (2017) views on the ontological nature of the all-pervading spiritual force contradict his claim that soft perennialism does not establish hierarchies among religious traditions or states. To begin, he asserted that although the various traditions naturally offer different perspectives and conceptualizations, the universal spiritual force is both impersonal and immanent to the world. Moreover, following Forman's (1998a) perennial psychology, S. Taylor proposed that this universal force is experienced in states of deep meditation as a pure consciousness event. Thus, while the universal force has actually the same immanent quality and entails the same experience for all people, it is diversely interpreted, for example, as God by Christianity, Islam, and Judaism; *brahman* by Hinduism; or *wakan-taka* by the Lakota. As S. Taylor wrote, "The concepts [e.g., God, *brahman*] can be seen as a metaphysical construction or conceptualisation of a more fundamental, basic, and simple *quality* that is not *in itself* metaphysical" (All-Pervading Spiritual Force section, para. 4). In other words, traditions that attribute transcendent, metaphysical, or personal qualities to this force are misinterpreting its nature, that is, distorting their experience through the projection of doctrinal beliefs: "The [force] *may* be interpreted in absolutist terms, when it is integrated into a metaphysical or philosophical system, and become conceptualised as a transcendent and objective domain of reality" (All-Pervading Spiritual Force section, para. 11).

First and foremost, this account is contingent on a naive—and highly discredited—view of the relationship between experience and conceptualization, according to which spirituality is phenomenologically the same for all people, but nonexperiential variables affect its interpretation and description (e.g., Smart, 1980). Like Taylor (2017), Smart (1980) contended that, although there is a diversity of contextually mediated spiritual experiences, they are all variations of the same universal experience of "consciousness purity." This view problematically overlooks the radically dialectical relationship between experience and interpretation, where "all experience becomes *interpreted* experience, while all interpretation is mediated by experience" (Dupré, 1996, pp. 3–4; see also Almond, 1982; Gadamer, 1990; Kripal, 2001, 2006a). Aware of this interrelation, S. Taylor conceded that

> no experience can exist without some degree of interpretation and conceptualization. . . . But there are degrees of mediation, and without the overlying conceptual frameworks of

spiritual traditions or metaphysical systems, these ranges of experience can be viewed in a more fundamental form. (At the same time, this doesn't mean that the less unmediated experiences are more valid—it's simply a different but equally valid form of expression.) (Nature of "Soft" Perennialism section, para. 13)

This passage is both disconcerting and arguably contradictory. On the one hand, it serves to reinforce S. Taylor's unjustified view that immanent interpretations of the universal force are somehow more fundamental or less mediated than transcendent ones. On the other hand, the assertion that "less unmediated experiences" (Nature of "Soft" Perennialism section, para. 13) are as valid as mediated ones controverts his claim that many traditions wrongly portray the immanent force in transcendent terms due to doctrinal (mis)interpretations.

S. Taylor (2017) seems to want to have it both ways: He wants to favor immanence (less mediated, more fundamental) over transcendence (more mediated, less fundamental), and simultaneously avoid hierarchies by saying that more and less mediated accounts are "different but equally valid forms of expression" (Nature of "Soft" Perennialism section, para. 13). From a participatory perspective, however, mediation stops being a problem (i.e., a distorting source of doctrinal projection on a more fundamental reality or experience) because interpretive frameworks are seen as the vehicles through which reality or the mystery manifests in the locus of the human (Ferrer, 2002). In other words, in a participatory context, mediating factors become the very means that enable human beings to directly participate in the self-disclosure of the world and the mystery (Panikkar, 1996; R. Tarnas, 1991). Of course, this does not mean that all mediating frameworks and associate enactions have the same value or are equally valid. Some of them are more valid than others, not because they better represent a more fundamental experiential essence or "objective" reality, but because they more fully and efficiently foster the wholeness, well-being, harmonious relations, and survival of a greater number of sentient beings.

The second problematic aspect is S. Taylor's (2017) characterization of the universal spiritual force as immanent and impersonal—while also linking the experience of the universal force with meditative states of pure consciousness and apophatic (or negative) spiritualities. These assertions de facto contradict S. Taylor's declaration that his soft perennialism does not lead to hierarchical gradations of spiritual traditions or states. To declare that the universal spiritual force is impersonal immediately demotes the many theistic traditions that attribute personal qualities to the ultimate mystery. Likewise, S. Taylor's association of the experience of the universal spiritual force with both pure consciousness and apo-phatic union favors monistic and formless spiritualities over theistic and visionary ones, among others. Lastly, to claim that the ultimate spiritual force is immanent privileges traditions holding this-worldly accounts of the mystery (e.g., Taoist, Zen, Indigenous) over transcendental ones (e.g., Advaita Vedanta, Christianity, Islam). In this regard, S. Taylor wrote that "It [the spiritual force] is not transcendent but immanent. In other words, *this all-pervading force does not have to be interpreted as a transcendent other, and is only done so when such an interpretation accords with metaphysical and religious systems*" (All-Pervading Spiritual Force section, para. 12). However, proponents of the transcendent nature of the mystery might retort, "It [the spiritual force] is not immanent but transcendent. In other words, this all-pervading force does not have to be interpreted as an immanent energy, and is only done so when such an interpretation accords with metaphysical and religious systems."

In my view, no amount of phenomenological or textual data can settle these conflicting views. A way out, as I suggest in this volume's Postscript, is not to opt for one or the other account (immanent or transcendent, personal or impersonal, etc.), but rather to shift from inter-pretation to enaction, embrace multiple enactions of the mystery, posit the undetermined nature of the mystery, reject the dualism between the mystery and its enactions, and deconstruct the immanent/transcendent dichotomy.

A Mysterious Experiential Realm

S. Taylor's (2017) soft perennialism reifies a mysterious experiential realm that might perpetuate the myth of the given in spiritual discourse. According to S. Taylor's perspectival perennialism, the various spiritual traditions or practitioners explore different areas of the same landscape, thus gaining access to situated perspectives of the same territory. In his words:

There are different groups of people—corresponding to dif-ferent spiritual traditions—exploring different areas of the landscape, moving across different sides of the mountainside. They all have different vantage points and different perspec-tives, and they all experience and interact with the landscape in different ways, from their own viewpoints. Some of their interpretations may differ markedly, because of their different views. Even within the different groups, individual psychological differences may lead to different experiences and different interpretations. But despite these differences of perspective and interpretation, it is still *essentially the same landscape*. ("Soft" Perennialism section, para. 8)

In contrast to traditional metaphysical territories, however, S. Taylor's landscape is a "psychological or experiential realm underlying spiritual traditions, and which can exist outside them" ("Soft" Perennialism section, para. 5). In other words, the landscape is made by "ranges of potential psychological experience" ("Soft" Perennialism section, para. 8) that are latently accessible to all human beings. S. Taylor proposed that the postulation of this open-ended (i.e., in the sense of not obliging any particular spiritual endpoint) but shared landscape is required to account for the strong similarities in spiritual processes he has identified.

Although S. Taylor's (2017) proposal could be seen as preserving the myth of the given (Sellars, 1963) in spiritual discourse, this may not necessarily be the case. In the context of spiritual knowing, the myth of the given erroneously attributes to spiritual referents or spiritual states a number of pregiven features independent of human cognition (for discussions, see Ferrer, 2000, 2002; Wilber, 2005). S. Taylor's allegiance to this myth might be inferred from his claim that the spiritual landscape has a pregiven nature that "precedes interpretation and conceptualization by spiritual traditions" (Abstract, para. 1). Nevertheless, the participatory approach also accepts that once a particular spiritual shore has been enacted, it becomes potentially accessible and, in a way, "given" to the entire human species (see chapters 8 and 9; Ferrer, 2002). This account, I argued, is necessary to explain the well-documented transcultural access to apparently given spiritual symbols and realities (see chapter 8; Grof, 1988a, 1998), and it could also serve to explain similarities in processes of spiritual awakening.

But then, in what way might S. Taylor's (2017) soft perennialism be prey to the myth of the given? To be sure, S. Taylor's experiential emphasis and adoption of the participatory emancipation from a single or final goal for spiritual development free his proposal from the most rigid versions of the myth. However, he remained silent about an important question: the origins of his experiential landscape. If S. Taylor thinks of this landscape as either independent from human history or innate to human nature, then the myth of the given is alive and well in his project. If instead he sees the spiritual landscape as a dynamic and evolving field of experiential potentialities enacted through human history, then his proposal is free of the myth—although it then becomes indistinguishable from the aforementioned participatory account.

In sum, although I believe that participatory enaction explains more parsimoniously the strong similarities identified by S. Taylor (2017) than a mysterious experiential realm (which could be easily reified or objectified), it is likely that S. Taylor and I are talking about the same phenomenon in different terms (cf. Wilber's [2006] Kosmic habits; see chapter 9). If this is the case, however, such a convergence refutes S. Taylor's view that "Ferrer's model is unable to account for the strong similarities between spiritual traditions' conceptions of the process of awakening or expansion" (Nature of "Soft" Perennialism section, para. 12). For a related discussion of S. Taylor's proposal, see Hartelius (2017).

In any event, S. Taylor's (2017) soft perennialism should be regarded as an important advance in the ongoing perennialist/participatory dialogue (e.g., Abramson, 2014a, 2015; Alderman, 2011, 2012a, 2012b; Hartelius, 2015a, 2015b, 2016). His identification of a number of common elements in transformative spiritual processes should instigate further research, and his call for both phenomenological studies of spiritual awakening and the importance of nonreligious spiritual perspectives in transpersonal scholarship should not go unanswered.

NOTES

INTRODUCTION

1. Some historical roots of participatory thinking are discussed in Ferrer and Sherman (2008a), Sherman (2008, 2014a), and Kelly (2008). More recent precedents are the works of Barfield (1957), Buber (1970), Chaudhuri (1974, 1977), Berman (1981), Tambiah (1990), R. Tarnas (1991), Heron (1992, 1998), Panikkar (1993), Reason (1994), Skolimowski (1994), Kremer (1994), and Abram (1996). See also the two *ReVision* monographs *Toward a Participatory Worldview, Part 1 and 2* (Torbert & Reason 2001; Reason & Torbert 2001), which include R. Tarnas's important elucidation of the various meanings of the term *participation*; as well as the two *ReVision* monographs *The Participatory Turn, Parts 1 and 2* (Lahood, 2007c), and Cabot's (2014) "participatory spirituality" entry in Leeming's (2014) *Encyclopedia of Psychology and Religion*. Other important participatory works on religion and spirituality include Evans (1993), Burns (2002), and Miner (2004). For references to participatory thinkers in contemporary transpersonal studies and related fields, see chapter 1.

2. I should clarify the meaning of the term *transpersonal* as used in this volume's subtitle. Etymologically, the prefix *trans-* means beyond or through. *Transpersonal* was originally coined in the field of transpersonal psychology to refer to experiences, motivations, developmental stages (e.g., cognitive, moral, emotional, interpersonal), modes of being, and other phenomena that include but transcend the sphere of the individual or biographical personality, self, or ego (see Maslow, 1968; Sutich, 1976; Vich, 1990; Walsh, 1993). Although debate over the definition of transpersonal psychology has received much attention among scholars (e.g., Caplan, Hartelius, & Rardin, 2003; Hartelius, Rothe, & Roy, 2013; Shapiro, Lee, & Gross, 2002), here I use the term *transpersonal* in a broad and open-ended manner to convey a particular theoretical perspective: one accepting that human beings cocreatively participate in the unfolding of the *mystery* or generative power of life, the cosmos, or reality (for discussions of the term *mystery*, see chapter 1 and Postscript). In this participatory understanding, Tarnas (2002) observed, *transpersonal* "multivalently acknowledges the sacred dimension of life dynamically moving beyond as well as within, through, and by way of the human person in a manner that is mutually transformative, complexly creative, opening to a fuller participation in the divine creativity" (p. xv). Readers unacquainted with the field of transpersonal psychology can consult the aforementioned sources, as well as Washburn (1994), Scotton,

Chinen, and Battista (1996), Ferrer (2002), M. Daniels (2005), and Friedman and Hartelius (2013).

CHAPTER ONE. PARTICIPATORY SPIRITUALITY AND TRANSPERSONAL THEORY

1. To be completely accurate, the book appeared in October 2001, after the publication of a series of essays introducing my participatory perspective (e.g., Ferrer, 1998a, 1998b, 2000a, 2000b, 2001). I wrote *Revisioning* during 1994–98 and defended it as my doctoral dissertation in 1999 (Ferrer, 1999).

2. In addition to the influence of many spiritual, psychological, and philosophical schools and my own lived spiritual inquiry, my participatory perspective is particularly indebted to R. Tarnas's (1991) participatory epistemology, Maturana and Varela's enactive paradigm of cognition (Maturana & Varela, 1987; Varela et al., 1991), Albareda and Romero's (2001) Holistic Transformation (see chapter 4), Kremer's (1994) participatory Indigenous studies, and Panikkar's (1984, 1988, 2014) pluralistic account of religion. Exchanges with the pioneer participatory thinker and practitioner Heron (1992, 1998, 2006) helped me to develop and refine my perspective in significant ways. Important aspects of my work also emerged in contradistinction to Wilber's (1995) integral theory and other classical transpersonal models.

3. Although *Revisioning* was translated into Spanish, Russian, and Italian, as well as widely discussed on the World Wide Web, I limit this assessment, with a few exceptions, to scholarly books and journal articles written in the Anglophone world. A helpful, electronic resource for participatory spirituality is Bauwens's Peer-to-Peer Foundation (http://p2pfoundation.net).

4. My use of the term *enactive* is inspired by Varela et al.'s (1991) innovative articulation of a nonrepresentational paradigm of cognition (see also Frisina, 2002; Thompson, 2007). The participatory formulation adapts and extends the enactive paradigm—originally limited to the perceptual cognition of the natural world—to account for the emergence of ontologically rich religious realms, which are cocreated by human multidimensional cognition and the mystery or generative force of life or the cosmos. By including the epistemic role of all human ways of knowing (e.g., somatic, emotional, imaginal, archetypal) in the enactive process, participatory theory also extends the perceptual cognitivist focus of the original enactive paradigm. For other discussions of spiritual knowing as enactive, see Kelly (2008), Irwin (2008), and Wilber (1995), and for an important synthesis of bio-cognitive, phenomenological, and transpersonal participatory accounts of enaction, see Malkemus (2012).

5. Cf. Chaudhuri's (1977) individuality, relatedness, and transcendence aspects of the human person (see also Shirazi, 2005), and Heron's (2006, 2007) enlivenment, engagement, and enlightenment modes of spiritual inquiry.

6. The language of *equi*primacy, *equi*potentiality, and *equi*pluralism can raise the specter of Wilber's (1995, 2002) critique of the so-called green meme

in spiritual discourse, with its problematic emphasis on antihierarchical egalitarianism. For a response to Wilber's "green meme" charge of the participatory approach, see Ferrer (2002, pp. 223–226) and below, and for a critique of Wilber's misleading use of the "green meme" by one of Claire Graves's students, see Todorovic (2002). See also Butters (2015) for a historical overview of both Graves's (1970, 1974) model and its successor Spiral Dynamics (which introduced the term *green meme*; Beck & Cowan, 1996), as well as a discussion of Wilber's various misrepresentations of this body of work.

7. I stress "potentially" to convey that every spiritual tradition—even those traditionally promulgating disembodied or world-denying doctrines and practices—can be legitimately re-envisioned from the perspective of more holistic understandings (see chapters 9 and 10). Think, for example, of Patanjali's yoga system—originally aimed at the arguably dissociative self-identification with a pure consciousness or universal Self (*purusa*) in isolation (*kaivalyam*) from body, mind, and nature (*prakrti*), yoga is nowadays conceptualized and practiced globally in strongly integrative and embodied ways (e.g., Horton, 2012; Horton & Harvey, 2012; Whicher, 1998). For an in-depth historical account of the transformations of yoga practice in the West, see Singleton (2010).

8. See this volume's Postscript for an extended discussion of how overcoming the dualism of the mystery and its enactions not only fosters a more genuine religious pluralism, but also minimizes sectarianism in participatory spirituality.

9. Although there are important differences (see Cabot, 2015), the participatory affirmation of a multiplicity of ontologically rich spiritual worlds is aligned with contemporary anthropology's "ontological turn" (Henare, Holbraad, & Wastell, 2007; Holbraad, 2012); consider, for example, Descola's (2013) multiple ontologies and Viveiros de Castro's (2014, 2015) account of Amerindian multinaturalism. Although Holbraad and other anthropologists would resist the charge, Heywood's (2012) contention that "insisting on the 'reality' of multiple worlds commits you to a meta-ontology in which such worlds exist" (146) parallels the participatory openness to a multidimensional cosmos. In any event, as Cabot's (2011, 2015) important work showed, participatory-enactive approaches are more radically pluralistic—and ontologically thick—than those of modern anthropologists.

10. As J. Heron (personal communication, May 8, 2011) perceptively noted, the dissociation, egocentricism, and eco-socio-political tests are related to the intrapersonal, transpersonal, and interpersonal dimensions of participatory spirituality, respectively (see Table 1.1).

11. It is noteworthy that Washburn (2003b) endorsed the participatory affirmation of a creative dialectical relationship between spiritual universalism and pluralism (see also Puhakka, 2008), and M. Daniels (2009) suggested the natural alignment between spiral-dynamic and participatory perspectives. I concur. These perspectives' emphasis on embodiment, relatedness, and instinctual/spiritual integration renders likely their future integration. An important theoretical difference lies between Washburn's (1995) neo-Kantian agnosticism

toward the ontological status of spiritual realities and the participatory avowal of their cocreated ontological value (for discussions of transpersonal neo-Kantianism, see chapters 2 and 9). As Ianiszeskwi (2010) argued, however, the spiral-dynamic and participatory orientations might be coherently integrated via linking Washburn's (1995) Dynamic Ground with a postulated participatory Noetic Field that is the source of ontologically rich enacted spiritual realities.

12. Participatory pluralism is Dale's (2014) sixth and most recent agglomeration, with neo-perennialism as the fifth and the transpersonal East-West synthesis as the fourth. He also identified three earlier agglomerations in transpersonal thinking: a premodern mystical world philosophy as the first agglomeration, nineteenth-century German idealism as the second, and twentieth-century early introspectionist/cognitive science as the third. For a critical appreciation of Dale's own pluralistic transpersonal vision, see Ferrer (2015).

13. For some historical roots of participatory thinking in premodern and modern times, see Ferrer and Sherman (2008a), Sherman (2008, 2014a), and Kelly (2008). For references on more recent participatory authors and works, see Introduction, note 1, as well as Cabot (2014) and Hartelius and Ferrer (2013).

14. Participatory thinking is also alive in other fields such as qualitative research (e.g., Hiles, 2008; Reason & Bradbury, 2008), ecopsychology (e.g., Abram, 1996; W. W. Adams, 2010a, 2010b; H. Walker, 2012), anthropology (e.g., Lahood, 2007c; Tambiah, 1990), relational and postrelational psychoanalysis (R. S. Brown, 2016), and contemporary Christian theology and spirituality (e.g., Burns, 2002; Dreyer & Burrows, 2005; Miner, 2004), among others.

15. I do not suggest that all these authors necessarily identify themselves as participatory scholars, but rather that they have endorsed, supported, or developed participatory perspectives in transpersonal and spiritual discourse. Participatory thinking, as I argue in the conclusion to this chapter, tends to crystallize not so much in a formalized school of thought granting its members a sense of distinct identity, but in a participatory sensibility to spirituality and scholarship informing a network of extraordinarily diverse scholar-practitioners.

16. In addition to being reprinted in many publications (e.g., *Revision*, *Kosmos*, and *Studies in Holistic Education*), the article catalyzed a number of invited keynote and plenary presentations at major national and international educational conferences, such as the Fourth International Conference on the New Paradigm of Science in Education, University of Baja California (UABC) in Mexicali (Mexico, 2005); the International Transformative Learning Conference, Michigan State University (East Lansing, Michigan, 2005); the Annual Conference of Holistic Education, Ritsumeikan University (Kyoto, Japan, 2009); and the First International Conference in Indonesia for Humanities and Transpersonal Psychology, Udayana University (Bali, Indonesia, 2015).

17. In subsequent writings, I clarified my perspective on this issue:

I am not suggesting the existence of a "moral perennialism" resting on a supposedly ethical common religious past. By contrast, I propose that any future global ethics will very likely not emerge from our highly diverse and ambiguous moral religious history, but rather from our critical reflection on such history in the context of our present-day moral intuitions. (Ferrer, 2008, p. 143)

18. Notably, *Revisioning* anticipated and addressed Wilber's critical points; for a response to the charge of performative self-contradiction, see Ferrer (2002, pp. 179–81; see also Ferrer, 1998a) and for a response to the "green meme" charge, see Ferrer (2002, pp. 223–226). Wilber (2002) has not responded to these rejoinders, nor has he re-engaged his response (Wilber 1998) to my earlier critique of his spiritual epistemology (Ferrer 1998b), which is also addressed in Ferrer (2002, pp. 66–69). In subsequent works, however, Wilber stopped using Popperian falsifiability as demarcation criterion between genuine and dogmatic spiritual knowledge—a central target of my critique—so I can only assume that the critique was effective even if Wilber never acknowledged its validity. Arguably, the participatory critique significantly contributed to Wilber's departure from the field of transpersonal psychology and related announcement of its demise (see Ferrer & Puente, 2013).

19. For an extended discussion, see chapter 9. See also Abramson (2014a) for a response to Hartelius and Ferrer's (2013) participatory critique of Wilber's work, as well as the ensuing exchange between Whomsley (2014), Abramson (2014b, 2015), and Hartelius (2015a, 2015b). In my view, Hartelius's (2015a) essay summarizes and conclusively settles many of the central issues discussed around Wilber's work in the last two decades. For other criticisms of the participatory approach from Dzogchen and traditionalist perspectives, see Capriles (2013) and Sugobono (2013), respectively.

20. In my view, B. Tarnas (2016) offered a more cogent and integrative account of the relationship between the participatory approach and archetypal cosmology. Unfortunately, publication deadlines do not allow me to engage her essay here as it surely deserves. See also R. Tarnas (2012) for a participatory (re-)interpretation of the nature of archetypes (mythic, psychic, and cosmic) as radically pluralistic, indeterminate, and enactive.

21. Gleig and Boeving (2009) traced the origins of this metaphysics to the modern psychoanalytic ideal of an intimate autonomy "allowing for connection without the loss of individuality" (p. 68). For the romantic and mystical roots of this account, see Kirschner (1996).

CHAPTER TWO. TRANSPERSONAL PSYCHOLOGY, SCIENCE, AND THE SUPERNATURAL

1. While strongly advocating for quantitative (e.g., psychometric) studies, transpersonal scientists regard most qualitative approaches as scientific (e.g., Friedman, 2013a; MacDonald & Friedman, 2013). I therefore use the terms *scientific* and *empirical* interchangeably to include both quantitative and qualita-

tive research. As Dale (2014) compellingly argued, however, mainstream (linear) quantitative methods should be supplemented with nonlinear methodologies in the study of transpersonal phenomena. Since essential aspects of transpersonal experience and development are nonlinear (i.e., indeterministic and thus defying statistical predictability), they cannot be captured by the conventional quantitative methods of mainstream psychology (Dale, 2014; see also Almendro, 2014; Almendro & Weber, 2012). In other words, because transpersonal trajectories are developmentally atypical, individual case studies are more informative about transpersonal growth than are statistical analyses based on group studies. For Dale, the application of the nonlinear methods emerging from twenty-first-century mathematics, physics, and systems biology leads to "a transpersonal psychology based around plurality and complexity rather than universal structuralism" (p. 37). For further contrasts between participatory pluralism and universal structuralism, see Dale's important work and chapter 9 in this book.

2. This is in itself a rather peculiar claim: to wit, are not theoretical physicists *physicists?* Are not the publishing authors in the *Journal of Theoretical Biology* biologists? Note also that accepting Friedman's (2002, 2013a) proposal would forbid use of the term *psychologies* for (1) the many schools of the depth psychological tradition (e.g., classical, contemporary, and intersubjective psychoanalysis; Jungian, analytic, and archetypal psychologies; object-relations theory and self-psychology); (2) the robust nonempirical subfields of contemporary psychology (e.g., theoretical psychology, critical psychology, liberation psychology, or psychology of science); and (3) central elements of evolutionary psychology, ecological psychology, cultural psychology, comparative and cross-cultural psychology, indigenous psychologies, and phenomenological, existential, and hermeneutic psychologies. In this regard, Slife and Williams (1997) listed more than a dozen of academic psychological journals "devoted entirely, or in part, to theoretical work" (p. 125). Finally, it is unclear how Friedman's scientific transpersonal psychology would be different from disciplines such as the psychology of religion or the scientific study of religion. Despite Friedman's (2002) de jure pronouncement against such a possibility, his proposal seems inevitably to lead to the gradual dissolution of the field into these mainstream fields—perhaps becoming a kind of fringe subfield dealing with those particular spiritual experiences called *transpersonal.*

3. Although naturalism is widely regarded today as essential to the modern scientific worldview (e.g., Mahner, 2012; Schafersman, 1997), the association of naturalism and science was largely historically contingent (Bilgrami, 2010; Kubrin, 1980). Science has the potential to operate with supernaturalistic assumptions as evidenced by the many past scientific explanations (even Newton's) appealing to supernaturalistic factors (S. Clarke, 2009). For a defense of science's potential openness to both naturalistic and supernaturalistic worldviews, see Fishman (2007).

4. Although usually hand-in-hand, naturalism and materialism are not synonymous. Whereas all materialists are naturalists of some sort, one can be a naturalist without committing to materialism or to the view that all that truly

exists is made of matter. Expanded or liberal forms of naturalism embrace the reality of nonmaterial entities such as numbers, psychological states, and perceptions (see De Caro & Macarthur, 2004b, 2010; Nagel, 2012; Schafersman, 1997).

5. My endorsement of van Fraassen's (2002) account of the ideological status of naturalism and materialism does not mean that I subscribe to his constructive empiricism (2002, 2008), which results in the rejection of all metaphysical considerations about nature and reality. For a cogent rebuttal to van Fraassen's critique of metaphysics, see Chakravartty (2007, pp. 20–26).

6. Physicalism is a narrower stance than materialism: The latter is the view that only matter exits, and the former holds that the microentities studied by physics are ontologically or explanatorily primary (see J. Dupré, 1995).

7. Nagel (2012) agrees: "Such a world view [reductionist and materialist naturalism] is not a necessary condition of the practice of any of those sciences [biology, chemistry, and physics], and its acceptance or nonacceptance would have no effect on most scientific research" (p. 4). The failure of psychophysical reductionism, Nagel continued, shows that materialist naturalism "is ripe for displacement" (p. 12). For Nagel, the most cogent alternative is to conceive that mind is "a basic aspect of nature" (p. 16).

8. Naturalism can also be religious in the sense that nature can be understood religiously and evoke religious feelings—for contemporary articulations of religious naturalism, see Crosby (2002), Hogue (2010), and Stone (2008). Religious traditions, such as certain Zen schools, that do not posit metaphysical or supernatural referents could also be included within this category.

9. Discussing the scientific dismissal of paranormal evidence, Friedman and Hartelius (2013b) made a strikingly similar point: "If a modern metaphysics is imposed on research (cf. Mahner, 2012), then those very aspects of the phenomena will necessarily be discounted a priori, and the knowledge that might be generated from them will be lost. Evidence challenging the de facto metaphysical assumptions that tend to accompany science is disallowed on the grounds that it challenges those assumptions—rather like a judge who refuses to consider a motion to recuse him- or herself" (p. xxv).

10. This proposal is not new. M. Daniels (2005) wrote: "As transpersonal psychologists, we should aim to bracket as far as possible ALL metaphysical assumptions in what should essentially become a phenomenological examination of experiences of transformation" (p. 230; see also M. Daniels, 2001). Similarly, adopting Jung's neo-Kantianism (Nagy, 1991), Washburn (1995) pointed out: "We simply cannot know . . . whether the power of the Ground, in addition to being an intrapsychic phenomenon, is also an extrapsychic (metaphysical, cosmic) noumenon" (p. 130). For a transpersonal critique of this position, see Lancaster (2002).

11. In neo-Kantianism, Krijnen and Zeidler (2014) wrote,

epistemology functions as *philosophia prima*. As *philosophia prima*, epistemology does not only have a specific content or subject matter.

Beyond that it has a fundamental relevance for the whole system of philosophy, as it predetermines its method and basic concepts. (para. 2)

Strictly speaking, neo-Kantianism was a highly pluralistic philosophical movement—dominant in Europe between 1870 and 1930—developed at the Marburg School (e.g., Hermann Cohen, Paul Natorp, and Ernst Cassirer; see Beiser, 2015; Kohenke, 1991) and the Southwest German School (e.g., Wilhelm Windelband, Heinrich Rickert, Emil Lask; see Beiser, 2015; Kohenke, 1991). As Makkreel and Luft (2009) showed in their anthology on the impact of neo-Kantianism on contemporary philosophy, this orientation influenced key modern developments such as Kuhn's (1970) notion of scientific paradigm, Sellars's (1963) challenge to the myth of the given, and aspects of Gadamer's (1990) hermeneutics (despite the latter's explicit criticisms of neo-Kantianism). For critical discussions of neo-Kantianism in transpersonal and religious studies, see Adam (2002), Blum (2014), Ferrer (2000a, 2002), Ferrer and Sherman (2008a), Forgie (1985), Forman (1999), R. King (1999), and Schilbrack (2014a).

12. After a balanced discussion of the philosophical foundations of scientific transpersonal psychology, MacDonald (2013) also assumed a neo-Kantian epistemology. This is evident in his accepting the Western dualism between the world of appearances (human perception) and reality (the world as-it-really-is; p. 313), as well as the derived dualism of map and territory. Although the reality-and-appearances dualism is not strictly equivalent to the Kantian two-worlds doctrine (Schilbrack, 2014a; van Fraaseen, 2008), identical skeptical consequences emerge when such a reality behind appearances is considered to be cognitively inaccessible.

13. Friedman's views are strongly reminiscent of Katzian constructivism (see chapter 8), whose Jewish leanings have been exposed by religious studies scholars (see Evans, 1989; R. King, 1999; H. Smith, 1987). In addition, metaphysical agnosticism has been denounced as "cryptotheological," or inadvertently perpetuating theological agendas in its implicitly positing a single transcendental referent about which scholars need to remain agnostic (Fitzgerald, 2000).

14. For critical overviews of the debate between proponents of Katz's (1978b, 1983a) contextualism and advocates of Forman's (1990, 1998b) neo-perennialism in the study of mysticism, see R. King (1999), M. T. Adam (2002), Ferrer (2000a, 2002), and Studstill (2005). See also chapter 8 in this volume.

15. For critiques of objectivism, see Bernstein (1985), Bordo (1987), and Megill (1994).

16. But then, why not to go all the way and replace folk psychological language with scientific brain jargon, as Churchland (1986) famously proposed (i.e., talk about neural dynamics instead of beliefs or feelings)? I suspect that Friedman would reject such an eliminative materialist project, but his proposal is congruent with it—especially considering modern science's allegiance to ontological materialism and reductionism (MacDonald, 2013; Mahner, 2012).

NOTES TO CHAPTER TWO

17. For a thorough account of how Lakoff and Johnson's (1999) "embodied realism" paves a middle way between objectivism and postmodern relativism in both the sciences and the humanities, see Slingerland (2008). On embodied cognitive science in general, see Varela et al. (1991), Chemero (2009), and L. H. Shapiro (2014).

18. Cf. Schilbrack (2014a): "Kant's distinction does not *challenge* the alleged metaphysical desire to describe a noumenal reality but rather *invents* it" (p. 173n5). The patriarchal foundations of the Cartesian-Kantian legacy could also be explored (cf. R. Tarnas, 1991). Discussing the modern conceptualization of mysticism, for example, Jantzen (1995) denounced the androcentricism of this existential stance: "Feminists . . . have demonstrated the extent to which the Cartesian/Kantian 'man of reason' is indeed male" (pp. 343–344). On the masculinized origins of Cartesian thinking, see also Bordo (1987).

19. Supporting the ongoing (and arguably highly political) "scientification" and "biologizing" of psychology (e.g., Slife & Williams, 1997; Teo, 2005; Ward, 2002) that is characteristic, for example, of the American Psychological Association (APA), Friedman (2002, 2013a) sees psychology more as a natural science (like biology, chemistry, and physics) than a social or human science (like anthropology or sociology). In my view, psychology's focus on socially situated, biologically mediated, and arguably spiritually informed behavior and experience makes the discipline a natural, human, social, and spiritual science— a highly integrative field calling for a plurality of epistemic frameworks and methodological approaches beyond the exclusive scientific empiricism of the natural sciences (cf. Giorgi, 1970; Heron, 1998; Polkinghorne, 1983; Slife & Williams, 1997).

20. Moving past the Two Cultures split does not overlook the different epistemic sensibilities and discursive styles of the various scientific and humanist disciplines. In this approach, rather, such different sensibilities operate not only between but also within the sciences and the humanities; in addition, they are all equally important in the human search for knowledge, meaning, and understanding. For a lucid discussion of Two Cultures stereotypes, conflicts, and polarizations, see B. H. Smith (2005).

21. For J. Dupré (1995, 2004), there are not two or one grand cultures but a multiplicity of overlapping subcultures of inquiry—or "epistemic cultures," in Knorr-Cettina's (1999) terms—that may (or may not) share epistemic virtues (e.g., coherence, empirical accountability, elegance, simplicity) and normative virtues (e.g., critique of androcentric and ethnocentric biases). The debunking of the myth of the unity of science brought forth by this conception of shared epistemic virtues paradoxically delivers "a kind of unity of knowledge" (J. Dupré, 1995, p. 243).

22. Incidentally, Friedman (2013a) misapprehended the nature of my participatory proposal as building "silos that separate, abnegating the possibility of finding useful connections" (p. 303) among spiritual traditions that lead to "considering all transpersonal systems as incommensurate" (p. 303). In my work,

however, I not only criticized constructivism's "myth of the framework," which might lead to such undesirable outcomes (Ferrer, 2000a, 2002), but also argued that participatory pluralism allows and even encourages doctrinal, practical, and even ontological hybridizations among traditions (see chapter 10).

In addition, contra Friedman's (2013a) suggestion that my proposal leads to the uncritical appraisal of local understandings, a participatory epistemology provides ample resources for the criticism of religious traditions (e.g., Ferrer, 2002, 2008; Ferrer & Sherman, 2008a; see also chapters 3 and 10). The participatory endorsement of "the diversity of all spiritual traditions as seen on their own terms" (Friedman, 2013a, p. 303) should be understood not as eschewing criticism, but rather as both avoiding reductionist distortions of such a diversity (e.g., by perennialism) and affirming a potential plurality of equally holistic and emancipatory spiritual enactions of self, relationships, and world (equiplurality principle; see chapters 1 and 9).

23. In this context, Wilber's (2006) postmetaphysical reduction of spiritual realms to the individual's interiors fails to bridge the gap (see chapter 9; Hartelius, 2015a; Hartelius & Ferrer, 2014).

24. Note that the overcoming of Kantian assumptions automatically eschews the very idea of a metaphysical dimension "supernaturally" existing beyond or behind the realm of appearances (see Hartelius & Ferrer, 2013), even though such a "realm of appearances" (which then becomes "reality" itself) might be substantially deeper and broader than the one accepted by modern scientific naturalism.

25. Although its origins are uncertain, *astral doctor* (or *spirit doctor*) is demonstrably an etic term and Indigenous peoples use different local terms to refer to such reportedly nonphysical entities. The Matsigenka of Southern Peru, for example, call their spirit allies *Sangariite*—those "elusive, luminous beings" that can be seen "under the influence of hallucinogens plants" (Shepard, 2014, p. 23). In the context of Peruvian *vegetalismo*, after discussing several types of animal spirits, Luna (1986) wrote about helping spirits that are always seen in human form: "they are either the spirits of the plant teachers or . . . *maestros de la medicina* (masters of medicine), which include Indian and mestizo shamans . . . famous deceased Western doctors, wise men from distant countries, and even beings from other planets, solar systems and galaxies" (p. 94).

26. At the time of both the interview and its publication, I was unaware of a number of serious sexual misconduct charges—many of which emerged several years later—being made against Arévalo and several of his apprentices working at Arévalo's centers in Iquitos, Peru. Given the seriousness of the charges, scholarly and ethical responsibility compels me to urge individuals interested in working with Arévalo or visiting his centers to carry out their own independent research regarding these charges before proceeding to work with him or his apprentices in Iquitos. This proviso does not obviously apply to Arévalo's disciples offering ceremonies in impeccable ethical ways. Whereas I firmly believe that published interview (Ferrer, 2013) contains valuable information about

Shipibo *vegetalismo* and cosmology, the interview should in no way be read as my promotion of Arévalo's shamanic practice or encouragement to work with him. I thank my students at California Institute of Integral Studies (CIIS), San Francisco, for crucial exchanges leading to my taking action about this very important issue. For a balanced discussion of the unfortunately increasing cases of sexual transgression in Indigenous shamanic contexts, see Peluso (2014).

27. The mainstream scientific explanation of some of these entheogenic phenomena (in particular, visions of geometric patterns such as spirals or spiderwebs) is that they are determined by the form of the retino-cortical map and the architecture of the visual cortex (e.g., Bresloff, Cowan, Golubitsky, Thomas, & Wiener, 2002; Klüver, 1966; Siegel & Jarvik, 1975). In support of this hypothesis, Bresloff, Cowan, Golubitsky, Thomas, and Wiener (2002) wrote, "In most cases, the images are seen in both eyes and move with them, but maintain their relative positions in the visual field. We interpret this to mean that they are generated in the brain" (p. 474).

This account, however, cannot explain the shared, interactive nature of either certain types of entheogenic geometric visions or more elaborated visions, such as the astral doctors or other nonphysical entities. As Reichel-Dolmatoff (1978) showed in his classical study of ayahuasca visions in the Tukano people of Colombia, while the geometrical patters of the first hallucinatory stage strikingly corresponded to the shape of phosphenes (i.e., light patterns originated within the eye and the brain) as depicted by Knoll, Kluger, Hofer, & Lawder (1962), these patterns cannot account for the more elaborated visions of the second and third stages—in particular those involving encounters with supernatural beings or mythological reenactments of the creation of the universe. In addition, from a participatory perspective, even if some of these so-called *entoptic phenomena* (from the Greek, "within vision"; see Klüver, 1966; Lewis-Williams & Dowson, 1988) match the structure of the optic system or visual cortex, this fact does not preclude the possibility that those systems mediate (vs. simply produce) the enacted perception of independent or cocreated energetic dimensions of reality. This participatory account would be consistent with mystical and esoteric visions of the human body as an organ of divine or spiritual revelation (see chapter 3).

28. However, Grof's (1988) reported transcultural access, in nonordinary states of consciousness, to both the imagery and the (esoteric, at times) meaning of spiritual symbols, rituals, and cosmologies belonging to specific religious worlds without participants' previous exposure to those symbols arguably challenges such a naturalistic reading (see chapter 8).

29. It is noteworthy that the trajectories of two of the most prominent figures of twentieth-century entheogenic culture—psychedelic priest Terence McKenna and visionary artist Alex Grey—were significantly shaped by shared entheogenic visions. McKenna's shared entheogenic experiences with his younger brother Dennis took place in 1971 at La Chorrera, Colombia, and prefigured the major themes developed in his lifework (D. McKenna, 2012;

T. McKenna, 1993). Grey's shared vision is recounted by his wife Allyson:

> On an LSD trip with Alex on June 3rd, 1976, we simultaneously shared a vision of the vista of interconnected fountains and drains flowing in a pattern that spread infinitively in all directions. . . . For both of us, this was clearly our life's most profound revelation. As the most important message we could impart to the world, as artists this higher vision would become the subject of our work for a lifetime. (cited in Slattery, 2015, p. 242)

Also relevant to this discussion is the controversial body of evidence on (non-entheogenic) collectively perceived apparitions, some of which have reportedly been described from different perceptual angles (e.g., Cunningham, 2011b).

30. For a historical account of the "naturalization" of hallucinations, see Berrios (2005). As Aleman and Larøi (2008) explained, "Increasingly, mystical visions and similar experiences were no longer seen as the communication of supernatural origin. Instead, natural explanations were advanced" (p. 14). For the medieval origins and development of the distinction between the natural and the supernatural in the West, see de Lubac (1967) and Bartlett (2008).

31. The "and/or" of this sentence is crucial, particularly in the context of spiritual inquiry. On the one hand, it may be plausible to consider intersubjective consensus as a central epistemic standard in the context of what I call, paraphrasing Kuhn (1970), a single tradition's *normal spiritual inquiry*. In other words, when spiritual practice is managed by a prevailing spiritual paradigm and something akin to a correspondence theory of truth is operative (e.g., between practitioners' insights and the tradition's mapped "stages of the path"). On the other hand, it should be obvious that intersubjective agreement is probably an inappropriate test not only among traditions (which bring forth different and often incompatible spiritual insights), but also in periods of *revolutionary spiritual inquiry* within one tradition, in which anomalies in relation to accepted doctrines arise and new paradigms of spiritual understanding are developed (e.g., it is likely that neither the Buddha's enlightenment nor the claims of the more radical Christian mystics could have been intersubjectively corroborated in their respective times and contexts). In the latter case, the search for more pragmatic avenues to legitimize spiritual knowledge claims becomes imperative (see chapter 9; Ferrer, 2002).

32. Similarly, Kripal (2014) recommended the following to students of comparative religion: "We also need to beware of projecting the western categories of the 'natural' and the 'supernatural' onto religious worldviews in which such divisions are simply not operable. We have suggested instead that you employ the category of the 'super natural'" (p. 172). Indeed, commenting on a number of visions of other "realities," the Dagara (Burkina Faso, Africa) scholar and healer Somé (1995) wrote: "Enlarging one's vision and abilities has nothing supernatural about it, rather it is 'natural' to be a part of nature and to participate in a wider understanding of reality" (p. 226).

33. The use of entheogens as inquiry tools is justified by modern cognitive psychological studies (Shanon, 2002), transpersonal research proposals (Friedman, 2006; Roberts & Hruby, 2002), and Indigenous accounts of the power of entheogens to make subtle entities or phenomena visible (e.g., Harner, 1973; Shepard, 2014; Turner, 1992). Interestingly, despite receiving enthusiastic support from transpersonal psychologists for decades, Tart's (1972) state-specific scientific research program never took off. I strongly suspect that the problem was that accessing deep meditative states in a stable manner, let alone the various visionary realms mapped by religious traditions, can take an entire life of practice. Put bluntly, transpersonal researchers have the maps and the vehicle but not the fuel. Given the widely documented access to spiritual states and realms entheogens provide (e.g., Grof, 1985; Merkur 1998; Shanon, 2002; Strassman, 2001), I suggest that Tart's program could be revitalized by the cautious but systematic use of entheogens as inquiry tools. Despite the current revival of governmentally sanctioned psychedelic research (Friedman, 2006; Langlitz, 2013; Roberts & Winkelman, 2013), the use of most entheogens in the United States is still illegal, so this proposal should be seen as strictly epistemological and by no means recommending unlawful research.

CHAPTER THREE. TOWARD A FULLY EMBODIED SPIRITUAL LIFE

1. Important discussions have appeared in the literature since the publication of the first version of this chapter (Ferrer, 2006). Perhaps the most thorough consideration of an embodied spirituality is the one offered by Masters (2010), but see also Heron's (2007) participatory spirituality (2007), Kripal's (2007) enlightenment of the body, Lanzetta's (2005) embodied feminine mysticism, and Ray's (2008) critique of Buddhist disembodied practice. Although not focused on spiritual practice, Fuller's (2008) work is a mine of rich information and reflection on the bodily sources of spiritual experience. Previous valuable resources include Dürckheim (1962), Donnelly (1982), Evans (1993), J. B. Nelson (1978, 1992), and Washburn (1995, 2003a), as well as the body spirituality that can be drawn from classical and contemporary works in the field of Somatics (see D. Johnson, 2005).

2. I presented earlier versions of this chapter in a keynote address at the 2006 conference, Mindfulness: Scientific and Spiritual Perspectives, University of Witten-Herdecke, Germany, and as a plenary address at the Esoterika 2007 Festival: Prague Gateways, Prague, Czech Republic.

3. I take advantage of the publication of this essay in this anthology to credit Ramón V. Albareda's teachings on embodied spirituality as an important source of the following account, even if due to their oral nature it has not been always possible to document them bibliographically.

4. The chakras (or *cakras*), whose number varies across the traditions, are the living body's subtle energetic centers that store and channel the vital

force (*prana-shakti*) of the individual. The Indian tantric tradition identifies six of these centers, located respectively at the base of the spine (*muladhara*), the pelvic sexual area (*svadhisthana*), the solar plexus (*manipura*), the heart (*anahata*), the throat (*visuddha*), and in the center of the eyebrows or "third eye" (*ajna*) (Basu, 1986). Whereas all these centers were considered in many religious practices, the overriding tendency has been to transmute the primary expressions of the vital force—connected to the lower chakras—into the subtle qualities and ecstasies of the heart and consciousness—connected to the higher chakras.

5. In the Postscript, I argue that the open naturalism introduced in chapter 2 problematizes the traditional opposition between the categories of transcendence and immanence. Generally speaking, whereas the term *immanent* can be unambiguously used to describe spiritual sources located within—or emerging from—physical matter, body, and nature, the term *transcendent* is a highly polythetic (i.e., heterogeneous) or even homonymic term. Specifically, the term *transcendent* has at least three related but independent meanings: (1) metaphysically supernatural dimensions or realities (i.e., allegedly existing beyond the "natural" world); (2) spiritual orientations connected to the overcoming of so-called gross, instinctive, or primary human dimensions or attributes (e.g., sexuality, mortal body, certain emotional states), often through the achievement of transcending states of consciousness or being; and (3) spiritual sources or energies that transcend (i.e., go beyond) human structures and personal individuality with no necessary metaphysical connotations (e.g., sources existing in nature or the cosmos; here, transcendence becomes immanence). In my work, I reject the first definition, opting for a wider naturalistic framework that is open to the feasibility of a multidimensional cosmos and associated subtle worlds; critique the second on pragmatic grounds as not being a fully embodied or integrative spiritual approach, and so one that can lead to unnecessary suffering; and embrace the existence of the third.

6. Furthermore, in light of the Indian account of the primordial vital force (*shakti*) as feminine and of consciousness (*shiva*) as masculine, certain traditional tantric practices can be seen as a kind of internalized patriarchy in which feminine energies are used at the service of masculine goals and expressions. This account should not be taken as descriptive of all tantric and neo-tantric practices, but only of those seeking to transmute vital/sexual energies into disembodied states of consciousness. It should be obvious that both Tantra and neo-Tantra are practiced today with more embodied and integrative aspirations. For a fascinating genealogy of the transformations of Tantra in the context of the dialectical encounter between East and West, Indigenous traditions and scholarly imaginations, see Urban (2003).

7. This possibility is arguably connected to the contemporary revisioning of many religious traditions, such as Fox's (1988) Creation Spirituality for Christianity, Lerner's (1994, 2000) Jewish Renewal and Emancipatory Spirituality, or Rothberg's (1998) Socially Engaged Buddhism. These and many other spiritual leaders and authors propose reconstructions of their traditions that

seek to integrate human dimensions that had been hitherto inhibited, repressed, or even proscribed (such as the role of women and feminine values, body appreciation and sensual desire, or intimate relationships and sexual diversity). The importance of grounding an integrated spiritual life in primary potentials and instinctual life is also central to Washburn's (1995, 2003a) spiral-dynamic model of transpersonal development, as well as to Chaudhuri's revision of Sri Aurobindo's integral yoga (Shirazi, 2001).

8. Of course, the "structural" correspondence between body and cosmos should not be taken in a geometrical or quantitative fashion (à la Leonardo da Vinci's *Vitruvian Man*), but in a dynamic and qualitative one (i.e., body and cosmos as having interiority, consciousness and energy, telos). Whereas modern science does not support the strictly structural parallels posited by some ancient traditions, scientists have established that many equations, patterns, and symmetries are shared by both the (subatomic) microcosm and the (astronomical) macrocosm (for examples, see Wilczek, 2016). As Wilczek (2016), a Nobel laureate in physics, observed, "We humans are poised between Microcosm and Macrocosm, containing one, sensing the other, comprehending both" (p. 323).

9. For a discussion of some of the possible implications of this integration for intimate relationships, see Ferrer (2007). In a forthcoming book, I offer a fuller treatment of this important topic (Ferrer, 2016).

10. This proposal is in accord with many mystical teachings, such as those regarding the creative role of the primordial *shakti* or *kundalini* in Hindu tantra, the generative power attributed to *chi* energy in Taoism, or even the motivation behind *virginae subintroductae* (or celibate marriages) in the early Christian church (see Ferrer & Sherman, 2008a).

CHAPTER FOUR. A NEW LOOK AT INTEGRAL GROWTH

1. What counts as *integral* or *integrative* practice is of course contingent on the explicit or implicit criteria used by researchers. For a valuable review of other psychospiritual integrative practices selected using different criteria than mine—including mindfulness-based stress reduction, prayer, and Transcendental Meditation—see Wall, Nye, and FitzMedrud (2013). More aligned with this chapter's standards, M. Daniels (2013) identified four important developments toward a truly integral practice: Sri Aurobindo's (1993) Integral Yoga, Leonard and Murphy's (1995) Integral Transformative Practice, Wilber's Integral Life Practice (Wilber, Patten, Leonard, & Morelli, 2008), and Albareda and Romero's Holistic Integration (called Holistic Transformation in this chapter; see note 8) as important developments toward a truly integral practice.

2. For accounts of the Indian tantric sources of Murphy's (1993) integral approach, see Kripal (2005, 2007). See also Taves (2005) for a lucid discussion of Murphy's overall approach to metanormal or extraordinary functioning, and Vieten et al. (2014) for an empirical study of the impact of Murphy and Leonard's

ITP program on practitioners' health, well-being, and self-transcendence.

3. Although mirror images of each other, there is an important difference between Orientalism and Occidentalism. As Fazlhashemi (2013) pointed out, whereas Orientalism is generally thought to have emerged as means of justifying the Western hegemony over the Orient (e.g., Said, 1979), Occidentalism emerged from the need to shape the identity of the vulnerable and the weak in opposition to, for example, a stereotyped decadent and materialistic West. For more nuanced portraits of Orientalism and, by extrapolation, Occidentalism, see J. J. Clarke (1997) and R. King (1999).

4. I place *masculine* and *feminine* within quotation marks to problematize the still common practice of linking these terms and culturally associated qualities to binary constructions of biological sex (man/woman) or gender (male/female). The transgender cultural revolution (e.g., Butler 2004; Stryker, 2008; Thurer, 2005) has demonstrated conclusively that such binary constructs are not only misleading, but also oppress an increasing number of individuals who do not identify with either polar reality. Thus, although for narrative purposes I attach specific qualities to these terms (e.g., gestating and birthing to the "feminine"), I am suggesting neither that those qualities are connected to particular biological sexes or genders, nor that masculine and feminine can be essentialized in any generic or universal fashion. Aware of these issues, Romero and Albareda (2001) used the terms *centripetal* and *centrifugal* to refer to the qualities commonly associated with the feminine and the masculine, respectively.

5. This is not a criticism of yoga practice, but a reaffirmation and vindication of its organic, energetic roots and potential prospects. Interestingly, Sovatsky (1994) reported that some yoga texts state there are 840,000 yoga *asanas*. For a thorough account of the eminently Western origins of modern yoga *asana* practice, see Singleton (2010).

6. Since 2000, Holistic Transformation has been taught in the United States at California Institute of Integral Studies (CIIS), San Francisco; Sophia University (previously the Institute of Transpersonal Psychology), Palo Alto; Esalen Institute, Big Sur; Open Center, New York; and through many groups of integral growth in the Bay Area of San Francisco. Holistic Transformation was also presented at the 2004 Parliament of the World's Religions, Barcelona, Spain, as well as in many national and international scholarly conferences.

7. Although a body of knowledge has gradually emerged from the work (Albareda & Romero, 1991, 1999; Romero & Albareda, 2001; Malkemus & Romero, 2012), Holistic Transformation is offered virtually free from ideological or metaphysical baggage. It is probably this nonsectarian character of the work that makes it appealing to people from very diverse psychological, social, cultural, and spiritual orientations, who, according to R. V. Albareda and M. T. Romero (personal communication, May 25, 2002), usually report bringing a renewed sense of creative vitality back to their personal lives, professions, communities, or traditions.

8. Because of its distinctive inclusion of sexuality (understood as

vital-primary energy or life force), Holistic Transformation was originally called Holistic Sexuality. Although I have used Holistic Integration elsewhere to refer to this work (Ferrer, 2003), I agree with Malkemus and Romero (2012) that Holistic Transformation is a more felicitous term.

9. As modern consciousness research shows, for example, human consciousness can not only access but also understand spiritual insights, esoteric symbols, mythological motifs, and cosmologies belonging to specific religious worlds even without previous exposure to them (see chapter 8).

10. Holistic Transformation needs to be distinguished from tantric and neo-tantric practices in which sexual energies are used as fuel to catapult human consciousness to expanded, transcendent, or even transhuman states (e.g., Feuerstein, 1998; White, 2000). In addition, and for the reasons outlined below, Holistic Transformation avoids conventional sexual exchange among practitioners. For further discussion of the differences between Holistic Transformation and Tantra, see Kripal (2008).

11. Any undocumented claim attributed to Albareda and Romero hereafter derives from their oral teachings at Holistic Transformation workshops. I attended a number of Albareda and Romero's week-long workshops in Spain (1993–99); translated several of their workshops at Esalen Institute, Big Sur, California (2001–03); co-facilitated (with Romero) two seven-month course cycles in Oakland, California (2001–03); and co-presented the work at the 2004 Parliament of the World's Religions, Barcelona, Spain. I have also offered many workshops introducing aspects of this body of work at many national and international conferences, as well as developed a method of Embodied Spiritual Inquiry that uses some of Holistic Transformation's interactive meditations as inquiry tools (see chapter 7).

12. Note that none of these authors claim that a strict correspondence exists between these bodily areas and the various human attributes. A human being is a multidimensional unity and any attribute or associated way of knowing can therefore potentially manifest throughout the entire organism. This fact does not preclude, however, that sustained contact with certain bodily areas tends to facilitate in most individuals access to specific experiential worlds; after all, it is generally easier to feel one's emotions when being touched in the heart than in the toes or the nose. Malkemus and Romero (2012) put it this way: "While being profoundly interwoven within the flow of full-bodied living, each center reflects specific experientially discernable characteristics that are related to specific regions in the human form" (p. 34).

13. The significance of context cannot be emphasized enough. Holistic Transformation embraces an ecological approach in which many factors come into play to facilitate the appropriate conditions for these contemplative practices. Therefore, their transformative power is to a large extent due to the carefully crafted context provided in the work, and it is likely that, without the pertinent set and setting, most of the practices may be not only sterile but also potentially confusing or problematic. The structure and safety provided by the

context, as well as the emphasis placed on mindfulness, necessary boundaries, and gradual integration, makes Holistic Transformation stand in sharp contrast to many of the interactive and group explorations developed in the 1960s.

14. Of course, knowing when to stop a practice, or being able to stop it, requires a learning curve for some individuals. If stopping a practice is especially hard for a participant, this difficulty is simply taken as one more area to explore and work on. In this case, the practitioner may be encouraged to carry out some practices specifically designed to gain discrimination and reinforce her capability of expression and boundary setting.

CHAPTER FIVE. THE FOUR SEASONS OF INTEGRAL EDUCATION

1. Earlier versions of parts of this chapter were presented at California Institute of Integral Studies (CIIS), San Francisco, with the titles "Integral Education at the New Millennium" (Ferrer & Romero, April 2003) and "A Participatory Inquiry into Integral Education" (Ferrer, April 2004). Also, Ferrer presented some sections of the chapter at the Fourth Conference on Integral Psychology, Auroville, India, January 2005, and the British Psychological Society Quinquennial Conference: Psychology of the 21st Century, University of Manchester, United Kingdom, March 2005, with the titles "The Transformation of the Embodied Mind in Integral Education," and "The Transformation of the Embodied Mind: A Transpersonal Participatory Model," respectively.

2. Although we frame most of this chapter in the context of gradu-ate-level Western education, the following ideas may also be relevant for other educational levels, practices, and cultures.

3. See J. P. Miller (1996, 1999) for valuable discussions of the nature and contents of holistic and spiritual curricula.

4. In *Manifesto of Transdisciplinarity*, Nicolescu (2002) wrote: "Transdis-ciplinary education revalues the role of intuition, imagination, sensibility and the body in the transmission of knowledge" (p. 150).

5. As I indicate in chapter 4, the term *cognicentrism* refers here to the privileged position of the rational-analytical mind (and its associated instrumen-tal reason and Aristotelian logic) in the modern Western world over and above other ways of knowing, such as somatic, vital, emotional, aesthetic, imaginal, visionary, intuitive, and contemplative. This usage of the term *cognicentrism* does not of course suggest that the other human dimensions are not cognitive in the sense of not being able to enact or apprehend knowledge. Actually, a chief distinguishing tenet of participatory education is precisely that all human attri-butes are creative organs of knowledge and thus endowed with epistemic powers.

6. For discussions of assessment and validity in multidimensional inquiry, see Anderson (2000), Anderson and Braud (2011), Braud (1998), Heron (1999), and Kremer (1992a, 1992b).

7. Discussion of the crucial relationship between epistemic and political

participation in academia is beyond the scope of this chapter. Briefly, as education moves from its current mind-centeredness to multidimensional knowing, the traditional unilateral assessment by teachers may undergo serious scrutiny and move toward a more integral approach involving teachers' evaluations and self- and peer assessment. The attempt to implement a participatory integral education in the context of nonparticipatory academic politics may be not only incoherent but also ultimately self-defeating. See Heron (2002) for a provoking discussion of this fundamental issue; see Freire (1970/1996, 1998) for discussions of the transformation of the traditional relationship between teachers and students.

8. We derive the images of the four seasons and planting a seed from Albareda and Romero's approach to integral growth and training (see chapter 4). Ferrer and Romero adapted the images for academic context in lectures, graduate courses, and pedagogical experiments at North American alternative educational institutions such as California Institute of Integral Studies (CIIS) in San Francisco and Sophia University (previously the Institute of Transpersonal Psychology) in Palo Alto, both located in California. The image of "planting a seed" is also central in the research methodology called organic inquiry (Clements, Ettling, Jenett, & Shields, 1998), and P. J. Palmer (2000) used the metaphor of the four seasons in a pedagogical context in his evocative essay, "There is a season."

9. *Vital seeds* are the virtually infinite life potentials (genetic dispositions, in scientific language) stored in the vital world of each human being. Although a limited number of these potentials can be actualized in a lifetime, others can be passed on—biologically and energetically—to one's progeny, transmitted to others through teaching or mentoring, or embodied in a variety of creative fruits (e.g., social projects, art, books) that can activate the vital seeds of others in the future.

10. See hooks (1994) and Pryer (2001) for compelling discussions about the pedagogical value of the inclusion of eros in academic teaching.

11. We do not suggest an association between vital/heart and the "feminine," and body/mind and the "masculine." Regardless of gender, both "masculine" and "feminine" principles can manifest in and through all human dimensions in many ways (e.g., as centrifugal action and receptive presence in the body, as the capability to energetically impregnate and gestate in the vital world, as the expression and reception of feelings and emotions in the heart, as speaking and listening on the mental level, prayer and receptive meditation in contemplative consciousness). This apparent incoherence emerges from working simultaneously with different symbolic systems that, although helpful in expressing fundamental features of the model presented, are not in total synchrony with each other. See Rothberg (1999) for a lucid discussion of the need to combine feminine and masculine qualities and to incorporate the nonmental worlds in integral education.

12. The notion of a distinct "spiritual intelligence" is controversial; for

discussions, see Emmons (2000a, 2000b), Gardner (2000), and Edwards (2003).

13. For a description of some experiential practices Ferrer has used for this purpose in a number of pedagogical experiments, see chapters 6 and 7.

14. I am indebted for this image to the Spanish transpersonal psychologist O. García (personal communication, November 8, 1991), who originally used it in a psychotherapeutic context.

CHAPTER SIX. TEACHING MYSTICISM FROM A PARTICIPATORY PERSPECTIVE

1. On the history and educational mission of CIIS, see McDermott (2005), Subbiondo (2005, 2011), and Wexler (2005, 2011). Subbiondo (2006) outlined ten principles of integral education drawn from a course of my design. For the current mission statement of the Institute, see www.ciis.edu.

2. For a description of the programs' curricula and courses, see http://www.ciis.edu/academics/graduate-programs/east-west-psychology.

3. Space does not allow me to discuss here the relationship between epistemic and political participation in higher education not only in course design but also regarding assessment. For a provocative essay on participatory assessment see Heron (1988).

4. For an extended discussion of the differences between mind-centered, bricolage, and participatory approaches, see chapter 5.

5. For discussions of validity and assessment in multidimensional inquiry, see Anderson and Braud (2011), Braud (1998), and Heron (1988, 1996).

6. For examples of some of these practices, see chapters 4 and 7, and for reports of fuller participatory inquiries developed in my course "Embodied Spiritual Inquiry," see Osterhold et al. (2007) and Sohmer et al. (forthcoming). For narrative accounts of students' transformative learning experiences in a version of this course I taught at Ritsumeikan University, Kyoto, Japan, see Nakagawa and Matsuda (2010).

7. At a recent Conference on Contemplative Studies, I offered an invited talk ("Critical Subjectivity After the Participatory Turn," University of San Diego, San Diego, California, November 2014) on the importance and challenges of critical subjectivity for contemplative studies, in which I distinguished between "subjectivity as critical" (i.e., the subjective resources of critical perspectives) and "the critique of subjectivity" (i.e., critical awareness toward one's own subjective experience). For valuable discussions of critical subjectivity in the human sciences and spiritual inquiry, see Heron (1996, 1998).

8. I cannot elaborate on this point here, but I also indicate the striking parallels between M. Johnson's (1987) cognitive theory of the imagination—as an epistemic bridge between the embodied and the mental—and esoteric and mystical takes on the epistemic role of the active Imagination (to be distinguished from "imagination" or merely mental fantasizing) in raising sensual/

perceptual experience to a visionary status in that isthmus between physical and spiritual realms that Corbin (1995, 1998) called *mundus imaginalis* (see Ferrer & Sherman, 2008a).

9. For a thorough account of the incorporation of art into scholarly inquiry, see Sullivan (2010).

10. To increase their understanding of the practice, students read Arico (1999).

11. For example, as identified by Paul and Elder (2002). A notable exception is the critical thinker's (over)reliance on discursive reason as the final arbiter of truth claims.

12. See also Romanyshyn's (2007) important account of research with soul in mind and articulation of an alchemical hermeneutics.

13. Cf. Taves's (2003) sustained argument for "the value of cultivating both the engaged and detached roles relative to the study of spirituality and for the value of learning to move back and forth between these roles" (p. 187).

14. In a later work, although affirming the import of insider perspectives, Kripal (2006b) privileged the outsider standpoint in the study of religion. My own view is that each case needs to be assessed independently, and that no a priori or generic hierarchical relationship between these standpoints can be legitimately established to ascertain what the privileged interpretation of a religious phenomenon (say a Kalua tantric ritual or a Shipibo ayahuasca ceremony) may be. Paraphrasing Kripal, I would argue that it is as important to let go of the pride of the insider and embrace the gnosis of the outsider, as it is to let go of the pride of the outsider and embrace the gnosis of the insider.

15. Space has not allowed me to discuss the challenges involved in implementing participatory pedagogies, such as overcoming of cognicentrism, avoiding anti-intellectualism, cultivating an effective critical subjectivity, or integrating in the classroom difficult personal materials that may be activated as students engage nonmental worlds. For a discussion of some of these challenges, see chapter 5, Barnard (1999), and Heron (1996, 1998).

16. The gnostic epistemology outlined by Kripal (2006b) is another example of a contemporary approach to the study of religion that relies not only on reason and the critical intellect, but also on the symbolic and contemplative, the mystical body and its erotic energies.

CHAPTER SEVEN. EMBODIED SPIRITUAL INQUIRY

1. I am grateful to Ross Baumann and Olga R. Sohmer, doctoral students at California Institute of Integral Studies (CIIS), for their valuable contributions to the contents of this chapter. I also thank Marina T. Romero and John Heron for their steady support in the development of Embodied Spiritual Inquiry as a graduate course and a cooperative inquiry method, respectively.

2. Although Embodied Spiritual Inquiry can be engaged as a spiritual or contemplative practice in itself, this chapter describes its application as a

learning and inquiry method in the context of higher graduate education. Even when applied as an inquiry method, however, Embodied Spiritual Inquiry can facilitate spiritual states that are phenomenologically similar to those described by many contemplative traditions, such as oneness, communion, and nonduality (see Osterhold et al., 2007). This is in itself rather remarkable since many traditions—in particular those traditions holding gradual (vs. sudden) approaches to enlightenment (see Gregory, 1991; Rawlinson 1997) emphasize that in most cases the achievement of such states requires many years of contemplative practice. See also chapter 4 for an account of some of Embodied Spiritual Inquiry's exercises as integral transformative practices.

3. For a problematization of the terms *masculine* and *feminine*, see chapter 4, note 4.

4. Is this intersubjective field generated through the interaction of two or more individual subjectivities (e.g., Gillespie & Cornish, 2010; Mead, 1934) or does it have a preexisting ontological nature out of which those individual subjectivities emerge (e.g., Buber, 1970; de Quincey, 2000, 2010; Sarath, 2013)? Although this chapter is not the place to discuss such ontological considerations in any detail, the ESI evidence suggests an arguably conciliatory, "both/and" response to the above question. From this perspective, whereas broader fields of consciousness may be foundational to participatory individual subjectivities, the specific features of any intersubjective field are largely enacted by the particular, conscious and unconscious dispositions (e.g., energies, emotions, intentions) of the interactive players. In this regard, in addition to de Quincey's (2010) and Sarath's (2010) works, see Ferrer's (2002) discussion of the multilocal nature of transpersonal events, as well as the consideration of the phenomenon of "transpersonal morphic resonance," below.

5. For some examples of participatory validity tests, see chapters 1 and 10.

CHAPTER EIGHT. STANISLAV GROF'S CONSCIOUSNESS RESEARCH AND THE MODERN STUDY OF MYSTICISM

1. I first presented a longer version of this chapter in 2000 at the Esalen Institute's Grof Transpersonal Conference (Big Sur, California); then I presented an updated version at the 2014 conference, Expanding and Reenchanting the Psyche: The Pioneering Thought of Stanislav Grof, at California Institute of Integral Studies (CIIS), San Francisco, California.

2. For two accounts of this movement, see the partisan study by Oldmeadow (2004) and the far superior work by Sedgwick (2004).

3. Both this perspectival perennialism and metaphysical agnosticism are overcome by the participatory approach's adoption of the enactive paradigm: enactive spiritual cognition is an antidote for perspectival perennialism, and affirmation of the nonduality of the mystery and its enactions counteracts metaphysical agnosticism. For an updated summary of Katz's contextualism, see Katz

(2004); for a revealing discussion of Katz's metaphysical agnosticism as central to his weak version of mediation, see Hammersholt (2013). See Ferrer (2002) for a more detailed analysis of the Cartesian and neo-Kantian roots of perennialism and contextualism, respectively. Essentially, I argued that whereas perennialism subscribes to the myth of the given (Sellars, 1963) and contextualism to the myth of the framework (Popper, 1994), Davidson's (1984) dismantling of the dualism of framework and reality (or scheme-content) renders both myths unintelligible and paves the way for more participatory considerations of spiritual knowing (see also Ferrer & Sherman, 2008a).

4. Note that transcultural similarities in myths that cannot be explained by historical or cultural diffusion are today thought to derive, not from any Jungian "collective unconscious" or related notions of human "psychic unity," but rather from our "shared humanity" or "shared life experience" (e.g., birth, body, sexual desire, procreation, parenting, pain, loss, death; see Doniger, 1998, p. 61). Some of Grof's (1998, 2006) reported cases, however, arguably challenge this mainstream account and, in my view, should be carefully studied by modern comparative mythologists.

5. For Campbell's changing views on Jung's approach to mythology, see Rensma (2009).

6. Although a few of Grof's (1998, 2006) reported cases dramatically challenge both the strong thesis of mediation in mysticism studies and the "shared humanity" model in comparative mythology (e.g., Doniger, 1998), many scholars may legitimately request additional evidence before accepting alternative transpersonal explanations. In other words, a systematic research program is imperative to turn these anecdotal cases into thoroughly documented evidence that can be presented to the scientific community.

7. Grof's (1998) proposal closely follows Huxley's (1954; Horowitz & Palmer, 1980) belief that his psychedelic self-experimentation provided corroboration for both a transcultural mystical experience and attendant perennialist metaphysics. In addition to Zaehner's (1980) classical Christian critique of Huxley's psychedelic perennialism, see Halbfass (2001) and Wezler (2001) for two critical accounts of Huxley's views on Indian religion shaped by his psychedelic experiences. The latest version of this idea comes from Langlitz (2013), who suggested that contemporary psychedelic research "point[s] to a new form of perennialism that reconciles biology and spirituality" (p. 260)—a *neurobiologia perennis* or mystic materialism based on the universality of the human brain, DNA, or neurochemical makeup.

8. Abramson (2015) claimed that the participatory postulation of both a diversity of spiritual ultimates and a mystery (out of which those ultimates are enacted through human cocreative participation) is equivalent to perspectival perennialism. In my view, three things differentiate the participatory approach from perspectival perennialism. First, the participatory approach rejects the myth of the given. (Note that even when traditionalist scholars speak about an ineffable or transconceptual spiritual Ultimate, they immediately—and

arguably contradictorily—qualify it, stating that it is nondual or that Advaita Vedanta offers, through its notion of *nirguna Brahman*, the best articulation of the perennial wisdom). Second, the participatory approach adopts an enactive paradigm of cognition, according to which the various spiritual ultimates are not perspectives of a single spiritual Ultimate, but rather enactions bringing forth ontological realities. Third, and perhaps most crucially, by overcoming of the dualism of the mystery and its enactions, the participatory approach avoids the traditionalist (and neo-Kantian) duality between religions' relative absolutes and the Absolute supposedly existing behind them (see Postscript). For a thorough rebuttal of Abramson's (2015) view, see Hartelius (2015a, 2015b). See also Merlo (2011) for some interesting reflections on how a hypothetical nondogmatic, nonhierarchical, and noninclusivist perennialism may be consistent with the participatory approach. S. Taylor's (2017) recent attempt to reconcile perennialist and participatory approaches is discussed in Appendix 2.

9. Applying an entheogenic, psychohistorical lens to Grof's (1998) allegiance to a Hindu cosmology, it is noteworthy that his two reportedly most transformational experiences (including his first ego-death) took place through entheogenic encounters with the Hindu God Shiva. In Grof's (2006) own words: "I considered Shiva to be the most important personal archetype because the two most powerful and meaningful experiences I have ever had in my psychedelic sessions involved this Indian deity" (p. 30).

10. The most nuanced defense of a qualified version of the "common core" theory is due to Forman (1990, 1998b, 1999), who, together with his collaborators, presented compelling evidence for the occurrence of a "pure consciousness event" in many, although by no means all, contemplative traditions. Naturally, the ontological and spiritual status of such an event is valued quite differently across traditions.

11. Consider, for example, the Buddhist tradition. For discussions highlighting the diversity of Buddhist views about the nature of ultimate reality, see Hopkins (1988), Cook (1989), and Küng (1989). See also W. L. King (1974) for an analysis of differences between Mahayana and Theravada accounts of *nirvana*, Chen (1972) for distinctions among Buddhist enactions of emptiness (*sunyata*), and Komarovski (2015) for an account of Tibetan Buddhism's conflicting views of ultimate reality and its realization. For a general introduction to some of the controversies among Buddhist schools regarding the substantiality of ultimate reality, see Chinchore (1995).

12. Varela et al. (1991) understood *enaction* as an embodied action that brings forth a domain of distinctions as the result of the mutual specification of organism and its natural environment, limiting thereby the scope of their proposal to the perceptual cognition of the sensoriomotor world. Participatory formulations adapt and extend the enactive paradigm to account for the emergence of ontologically rich spiritual realms (i.e., subtle worlds or domains of distinctions) cocreated by human multidimensional cognition and the genera-

tive force of life or the mystery (Ferrer, 2002, 2008; Ferrer & Sherman, 2008a; Kelly, 2008; Irwin, 2008). For further refinements of the enactive paradigm, see Thompson (1996, 2007). See also Frisina (2002) for a lucid account of both classic and contemporary, Asian and Western perspectives of the emerging nonrepresentational paradigm of cognition.

13. I am merely suggesting that liberation from self-centeredness is an ideal (or aspiration) shared by virtually all contemplative traditions. Whether such an ideal is ever actualized in practice is an empirical question to be explored through both the historical study of religious communities and biographies, as well as research into the effectiveness of contemporary religious practices in fostering such a transformation.

14. What does happen after death? If one accepts the feasibility of some sort of postmortem survival, would not such an experience validate a single religious after-death scenario (e.g., Christian Heaven) and refute the others (e.g., Buddhist Pure Lands or merging with the Absolute), thus providing ultimate verification of the superiority of one religion's cosmology over the rest? Not necessarily. Although I have not in my work discussed this crucial question, I concur with Barnard's (2011) important participatory reflections, which deserve to be quoted at length:

> It seems quite likely to me that how we envision postmortem existence, the variety of religious beliefs (both conscious and pre-conscious) that we have about what will happen after death (e.g., reincarnation, sensual heavens, ghostly shadow worlds, merger with God, etc.), as well as our own conscious and subconscious beliefs about what we deserve and how compassionate or not we believe the "unseen world" to be, will strongly shape the quality and form of our postmortem experience. I do not think that there is just some utterly objective after death realm of experience "out there" or "up there" waiting for us. Instead, I am convinced that our level of imagination (or lack of it), the audacity of our hopes or the tenacity of our fears, the complex layering of our beliefs (especially our subconscious beliefs and assumptions) will help to create a unique after-death quality of experience for each of us.
>
> I want to be clear, however. I do not think that our postmortem experience will be utterly plastic, that it will be simply subjective. Instead, similar to our current level of experience, I think that our postmortem existence will be a subjective *and* objective *co-created* reality, or more accurately, that it will be a reality in which the subject/object dichotomy itself will be transcended even more completely and obviously than is currently possible on this level of reality. I imagine that after death we will "arrive" in a dimension of reality that has a degree of "otherness," that "pushes back" in a way that is similar to our current level of physical existence;

however, this dimension of experience will be powerfully shaped and formed by the ongoing creative continuity of our memories, hopes, fears, beliefs—on both conscious and subconscious levels. What this co-created, participatory notion of after-death experience implies is that our after-death experience will most likely be extremely variable—a variability that the plurality of different cultural beliefs about the afterlife both reflects, and more subtly, helps to shape. (p. 261)

To appreciate the diversity of postmortem scenarios in one single tradition (Buddhism), see Becker (1993); for a fascinating visual tour of different visions of paradise across traditions, see Scafi (2013). See also Zuleski (1987) for an account of how historical, cultural, and social variables shape (enact?) the experiences of visionary journeys to the afterlife.

15. I am not saying that spiritual insights are incommensurable, but merely that it may be seriously misguided to compare them according to any preestablished spiritual hierarchy. Although "higher" and "lower" spiritual insights may exist both within and between religious traditions, I suggest that these qualitative distinctions need to be elucidated through spiritual inquiry, interreligious dialogue, and the assessment of their emancipatory power of self, relationships, and world, and not determined from the perspective of overarching metaphysical schemes telling, in an a priori and ultimately doctrinal manner, which insights and traditions are superior or inferior. As I see it, the validity of spiritual insights does not rest in their accurate matching with any pregiven content, but in the quality of selfless, integrated, and eco-socio-political awareness disclosed and expressed in perception, thinking, and action (see chapters 1 and 10). In this way, both pernicious relativisms and religious anarchies are effectively undermined (see Ferrer, 2002, 2008).

16. Merkur's (1998) psychoanalytic account of psychedelic experiences is ultimately reductionistic. For Merkur, all psychedelic experiences are pseudo-hallucinations explicable in terms of intense intrapsychic fantasying. In his own words: "Psychedelic unions are all experiences of imagination" (p. 156). What Merkur does not perhaps realize is that many mystics sharply distinguished the noetic faculty known as the active Imagination from "imagination" or merely mental fantasizing. According to these mystics, the function of active Imagination is to raise sensual/perceptual experience to an imaginal level in that isthmus between physical and spiritual realms that Corbin (1995, 1998) called *mundus imaginalis*. On the epistemic status of imagination in Islamic mysticism, see Chittick (1994b). For a contemporary, nonreductive account of human imagination and its centrality in promoting human transformation, see Varela and Depraz (2003).

17. Note that a participatory framework can be also seen as more coherent with the open-ended approach of Grof's Holotropic Breathwork practice (Grof, 1988a; S. Grof & C. Grof, 2010), whose deep trust in the organic unfolding of

each person's psychospiritual trajectory supports the participatory emphasis on enacted spiritual paths, cosmological hybridization, and spiritual individuation. In this light, one might argue that an unnecessary tension exists between Grof's theory (neo-Advaita cosmology) and praxis (Holotropic Breathwork).

18. For a more general participatory account of psychedelic consciousness, see Segall (2013).

CHAPTER NINE. PARTICIPATION, METAPHYSICS, AND ENLIGHTENMENT

1. See Stoeber (1994) for a contemporary argument of the superiority of theistic dual states over monistic nondual ones. Similarly, Buber (1947/2006) regarded the I/Thou relationship with God as spiritually higher than the monistic experience of nonduality, and Zaehner (1957/1980) argued that the monistic ideal is transcended in theistic mysticism, considering Sankara's monistic liberation (*moksa*) a primitive stage in the process of deification. More recently, Wilber's (1995) ranking of nondual mysticism over theism and other contemplative paths has been critiqued and rebutted by Helminiak (1998), G. Adams (2002), and, perhaps most effectively, by Schlamm (2001), who used Rawlinson's (1997, 2000) typology of mystical orientations to show the arbitrariness and doctrinal nature of such rankings.

2. Both Wilber's account of nondual realization—built upon monistic belief in the ultimate identity between one's true Self and the divine—and his stage model drew heavily from the writings of Franklin Jones (aka Adi Da), a Western adept of Hinduism (see B. Daniels, 2005). Elsewhere, I argued for the importance of distinguishing between different forms of nonduality usually conflated by Wilber; for example, the Hindu Atman-Brahman nonduality and the Buddhist nonduality of emptiness (*sunyata*) are conceptually, experientially, and ontologically distinct (Ferrer, 2002; cf. Fenton, 1995). Similarly, considering the Soto Zen founder Dogen's nonduality, Harmless (2008) wrote that although "he pointed to the radically nondual, it cannot be presumed he is speaking of a oneness within ultimate reality that is anything like what Christians or Muslims speak of, much less what Hindus mean when they speak of a deeper monism" (p. 253).

3. This type of move—unfortunately, frequent in Wilber's work—partly explains why Wilber is mostly ignored in the field of religious studies. Although Wilber cannot be unaware that Underhill's *unitive life* has nothing to do with his own *nondual realization*, he nonetheless equates them to defend the universal validity of his model. Even if Underhill's map would fit Wilber's, her overall characterization of Christian mysticism in terms of mystical union is today recognized as a historical distortion (Harmless, 2008; McGinn, 1991). Historically, the Christian mystical path had many goals (e.g., spiritual marriage, the birth of the Word in the soul, the vision of God, deification, *unio mystica*, the direct feeling of the presence of God), but Wilber's nonduality was not one

of them. For instance, St. Bonaventure, one of the greatest cartographers of the Christian path, depicted the final spiritual stage as an ecstatic union with the salvific suffering of Christ: "For Bonaventure, union meant sharing in the radical self-emptying, self-abnegating union with Christ crucified" (Harmless, 2008, p. 252). For discussions of the varieties of mystical union between the soul and God in the Semitic traditions, see Idel and McGinn (1996) and McGinn (2005).

4. For a nuanced account of the differences between Eastern and Christian nondualities, see Barnhart (2001). Whereas in the East nonduality (whether of self and God, or self and world) is taken to be the ontologically given nature of things to be realized by the mystic, when and if insinuated in the West, nonduality becomes a new historical ontological reality that did not exist before. In Christianity, mystical union with God was generally conceived in this same spirit. Commenting on Jan van Ruuesbroec's mysticism, for example, L. Dupré (1996) wrote: "By its dynamic quality, the mystical experience surpasses the mere awareness of an already present, ontological union. The process of loving devotion *realizes* what existed only as potential in the initial stage, thus creating a *new* ontological reality" (p. 20).

5. Unless indicated otherwise, all mention of Rowan, Daniels, and Fontana in this chapter refers to Rowan, Daniels, Fontana, and Walley (2009).

6. Wilber's (1995) and Marion's (2000) use of Eckhart as representing a nondual mysticism parallel to Ramana Maharshi's is distorting. In contrast to Ramana's absolute monism, Eckhart's account of the mystical union with God maintained the formal duality between the soul and the divine: "Eckhart's notion of indistinct union . . . is fundamentally dialectical, that is to say, union with God is indistinct in the ground, but we always maintain a distinction from God in our formal being . . . even in the ultimate union in heaven, Eckhart insists, this distinction will remain" (McGinn, 2001, p. 148; see also Harmless, 2008). As Schlamm (2001) pointed out, Wilber's treatment of St. Teresa is equally problematic: "What Wilber has done is to superimpose his developmental model on to Teresa's journey . . . and has thereby distorted both the texture and the content of her spiritual testimony" (p. 30).

7. Although Eckhart developed a new terminology with his language of "the ground" (*grunt*), the revolutionary nature of his mysticism tends to be exaggerated in popular circles. Eckhart's metaphysics of emanation and return has a long pedigree in the Christian tradition (e.g., Origen, Pseudo-Dionysius, Bonaventure), his articulation of an indistinct union with God was inspired by the Beguine mystics (especially Marguerite Porete), and his teaching on the unceasing birth of God in the soul goes back to Origen, as Eckhart acknowledged in one of his sermons (Harmless, 2008; McGinn, 1994, 2001).

8. This is not to say there were not heretical mystics who challenged traditional authority (Cupitt, 1998; Kripal, 2006a), but simply that, in light of the available historical evidence, those were rather anomalous.

9. I wrote *Revisioning* between 1994 and 1998 and defended it as my

doctoral dissertation in 1999 (Ferrer, 1999a). Despite its 2002 publication date, the book actually came out in October of 2001, shortly after R. Tarnas's (2001) preview in *The Journal of Transpersonal Psychology*. Earlier introductions to my participatory approach and critical perspectives on Wilber's work appeared in Ferrer (1998b, 2000a, 2000b, 2001).

10. The Christian theologian Vroom (1996) got to the heart of this problem: "If a Zen master states that faith in God is only halfway down the road to ultimate wisdom because the idea of a separate being, distinguished from the world in which we live, is naive and betrays attachment to the self, then I see no philosophical ground for concluding that Zen and Christianity refer to the same divine or 'empty' transcendence" (p. 148).

11. Since Wilber's nonduality is admittedly different than traditional versions, even nondual practitioners may need to strike this bargain in order to qualify as proper suitors of his final realization.

12. As feminist analyses suggested, these rankings also might reveal a patriarchal bias. For the patriarchal roots of the historical denigration of visionary forms of mysticism, see Hollywood (2002) and Jantzen (1995), and for a suggestion that the common association between monism and mysticism may be a product of the male psyche, see Jantzen (1989).

13. As described by a prominent member of Wilber's Integral Institute, requesting anonymity (personal communication, May 16, 2008).

14. I decided not to respond to Wilber's (2002) critique because each of his substantial points had already been anticipated and addressed in *Revisioning* (e.g., the green-meme critique, the charge of performative self-contradiction; for discussion, see chapter 1).

15. Although a philosophical divide is often traced between "representationalist realists" and "antirepresentationalist constructivists" who tend to reject realism (e.g., Rorty, 2004), this generally valid polarization becomes fallacious if taken to be normative. As Engler (2004) showed in an instructive essay, constructivism—although challenging the correspondence between linguistic signs and independent facts—is not necessarily antirealist or relativistic. For a recent, sophisticated realist-constructivist synthesis in international relations theory, see Barkin (2010). More attuned to participatory standpoints, Miner (2004) offered an account of knowledge as *true construction* that takes human creative pursuits to be participating in divine knowledge and creation.

16. In *The Empirical Stance* (2002), the philosopher of science van Fraassen offered the most cogent and, in my opinion, definitive exposition of the ideological nature of associating scientific empiricism with naturalistic and materialistic metaphysical theories (see chapter 2).

17. For critical discussions of neo-Kantianism in transpersonal and religious studies, see Ferrer (2000a, 2002) and Ferrer and Sherman (2008a), and for an often overlooked but important analysis of the "radically subjectivist neo-Kantianism" (Nagy, 1991, p. 365) that shaped Jung's metaphysical agnosticism, see Nagy (1991). See also Kelly (1993) for a proposed dissolution of the

Kantianism affecting Jungian views of the archetypes. For a critical analysis of the arguably disembodied roots of the Kantian two-worlds dualism, see chapter 2.

18. For a questioning of the *post*metaphysical nature of Wilber's (2006) approach, see Hartelius and Ferrer (2013) and Hartelius (2015a, 2015b).

19. I am equally puzzled by Rowan's claim that Wilber "invented the idea of these quadrants [AQAL model]" (Rowan et al., p. 41). Put together Schumacher's (1977) four fields of knowledge—interior/exterior of myself, interior/exterior of other beings and the world—or any pantheist's inner/outer dimensions (see D. S. Clarke, 2004), and Jantsch's (1980) micro/macro evolutions, then add a pinch of Koestler's (1976) holonic logic, and *voilà*, you have the basic AQAL framework. Wilber (1995) gave due acknowledgment to most of these influences in his elaboration of the AQAL model, except perhaps to Schumacher, whose own four-quadrant model is closest to Wilber's. Note also how heavily Wilber drew his critique of the modern flatland, neo-perennialism, and three-eyes epistemology from Schumacher's "loss of the *vertical dimension*" (pp. 10–14), evolutionary "Levels of Being" (pp. 15–26), and theory of *adaequatio* (pp. 39–60), respectively. Conceptually speaking, therefore, much of what is valuable in the model is not new; unfortunately, what is new is arguably problematic (e.g., Wilber's developmental map and hierarchical spiritual gradations). Nonetheless, although I take issue with Rowan's claim that Wilber invented something new in the AQAL model, Wilber has played an important role in spreading these ideas and some integral scholars are exploring the applicability of the AQAL model to important issues (e.g., Esbjörn-Hargens, 2010). As I believe Wilber himself would admit, his particular genius manifests not in invention, but in the integration of others' ideas.

20. For two anthologies exploring the implications of postmetaphysical thought for religious studies, see Wrathall (2003) and Bloechl (2003). Earlier discussions appeared in Ruf (1989). See chapter 2 in this volume for a proposed overcoming of the natural/supernatural dichotomy, and the Postscript for a proposal to talk about so-called metaphysical or transcendent realities in terms of *subtle worlds*.

21. See Shanon (2002, pp. 69–85) for descriptions of a variety of these "open-eye visualizations." In my experience, the psychoactive brew ayahuasca (*yagé*) and the cactus San Pedro (*wachuma*) are especially conducive to such external visions. In chapter 2 of this book, I examine the epistemological challenge of intersubjective external visions for modern scientific naturalism.

22. See Barnard (2007, 2011) for a powerful participatory case regarding the feasibility of a diversity of cocreated postmortem scenarios. In a similar spirit, Loy (2010) wrote:

the Christian Heaven, the Pure Land of Buddhism, are we suddenly whisked away to them, or do we gain them by becoming the kind

of person who would live in such a place? . . . If the world is made
of stories, who knows what our best stories might accomplish? If
we ourselves are Buddha, who but us can create Pure Land? (pp.
102–103)

23. Perennialists may assume that practitioners from different traditions
encounter the same entities (putatively existing in a shared spiritual universe),
and that the entities' various outlooks are contingent on the practitioners'
particular belief systems, conceptual schemes, or interpretations (e.g., Sogyal
Rinponche, 1992). Similarly, scholars with neo-Kantian leanings may appeal to
different phenomenal appearances of the same noumenal realities (e.g., Hick,
1989), structuralist thinkers may refer to plural surface manifestations of the
same deep structure or structural level (e.g., D. Anthony, 1982; Wilber, 1995,
1996b), and Jungians may write about culturally specific manifestations of the
same universal archetypes (after Jung, 1969; e.g., Grof, 1988a). Exemplifying this
overall approach, Sogyal Rinponche (1992) wrote of the deities encountered in
the *bardos* (realms in between lives): "They are not unique to Tibetans; they
are a universal and fundamental experience, but the way they are perceived
depends on our conditioning. . . . for Christian practitioners, the deities might
take the form of Christ or the Virgin Mary" (p. 284).

After dispensing with the dualism of framework and reality underlying the
above explanations, the participatory approach—through its enactive account of
spiritual knowledge (Ferrer, 2002, 2008)—overcomes all these problematic dualisms and reductionisms. Although I recognize that some of the above accounts
can initially have a certain intuitive force (after all, people can have different
perspectives and interpretations of the same phenomenon in the natural and
social worlds), a deeper examination reveals the limitations of these dualistic
proposals. It is plausible to consider that a sensorially vague or diffuse being
of light (e.g., the ayahuasca's astral doctor I describe in chapter 2) could be
perceived as an angel by a Christian practitioner. However, it is much less convincing to establish meaningful equivalences among the highly specific spiritual
visions that these dualistic proposals agglutinate within a particular structural,
archetypal, or noumenal reality. Consider, for example, the very specific image
of a Tibetan Buddhist *dakini*. To be sure, a *dakini* can manifest in a variety of
ways—from an ugly beggar woman to a beautiful golden consort—but it would
most likely be a serious mistake to equate, whether structurally or archetypally,
the wisdom *dakini* Vajrayogini (a three-eyed, semi-wrathful, red-skinned naked
female with cemetery ornaments and a hooked knife; Simmer-Brown, 2002) with
the Virgin Mary or the Hindu Goddess Lakshmi. In contrast to these dualistic
solutions and their forced equivalences, I propose that it is both more cogent and
less reductionist to consider such religious figures as different enacted, cocreated,
or perhaps independent entities or phenomena.

24. Note here that the Dalai Lama's account of liberation is different

from Wilber's:

> Liberation in which "a mind that understands the sphere of reality annihilates all defilements in the sphere of reality" is a state that *only* [italics added] Buddhists can accomplish. This kind of *moksa* or *nirvana* is *only* [italics added] explained in the Buddhist scriptures, and is achieved *only* [italics added] through Buddhist practice. (Tenzin Gyatso, 1988, p. 23)

While celebrating the existence of different religions to accommodate the diversity of human karmic dispositions, the Dalai Lama contended that final liberation can only be achieved through the emptiness practices of his own school of Tibetan Buddhism, implicitly situating all other spiritual choices as lower—a view that he believes all other Buddhists and religious people will eventually accept (see chapter 10; D'Costa, 2000).

25. I mean no disrespect or condescension. When looking at this religious past, it is important to avoid falling into what Barfield called a "chronological snobbery" that excoriates past spiritualities as deficient when considered from the perspective of modern standards (as cited in Lewis, 1955/2012, p. 125). The point here is that many, although by no means all, past disembodied spiritual trends may have been appropriate and even inevitable in their particular historical and cultural contexts.

26. In this context, spiritual practice is aimed either at accessing such overriding realities (ascent paths, e.g., classic Neo-Platonic mysticism) or at bringing such spiritual energies down to earth to transfigure human nature or the world (descent paths, e.g., central elements of Sri Aurobindo's [1993] integral yoga; cf. Heron, 1998, 2006). Here, monopolar descent is different from the traditional descending paths that search for spiritual fulfillment in nature or the world (M. Daniels, 2009; Wilber, 1995).

27. As Kelly (1998) and Washburn (1998) pointed out, however, Wilber's (1996b) holarchical logic cannot account for important aspects of human development. See also Dale (2014) for a persuasive case about the nonlinear (i.e., atypical, indeterministic) nature of transpersonal development and the consequent failure of Wilber's (2000, 2006) essentially linear approach to account for it.

28. It is noteworthy that meditation and other contemplative practices are being reenvisioned today from the perspective of more holistic understandings (e.g., Horton, 2012; Ray, 2008; Rothberg, 2006, 2008; Urban, 2003; Whicher, 1998).

29. Perhaps aware of these limitations, Wilber currently recommends an Integral Life Practice (ILP) in which practitioners select practices from different modules corresponding to trainable human capacities, such as body, mind, spirit, sex, and relationships (see Wilber, 2006; Wilber et al., 2008). For a critical appraisal of Wilber's ILP, see chapter 4.

30. My emphasis on spiritual individuation should not be confused with what Bellah (Bellah, Madsen, Sullivan, Swidler, & Tipton, 1985) famously called *Sheilaism*—named after Sheila, a respondent who claimed to have her own private religion. By contrast, my sense is that the perspectives of spiritually individuated persons may naturally align with one another and shape spiritual networks and communities even across doctrinal differences—a communion or genuine unity-in-diversity of multiple spiritual perceptions (cf. Dale, 2014).

CHAPTER TEN. RELIGIOUS PLURALISM AND THE FUTURE OF RELIGION

1. Bernstein (1985) coined the term *Cartesian anxiety* to refer to the relativistic worries (e.g., about intellectual and moral chaos) derived from the failure to find secure foundations for human knowledge and morality. These worries, for Bernstein, are ultimately specious and need "to be questioned, exposed, and overcome" (p. 19). Here, I give the term a different twist to refer to the Cartesian (i.e., objectivist) roots of the disconcertment produced by the existence of a multiplicity of conflicting religious accounts supposedly referring to a single pregiven reality, however naturalistically or supernaturalistically such a reality is conceived. See chapter 2 and Postscript for problematizations of the natural/supernatural divide.

2. I deliberately offer no definition of "religion" in this chapter. I take the position that although definitions can be helpful as springboards for open-ended inquiry—when offered in a heuristic, provisional, and culturally situated fashion—they can also blind researchers and scholars to crucial elements of the studied phenomenon. This is especially so with a phenomenon as diverse and multifaceted as religion. As with terms such as *culture* and *experience* (or even *philosophy* and *science*), defining *religion* has become increasingly dubious today. A major problem is that any definition of religion will inevitably emphasize some religious phenomena, marginalizing one or another religious tradition, feature, or element—or, even worse, leaving them out. This is why an increasing number of scholars today adopt a "family resemblances" or polythetic approach to religion—or to specific religions—that highlights religions' inter- and intra-diversity and heterogeneity (e.g., Doniger, 2009; Harrison, 2006; Jain, 2014). For my part, and in alignment with this polythetic approach, instead of offering an a priori definition of such a protean concept, I opt to allow its meaning to gradually emerge in the text's discussion. For key discussions of the problems inherent in generic, universal, and essentialist definitions of religion, see W. C. Smith (1978), J. Z. Smith (1982), Asad (1993), McCutcheon (1997), and R. King (1999).

3. I presented earlier versions of this chapter in an invited talk for the Center for Spirituality and Health, University of Florida, 2006, and then as a keynote speech for The 17th International Transpersonal Association Conference, Moscow, Russia, 2010. See also Arévalo (2012) and Shirazi (2012) for two interviews I offered on interreligious exchange and the future of reli-

gion, respectively; for an essay exploring the implications of the participatory approach for interfaith chaplaincy, see Christy (2015). My views on these matters were enriched by serving as consultant for the research project Harnessing the Socially Transformative Power of Spiritual Assets for Healing and Building Compassionate Communities, convened in 2009 by the organization Religions for Peace at the United Nations (New York), in cooperation with the Fetzer Institute (Kalamazoo, Michigan), with the aim of solving global interreligious conflict. I thank the secretary general of Religions for Peace, Dr. William F. Vendley, for his kind invitation and the Fetzer Institute for financial funding.

4. The case of the Baha'i faith is far more complex than this account suggests. On the one hand, a strong inclusivism is explicit in certain Baha'i teachings; for example, in the affirmation that the revelation of its founder Bahá'u'lláh is "the last and highest in the stupendous evolution of man's [sic] collective life of man on this planet" (Rabbání, 1973, p. 163), and represents the culmination of the teachings of all prior monotheistic prophets (e.g., Moses, Jesus, Muhammad). In addition, the Baha'i claim that all religious practitioners "derive their inspiration from one Heavenly source, and are the subjects of one God" (Bahá'u'lláh, 1976, p. 217) can easily appear as a sign of monotheistic exclusivism. On the other hand, the Baha'i scholar Fazel (2003, 2008) argued that such a progressive view of religious evolution could be understood as a continuity of revelation focused, not on a belief in a personal God, but on individual spiritual transformation. This emphasis on transformation and the Baha'i stance against any final word in spiritual truth parallels central tenets of the participatory approach. In any event, it seems evident that both Baha'i foundational teachings and their contemporary interpretations house a diversity of inclusivist and pluralist attitudes toward other religions (Fazel, 2008). I thank R. Faber (personal communication, January 18, 2016) for kindly drawing my attention to this diversity.

5. For related discussions, see Yandell (1993), Heim (1995), and Alderman (2011). See Schilbrack (2014b) for an essay review of recent works on religious pluralism.

6. In this context, the peculiar case of the Tibetan "nonsectarian" (ris med) movement deserves special mention. On the one hand, whereas the highly diverse and syncretic ris med movement appreciated and encouraged the practice of admittedly different Buddhist approaches, its proponents followed the Dzogchen school in their more positive account of emptiness and Buddha nature as resplendent luminosity (Duckworth, forthcoming; Geoffrey, 1993; Ray, 2000). The assumption of this univocal goal reintroduces sectarianism (and, ultimately, inclusivist exclusivism) at the core of the Buddhist emancipatory enterprise in the sense that other Buddhist goals are indirectly rejected or demoted, rendering the ris med movement ecumenically pluralist within the Buddhist tradition. On the other hand, as D. Duckworth (personal communication, January 12, 2016) pointed out, the ris med endorsement of a variety of Buddhist teachings and practices may well function as a potential Trojan horse. In other words, given the generally admitted causal relationship between particular practices and enacted goals in Buddhism, a theory that holds there to be many paths

and one goal may be said in practice to foster, within the limits of Buddhist spiritual aspirations, a soteriological pluralism of many ends.

7. Ogilvy (2013) offered a generous account of participatory pluralism (or *new polytheism*, in his term) as the way "to embrace some form of spirituality that does justice to the multi-cultural condition of a globalized world" (p. 47; cf. Dale, 2014; Hollick, 2006). Ogilvy understands well how participatory pluralism overcomes the problems of both religious universalism (including its inherent competitive predicament among traditions) and ecumenical pluralism while not falling into relativistic dilemmas:

> Polytheism is different from a wishy-washy pluralism that trends toward abject relativism. It doesn't say *anything goes*. Instead it says, *some things excel. Not one, not all, but some*. There are *some* paths to holiness, not just one. There are *some* forms of enlightenment or salvation, not just one. (p. 45)

Nevertheless, I am not sure that Ogilvy fully grasped the ontological implications of participatory enaction, in the sense that it brings forth not only different states of enlightenment or salvation, but also multiple spiritual worlds and ultimates. Participatory pluralism is not only soteriological, but also ontological and, arguably, metaphysical. For a relational account of the participatory approach's enactive ontology, see Hartelius (2016).

8. I wrote these lines barely one week after the tragic Paris terrorist attacks killing 129 people on November 13, 2015. When claiming responsibility for the attacks, the Islamic State of Irak and the Levant (ISIL) referred to them as a religious raid (*ghazwa*) seeking to debilitate a perceived enemy of the Muslim world (Ibrahim, 2015).

9. Note that many traditions reject the idea of a gradual approach to liberation—and thus the very existence of stages in the path. For valuable discussions of gradual versus sudden approaches to enlightenment, see Gregory (1991), Rawlinson (1997), and Schlamm (2001).

10. I am indebted to M. Washburn for this important qualification (personal communication, November 4, 2001).

11. On the very different phenomenon of religious globalization (i.e., diasporas, transnational religions, and religions of plural societies), see Juergensmeyer (2003).

12. Note, however, that Harris (2014) offered a secularized, scientific version of Buddhism—which conveniently ignores nonscientific Buddhist teachings about cosmology, karmic retribution, or transmigration (Faure, 2009; Lopez, 2010, 2012)—as his proposed path to spirituality without religion.

13. In addition to these common roots, two other possible sources of spiritual unity are spirituality's arguable transformative telos (e.g., liberation from selfishness, achievement of human integration) and, as I elaborate below, the search for a spiritually based global ethics to respond effectively to the ecological, social, religious, and political challenges of the twenty-first century.

14. In addition, I find other tensions in Dale's (2014) work that are arguably due to the ongoing revision of his approach. First, he proposed three stages of spiritual development, based on increasing merger with the object of contemplation and leading to a state "akin to the Eastern notion of meditative samadhi" (p. 177). In addition to privileging nondual, formless, unitive paths over visionary and dual spiritual ones (see chapter 9), Dale originally stated that these stages "are common but not universal across traditions" (p. 176), but then wrote that they "provide a possible universal aspect of human spirituality" (p. 207). While Dale's stages are shared by contemplative traditions enacting a formless or nondual spiritual ultimate, as well as those aimed at achieving unitive absorption with the object of meditation, in my view they are far from being (even possibly) universal for human spiritual development. Indeed, Dale himself often argued in his book that such a development follows a multiplicity of trajectories. Second, in explicit alignment with the participatory approach, Dale acknowledged that there is no fixed or given spiritual reality (p. 261). However, he also stated that "reality is objective, in the style described in the perennialist literature. . . . All subjects draw towards the same peak, though none ever completely reach it" (pp. 192–193). These arguably inconsistent statements give with one hand what they take with the other: If spiritual reality is not given, then it cannot be objective in the way perennialist authors conceive it (see Ferrer, 2000a, 2002). Finally, Dale subscribed to neo-Kantian perennialism when he wrote: "The structure-of-the-whole [highest form of individual integrated organization] grows ever-closer to reality, but it can never reach reality as reality is unknowable except through the subject, and the perceptual constructions of the subject are constantly changing" (p. 192). This formulation perpetuates the neo-Kantian alienation from reality that an enactive account of spiritual cognition, and its attendant affirmation of the nonduality of the mystery and its enactions, arguably overcomes (see chapter 2). For a more detailed discussion of these tensions, as well as of the many merits of Dale's work, see Ferrer (2015).

15. This account does not exclude, of course, the possibility to complement, either in a concurrent or sequential fashion, one's favored spiritual path with practices or engagements that cultivate different human potentials and attributes. For participatory perspectives on integral spiritual practice, see chapters 4 and 9.

16. Smart (2003) is understandably suspicious of the possible ideological problems inherent to the imposition of a single ethics for the entire world. For discussions of the promises and pitfalls of a global ethics, see Twiss and Grelle (1998). See also Widdows (2014) for a general overview of the dilemmas of a global ethics, and Pogge and Horton (2008) for philosophical perspectives on appropriate responses to global problems.

POSTSCRIPT

1. In this context, see Duckworth's (2014b) creative engagement of the participatory approach to reinterpret Buddhist emptiness (*sunyata*) and Buddha nature (*tathagatagarbha*), as well as his related argument that participatory pluralism prevents emptiness (*sunyata*) from being the last work on the nature of ultimate reality (Duckworth, 2014a).

2. For a strikingly similar defense of an "apophatic pluralism" that neither privileges nor cannot be privileged over religious perspectives, see Rose (2013). See Schilbrack (2014b) for a critique of Rose's stance and a plea to "develop a cataphatic account of the nature of things in which reality is rich and complex enough that the metaphysical claims of more than one religion can be true" (pp. 6–7). While Schilbrack suggested that Griffin's (2005) process-oriented deep pluralism is an apt candidate to meet this challenge, I contend that participatory pluralism can house a wider array of metaphysical truths in a nonreductionist or less reductionist manner. For a brief critique of process theology's problematic conflation of the variety of religious metaphysical claims onto two or three ontological ultimates, see chapter 10.

3. For similar reasons, in the introduction to *The Participatory Turn* (Ferrer & Sherman, 2008a), we used the term *nondetermined*. I thank J. H. Sherman (personal communication, October 20, 2006) for making me aware of some of the problems with my early use of the term *indeterminate* to qualify the mystery.

4. I believe this account opens a potential ground for reconciliation between classical and contemporary proposals insisting on either the determinate or the indeterminate ultimate nature of the mystery. In addition to traditional religious arguments for one or other position (e.g., Arapura, 1981), see Bracken (1995, 2001) for a defense of the determinate nature of the ultimate mystery as a creative activity serving as ontological ground for everything that exists. See also Neville's (2013) most complete analytical argument for the indeterminate nature of the ultimately unknowable source out of which such an ontological creativity proceeds. Regarding these germane proposals, I stand with Bracken in preferring to identify the mystery with the very generative power of the cosmos or reality, avoiding thereby the wink to theism implicit in Neville's supposition of a transcendent source beyond such a creative force; see Neville (1991, 1993) for two earlier, less-developed versions of his proposal that reveal more explicitly its theistic propensities. With Neville, I believe that the affirmation of genuine creativity in the mystery—as well as the affirmation of that creativity in the mystery as it unfolds in and through intrapersonal, interpersonal, and transpersonal human and nonhuman enactions—may be more consistent with hypothesizing radical indeterminacy at the deepest core of its generative motor (Ferrer, 2008). In contrast to both Bracken and Neville, then, I see no conflict in upholding both a creative power as ultimate principle and an indeterminate core in such a power—"indeterminate" in the sense that any truly *genuine* innovation cannot

preexist in an a priori manner (e.g., in God's mind or creative master plan).

5. Duckworth's (forthcoming) essay offers a thorough discussion of the implications of my proposed distinction (Ferrer, 2008) between the *indeterminate* and the *undetermined* for interreligious relations.

6. This formulation also distances my position from the traditional-ist dualism between various "relative absolutes" (i.e., of the different religious worlds) and the Absolute in itself, which is posited to exist behind the reli-gions' absolutes as "the Godhead in Its Infinitude and Oneness . . . above all relativity" (Nasr, 1989, p. 294). Thus, when Abramson (2015) charged the participatory approach with conflating "the 'Absolute that is beyond all religious Absolutes' with the multiple Absolutes of the different traditions" (p. 42), he misunderstood that such a move is not a conflation but a deliberate overcoming of an arguably problematic spiritual dualism. This dualism of the mystery and its enactions is pernicious: It not only binds scholars and practitioners alike to objectivist and hierarchical frameworks, but also paves the way for interreligious exclusivism and spiritual narcissism (i.e., once a supra-ultimate Absolute is pos-ited, practitioners can—and often do—claim their own religion's Absolute to be the closer, better, or more accurate account of the supra-ultimate Absolute). In addition, as S. B. King (2001) observed, no religious practitioner would accept her professed spiritual ultimate to merely be a "relative absolute."

7. Cf. Habermas: "One society may be superior to another with reference to the level of differentiation of its economic or administrative system, or with reference to technologies and legal institutions. But it does not follow that we are entitled to value this society more highly *as a whole,* as concrete totality, as a form of life" (cited in Dews, 1986, p. 169).

8. For several works problematizing the polar opposition or antagonism between transcendence and immanence, see Placher (1996), Thatamanil (2006), and Nelstrom and Podmore (2013). See also Panikkar (2014) for distinctions between transcendent transcendence (e.g., the Christian God), transcendent immanence (e.g., the Hindu Brahman), immanent transcendence (e.g., Buddhist nirvana), and immanent immanence (e.g., traditional Chinese religion). Although Panikkar's typology is helpful, I believe that the intricate hybridity of its categories suggests the need to find a different language to speak about the various spiritual worlds and ultimates.

9. Combs, Arcari, and Krippner (2006) offered a useful account of the wide diversity of subtle worlds posited by shamanic and contemplative tradi-tions; they also argued that the ontological value of these realms is consistent with both contemporary scientific theories positing the existence of multiple universes (e.g., Leslie, 1989) and the holographic models of Bohm (1980) and Laszlo (2004).

10. In some passages of this book, however, I have used the term *tran-scendent* to refer not to any ontological or supernatural realm, but to energies, phenomena, or states of being that transcend (i.e., go beyond) human structures and personal individuality; this is the case, for example, of the transcendent

states of being pursued by disembodied spiritual approaches (see chapter 3) or the transcendent sources of the integral creative cycle (see chapter 5). For an elucidation of three different meanings of the term *transcendent*, see chapter 3, note 5.

11. This participatory, enactive account stands in contrast to perspectival explanations of the plurality of sensory and interpretive versions of a single or pregiven world. Representing this pluralist but still objectivist stance, Wilczek (2015) wrote: "the world does not provide its own unique interpretation. The world offers many possibilities for different sensory universes, which support different interpretations of the world's significance. In this way our so-called Universe is already a multiverse" (p. 14).

12. In traditionalist metaphysics, the subtle realm is similarly considered to be the intermediate plane (i.e., the etheric, astral home of nonphysical beings) positioned between terrestrial (i.e., material, phenomenal) and celestial (i.e., personally divine, transcendent) planes of reality. This shared ontological ladder leads to the Infinite—that is, the single, undifferentiated, ultimate reality variously called *nirguna Brahman, nirvana,* emptiness, or the Tao that cannot be spoken (H. Smith, 1976; see also B. Johnson, 1991).

13. In the introduction to his celebrated biography of Einstein's famous equation of mass and energy, Bodanis (2000) wrote: "Mass is simply the ultimate type of condensed or concentrated energy. Energy is the reverse: it is what billows out as an alternate form of mass under the right circumstances" (p. 2). I thank M. Washburn for suggesting this argumentative line (personal communication, June 13, 2014).

REFERENCES

Abram, D. (1996). *The spell of the sensuous: Perception and language in a more-than-human world*. New York, NY: Vintage.

Abram, D. (2007). Earth in eclipse: An essay on the philosophy of science and ethics. *ReVision: A Journal of Consciousness and Transformation, 29*(4), 10–22.

Abramson, J. (2014a). The misunderstanding and misinterpretation of key aspects of Ken Wilber's work in Hartelius and Ferrer's (2013) assessment. *Transpersonal Psychology Review, 16*(1), 3–12.

Abramson, J. (2014b). The misunderstanding and misinterpretation of key aspects of Ken Wilber's work in Hartelius and Ferrer's (2013) assessment: A response to the reviewer. *Transpersonal Psychology Review, 16*(1), 15–16.

Abramson, J. (2015). The emperor's new clothes: Ferrer isn't wearing any— Participatory is perennial. A reply to Hartelius. *Transpersonal Psychology Review, 17*(1), 38–48.

Achterberg, J., & Rothberg, D. (1998). Relationship as spiritual practice. In D. Rothberg & S. M. Kelly (Eds.), *Ken Wilber in dialogue: Conversations with leading transpersonal thinkers* (pp. 261–274). Wheaton, IL: Theosophical Publishing House.

Adam, M. T. (2002). A post-Kantian perspective on recent debates about mystical experience. *Journal of the American Academy of Religion, 70*(4), 801–818.

Adams, G. (2002). A theistic perspective on Ken Wilber's transpersonal psychology. *Journal of Contemporary Religion, 17*(2), 165–179.

Adams, G. (2003). Review of *Revisioning transpersonal theory: A participatory vision of human spirituality*, by Jorge N. Ferrer. *Journal of Contemporary Religion, 18*(3), 431–433.

Adams, G. (2011). Review of *The participatory turn: Spirituality, mysticism, religious studies*, edited by Jorge N. Ferrer and Jacob H. Sherman. *Journal of Contemporary Religion, 26*(1), 154–156.

Adams, W. A. (2006). Transpersonal heterophenomenology? *Journal of Consciousness Studies, 13*(4), 89–93.

Adams, W. W. (2010a). Bashō's therapy for Narcissus: Nature as intimate other and transpersonal self. *Journal of Humanistic Psychology, 50*(1), 38–64.

Adams, W. W. (2010b). Nature's participatory psyche: A study of consciousness in the shared earth community. *The Humanistic Psychologist, 38*(1), 15–39.

Akyalcin, E., Greenway, P., & Milne, L. (2008). Measuring transcendence: Extracting core constructs. *The Journal of Transpersonal Psychology*, 40(1), 41–59.

Albareda, R. V., & Romero, M. T. (1991). *Nacidos de la tierra: Sexualidad, origen del ser humano*. Barcelona, Spain: Hogar del Libro.

Albareda, R. V., & Romero, M. T. (1999). Sexualidad transpersonal y transcendente. In M. Almendro (Ed.), *La conciencia transpersonal* (pp. 218–242). Barcelona, Spain: Kairós.

Alderman, B. (2011). Kingdom come: Beyond inclusivism and pluralism, an integral post-metaphysical invitation. *Journal of Integral Theory and Practice*, 6(3), 14–31.

Alderman, B. (2012a). Opening space for translineage practice: Some ontological speculations. *Journal of Integral Theory and Practice*, 7(2), 49–71.

Alderman, B. (2012b). The participatory turn (Review of *The participatory turn: Spirituality, mysticism, religious studies* edited by Jorge N. Ferrer and Jacob H. Sherman). *Journal of Integral Theory and Practice*, 7(2), 120–126.

Aleman, A., & Larøi, F. (2008). *Hallucinations: The science of idiosyncratic perception*. Washington, DC: American Psychological Association.

Alexander, C., Heaton, D., & Chandler, H. (1994). Advanced human development in the Vedic psychology of Maharishi Mahesh Yogi: Theory and research. In M. Miller & S. Cook-Greuter (Eds.), *Transcendence and mature thought in adulthood* (pp. 39–70). Lanham, MD: Rowman & Littlefield.

Almaas, A. H. (1988). *The pearl beyond price: Integration of personality into being: An object relations approach*. Berkeley, CA: Diamond.

Almaas, A. H. (1996). *The point of existence: Transformations of narcissism in self-realization*. Boston, MA: Shambhala.

Almaas, A. H. (2002). *Spacecruiser inquiry: True guidance for the inner journey*. Boston, MA: Shambhala.

Almaas, A. H. (2004). *The inner journey home: Soul's realization of the unity of reality*. Boston, MA: Shambhala.

Almaas, A. H. (2014). *Runaway realization: Living a life of ceaseless discovery*. Boston, MA: Shambhala.

Almendro, M. (2004). *Psicología transpersonal: Conceptos clave*. Madrid, Spain: Ediciones Martínez Roca.

Almendro, M. (2014). *Chaos psychology and psychotherapy*. Houston, TX: The Written Spiral.

Almendro, M., & Weber, D. (2012). Dissipative processes in psychology: From psyche to totality. *International Journal of Transpersonal Studies*, 31(2), 1–22.

Almond, P. C. (1982). *Mystical experience and religious doctrine: An investigation of the study of mysticism in world religions*. New York, NY: Mouton.

Andersen, P. B., Emmeche, C., Finnemann, N. O., & Christiansen, P. V. (2001). *Downward causation: Minds, bodies and matter*. Aarhus, Denmark: Aarhus University Press.

Anderson, R. (2000). Intuitive inquiry: Interpreting objective and subjective data. *ReVision: A Journal of Consciousness and Transformation, 22*(4), 31–39.

Anderson, R. (2006). Body intelligence scale: Defining and measuring the intelligence of the body. *The Humanistic Psychologist, 34*(4), 357–367.

Anderson, R., & Braud, W. (2011). *Transforming self and others through research: Transpersonal research methods and skills for the human sciences and humanities.* Albany, NY: State University of New York Press.

Anderson, R., & Braud, W. (2013). Transpersonal research and future directions. In H. L. Friedman & G. Hartelius (Eds.), *The Wiley-Blackwell handbook of transpersonal psychology* (pp. 241–260). Malden, MA: John Wiley & Sons.

Anthony, D. (1982). A phenomenological structuralist approach to the scientific study of religion. *Revision: A Journal of Consciousness and Transformation, 5*(1), 50–66.

Anthony, D., Naranjo, C., Deikman, A., Fireman, B., Hastings, A., & Reisman, P. (1987). Many inner lands: An interview with Claudio Naranjo. In D. Anthony, B. Ecker, & K. Wilber (Eds.), *Spiritual choices: The problem of recognizing authentic paths to inner transformation* (pp. 193–209). New York, NY: Paragon.

Anthony, M. (2008). *Integrated intelligence: Classical and contemporary depictions of mind and intelligence and their educational implications.* Rotterdam, The Netherlands: Sense Publishers.

Apffel-Marglin, F. (2011). *Subversive spiritualities: How rituals enact the world.* New York, NY: Oxford University Press.

Arapura, J. G. (1981). Transcendent Brahman or transcendent void: Which is ultimately real? In A. M. Olson & L. S. Rouner (Eds.), *Transcendence and the sacred* (pp. 83–99). Notre Dame, IN: University of Notre Dame Press.

Arévalo, S. (2012). Ja no es tracta d'intercanviar pràctiques sinó de cocrear-ne. Entrevista a Jorge N. Ferrer. (The point is no longer to exchange practices, but to cocreate them: An interview with Jorge N. Ferrer). *Dialogal: Quaderns de l'Associació UNESCO per al Diàleg Interreligiós, 41*(11), 44–45.

Arico, C. (1999). The *lectio divina* tradition: Lost and found. In *A taste of silence: A guide to the fundamentals of centering prayer* (pp. 103–122). New York, NY: Continuum.

Asad, T. (1993). *Genealogies of religion: Discipline and reasons of power in Christianity and Islam.* Baltimore, MD: The John Hopkins University Press.

Assagioli, R. (1971). *Psychosynthesis: A manual of principles and techniques.* New York, NY: Viking Press.

Aurobindo, Sri. (1993). *The integral yoga: Sri Aurobindo's teaching and method of practice.* Twin Lakes, WI: Lotus Press.

Aurobindo, Sri. (2001). *The life divine* (6th ed.). Pondicherry, India: Sri Aurobindo Ashram.

Bache, C. M. (2000). *Dark night, early dawn: Steps to a deep ecology of mind.* Albany, NY: State University of New York Press.

Bache, C. M. (2008). *The living classroom: Teaching and collective consciousness.* Albany, NY: State University of New York Press.

Bahá'u'lláh (1976). *Gleanings from the writings of Bahá'u'lláh* (S. Effendi, Trans.). Wilmette, IL: Baha'i Publishing Trust.

Bailey, G., & Arthur, K. (2011, July). *Stabilizing presence: Using embodied spiritual inquiry and Enneagram attachment narratives to recognize and integrate spiritual experience.* Paper presented at the 16th Global Conference of the International Enneagram Association, Fort Lauderdale, FL.

Ball, M. W. (2008). *The entheogenic evolution: Psychedelics, consciousness and the awakening of the human spirit.* Medford, OR: Kyandara.

Banchoff, T., & Wuthnow, R. (Eds.). (2011). *Religion and the global politics of human rights.* New York, NY: Oxford University Press.

Barbezat, D. P., & Bush, M. (Eds.). (2013). *Contemplative practices in higher education: Powerful methods to transform teaching and learning.* San Francisco, CA: Jossey-Bass.

Barfield, O. (1957). *Saving the appearances: A study in idolatry.* London, United Kingdom: Faber and Faber.

Barkin, J. S. (2010). *Realist constructivism: Rethinking international relations theory.* New York, NY: Cambridge University Press.

Barks, C. (2002). *The soul of Rumi: A new collection of ecstatic poems.* New York, NY: HarperOne.

Barnard, G. W. (1994). Transformations and transformers: Spirituality and the academic study of mysticism. *Journal of Consciousness Studies, 1*(2), 256–260.

Barnard, G. W. (1999). Meditation and masks, drums and dramas: Experiential and participatory exercises in the comparative religions classroom. *Teaching Theology and Religion, 2*(3), 169–172.

Barnard, G. W. (2007, May). *Dreaming about the afterlife.* Paper presented at the Esalen Institute's Center for Theory and Research Conference on Survival After Death, Big Sur, CA.

Barnard, G. W. (2008). Pulsating with life: The paradoxical intuitions of Henri Bergson. In J. N. Ferrer & J. H. Sherman (Eds.), *The participatory turn: Spirituality, mysticism, religious studies* (pp. 321–348). Albany, NY: State University of New York Press.

Barnard, G. W. (2011). *Living consciousness: The metaphysical vision of Henri Bergson.* Albany, NY: State University of New York Press.

Barnard, G. W., & Kripal, J. J. (Eds.). (2002). *Crossing boundaries: Essays on the ethical status of mysticism.* New York, NY: Seven Bridges.

Barnhart, B. (2001). Christian self-understanding in the light of the East: New birth and unitive consciousness. In B. Barnhart & Y. Huang (Eds.), *Purity of the heart and contemplation: A monastic dialogue between Christian and Asian traditions* (pp. 291–308). New York, NY: Continuum.

Barnhart, B. (2008). One spirit, one body: Jesus' participatory revolution. In J. N. Ferrer & J. H. Sherman (Eds.), *The participatory turn: Spirituality, mysticism, religious studies* (pp. 265–291). Albany, NY: State University of New York Press.

Barrett, D. B., Kurian, G. T., & Johnson, T. M. (Eds.). (2001). *World Christian encyclopedia: A comparative survey of churches and religions in the modern world* (2nd ed., 2 Vols.). New York, NY: Oxford University Press.

Bartlett, R. (2008). *The natural and the supernatural in the Middle Ages* (The Wiles Lectures). New York, NY: Cambridge University Press.

Bastien, B. (2003). The cultural practice of participatory transpersonal visions: An Indigenous perspective. *ReVision: A Journal of Consciousness and Transformation, 26*(2), 41–48.

Bastien, B., & Kremer, J. W. (2004). *Blackfoot ways of knowing: The worldview of the Siksikaitsitapi.* Calgary, Canada: University of Calgary Press.

Basu, M. (1986). *Fundamentals of the philosophy of the Tantras.* Calcutta, India: Mira Basu Publishers.

Battista, J. R. (1996). Offensive spirituality and spiritual defenses. In B. W. Scotton, A. B. Chinen, & J. R. Battista (Eds.), *Textbook of transpersonal psychiatry and psychology* (pp. 250–260). New York, NY: Basic.

Bauwens, M. (2007). The next Buddha will be a collective: Spiritual expression in the peer-to-peer era. *ReVision: A Journal of Consciousness and Transformation, 29*(4), 34–45.

Beauregard, M. (2007). Mind does really matter: Evidence from neuroimaging studies of emotional self-regulation, psychotherapy, and placebo effect. *Progress in Neurobiology, 81*(4), 218–236.

Beck, D., & Cowan, C. (1996). *Spiral Dynamics: Mastering values, leadership, and change.* Malden, MA: Blackwell.

Becker, C. B. (1993). *Breaking the circle: Death and the afterlife in Buddhism.* Carbondale, IL: Southern Illinois University Press.

Beena, C. (1990). *Personality typologies: A comparison of Western and ancient Indian approaches.* New Delhi, India: Commonwealth Publishers.

Beiser, F. C. (2015). *The genesis of neo-Kantianism, 1796–1880.* New York, NY: Oxford University Press.

Bellah, R. N., Madsen, R., Sullivan, W. M., Swidler, A., & Tipton, S. M. (Eds.). (1985). *Habits of the heart: Individualism and commitment in American life.* Berkeley, CA: University of California Press.

Bellegarde-Smith, P., & Michel, C. (Eds.). (2006). *Haitian Vodou: Spirit, myth, and reality.* Bloomington, IN: Indiana University Press.

Benhabib, S. (2002). *The claims of culture: Equality and diversity in the global era.* Princeton, NJ: Princeton University Press.

Berman, M. (1981). *The reenchantment of the world.* Ithaca, NY: Cornell University Press.

Bernstein, R. J. (1985). *Beyond objectivism and relativism: Science, hermeneutics, and praxis.* Philadelphia, PA: University of Pennsylvania Press.

Berrios, G. E. (2005). On the fantastic apparitions of vision by Johannes Müller. *History of Psychiatry, 16*(2), 229–246.

Berthrong, J. H. (1999). *The divine deli: Religious identity in the North American cultural mosaic.* Maryknoll, NY: Orbis.

Bhagat, M. G. (1976). *Ancient Indian asceticism.* New Delhi, India: Munshiram Manoharlal Publishers.

Bhaskar, R. (1989). *Reclaiming reality.* New York, NY: Verso.

Biale, D. (1992). *Eros and the Jews: From Biblical Israel to contemporary America.* New York, NY: Basic Books.

Bidwell, D. R. (2015). Enacting the spiritual self: Buddhist-Christian identity as participatory action. *Spiritus: A Journal of Christian Spirituality, 15*(1), 105–112.

Bilgrami, A. (2010). The wider significance of naturalism: A genealogical essay. In M. De Caro & D. Macarthur (Eds.), *Naturalism and normativity* (pp. 23–54). New York, NY: Columbia University Press.

Bloechl, J. (Ed.). (2003). *Religious experience and the end of metaphysics.* Bloomington, IN: Indiana University Press.

Blum, J. N. (2014). The science of consciousness and mystical experience: An argument for radical empiricism. *Journal of the American Academy of Religion, 82*(1), 150–173.

Bodanis, D. (2000). *E=mc²: A biography of the world's most famous equation.* New York, NY: Walker.

Bohm, D. (1980). *Wholeness and the implicate order.* Boston, MA: Routledge and Kegan Paul.

Bohm, D. (1996). *On dialogue.* (L. Nichol, Ed.). New York, NY: Routledge.

Bonheim, J. (1997). *Aphrodite's daughters: Women's sexual stories and the journey of the soul.* New York, NY: Fireside.

Bordo, S. (1987). *The flight to objectivity: Essays on Cartesianism and culture* (SUNY series in philosophy). Albany, NY: State University of New York Press.

Borella, J. (1995). René Guénon and the traditionalist school. In A. Faivre & J. Needleman (Eds.), *Modern esoteric spirituality* (Vol. 21, World spirituality: An encyclopedic history of the religious quest, pp. 330–358). New York, NY: Crossroad.

Bostic, J. R. (2001). Mystical experience, radical subjectification, and activism in the religious traditions of African American women. In J. K. Ruffing (Ed.), *Mysticism and social transformation* (pp. 143–158). Syracuse, NY: Syracuse University Press.

Boucouvalas, M. (1999). Following the movement: From transpersonal psychology to a multi-disciplinary transpersonal orientation. *The Journal of Transpersonal Psychology, 31*(1), 27–40.

Boyer, E. L. (1990). *Scholarship reconsidered: Priorities of the professoriate* (1990 Special Report of the Carnegie Foundation for the Advancement of Teaching). Princeton, NJ: Carnegie Foundation for the Advancement of Teaching.

Bracken, J. A. (1995). *The divine matrix: Creativity as link between East and West.* Maryknoll, NY: Orbis.

Bracken, J. A. (2001). *The one in the many: A contemporary reconstruction of the God-world relationship.* Grand Rapids, MI: William B. Eerdmans Publishing Company.

Bragdon, E. (1990). *The call of spiritual emergency: From personal crisis to personal transformation.* San Francisco, CA: Harper & Row.

Braud, W. (1998). An extended view of validity. In W. Braud & R. Anderson (Eds.), *Transpersonal research methods for the social sciences: Honoring human experience* (pp. 213–237). Thousand Oaks, CA: SAGE.

Braun, W. (2000). Religion. In W. Braun & R. T. McCutcheon (Eds.), *Guide to the study of religion* (pp. 3–18). New York, NY: Cassell.

Braybrooke, M. (1998). *Faith and interfaith in a global age.* Grand Rapids, MI: CoNexus.

Bressloff, P. C., Cowan, J. D., Golubitsky, M., Thomas, P. J., & Wiener, M. C. (2002). What geometric visual hallucinations tell us about the visual cortex. *Neural Computation, 14,* 473–491.

Brooks, C., Ford, K., & Huffmann, A. (2013). Feminist and cultural contributions to transpersonal psychology. In H. L. Friedman & G. Hartelius (Eds.), *The Wiley-Blackwell handbook of transpersonal psychology* (pp. 612–625). Malden, MA: John Wiley & Sons.

Brown, P. (1988). *The body and society: Men, women, and sexual renunciation in early Christianity.* New York, NY: Columbia University Press.

Brown, R. S. (2013). Beyond the evolutionary paradigm in consciousness studies. *The Journal of Transpersonal Psychology, 45*(2), 159–171.

Brown, R. S. (2016). *Psychoanalysis beyond the end of metaphysics: Thinking towards the post-relational.* New York, NY: Routledge.

Brown, R. S. (2017). Bridging worlds: Participatory thinking in Jungian context. *Journal of Analytical Psychology, 62*(2), 284-302."

Bruce, S. (2002). *God is dead: Secularization in the West.* Malden, MA: Blackwell.

Buber, M. (1970). *I and thou* (W. A. Kaufmann, Trans.). New York, NY: Charles Scribner's Sons.

Buber, M. (2006). *Between man and man.* New York, NY: Routledge. (Original work published 1947).

Burns, C. P. E. (2002). *Divine becoming: Rethinking Jesus and incarnation.* Minneapolis, MN: Fortress.

Buruma, I., & Margalit, A. (2004). *Occidentalism: The West in the eyes of their enemies.* New York, NY: Penguin.

Butler, J. (2004). *Undoing gender.* New York, NY: Routledge.

Butler, K. (1990). Encountering the shadow in Buddhist America. *Common Boundary, 18*(3), 15–22.

Butter, A. M. (2015). A brief history of Spiral Dynamics. *Approaching Religion, 5*(2), 67–78.

Bynum, C. W. (1995). *The resurrection of the body in Western Christianity, 200–1336* (No. 15). New York, NY: Columbia University Press.

Byrne, P. (1999). The study of religion: Neutral, scientific, or neither? In R. T.

McCutcheon (Ed.), *The insider/outsider problem in the study of religion* (pp. 248–259). New York, NY: Cassell.

Cabezón, J. I. (2006). The discipline and its other: The dialectic of alterity in the study of religion. *Journal of the American Academy of Religion, 74*(1), 21–38.

Cabot, Z. (2011). *Ecologies of participation: Between shamans, diviners, and metaphysicians* (Doctoral dissertation). California Institute of Integral Studies, San Francisco, CA.

Cabot, Z. (2014). Participatory spirituality. In D. A. Leeming (Ed.), *Encyclopedia of psychology and religion* (2nd ed., Vol. 2, pp. 1290–1295). New York, NY: Springer.

Cabot, Z. (2015). *Ecologies of participation: In between shamans, mystics, and diviners.* Unpublished manuscript.

Caldwell, C. (2014). Mindfulness and bodyfulness: A new paradigm. *The Journal of Contemplative Inquiry, 1*, 69–88.

Campbell, C. (1999). The Easternization of the West. In B. R. Wilson & J. Cresswell (Eds.), *New religious movements: Challenge and response* (pp. 35–48). New York, NY: Routledge.

Caplan, M. (1999). *Halfway up the mountain: The error of premature claims to enlightenment.* Prescott, AZ: Hohm.

Caplan, M. (2002). *To touch is to live: The need for genuine affection in an impersonal world.* Prescott, AZ: Hohm.

Caplan, M., Hartelius, G., & Rardin, M. A. (2003). Contemporary viewpoints on transpersonal psychology (forum). *The Journal of Transpersonal Psychology, 35*(2), 143–162.

Capriles, E. (2013). Appendix III. Is Jorge Ferrer's "participatory vision" really inclusive? In *The beyond mind papers: Transpersonal and metatranspersonal theory: A critique of the systems of Wilber, Washburn and Grof: And an outline of the Dzogchen path to definitive true sanity* (Vol. 4, pp. 149–182). Nevada City, CA: Blue Dolphin.

Caputo, J. D. (1997). *The prayers and tears of Jacques Derrida: Religion without religion.* Bloomington, IN: Indiana University Press.

Caputo, J. D. (2001). *On religion.* New York, NY: Routledge.

Carlson, T. A. (1999). *Indiscretion: Finitude and the naming of God.* Chicago, IL: University of Chicago Press.

Carpenter, D. (1995). *Revelation, history, and the dialogue of religions: A study of Bhartrhari and Bonaventure.* New York, NY: Orbis.

Chakravartty, A. (2007). *A metaphysics for scientific realism: Knowing the unobservable.* New York, NY: Cambridge University Press.

Chalquist, C. (2009). Review of *The participatory turn: Spirituality, mysticism, religious studies* edited by Jorge N. Ferrer and Jacob H. Sherman. *The Journal of Transpersonal Psychology, 41*(1), 98–100.

Chaudhuri, H. (1974). *Being, evolution, and immortality: An outline of integral philosophy.* Wheaton, IL: The Theosophical Publishing House.

Chaudhuri, H. (1977). *The evolution of integral consciousness*. Wheaton, IL: The Theosophical Publishing House.

Chemero, A. (2009). *Radical embodied cognitive science*. Cambridge, MA: The MIT Press.

Chen, C. M. (1972). *The subtle discrimination between the practices of sunyata in Hinayana, Mahayana and Vajrayana* (Chenian booklet series, Jivaka, Trans.). Kalinpang, India: Chen.

Chinchore, M. R. (1995). *Anattā/Anātmatā: An analysis of Buddhist anti-substantialist crusade* Delhi, India: Sri Satguru.

Chittick, W. C. (1994a). Microcosm, macrocosm, and perfect man. In *Imaginal worlds: Ibn al-'Arabī and the problem of religious diversity* (pp. 31–38). Albany, NY: State University of New York Press.

Chittick, W. C. (1994b). *Imaginal worlds: Ibn al-'Arabī and the problem of religious diversity*. Albany, NY: State University of New York Press.

Chittick, W. C. (2008). Ibn al-'Arabī on participating in the mystery. In J. N. Ferrer & J. H. Sherman (Eds.), *The participatory turn: Spirituality, mysticism, religious studies* (pp. 245–264). Albany, NY: State University of New York Press.

Christy, D. (2015). Ignoring the Buddha and yelling at God: Reflections for interfaith chaplaincy. *Interfaith Ramadan* (June). Retrieved from http://www.interfaithramadan.com/2015/06/ignoring-buddha-and-yelling-at-god.html.

Churchland, P. S. (1986). *Neurophilosophy: Toward a unified science of the mind-brain*. Cambridge, MA: The MIT Press.

Clark, A. (1997). *Being there: Putting brain and world back together again* (1st ed.). Cambridge, MA: The MIT Press.

Clarke, C. (2009). The reinvention of religion. (Review of *The participatory turn: Spirituality, mysticism, religious studies* edited by Jorge N. Ferrer and Jacob H. Sherman). *Network Review: Journal of the Scientific and Medical Network, 100*, 55–57.

Clarke, D. S. (Ed.). (2004). *Panpsychism: Past and recent selected readings*. Albany, NY: State University of New York Press.

Clarke, J. J. (1994). *Jung and Eastern thought: A dialogue with the Orient*. New York, NY: Routledge.

Clarke, J. J. (1997). *Oriental enlightenment: The encounter between Asian and Western thought*. New York, NY: Routledge.

Clarke, J. J. (2000). *The Tao of the West: Western transformations of Taoist thought*. New York, NY: Routledge.

Clarke, P. B. (2006). *New religions in global perspective: A study of religious change in the modern world*. New York, NY: Routledge.

Clarke, S. (2009). Naturalism, science and the supernatural. *Sophia, 48*(2), 127–142.

Clements, J., Ettling, D., Jenett, D., & Shields, L. (1998). *Organic inquiry: If research was sacred.* Palo Alto, CA: Serpentine.

Cobb, J. B. Jr. (1975). *Christ in a pluralistic age.* Philadelphia, PA: Westminster.

Cobb, J. B. Jr. (1996). Metaphysical pluralism. In J. Prabhu (Ed.), *The intercultural challenge of Raimon Panikkar* (pp. 46–57). Maryknoll, NY: Orbis.

Cobb, J. B. Jr. (1999). *Transforming Christianity and the world: A way beyond absolutism and relativism* (P. F. Knitter, Ed.). Maryknoll, NY: Orbis.

Cohen, A. (1999). Integrating the big bang: An interview with Michael Murphy. *What is Enlightenment magazine, 15,* 82–96, 156–159. Retrieved from http://www.wie.org/j15/murphy.asp.

Cohen, S. J. (1993). *The holy letter: A study of Jewish sexual morality.* Northvale, NJ: Jason Aronson.

Collins, M. (2010). Engaging transcendent actualization through occupational intelligence. *Journal of Occupational Science, 17*(3), 177–186.

Collins, S. (1998). *Nirvana and other Buddhist felicities.* New York, NY: Cambridge University Press.

Combs, A., Arcari, T., & Krippner, S. (2006). All the myriad worlds: Life in the Akhasic plenum. *World Futures, 62,* 1–11.

Conner, R. P. (2007). Of travelers, roads, voyages, and rafts: A meditation on participation. *ReVision: A Journal of Consciousness and Transformation, 29*(3), 18–28.

Cook, F. H. (1989). Just this: Buddhist ultimate reality. *Buddhist-Christian Studies, 9,* 127–142.

Cooper, J. (2007). *Cognitive dissonance: Fifty years of a classic theory.* Los Angeles, CA: SAGE.

Corbin, H. (1995). *Mundus Imaginalis: Or the imaginary and the imaginal.* In H. Corbin (Ed.), *Swedenborg and esoteric Islam* (L. Fox, Trans., pp. 1–33). West Chester, PA: Swedenborg Foundation.

Corbin, H. (1998). A theory of visionary knowledge. In *The voyage and the messenger: Iran and philosophy* (J. Rowe, Trans., pp. 117–134). Berkeley, CA: North Atlantic Books.

Cousins, E. H. (1992). *Christ of the 21st century.* Rockport, MA: Element.

Coward, H. (2000). Religious pluralism and the Baha'i faith. In *Pluralism in world religions: A short introduction* (pp. 85–100). Rockport, MA: Oneworld.

Crosby, D. A. (2002). *A religion of nature.* Albany, NY: State University of New York Press.

Cunningham, P. F. (2007). The challenges, prospects, and promise of transpersonal psychology. *International Journal of Transpersonal Studies, 26,* 41–55.

Cunningham, P. F. (2011a). *Bridging psychological science and transpersonal spirit: A primer of transpersonal psychology.* Retrieved from http://www.rivier.edu/faculty/pcunningham/Research/A%20Primer%20of%20Transpersonal%20Psychology.pdf.

Cunningham, P. F. (2011b). The apparition at Medjugorje: A transpersonal interpretation (Pt 1–2). *The Journal of Transpersonal Psychology, 43,* 50–103.

Cunningham, P. F. (2015). Empirical rationalism and transpersonal empiricism:

Bridging the two epistemic cultures of transpersonal psychology. *The Journal of Transpersonal Psychology*, *47*(1), 83–120.

Cupitt, D. (1997). *After God: The future of religion*. New York, NY: Basic.

Cupitt, D. (1998). *Mysticism after modernity*. Malden, MA: Blackwell.

D'Costa, G. (Ed.). (1990). *Christian uniqueness reconsidered: The myth of a pluralistic theology of religions*. Maryknoll, NY: Orbis.

D'Costa, G. (2000). The near-triumph of Tibetan Buddhist pluralist-exclusivism. In *The meeting of religions and the Trinity* (pp. 72–95). Maryknoll, NY: Orbis.

Dale, E. J. (2014). *Completing Piaget's project: Transpersonal philosophy and the future of psychology*. St. Paul, MN: Paragon House.

Daniels, B. (2005). Nondualism and the divine domain. *International Journal of Transpersonal Studies*, *24*, 1–15.

Daniels, M. (2001). On transcendence in transpersonal psychology. *Transpersonal Psychology Review*, *5*(2), 3–11.

Daniels, M. (2005). *Shadow, self, spirit: Essays in transpersonal psychology*. Charlottesville, VA: Imprint Academic.

Daniels, M. (2009). Perspectives and vectors in transpersonal development. *Transpersonal Psychology Review*, *13*(1), 87–99.

Daniels, M. (2013). Traditional roots, history, and evolution of the transpersonal perspective. In H. L. Friedman & G. Hartelius (Eds.), *The Wiley-Blackwell handbook of transpersonal psychology* (pp. 23–43). Malden, MA: John Wiley & Sons.

Davidson, D. (1984). *Inquiries into truth and interpretation*. New York, NY: Oxford University Press.

Davies, J. A. (2014). Relational Dharma: A modern paradigm of transformation: A liberating model of intersubjectivity. *The Journal of Transpersonal Psychology*, *46*(1), 92–121.

Dawkins, R. (2006). *The God delusion*. Boston, MA: Houghton Mifflin.

Dawson, A. (2013). *Santo Daime: A new world religion*. New York, NY: Bloomsbury Academics.

De Brujin, J. T. P. (1997). *Persian Sufi poetry: An introduction to its mystical use*. Richmond, United Kingdom: Curzon.

De Caro, M., & Macarthur, D. (2004a). Introduction: The nature of naturalism. In M. De Caro & D. Macarthur (Eds.), *Naturalism in question* (pp. 1–17). Cambridge, MA: Harvard University Press.

De Caro, M., & Macarthur, D. (Eds.). (2004b). *Naturalism in question*. Cambridge, MA: Harvard University Press.

De Caro, M., & Macarthur, D. (Eds.). (2010). *Naturalism and normativity*. New York, NY: Columbia University Press.

De Lubac, H. (1967). *The mystery of the supernatural* (R. Sheed, Trans.). New York, NY: Crossroad.

De Quincey, C. (2000). Intersubjectivity: Exploring consciousness from the second-person perspective. *The Journal of Transpersonal Psychology*, *32*(2), 135–155.

De Quincey, C. (2010). *Radical nature: The soul of nature* (2nd. ed.). Rochester, VT: Park Street Press.

Deleuze, G., & Guattari, F. (1987). *A thousand plateaus: Capitalism and schizo phrenia* (B. Massumi, Trans.). Minneapolis, MN: University of Minnesota Press.

Dennett, D. (2006). *Breaking the spell: Religion as a natural phenomenon.* New York, NY: Viking.

Derrida, J. (1976). *Of grammatology* (1st American ed., G. C. Spivak, Trans.). Baltimore, MD: Johns Hopkins University Press.

Derrida, J. (1981). *Positions* (A. Bass, Trans.). Chicago, IL. University of Chicago Press.

Descola, P. (2013). *Beyond nature and culture* (J. Lloyd, Trans.). Chicago, IL: University of Chicago Press.

Devenish, S. C. (2012). *Seeing is believing: The eye of faith in a visual world.* Eugene, OR: Wipf & Stock Publishers.

Dews, P. (Ed.). (1986). *Autonomy and solidarity: Interviews with Jürgen Habermas.* London, United Kingdom: New Left Books.

DiPerna, D. (2012). Integral religious studies in developmental context. *Journal of Integral Theory and Practice, 7*(2), 1–18.

Doniger, W. (1998). *The implied spider: Politics and theology in myth.* New York, NY: Columbia University Press.

Doniger, W. (2009). *The Hindus: An alternative history.* New York, NY: Oxford University Press.

Donnelly, D. H. (1982). The sexual mystic: Embodied spirituality. In M. E. Giles (Ed.), *The feminist mystic and other essays on women and spirituality* (pp. 120–141). New York, NY: Crossroad.

Dreyer, E. A., & Burrows, M. S. (Eds.). (2005). *Minding the spirit: The study of Christian spirituality.* Baltimore, MD: Johns Hopkins University Press.

Duckworth, D. (2014a). How nonsectarian is "nonsectarian"?: Jorge Ferrer's religious pluralist alternative to Tibetan Buddhist inclusivism. *Sophia, 53*(3), 339–348.

Duckworth, D. (2014b). Onto-theology and emptiness: The nature of Buddha-nature. *Journal of the American Academy of Religion, 82*(4), 1070–1090.

Duckworth, D. (forthcoming). Buddhism and beyond: The question of pluralism. In A. Vélez de Cea (Ed.), *Buddhist responses to religious diversity.* Albany, NY: State University of New York Press.

Duhem, P. M. M. (1991). *The aim and structure of physical theory.* Princeton, NJ: Princeton University Press. (Original work published 1954).

Dupré, J. (1995). *The disorder of things: Metaphysical foundations of the disunity of science.* Cambridge, MA: Harvard University Press.

Dupré, J. (2004). The miracle of monism. In M. De Caro & D. Macarthur (Eds.), *Naturalism in question* (pp. 36–58). Cambridge, MA: Harvard University Press.

Dupré, L. (1987). Mysticism. In M. Eliade (Ed.), *The encyclopedia of religion* (Vol. 10, pp. 245–261). New York, NY: MacMillan.

Dupré, L. (1996). *Unio mystica*: The state and the experience. In M. Idel & B. McGinn (Eds.), *Mystical union in Judaism, Christianity, and Islam: An ecumenical dialogue* (pp. 3–23). New York, NY: Continuum.

Dürckheim, K. G. (1962). *Hara: The vital center of man.* Rochester, VT: Inner Traditions.

Edelstein, S. (2011). *Sex and the spiritual teacher: Why it happens, when it's a problem, and what we all can do.* Boston, MA: Wisdom Publications.

Edwards, A. C. (2003). Response to the spiritual intelligence debate: Are some conceptual distinctions needed here? *The International Journal for the Psychology of Religion, 13*(1), 49–52.

Eliade, M. (1959). *The sacred and the profane.* New York, NY: Harcourt Brace Jovanovich.

Eliade, M. (1989). *Cosmos and history: The myth of the eternal return* (W. R. Trask, Trans.). London, United Kingdom: Arkana. (Original work published 1959).

Elkins, D. N. (1998). *Beyond religion: A personal program for building a spiritual life outside the walls of traditional religion.* Wheaton, IL: Theosophical Publishing House.

Eller, C. (1993). *Living in the lap of the Goddess: The feminist spirituality movement in America.* New York, NY: Crossroad.

Ellis, B. D. (2009). *The metaphysics of scientific realism.* Durham, United Kingdom: Acumen.

Emmons, R. A. (1999). *The psychology of ultimate concern: Motivation and spirituality in personality.* New York, NY: Guilford Press.

Emmons, R. A. (2000a). Is spirituality an intelligence? Motivation, cognition and the psychology of ultimate concern. *The International Journal for the Psychology of Religion, 10*(1), 3–26.

Emmons, R. A. (2000b). Spirituality and intelligence: Problems and prospects. *The International Journal for the Psychology of Religion, 10*(1), 57–64.

Eng, P. (2016). Saints run mad 2.0: Further deliberations on addictions recovery through a transpersonal lens. *Pastoral Psychology, 65*(2), 197–213.

Engler, S. (2004). Constructionism versus what? *Religion, 34*(4), 291–313.

Esbjörn-Hargens, S. (Ed.). (2010). *Integral theory in action: Applied, theoretical, and constructive perspectives on the AQAL model.* Albany, NY: State University of New York Press.

Evans, D. (1989). Can philosophers limit what mystics can do?: A critique of Steven Katz. *Religious Studies, 25*(01), 53–60.

Evans, D. D. (1993). *Spirituality and human nature.* Albany, NY: State University of New York Press.

Faith, E. (2007). Reading, dialogue, healing, a path of growth beyond past, present. *AAP News: The Newsletter of the Association for the Advancement of Psychosynthesis* (August), 4.

Faivre, A. (1994). *Access to Western esotericism.* Albany, NY: State University of New York Press.

Faure, B. (1993). *Chan insights and oversights: An epistemological critique of the Chan tradition.* Princeton, NJ: Princeton University Press.

Faure, B. (1998). *The red thread: Buddhist approaches to sexuality.* Princeton, NJ: Princeton University Press.

Faure, B. (2009). *Unmasking Buddhism.* Malden, MA: Wiley-Blackwell.

Fazel, S. (2003). Religious pluralism and the Baha'i faith. *Interreligious Insight,* 1(3), 42–49.

Fazel, S. (2008). Baha'i approaches to Christianity and Islam: Further thoughts on developing an inter-religious dialogue. *Baha'i Studies Review, 14,* 41–53.

Fazlhashemi, M. (2013). Occidentalism. In J. Svartvik & J. Wiren (Eds.), *Religious stereotyping and interreligious relations* (pp. 85–96). New York, NY: Palgrave Macmillan.

Fenton, J. Y. (1995). Mystical experience as a bridge for cross-cultural philosophy of religion: A critique. In T. Dean (Ed.), *Religious pluralism and truth: Essays on cross-cultural philosophy of religion* (pp. 189–204). Albany, NY: State University of New York Press.

Ferendo, F. J. (2007). *Holistic perspectives and integral theory: On seeing what is.* Westerly, RI: Process Publishing.

Ferrer, J. N. (1998a). Beyond absolutism and relativism in transpersonal evolutionary theory. *World Futures: The Journal of General Evolution, 52*(3–4), 239–280.

Ferrer, J. N. (1998b). Speak now or forever hold your peace. A review essay of Ken Wilber's *The marriage of sense and soul: Integrating science and religion. The Journal of Transpersonal Psychology, 30*(1), 53–67.

Ferrer, J. N. (1999). *Revisioning transpersonal theory: An epistemic approach to transpersonal and spiritual phenomena* (Doctoral dissertation). California Institute of Integral Studies, San Francisco, California. Retrieved from http://search.proquest.com/docview/619564487?accountid=25260 (Order No. AAI9949443).

Ferrer, J. N. (2000a). The perennial philosophy revisited. *The Journal of Transpersonal Psychology, 32*(1), 7–30.

Ferrer, J. N. (2000b). Transpersonal knowledge: A participatory approach to transpersonal phenomena. In T. Hart, P. L. Nelson, & K. Puhakka (Eds.), *Transpersonal knowing: Exploring the farther reaches of consciousness* (pp. 213–252). Albany, NY: State University of New York Press.

Ferrer, J. N. (2001). Toward a participatory vision of human spirituality. *ReVision: A Journal of Consciousness and Transformation, 24*(2), 15–26.

Ferrer, J. N. (2002). *Revisioning transpersonal theory: A participatory vision of human spirituality.* Albany, NY: State University of New York Press.

Ferrer, J. N. (2003). Integral transformative practice: A participatory perspective. *The Journal of Transpersonal Psychology, 35*(1), 21–42.

REFERENCES 327

Ferrer, J. N. (2006). Embodied spirituality, now and then. Tikkun: Culture, Spirituality, Politics, 21(3), 41–45, 53–64.
Ferrer, J. N. (2007). Spirituality and intimate relationships: Monogamy, polyamory, and beyond. Tikkun: Culture, Spirituality, Politics, 22(1), 37–43, 60–62.
Ferrer, J. N. (2008). Spiritual knowing as participatory enaction: An answer to the question of religious pluralism. In J. N. Ferrer & J. H. Sherman (Eds.), The participatory turn: Spirituality, mysticism, religious studies (pp. 135–169). Albany, NY: State University of New York Press.
Ferrer, J. N. (2010). The plurality of religions and the spirit of pluralism: A participatory vision of the future of religion. International Journal of Transpersonal Studies, 28(1), 139–151.
Ferrer, J. N. (2011, November). Participation and contemplation in the teaching of religion and spirituality. In J. N. Ferrer, J. H. Sherman, S. T. Malkemus, A. Klein, & B. Lanzetta (Panelists), Contemplative studies from a participatory perspective: Embodiment, relatedness, and creativity in contemplative inquiry. Annual meeting of the American Academy of Religion, San Francisco, CA.
Ferrer, J. N. (2013). Faith in Ayahuasca: An interview with Shipibo Shaman Guillermo Arevalo. Sacred Hoop, 80, 14–19.
Ferrer, J. N. (2014a, November). Critical subjectivity after the participatory turn. Paper presented at the Conference on Contemplative Studies. University of San Diego, San Diego, CA.
Ferrer, J. N. (Panel Respondent). (2014b, November). Contemplative stage models: Comparative and psychological perspectives. In S. Heine, L. Komjathy, B. Bogin, W. Meninger, & M. Larson-Harris (Panelists), Maps of transformation: Ox herding, horse taming, and stages on the contemplative path. Annual meeting of the American Academy of Religion, San Diego, CA.
Ferrer, J. N. (2015). Neo-Piagetian transpersonal psychology: Dancing in-between pluralism and perennialism. Essay review of Edward J. Dale's Completing Piaget's project: Transpersonal philosophy and the future of psychology. The Journal of Transpersonal Psychology, 47(1), 124–138.
Ferrer, J. N. (2016). A finer love: Sexuality, spirituality, and the evolution of intimate relationships. Manuscript in preparation.
Ferrer, J. N., Albareda, R. V., & Romero, M. T. (2004). Embodied participation in the mystery: Implications for the individual, interpersonal relationships, and society. ReVision: A Journal of Consciousness and Transformation, 27(1), 10–18.
Ferrer, J. N., & Puente, I. (2013). Participation and spirit: An interview with Jorge N. Ferrer. Journal of Transpersonal Research, 5(2), 97–111.
Ferrer, J. N., Romero, M. T., & Albareda, R. V. (2005). Integral transformative education: A participatory proposal. Journal of Transformative Education, 3(4), 306–330.

Ferrer, J. N., & Sherman, J. H. (2008a). Introduction: The participatory turn in spirituality, mysticism, and religious studies. In J. N. Ferrer & J. H. Sherman (Eds.), *The participatory turn: Spirituality, mysticism, religious studies* (pp. 1–78). Albany, NY: State University of New York Press.

Ferrer, J. N., & Sherman, J. H. (Eds.). (2008b). *The participatory turn: Spirituality, mysticism, religious studies*. Albany, NY: State University of New York Press.

Ferrer, J. N., & Sohmer, O. R. (2017). Embodied spiritual inquiry: A radical approach to second-person contemplative education. In O. Gunnlaugson, E. W. Sarath, H. Bai, & C. Scott (Eds.), *The intersubjective turn: Theoretical approaches to contemplative learning and inquiry across disciplines* (pp 15-35). Albany, NY: State University of New York Press.

Feuerstein, G. (1991). The shadow of the enlightened guru. In C. Zweig & J. Abrams (Eds.), *Meeting the shadow: The hidden power of the dark side of human nature* (pp. 148–150). New York, NY: Jeremy Tarcher.

Feuerstein, G. (1998). *The yoga tradition: Its history, literature, philosophy, and practice*. Prescott, AZ: Hohm.

Feuerstein, G. (2006). *Holy madness: Spirituality, crazy-wise teachers, and enlightenment* (Rev. ed.). Prescott, AZ: Hohm.

Fine, L. (1992). Purifying the body in the name of the soul: The problem of the body in sixteenth-century Kabbalah. In H. Eilberg-Schwartz (Ed.), *People of the body: Jews and Judaism from an embodied perspective* (pp. 117–142). Albany, NY: State University of New York Press.

Fingelkurts, A. A., & Fingelkurts, A. A. (2009). Is our brain hardwired to produce God or is our brain hardwired to perceive God?: A systematic review on the role of the brain in mediating religious experience. *Cognitive Processing, 10*(4), 293–326.

Fishman, Y. I. (2007). Can science test supernatural worldviews? *Science and Education, 18*(6–7), 813–837.

Fitzgerald, T. (1996). Religion, philosophy, and family resemblances. *Religion, 26*, 215–236.

Fitzgerald, T. (2000). *The ideology of religious studies*. New York, NY: Oxford University Press.

Flood, G. (1999). *Beyond phenomenology: Rethinking the study of religion*. New York, NY: Cassell.

Flood, G. (2000). The purification of the body. In D. G. White (Ed.), *Tantra in practice* (pp. 507–520). Princeton, NJ: Princeton University Press.

Forest, J. (1993). A Christian perspective on spirituality in light of the lives of Dorothy Day and Thomas Merton. *Revision: A Journal of Consciousness and Transformation, 15*(3), 115–120.

Forgie, J. W. (1985). Hyper-Kantianism in recent discussions of mystical experience. *Religious Studies, 21*(2), 205–218.

Forman, R. K. C. (1989). Paramārtha and modern constructivists on mysticism: Epistemological monomorphism versus duomorphism. *Philosophy East and West, 39*, 393–418.

Forman, R. K. C. (Ed.). (1990). *The problem of pure consciousness: Mysticism and philosophy*. New York, NY: Oxford University Press.

Forman, R. K. C. (1998a). Introduction: Mystical consciousness, the innate capacity, and the perennial philosophy. In R. K. C. Forman (Ed.), *The innate capacity: Mysticism, psychology, and philosophy* (pp. 3–44). New York, NY: Oxford University Press.

Forman, R. K. C. (Ed). (1998b). *The innate capacity: Mysticism, psychology, and philosophy*. New York, NY: Oxford University Press.

Forman, R. K. C. (1999). *Mysticism, mind, consciousness*. Albany, NY: State University of New York Press.

Forman, R. K. C. (2004). *Grassroots spirituality: What it is, why it is here, where it is going*. Charlottesville, VA: Imprint Academic.

Forsthoefel, T. A., & Humes, C. A. (Eds.). (2005). *Gurus in America*. Albany, NY: State University of New York Press.

Fort, A. O. (1998). *Jivanmukti in transformation: Embodied liberation in Advaita and neo-Advaita*. Albany, NY: State University of New York Press.

Fox, M. (1988). *The coming of the cosmic Christ: The healing of Mother Earth and the birth of a global renaissance*. San Francisco, CA: Harper & Row.

Fox, M. (2002). *Creativity: Where the divine and the human meet*. New York, NY: Jeremy P. Tarcher/Putnam.

Freeman, A. (2006). A Daniel comes to judgment?: Dennett and the revisioning of transpersonal theory. *Journal of Consciousness Studies, 13*(3), 95–109.

Freeman, A. (2007). What is mystical experience? *Sofia—The Sea of Faith Magazine, 84*. Retrieved from http://www.sofn.org.uk/sofia/84mystical.html.

Freinkel, P. D. (2015). Singing and participatory spirituality. *International Journal of Transpersonal Studies, 34*(1–2), 152–166.

Freire, P. (1996). *Pedagogy of the oppressed*. New York, NY: Penguin. (Original work published 1970).

Freire, P. (1998). *Pedagogy of freedom: Ethics, democracy, and civic courage*. Lanham, MA: Rowman & Littlefield.

Friedman, H. L. (1983). The Self-Expansiveness Level Form: A conceptualization and measurement of a transpersonal construct. *The Journal of Transpersonal Psychology, 15*(1), 37–50.

Friedman, H. L. (2002). Transpersonal psychology as a scientific field. *International Journal of Transpersonal Studies, 21*, 175–187.

Friedman, H. L. (2006). The renewal of psychedelic research: Implications for humanistic and transpersonal psychology. *The Humanistic Psychologist, 34*(1), 39–58.

Friedman, H. L. (2009). Xenophilia as a cultural trap: Bridging the gap between transpersonal psychology and religious/spiritual traditions. *International Journal of Transpersonal Studies, 28*(1), 107–111.

Friedman, H. L. (2013a). The role of science in transpersonal psychology: The advantages of middle-range theory. In H. L. Friedman & G. Hartelius (Eds.), *The Wiley-Blackwell handbook of transpersonal psychology* (pp. 300–311). Malden, MA: John Wiley & Sons.

Friedman, H. L. (2013b). Transpersonal self-expansiveness as a scientific construct. In H. L. Friedman & G. Hartelius (Eds.), *The Wiley-Blackwell handbook of transpersonal psychology* (pp. 203–222). Malden, MA: John Wiley & Sons.

Friedman, H. L., & Hartelius, G. (2013a). (Eds.), *The Wiley-Blackwell handbook of transpersonal psychology*. Malden, MA: Wiley Blackwell.

Friedman, H. L., & Hartelius, G. (2013b). Editors' introduction: The promise (and some perils) of transpersonal psychology. In H. L. Friedman & G. Hartelius (Eds.), *The Wiley-Blackwell handbook of transpersonal psychology* (pp. xxiii–xxxii). Malden, MA: John Wiley & Sons.

Friedman, H. L., Krippner, S., Riebel, L., & Johnson, C. (2010). Models of spiritual development. *The International Journal of Transpersonal Studies, 29*(1), 53–70.

Frisina, W. G. (2002). *The unity of knowledge and action: Toward a nonrepresentational theory of knowledge*. Albany, NY: State University of New York Press.

Fuller, R. C. (2001). *Spiritual but not religious: Understanding unchurched America.* New York, NY: Oxford University Press.

Fuller, R. C. (2002). Review of *Revisioning transpersonal theory: A participatory vision of human spirituality* by Jorge N. Ferrer. *Religious Studies Review, 28*(4), 342.

Fuller, R. C. (2008). *Spirituality in the flesh: Bodily sources of religious experiences.* New York, NY: Oxford University Press.

Gadamer, H-G. (1990). *Truth and Method* (2nd rev. ed.). (J. Weinsheimer & D. G. Marshall, Trans.). New York, NY: Crossroad.

Galian, L. (2004). *The centrality of the divine feminine in Sufism*. Retrieved from http://home.earthlink.net/~drmljg/id8.html.

Gardner, H. (1993). *Frames of mind: The theory of multiple intelligences*. New York, NY: Basic. (Original work published 1983).

Gardner, H. (2000). A case against spiritual intelligence. *International Journal for the Psychology of Religion,10*(1), 27–34.

Gebser, J. (1986). *The ever-present origin* (N. Barstad & A. Mikunas, Trans.). Athens, OH: Ohio University Press.

Geoffrey, S. (1993). *Civilized shamans: Buddhism in Tibetan societies*. Washington, DC: Smithsonian Institution Press.

Ghanea-Hercock, N. (Ed.). (2010). *Religion and human rights*. New York, NY: Routledge.

Gier, N. (2008). *Spiritual titanism: Indian, Chinese, and modern perspectives.* Albany, NY: State University of New York Press.

Gillespie, A., & F. Cornish (2010). Intersubjectivity: Towards a dialogical analysis. *Journal for the Theory of Social Behavior, 40*(1), 19–46.

Gimello, R. M. (1983). Mysticism in its contexts. In S. T. Katz (Ed.), *Mysticism and religious traditions* (pp. 61–88). New York, NY: Oxford University Press.

Giorgi, A. (1970). *Psychology as a human science: A phenomenologically based approach*. New York, NY: Harper & Row.

Gleig, A. (2009). A. H. Almaas's approach: Divine individualism or mystical humanism? *Fieldwork in Religion*, 4(1), 67–85.

Gleig, A. (2011a). Review of *The participatory turn: Spirituality, mysticism, religious studies*, edited by Jorge N. Ferrer and Jacob H. Sherman. *Alternative Spirituality and Religion Review*, 2(1), 125–128.

Gleig, A. (2011b). The participatory turn: Thinking beyond the philosophies of consciousness and constructivism in the study of religion [Review of *The participatory turn: Spirituality, mysticism, religious studies*, edited by Jorge N. Ferrer and Jacob H. Sherman]. *Spiritus: A Journal of Christian Spirituality*, 11(1), 146–148.

Gleig, A. (2012). Researching new religious movements from the inside out and the outside in: Methodological reflections from collaborative and participatory perspectives. *Nova Religio: The Journal of Alternative and Emergent Religions*, 16(1), 88–103.

Gleig, A., & Boeving, N. G. (2009). Spiritual democracy: Beyond consciousness and culture [Review of *The participatory turn: Spirituality, mysticism, religious studies*, edited by Jorge N. Ferrer and Jacob H. Sherman]. *Tikkun: Culture, Spirituality, Politics* (May/June), 64–68.

Gleig, A., Ferrer, J. N., Sherman, J. H., Barnard, W. G., Lanzetta, B., Irwin, L., & Kripal, J. (Panel). (2010, October). *The Participatory turn: Studying religion beyond the philosophies of consciousness and constructivism.* Presented at the 2010 American Academy of Religion Annual Meeting, Atlanta, GA.

Goddard, G. (2005). Counterpoints in transpersonal theory: Toward an astrological resolution. *ReVision: A Journal of Consciousness and Transformation*, 27(3), 9–19.

Goddard, G. (2009). *Transpersonal theory and the astrological mandala: An evolutionary model.* Victoria, BC: Trafford.

Goenka, S. N. (1998). *Sattipaṭṭhāna Sutta discourses.* Seattle, WA: Vipassana Research Publications.

Gold, D. (2003). *Aesthetics and analysis in writing on religion: Modern fascinations.* Berkeley, CA: University of California Press.

Goldberg, E. (2010). Review of *The participatory turn: Spirituality, mysticism, religious studies*, edited by Jorge N. Ferrer and Jacob H. Sherman. *Sophia*, 49(2), 309–310.

Grace, F., Sherman, J. H., Ferrer, J. N., Malkemus, S., Klein, A., & Lanzetta, B. (Panel). (2011, November). *Contemplative studies from a participatory perspective: Embodiment, relatedness, and creativity in contemplative Inquiry.* Presented at the 2011 American Academy of Religion Annual Meeting, San Francisco, CA.

Graves, C. W. (1970). Levels of existence: An open system theory of values. *Journal of Humanistic Psychology*, 10(2), 131–155.

Graves, C. W. (1974). Human nature prepares for a momentous leap. *The Futurist* (April), 72–87.

Gregory, P. N. (Ed.). (1987). *Sudden and gradual approaches to enlightenment in*

Chinese thought. Honolulu, HI: University of Hawaii Press.

Griffin, D. R. (Ed.). (2005). *Deep religious pluralism.* Louisville, KY: Westminster/ John Knox.

Grof, C., & Grof, S. (1990). *The stormy search for the self: A guide to personal growth through transformational crisis.* Los Angeles, CA: J. P. Tarcher.

Grof, S. (1975). *Realms of the human unconscious: Observations from LSD research.* New York, NY: Viking.

Grof, S. (1985). *Beyond the brain: Birth, death, and transcendence in psychotherapy.* Albany, NY: State University of New York Press.

Grof, S. (1988a). *The adventure of self-discovery: Dimensions of consciousness and new perspectives in psychotherapy and inner exploration.* Albany, NY: State University of New York Press.

Grof, S. (1988b). Modern consciousness research and human survival. In S. Grof (Ed.), *Human survival and consciousness evolution* (pp. 57–78). Albany, NY: State University of New York Press.

Grof, S. (1993). *The holotropic mind: The three levels of human consciousness and how they shape our lives.* San Francisco, CA: HarperSanFrancisco.

Grof, S. (1996). Ken Wilber's spectrum psychology: Observations from clinical consciousness research. In D. Rothberg & S. Kelly (Eds.), *Ken Wilber in dialogue: Conversations with leading transpersonal thinkers* (pp. 85–116). Wheaton, IL: Theosophical Publishing House.

Grof, S. (1998). *The cosmic game: Explorations of the frontiers of human consciousness.* Albany, NY: State University of New York Press.

Grof. S. (2000). *Psychology of the future: Lessons from modern consciousness research.* Albany, NY: State University of New York Press.

Grof, S. (2006). *When the impossible happens: Adventures in non-ordinary realities.* Louisville, CO: Sounds True.

Grof, S. (2012). *Healing our deepest wounds: The holotropic paradigm shift.* Newcastle, WA: Stream of Consciousness.

Grof, S. (2013). Revision and re-enchantment of psychology: Lessons from half a century of consciousness research. In H. L. Friedman & G. Hartelius (Eds.), *The Wiley-Blackwell handbook of transpersonal psychology* (pp. 91–120). Malden, MA: John Wiley & Sons.

Grof, S., & Grof, C. (Eds.). (1989). *Spiritual emergency: When personal transformation becomes a crisis.* Los Angeles, CA: J. P. Tarcher.

Grof, S., & Grof, C. (2010). *Holotropic breathwork: A new approach to self-exploration and therapy.* Albany, NY: State University of New York Press.

Gross, R. M., & Muck, T. C. (Eds.). (2003). *Christians talk about Buddhist meditation, Buddhists talk about Christian prayer.* New York, NY: Continuum.

Gunnlaugson, O. (2009a). *Exploring presencing as a contemplative framework for inquiry in higher education classrooms* (Doctoral dissertation). The University of British Columbia, Vancouver, Canada. Retrieved from https://circle. ubc.ca/bitstream/handle/2429/16644/ubc_2010_spring_gunnlaugson_carl.

pdf?sequence=1.

Gunnlaugson, O. (2009b). Establishing second-person forms of contemplative education: An inquiry into four conceptions of intersubjectivity. *Integral Review*, 5(1), 25–50.

Gunnlaugson, O. (2011). Advancing a second-person contemplative approach for collective wisdom and leadership development. *Journal of Transformative Education*, 9(1), 3–20.

Haar Farris, M. S. (2010). *Participatory wisdom in religious studies: Jacques Derrida, philo-sophia, and religious pluralism* (Doctoral dissertation). Graduate Theological Union, Berkeley, California. (Order No. 3416583).

Habermas, J. (1984). *The theory of communicative action: Reason and the rationalization of society* (Vol. 1, T. McCarthy, Trans.). Boston, MA: Beacon.

Habermas, J. (2008). *Between naturalism and religion: Philosophical essays*. Malden, MA: Polity Press.

Hakeda, Y. S. (1972). *Kūkai: Major works*. New York, NY: Columbia University Press.

Halbfass, W. (1988). *India and Europe: An essay in understanding*. Albany, NY: State University of New York Press.

Halbfass, W. (1991). *Tradition and reflection: Explorations in Indian thought*. Albany, NY: State University of New York Press.

Halbfass, W. (2001). Mescaline and Indian philosophy: Aldous Huxley and the mythology of experience. In C. C. Barfoot (Ed.), *Aldous Huxley between East and West* (pp. 221–236). New York, NY: Rodopi.

Hamilton, M. (2002). The Easternisation thesis: Critical reflections. *Religion*, 32(3), 243–258.

Hammer, O. (2001). Same message from everywhere: The sources of modern revelation. In M. Rothstein (Ed.), *New age religion and globalization* (pp. 42–57). Aarhus N, Denmark: Aarhus University Press.

Hammersholt, T. (2013). Steven T. Katz's philosophy of mysticism revisited. *Journal of the American Academy of Religion*, 81(2), 467–490.

Hanegraaff, W. J. (1998). *New age religion and Western culture: Esotericism in the mirror of secular thought*. Albany, NY: State University of New York Press.

Harmless, W. (2008). *Mystics*. New York, NY: Oxford University Press.

Harner, M. J. (1973). *Hallucinogens and shamanism*. New York, NY: Oxford University Press.

Harner, M. (1980). *The way of the shaman*. New York, NY: Harper & Row.

Harris, S. (2004). *The end of faith: Religion, terror, and the future of religion*. New York, NY: W. W. Norton.

Harris, S. (2014). *Waking up: A guide to spirituality without religion*. New York, NY: Simon & Schuster.

Harrison, V. (2006). The pragmatics of defining religion in a multi-cultural world. *The International Journal for Philosophy of Religion*, 59(3), 133–152.

Hartelius, G. (2006). All that glisters is not gold: Heterophenomenology and transpersonal theory. *Journal of Consciousness Studies, 13*(6), 63–77.

Hartelius, G. (2015a). A startling new role for Wilber's integral model: Or, how I learned to stop worrying and love perennialism. (A response to Abramson). *Transpersonal Psychology Review, 17*(1), 25–37.

Hartelius, G. (2015b). Participatory thought has no emperor and no Absolute— A further response to Abramson. *Transpersonal Psychology Review, 17*(1), 49–53.

Hartelius, G. (2016). Participatory transpersonalism: Transformative relational process, not the structure of ultimate reality. *International Journal of Transpersonal Studies, 35*(1), iii–ix.

Hartelius, G. (2017). Taylor's soft perennialism: A primer of perennial flaws in transpersonal scholarship. *International Journal of Transpersonal Studies, 35*(2), 42–47.

Hartelius, G., & Ferrer, J. N. (2013). Transpersonal philosophy: The participatory turn. In H. L. Friedman & G. Hartelius (Eds.), *The Wiley-Blackwell handbook of transpersonal psychology* (pp. 187–202). Malden, MA: John Wiley & Sons.

Hartelius, G., Harrahy, M., Crouch, C., Adler, H., Thouin, M., & Stamp, G. (forthcoming). Second-wave transpersonal psychology: Embodied, embedded, diverse, transformative. *The Journal of Transpersonal Psychology*.

Hartelius, G., Rothe, G., & Roy, P. (2013). A brand from the burning: Defining transpersonal psychology. In H. L. Friedman & G. Hartelius (Eds.), *The Wiley-Blackwell handbook of transpersonal psychology* (pp. 3–22). Malden, MA: Wiley Blackwell.

Harvey, A. (2002). *The direct path: Creating a personal journey to the divine using the world's spiritual traditions*. New York, NY: Harmony.

Harvey, P. (1995). *The selfless mind: Personality, consciousness and nirvana in early Buddhism*. Richmond, United Kingdom: Curzon.

Heaven, R. (2012). *Cactus of mystery: The shamanic powers of the Peruvian San Pedro cactus*. Rochester, VT: Park Street Press.

Heelas, P., & Woodhead, L. (2005). *The spiritual revolution: Why religion is giving way to spirituality*. Maiden, MA: Blackwell.

Heim, S. M. (1995). *Salvations: Truth and difference in religion*. Maryknoll, NY: Orbis.

Helminiak, D. A. (1998). *Religion and the human sciences: An approach via spirituality*. Albany, NY: State University of New York Press.

Henare, A., Holdbraad, M., & Wastell, S. (2007). *Thinking through things: Theorizing artefacts ethnographically*. London, United Kingdom: Routledge.

HERI Spirituality Project Team. (2005, April). Spirituality and higher education curriculum: The HERI syllabi project. *Spirituality in Higher Education Newsletter, 2*(2). Retrieved from http://www.spirituality.ucla.edu/publications/newsletters/2/syllabi.php.

Heron, J. (1988). Assessment revisited. In D. Boud (Ed.), *Developing student autonomy in learning* (2nd. ed., pp. 77–90). New York, NY: Nichols.

Heron, J. (1992). *Feeling and personhood: Psychology in another key*. Thousand

Oaks, CA: SAGE.

Heron, J. (1996). *Co-operative inquiry: Research into the human condition.* Thousand Oaks, CA: SAGE.

Heron, J. (1998). *Sacred science: Person-centered inquiry into the spiritual and the subtle.* Ross-on-Wye, United Kingdom: PCCS Books.

Heron, J. (1999). *The complete facilitator's handbook.* Sterling, VA: Kogan Page.

Heron, J. (2001). Spiritual inquiry as divine becoming. *ReVision: A Journal of Consciousness and Transformation, 24*(2), 32–41.

Heron, J. (2002, July). *Our process in this place.* Keynote speech at the International Conference of Organizational Spirituality titled Living spirit: New dimensions in work and learning. University of Surrey, United Kingdom. Retrieved from http://www.human-inquiry.com/Keynote2.htm.

Heron, J. (2006). *Participatory spirituality: A farewell to authoritarian religion.* Morrisville, NC: Lulu.

Heron, J. (2007). Participatory fruits of spiritual inquiry. *ReVision: A Journal of Consciousness and Transformation, 29*(3), 7–17.

Heron, J., & Lahood, G. (2008). Charismatic inquiry in concert: Action research in the realm of the between. In P. Reason & H. Bradbury (Eds.), *The SAGE handbook of action research: Participative inquiry and practice* (2nd ed., pp. 439–449). Thousand Oaks, CA: SAGE.

Heron, J., & Reason, P. (1997). A participatory inquiry paradigm. *Qualitative Inquiry, 3*(3), 274–294.

Heron, J., & Reason, P. (2001). The practice of co-operative inquiry: Research with rather than on people. In P. Reason & H. Bradbury (Eds.), *Handbook of action research: Participative inquiry and practice* (pp. 179–188). London, United Kingdom: SAGE.

Heron, J., & Reason, P. (2008). Extending epistemology within a co-operative inquiry. In P. Reason & H. Bradbury (Eds.), *The SAGE handbook of action research: Participative inquiry and practice* (2nd ed., pp. 366–380). Thousand Oaks, CA: SAGE.

Heschel, S. (1996). Bringing heaven down to earth. *Tikkun: A Bimonthly Jewish Critique of Politics, Culture, and Society, 11*(2), 48–56.

Heywood, P. (2012). Anthropology and what there is: Reflections on "ontology." *Cambridge Anthropology, 30*(1), 143–151.

Hick, J. (1989). *An interpretation of religion: Human responses to the transcendent.* New Haven, CT: Yale University Press.

Hick J., & Knitter, P. F. (Eds.). (1987). *The myth of Christian uniqueness: Toward a pluralistic theology of religions.* Maryknoll, NY: Orbis.

Hiles, D. R. (2008, November). *Participatory perspectives in counseling research.* Paper presented at the NCCR Conference, Newport, United Kingdom. Retrieved from www.psy.dmu.ac.uk/drhiles/.

Hill, C. (Ed.). (2006). Introduction: Contemplative practices and education (Special Issue). *The Teachers College Record, 108*(9), 1723–1732.

Hitchens, C. (2007). *God is not great: How religion poisons everything.* New York,

NY: Twelve.

Hocking, B., Haskell, J., & Linds, W. (2001). *Unfolding bodymind: Exploring possibility through education*. Brandon, VT: Foundation for Educational Renewal.

Hocking, W. E. (1956). *The coming world civilization*. New York, NY: Harper.

Hogue, M. S. (2010). *The promise of religious naturalism*. Lanham, MD: Rowman & Littlefield.

Holdbraad, M. (2012). *Truth in motion: The recursive anthropology of Cuban divination*. Chicago, IL: University of Chicago Press.

Holdrege, B. A. (1996). *Veda and Torah: Transcending the textuality of scripture*. Albany, NY: State University of New York Press.

Hollenback, J. B. (1996). *Mysticism: Experience, response, and empowerment*. University Park, PA: Pennsylvania State University Press.

Hollick, M. (2006). *The science of oneness: A worldview for the twenty-first century*. New York, NY: O Books.

Hollywood, A. M. (2002). *Sensible ecstasy: Mysticism, sexual difference, and the demands of history*. Chicago, IL: University of Chicago Press.

Hooks, B. (1994). *Teaching to transgress: Education as the practice of freedom*. New York, NY: Routledge.

Hopkins, J. (1988). Ultimate reality in Tibetan Buddhism. *Buddhist-Christian Studies, 8*, 111–129.

Horgan, J. (2004). *Rational mysticism: Spirituality meets science in the search for enlightenment*. New York, NY: Mariner Books.

Horowitz, M., & Palmer, C. (Eds.). (1999). *Moksha: Aldous Huxley's classical writings on psychedelics and the visionary experience*. Rochester, VT: Park Street Press. (Original work published 1979).

Horton, C. A. (2012). *Yoga Ph.D.: Integrating the life of the mind and the wisdom of the body*. Chicago, IL: Kleio Books.

Horton, C. A., & Harvey, R. (Eds.). (2012). *21st century yoga: Culture, politics, and practice*. Chicago, IL; Kleio Books.

Huxley, A. (1945). *The perennial philosophy*. New York, NY: Harper & Brothers.

Huxley, A. (1954). *The doors of perception and Heaven and hell*. New York, NY: Harper & Row.

Ianiszeskwi, P. (2010). Trans-Jungian psychology: An archetypal-noetic model of the psyche from the dialectic-dynamic paradigm and the participatory epistemology. *Journal of Transpersonal Research, 2*, 26–43.

Ibrahim, A. S. (2015). 4 ways ISIS grounds its actions in religion, and why it should matter (COMMENTARY). *The Washington Post*, 16 November 2015. Retrieved from https://www.washingtonpost.com/national/religion/4-ways-isis-grounds-its-actions-in-religion-and-why-it-should-matter-commentary/2015/11/16/d7e31278-8ca0-11e5-934c-a369c80822c2_story.html.

Idel, M., & McGinn, B. (Eds.). (1996). *Mystical union in Judaism, Christianity, and Islam: An ecumenical dialogue*. New York, NY: Continuum.

Ingram, P. O., & Streng, F. J. (Eds.). (2007). *Buddhist-Christian dialogue: Mutual renewal and transformation*. Eugene, OR: Wipf & Stock.

Irwin, L. (1994). *The dream seekers: Native American visionary traditions of the Great Plains*. Norman, OK: University of Oklahoma Press.

Irwin, L. (1996). *Visionary worlds: The making and unmaking of reality*. Albany, NY: State University of New York Press.

Irwin, L. (2008). Esoteric paradigms and participatory spirituality in the teachings of Mikhaël Aïvanhov. In J. N. Ferrer & J. H. Sherman (Eds.), *The participatory turn: Spirituality, mysticism, religious studies* (pp. 197–224). Albany, NY: State University of New York Press.

Jaenke, K. (2004). The participatory turn [Review of *Revisioning transpersonal theory: A participatory vision of human spirituality*, by Jorge N. Ferrer]. *Revision: A Journal of Consciousness and Transformation, 26*(4), 8–14.

Jaggar, A. M. (1990). Love and knowledge: Emotions in feminist epistemology. In A. M. Jaggar & S. R. Bordo (Eds.), *Gender/body/knowledge: Feminist reconstructions of being and knowing* (pp. 145–171). New Brunswick, NJ: Rutgers University Press.

Jain, A. R. (2014). *Selling yoga: From counterculture to pop culture*. New York, NY: Oxford University Press.

James, W. (1961). *The varieties of religious experience*. New York, NY: Collier Books. Macmillan. (Original work published 1902).

James, W. (2003). *Essays in radical empiricism*. Mineola, NY: Dover. (Original work published 1912).

Jantsch, E. (1980). *The self-organizing universe: Scientific and human implications of the emerging paradigm of evolution*. New York, NY: Pergamon.

Jantzen, G. M. (1989). "Where two are to become one": Mysticism and monism. In G. Vesey (Ed.), *The philosophy of Christianity* (pp. 147–166). New York, NY: Cambridge University Press.

Jantzen, G. M. (1995). *Power, gender, and Christian mysticism*. New York, NY: Cambridge University Press.

Jennings, W. H. (1996). Agape and *karuna*: Some comparisons. *Journal of Contemporary Religion, 11*(2), 209–217.

Jesse, R. (1996). Entheogens: A brief history of their spiritual use. *Tricycle, 6*(1), 61–64.

Johnson, B. (1991). The middle realm. In A. Sharma (Ed.), *Fragments of infinity: Essays in religion and philosophy. A festschrift in honour of professor Huston Smith* (pp. 109–115). Garden City Park, NY: Prism.

Johnson, D. H. (Ed.). (1995). *Bone, breath, and gesture: Practices of embodiment*. Berkeley, CA: North Atlantic Books.

Johnson, D. H. (2005). From sarx to soma: Esalen's role in recovering the body for spiritual development. In J. J. Kripal & G. W. Shuck (Eds.), *On the edge of the future: Esalen and the evolution of American culture* (pp. 250–267). Bloomington, IN: Indiana University Press.

Johnson, M. (1987). *The body in the mind: The bodily basis of meaning, imagina-*

tion, and reason. Chicago, IL: University of Chicago Press.

Jónsson, G. A. (1988). *The image of God: Genesis 1:26–28 in a century of Old Testament research*. (Old Testament series, L. Svendsen, Trans.). Lund, Sweden: Almqvist and Wiskell.

Juergensmeyer, M. (2000). *Terror in the mind of God: The global rise of religious violence*. Berkeley, CA: University of California Press.

Juergensmeyer, M. (Ed.). (2003). *Global religions: An introduction*. New York, NY: Oxford University Press.

Juergensmeyer, M., Kitts, M., & Jerryson, M. (Eds.). (2012). *The Oxford handbook of religion and violence*. New York, NY: Oxford University Press.

Jung, C. G. (1969). *Archetypes and the collective unconscious*. In H. Read (Ed.), *The collected works of C. G. Jung* (Vol. IX, Part I) (R. F. C. Hull, Trans.). Princeton, NJ: Princeton University Press.

Jung, C. G. (2009). *The red book = Liber novus*. (S. Shamdanasi, Ed. and Trans.). New York, NY: W. W. Norton.

Kaplan, S. (2002). *Different paths, different summits: A model for religious pluralism*. Lanham, MD: Rowman & Littlefield.

Kasulis, T. P. (1990). Kūkai (774–835): Philosophizing in the archaic. In F. E. Reynolds and D. Tracy (Eds.), *Myth and philosophy* (pp. 131–150). Albany, NY: State University of New York Press.

Kasulis, T. P. (2002). *Intimacy or integrity: Philosophy and cultural difference. The 1998 Gilbert Ryle lectures*. Honolulu, HI: University of Hawaii Press.

Katz, S. T. (1978a). Language, epistemology, and mysticism. In S. T. Katz (Ed.), *Mysticism and philosophical analysis* (pp. 22–74). New York, NY: Oxford University Press.

Katz, S. T. (Ed.). (1978b). *Mysticism and philosophical analysis*. New York, NY: Oxford University Press.

Katz, S. T. (Ed.). (1983a). *Mysticism and religious traditions*. New York, NY: Oxford University Press.

Katz, S. T. (1983b). The "conservative" character of mystical experience. In S. T. Katz (Ed.), *Mysticism and religious traditions* (pp. 3–60). New York, NY: Oxford University Press.

Katz, S. T. (1988). On mysticism. *Journal of the American Academy of Religion*, 56(4), 751–761.

Katz, S. T. (Ed.). (2000). *Mysticism and sacred scripture*. New York, NY: Oxford University Press.

Katz, S. T. (2004). Diversity and the study of mysticism. In P. Antes, A. W. Geertz, & R. R. Warne (Eds.), *New approaches to the study of religion: Textual, comparative, sociological, and cognitive approaches* (Vol. 2, pp. 189–210). Berlin, Germany: Walter de Gruyter.

Kauffman, S. A. (2008). *Reinventing the sacred: A new view of science, reason, and religion*. New York, NY: Basic.

Kazantzakis, N. (1965). *Report to Greco* (P. A. Bien, Trans.). New York, NY:

Simon & Schuster.

Kegan, R. (1998). *In over our heads: The mental demands of modern life*. Cambridge, MA: Harvard University Press.

Kelly, S. M. (1993). *Individuation and the absolute: Hegel, Jung, and the path toward wholeness*. New York, NY: Paulist.

Kelly, S. M. (1998). Revisioning the mandala of consciousness: A critical appraisal of Wilber's holarchical paradigm. In D. Rothberg & S. M. Kelly (Eds.), *Ken Wilber in dialogue: Conversations with leading transpersonal thinkers* (pp. 117–130). Wheaton, IL: Theosophical Publishing House.

Kelly, S. M. (2008). Participation, complexity, and the study of religion. In J. N. Ferrer & J. H. Sherman (Eds.), *The participatory turn: Spirituality, mysticism, religious studies* (pp. 113–133). Albany, NY: State University of New York Press.

King, M. (2009). *Postsecularism: The hidden challenge to extremism*. Cambridge, United Kingdom: James Clarke.

King, M. (2012). Review of *The participatory turn: Spirituality, mysticism, religious studies*, edited by Jorge N. Ferrer and Jacob H. Sherman. *Journal for the Study of Spirituality, 1*(2), 280–287.

King, R. (1999). *Orientalism and religion: Postcolonial theory, India, and "the mystic East."* New York, NY: Routledge.

King, S. B. (1988). Two epistemological models for the interpretation of mysticism. *Journal of the American Academy of Religion, 56*(2), 257–269.

King, S. B. (2001). The *Philosophia Perennis* and the religions of the world. In L. E. Hahn, R. E. Auxier, & L. W. Stone (Eds.), *The philosophy of Seyyed Hassein Nasr: The library of living philosophers* (Vol. 28, pp. 203–220). Chicago, IL: Open Court.

King, T. (Ed.). (1992). *The spiral path: Explorations in women's spirituality*. Saint Paul, MN: Yes International Publishers.

King, W. L. (1974). Zen as a vipassana-type discipline. In H. B. Partin (Ed.), *Asian religions: history of religions: 1974 proceedings* (pp. 62–79). Tallahassee, FL: American Academy of Religion.

Kirschner, S. R. (1996). *The religious and romantic origins of psychoanalysis: Individuation and integration in post-Freudian theory*. New York, NY: Cambridge University Press.

Klein, A. C. (1986). *Knowledge and liberation: Tibetan Buddhist epistemology in support of transformative religious experience*. Ithaca, NY: Snow Lion Publications.

Klein, J. T. (1990). *Interdisciplinarity: History, theory, and practice*. Detroit, MI: Wayne State University Press.

Klein, J. T. (1996). *Crossing boundaries: Knowledge, disciplinarities, and interdisciplinarities*. Charlottesville, VA: University Press of Virginia.

Klüver, H. (1966). *Mescal and mechanisms of hallucinations*. Chicago, IL:

University of Chicago Press. (Original work published 1928).

Knoll, M., Kugler, J., Hofer, O., Lawder, S. D. (1962). Effects of chemical stimulation of electrically-induced phosphenes on their bandwidth shape, number and intensity. *Confinia Neurologica, 23*, 201–226.

Knorr-Cetina, K. (1999). *Epistemic cultures: How the sciences make knowledge.* Cambridge, MA: Harvard University Press.

Knott, K. (2005). Insider/outsider perspectives. In J. R. Hinnells (Ed.), *The Routledge companion to the study of religion* (pp. 243–258). New York, NY: Routledge.

Koehnke, K. C. (1991). *The rise of neo-Kantianism: German academic philosophy between idealism and positivism.* New York, NY: Cambridge University Press.

Koestler, A. (1976). *The ghost in the machine.* New York, NY: Random House.

Kohn, L., & Miller, J. (2001). Ultimate reality: Chinese religion. In R. C. Neville (Ed.), *Ultimate realities: A volume in the Comparative Religious Ideas Project* (pp. 9–35). Albany, NY: State University of New York Press.

Komarovski, Y. (2015). *Tibetan Buddhism and mystical experience.* New York, NY: Oxford University Press.

Kremer, J. W. (1992a). The dark night of the scholar. *ReVision: A Journal of Consciousness and Transformation, 14*(2), 169–178.

Kremer, J. W. (1992b). Whither dark night of the scholar? *ReVision: A Journal of Consciousness and Transformation, 15*(1), 4–12.

Kremer, J. W. (1994). *Looking for Dame Yggdrasil.* Red Bluff, CA: Falkenflug.

Kremer, J. W. (2007). Ironies of true selves in trans/personal knowing: Decolonizing trickster presences in the creation of indigenous participatory presence. *ReVision: A Journal of Consciousness and Transformation, 29*(4) 23–33.

Krijnen, C., & Zeidler, K. W. (2014). Philosophy of science in neo-Kantianism (Universität Wien, November 29th–December 1st 2012). *Journal for General Philosophy of Science, 1-5.* Retrieved from http://dx.doi.org/10.1007/s10838-014-9279-z.

Kripal, J. J. (1999). Inside-out, outside-in: Existential place and academic practice in the study of North American guru-traditions. *Religious Studies Review, 25*(3), 233–238.

Kripal, J. J. (2001). *Roads of excess, palaces of wisdom: Eroticism and reflexibility in the study of mysticism.* Chicago, IL: University of Chicago Press.

Kripal, J. J. (2002). Debating the mystical as ethical: An Indological map. In G. W. Barnard & J. J. Kripal (Eds.), *Crossing boundaries: Essays on the ethical status of mysticism* (pp. 15–69). New York, NY: Seven Bridges.

Kripal, J. J. (2003). In the spirit of Hermes: Reflections on the work of Jorge N. Ferrer. *Tikkun: A Bimonthly Jewish Critique of Politics, Culture, and Society, 18*(2), 67–70.

Kripal, J. J. (2005). Reading Aurobindo from Stanford to Pondicherry: Michael Murphy and the Tantric transmission (1950–1957). In J. J. Kripal & G. W. Shuck (Eds.), *On the edge of the future: Esalen and the evolution of*

American culture (pp. 99–131). Bloomington, IN: Indiana University Press.

Kripal, J. J. (2006a). Mysticism. In R. A. Segal (Ed.), *The Blackwell companion to the study of religion* (pp. 321–335). Maiden, MA: Blackwell.

Kripal, J. J. (2006b). *The serpent's gift: Gnostic reflections on the study of religion.* Chicago, IL: University of Chicago Press.

Kripal, J. J. (2007). *Esalen: America and the religion of no religion.* Chicago, IL: The University of Chicago Press.

Kripal, J. J. (2008). The roar of awakening: The eros of Esalen and the Western transmission of Tantra. In W. J. Hanegraaff & J. J. Kripal (Eds.), *Hidden intercourse: Eros and sexuality in the history of Western esotericism* (pp. 479–519). Danvers, MA: Brill.

Kripal, J. J. (2010). *Authors of the impossible: The paranormal and the sacred.* Chicago, IL: The University of Chicago Press.

Kripal, J. J. (2014). *Comparing religions: Coming to terms.* Malden, MA: Wiley Blackwell.

Krishnamurti, J. (1996). *Total freedom: The essential Krishnamurti.* New York, NY: HarperSanFrancisco.

Kubrin, D. (1980). Newton's inside out! Magic, class struggle, and the rise of mechanism in the West. In H. Woolf (Ed.), *The analytic spirit: Essays in the history of science in honor of Henry Guerlac* (pp. 96–121). Ithaca, NY: Cornell University Press.

Kuhn, T. (1970). *The structure of scientific revolutions* (2nd ed.). Chicago, IL: University of Chicago Press.

Küng, H. (1988). Christianity and world religions: Dialogue with Islam. In L. J. Swidler (Ed.), *Toward a universal theology of religion* (pp. 192–209). Maryknoll, NY: Orbis.

Küng, H. (1989). Response to Francis Cook: Is it just this?: Different paradigms of ultimate reality in Buddhism. *Buddhist-Christian Studies, 9,* 143–156.

Küng, H. (1991). *Global responsibility: In search for a new world ethic.* New York, NY: Crossroad.

Küng, H., & Kuschel, K. (Eds.). (1993). *A global ethic: The declaration of the Parliament of the World's Religions* (Special Edition). New York, NY: Continuum.

Lachman, G. (2001). *Turn off your mind: The mystic sixties and the dark side of the Age of Aquarius.* New York, NY: The Disinformation Company.

LaFargue, M. (1992). Radically pluralistic, thoroughly critical: A new theory of religions. *Journal of the American Academy of Religion, 60*(4), 693–716.

Lahood, G. (2007a). One hundred years of sacred science: Participation and hybridity in transpersonal anthropology. *ReVision: A Journal of Consciousness and Transformation, 29*(3), 37–48.

Lahood, G. (2007b). The participatory turn and the transpersonal movement: A brief introduction. *ReVision: A Journal of Consciousness and Transformation, 29*(3), 2–6.

Lahood, G. (Ed). (2007c). The participatory turn, Part 1 and 2. (Monograph).

ReVision: A Journal of Consciousness and Transformation, 29(3–4).

Lahood, G. (2008). Paradise bound: A perennial tradition or an unseen process of cosmological hybridization? *Anthropology of Consciousness*, 19(2), 155–189.

Lahood, G. (2010a). Relational spirituality, part 1. Paradise unbound: Cosmic hybridity and spiritual narcissism in the "one truth" of New Age transpersonalism. *The International Journal of Transpersonal Studies*, 29(1), 31–57.

Lahood, G. (2010b). Relational spirituality, part 2. The belief in others as a hindrance to enlightenment: Narcissism and the denigration of relationship within transpersonal psychology and the New Age. *The International Journal of Transpersonal Studies*, 29(1), 58–78.

Lahood, G. (2015). Love's threshing floor: Sifting the participatory wheat from the perennial chaff in the transpersonal psychology "familiar" to Gestalt therapy. *Gestalt Journal of Australia and New Zealand*, 12(2), 17–45.

Lakoff, G., & Johnson, M. (1999). *Philosophy in the flesh: The embodied mind and its challenge to Western thought.* New York, NY: Basic.

Lancaster, B. L. (2002). In defence of the transcendent. *Transpersonal Psychology Review*, 6(1), 42–51.

Lancaster, B. L. (2004). *Approaches to consciousness: The marriage of science and mysticism.* New York, NY: Palgrave Macmillan.

Lancaster, B. L. (2008). Engaging with the mind of God: The participatory path of Jewish mysticism. In J. N. Ferrer & J. H. Sherman (Eds.), *The participatory turn: Spirituality, mysticism, religious studies* (pp. 173–195). Albany, NY: State University of New York Press.

Lancaster, B. L. (2013). Neuroscience and the transpersonal. In H. L. Friedman & G. Hartelius (Eds.), *The Wiley-Blackwell handbook of transpersonal psychology* (pp. 223–238). Malden, MA: John Wiley & Sons.

Langlitz, N. (2013). *Neuropsychedelia: The revival of hallucinogenic research since the decade of the brain.* Berkeley, CA: The University of California Press.

Lanzetta, B. (2005). *Radical wisdom: A feminist mystical theology.* Minneapolis, MN: Fortress.

Lanzetta, B. (2007). *Emerging heart: Global spirituality and the sacred.* Minneapolis, MN: Fortress.

Lanzetta, B. (2008). Wound of love: Feminine theosis and embodied mysticism in Teresa de Avila. In J. N. Ferrer & J. H. Sherman (Eds.), *The participatory turn: Spirituality, mysticism, religious studies* (pp. 225–244). Albany, NY: State University of New York Press.

Larson, G. J. (1969). *Classical Sāmkhya: An interpretation of its history and meaning.* Delhi, India: Motilal Banarsidass.

Laszlo, E. (2004). *Science and the Akhasic field: An integral theory of everything.* Rochester, VT: Inner Traditions.

Lattuca, L. R. (2001). *Creating interdisciplinarity: Interdisciplinary research and teaching among college and university faculty.* Nashville, TN: Vanderbilt

University Press.

Laudan, L. (1996). *Beyond positivism and relativism: Theory, method, and evidence*. Boulder, CO: Westview.

Lawlor, R. (1991). *Voices of the first day: Awakening in the aboriginal dreamtime*. Rochester, VT: Inner Traditions.

Leadbeater, C. W. (2005). *The astral plane: Its scenery, inhabitants, and phenomena*. New York, NY: Cosim Classics. (Original work published 1895).

Leavy, P. (2011). *Essentials of transdisciplinary research: Using problem-centered methodologies*. Walnut Creek, CA: Lest Coast Press.

Leder, D. (1990). *The absent body*. Chicago, IL: University of Chicago Press.

Leeming, D. A. (Ed.). (2014). *Encyclopedia of psychology and religion* (2nd ed., Vol. 2). New York, NY: Springer.

Left, L. (2003). *The Kabbalah of the soul: The transformative psychology and practices of Jewish mysticism*. Rochester, VT: Inner Traditions.

Lewis-Williams, J. D., & Dowson, T. A. (1988). The signs of our times: Entoptic phenomena in Upper Palaeolithic art. *Current Anthropology, 29*(2), 201–245.

Leonard, G., & Murphy, M. (1995). *The life we are given: A long-term program for realizing the potential of our body, mind, heart, and soul*. New York, NY: Jeremy P. Tarcher/Putnam.

Lerner, M. (1994). *Jewish renewal: A path of healing and transformation* (1st ed.). New York, NY: HarperPerennial.

Lerner, M. (2000). *Spirit matters*. Charlottesville, VA: Hampton Roads.

Leslie, J. (1989). *Universes*. London, United Kingdom: Routledge.

Lesser, E. (1999). *The new American spirituality: A seeker's guide*. New York, NY: Random House.

Lester, Y. (2002). Oh gods! An explosion of new religions will shake the 21st century. *The Atlantic Monthly* (February), 37–45.

Lewis, C. S. (2012). *Surprised by joy: The shape of my early life* (First Mariner Books ed.). New York, NY: Mariner Books. (Original work published 1955).

Lincoln, B. (1986). *Myth, cosmos, and society: Indo-European themes of creation and destruction*. Cambridge, MA: Harvard University Press.

Linden, D. J. (2015). *Touch: The science of hand, heart, and mind*. New York: Viking.

Lings, M., & Minnaar, C. (Eds.). (2007). *The underlying religion: An introduction to the perennial philosophy*. Bloomington, IN: World Wisdom.

Lopez, D. S. Jr. (2010). *Buddhism and science: A guide for the perplexed*. Chicago, IL: The University of Chicago Press.

Lopez, D. S. Jr. (2012). *The scientific Buddha: His short and happy life* (Terry Lectures). New Haven, CT: Yale University Press.

Loy, D. (1987). The *clôture* of deconstruction: A Mahāyāna critique of Derrida. *International Philosophical Quarterly, 27*(1), 59–80.

Loy, D. (1988). *Nonduality: A study in comparative philosophy*. New Haven, CT:

Yale University Press.

Loy, D. (2008). *Money, sex, war, karma: Notes for a Buddhist revolution*. Boston, MA: Wisdom.

Loy, D. (2010). *The world is made of stories*. Boston, MA: Wisdom.

Luna, L. E. (1986). *Vegetalismo: Shamanism among the mestizo population of the Peruvian Amazon*. Stockholm, Sweden: Almquist and Wiksell International.

Lutz, C. (1988). *Unnatural emotions: Everyday sentiments on a Micronesian atoll and their challenge to Western theory*. Chicago, IL: University of Chicago Press.

MacDonald, D. A. (2013). Philosophical underpinnings of transpersonal psychology as a science. In H. L. Friedman & G. Hartelius (Eds.), *The Wiley-Blackwell handbook of transpersonal psychology* (pp. 312–329). Malden, MA: John Wiley & Sons.

MacDonald, D. A., & Friedman, H. L. (2013). Quantitative assessment of transpersonal and spiritual constructs. In H. L. Friedman & G. Hartelius (Eds.), *The Wiley-Blackwell handbook of transpersonal psychology* (pp. 281–299). Malden, MA: John Wiley & Sons.

Mahner, M. (2012). The role of metaphysical naturalism in science. *Science and Education, 21*, 1437–1459.

Makkreel, R. A., & Luft, S. (Eds.). (2009). *Neo-Kantianism in contemporary philosophy*. Bloomington, IN: Indiana University Press.

Malkemus, S. A. (2012). Toward a general theory of enaction: Biological, transpersonal, and phenomenological dimensions. *The Journal of Transpersonal Psychology, 44*(2), 201–223.

Malkemus, S. A., & Romero, M. T. (2012). Sexuality as a transformational path: Exploring the holistic dimensions of human vitality. *International Journal of Transpersonal Studies, 31*(2), 33–41.

Marion, J. (2000). *Putting on the mind of Christ: The inner work of Christian spirituality*. Charlottesville, VA: Hampton Roads.

Marks, L. F. M. (2007). Great mysteries: Native North American religions and participatory visions. *ReVision: A Journal of Consciousness and Transformation, 29*(3), 29–36.

Marshall, P. (2005). *Mystical encounters with the natural world: Experiences and explanations*. New York, NY: Oxford University Press.

Maslow, A. H. (1968). *Towards a psychology of being* (2nd ed.). New York, NY: D. Van Nostrand.

Masters, R. A. (2000). Compassionate wrath: Transpersonal approaches to anger. *The Journal of Transpersonal Psychology, 32*(1), 31–52.

Masters, R. A. (2010). *Spiritual bypassing: When spirituality disconnects us from what really matters*. Berkeley, CA: North Atlantic Books.

Maturana, H. R., & Varela, F. J. (1987). *The tree of knowledge: The biological roots of human understanding*. Boston, MA: New Science Library.

McCutcheon, R. T. (1997). *Manufacturing religion: The discourse of sui generis religion and the politics of nostalgia*. New York, NY: Oxford University Press.

McCutcheon, R. T. (1999). Introduction: Part III: Reductionism and the study of religion. In R. T. McCutcheon (Ed.), *The insider/outsider problem in the study of religion: A reader* (pp. 127–132). New York, NY: Continuum.

McCutcheon, R. T. (2001). *Critics not caretakers: Redescribing the public study of religion*. Albany, NY: State University of New York Press.

McDaniel, J. (1992). The embodiment of God among the Bāuls of Bengal. *Journal of Feminist Studies in Religion*, 8(2), 27–39.

McDermott, R. (2005). An Emersonian approach to higher education. *ReVision: A Journal of Consciousness and Transformation*, 28(2), 6–17.

McDermott, R. (2008). Participation comes of age: Owen Barfield and the Bhagavad Gita. In J. N. Ferrer & J. H. Sherman (Eds.), *The participatory turn: Spirituality, mysticism, religious studies* (pp. 293–319). Albany, NY: State University New York Press.

McGinn, B. (1991). *The foundations of mysticism* (Vol. 1, The presence of God: A history of Western Christian mysticism). New York, NY: Crossroad.

McGinn, B. (Ed.). (1994). *Meister Eckhart and the Beguine mystics: Hadewijch of Brabant, Mechtild of Magdeburg, and Marguerite Porete*. New York, NY: Continuum.

McGinn, B. (2001). *The mystical thought of Meister Eckhart: The man from whom God hid nothing*. New York, NY: Crossroad.

McGinn, B. (2005). Mystical union in Judaism, Christianity, and Islam. In L. Jones (Ed.), *Encyclopedia of religion* (2nd ed., pp. 6334–6341). Detroit, MI: MacMillan Reference USA.

McGinn, B., & McGinn, P. F. (2003). *Early Christian mystics: The divine vision of the spiritual masters*. New York, NY: Crossroad.

McGrane, B. (1989). *Beyond anthropology: Society and the other*. New York, NY: Columbia University Press.

McIntosh, S. (2007). *Integral consciousness and the future of evolution: How the integral perspective is transforming politics, culture and spirituality*. St. Paul, MN: Paragon.

McKenna, D. (2012). *The brotherhood of the screaming abyss: My life with Terence McKenna*. St. Cloud, MN: North Star Press.

McKenna, T. (1993). *True hallucinations: Being an account of the author's extraordinary adventures in the devil's paradise*. San Francisco, CA: HarperSanFrancisco.

Mead, G. H. (1934). *Mind, self, and society from the standpoint of a social behaviorist*. (Charles Morris, Ed.). Chicago, IL: University of Chicago Press.

Megill, A. (Ed.). (1994). *Rethinking objectivity* (Annals of Scholarship). Detroit, MI: Wayne State University Press.

Mercadante, L. A. (2014). *Belief without borders: Inside the minds of the spiritual but not religious*. New York, NY: Oxford University Press.

Merkur, D. (1998). *The ecstatic imagination: Psychedelic experiences and the psychoanalysis of self-actualization*. Albany, NY: State University of New York

Press.

Merlo, V. (2011). Sobre el giro participativo [About the participatory turn]. *Journal of Transpersonal Research, 3,* 55–58.

Metzger, D. (1992). *Writing for your life: A guide and companion to the inner worlds.* San Francisco, CA: HarperSanFrancisco.

Metzner, R. (1999). *Green psychology: Transforming our relationship to the Earth.* Rochester, VT: Park Street Press.

Metzner, R. (Ed.). (2014). *The Ayahuasca experience: A sourcebook on the sacred vine of spirits* (3rd ed.). Rochester, VT: Park Street Press.

Miller, J. P. (1994). Contemplative practice in higher education: An experiment in teacher development. *Journal of Humanistic Psychology, 34*(4), 53–69.

Miller, J. P. (1996). *The holistic curriculum* (1st ed.). Toronto, ON: Ontario Institute for Studies in Education.

Miller, J. P. (1999). *Education and the soul: Towards a spiritual curriculum.* Albany, NY: State University of New York Press.

Miller, J. R. (2006). *Educating for compassion and action: Creating conditions for timeless learning.* Thousand Oaks, CA: SAGE.

Miller, R. (Ed.). (1991a). *New directions in education: Selections from Holistic Education Review.* Brandon, VT: Holistic Education Press.

Miller, R. (1991b). Introduction. In R. Miller (Ed.), *New directions in education: Selections from Holistic Education Review* (pp. 6–8). Brandon, VT: Holistic Education Press.

Miner, R. C. (2004). *Truth in the making: Creative knowledge in theology and philosophy.* New York, NY: Routledge.

Mishra, K. (1993). *Kashmir Śaivism: The central philosophy of Tantrism.* Cambridge, MA: Rudra.

Mitchell, D. W., & Wiseman, J. A. (Eds.). (1997). *The Gethsemani encounter: A dialogue on the spiritual life by Buddhist and Christian monastics.* New York, NY: Continuum.

Molz, M., & Gidley, J. (2008). A transversal dialogue on integral education and planetary consciousness: Markus Molz speaks with Jennifer Gidley. *Integral review, 4*(1), 47–70.

Mommaers, P., & van Bragt, J. (1995). *Mysticism: Buddhist and Christian: Encounters with Jan van Ruusbroec* (Nanzan Studies in Religion and Culture, 1st ed.). New York, NY: Crossroad.

Montagu, A. (1971). *Touching: The human significance of skin.* New York: Harper & Row.

Montuori, A. (2005a). Gregory Bateson and the challenge of transdisciplinarity. *Cybernetics and Human Knowing, 1,* 16–37.

Montuori, A. (2005b). Literature review as creative inquiry: Reframing scholarship as a creative process. *Journal of Transformative Education, 3*(4), 374–393.

Moore, P. (1978). Mystical experience, mystical doctrine, mystical technique. In S. T. Katz (Ed), *Mysticism and philosophical analysis* (pp. 101–131). New

York, NY: Oxford University Press.

Moore, T. (2014). *A religion of one's own: A guide to creating a personal spirituality in a secular world* (1st ed.). New York, NY: Gotham.

Moregan, C. M. (2008). *Beyond the threshold: After life beliefs and experiences in world religions.* New York, NY: Rowman & Littlefield.

Morin, E. (2008). *On complexity.* New York, NY: Hampton Press.

Mukherjee, J. K. (2003). *The practice of integral yoga: With copious hints for the pilgrims of the path.* Pondicherry, India: Sri Aurobindo International Centre for Education.

Murphy, M. (1993). *The future of the body: Explorations into the further evolution of human nature.* Los Angeles, CA: J. P. Tarcher/Perigee.

Nagatomo, S. (1992). *Attunement through the body.* Albany, NY: State University of New York Press.

Nagel, T. (2012). *Mind and cosmos: Why the materialist neo-Darwinian conception of nature is almost certainly false.* New York, NY: Oxford University Press.

Nagy, M. (1991). *Philosophical issues in the psychology of C. G. Jung.* Albany, NY: State University of New York Press.

Nah, D. S. (2013). *Religious pluralism and Christian theology: A critical evaluation of John Hick.* Cambridge, United Kingdom: James Clarke.

Nakagawa, Y., & Matsuda, Y. (Eds.). (2010). *Integral approach: Integral transformative inquiry.* Kyoto, Japan: Institute of Human Sciences, Ritsumekian University.

Nasr, S. H. (1989). *Knowledge and the sacred* (Gifford Lectures). Albany, NY: State University of New York Press.

Nasr, S. H. (1993). The *Philosophia Perennis* and the study of religion. In *The need for a sacred science* (pp. 53–68). Albany, NY: State University of New York Press.

Nasr, S. H. (2001). Reply to Sally B. King. In L. E. Hahn, R. E. Auxier, & L. W. Stone (Eds.), *The philosophy of Seyyed Hassein Nasr* (Vol. 28, The library of living philosophers, pp. 221–231). Chicago, IL: Open Court.

Nelson, J. B. (1978). *Embodiment: An approach to sexuality and Christian theology.* Minneapolis, MN: Augsburg.

Nelson, J. B. (1992). *Body theology* (1st ed.). Louisville, KY: Westminster/John Knox.

Nelson, L. E. (Ed.). (1998a). *Purifying the earthly body of God: Religion and ecology in Hindu India.* Albany, NY: State University of New York Press.

Nelson, L. E. (1998b). The dualism of nondualism: Advaita Vedānta and the irrelevance of nature. In L. E. Nelson (Ed.), *Purifying the earthly body of God: Religion and ecology in Hindu India* (pp. 61–88). Albany, NY: State University of New York Press.

Nelstrom, L., & Podmore, S. D. (Eds.). (2013). *Christian mysticism and incarnational theology: Between transcendence and immanence.* Burlington, VT: Ashgate.

Neville, R. C. (1982). *The Tao and the daimon: Segments of a religious inquiry.* Albany, NY: State University of New York Press.

Neville, R. C. (1991). *Behind the masks of God: An essay toward comparative theology*. Albany, NY: State University of New York Press.

Neville, R. C. (1993). *Eternity and time's flow*. Albany, NY: State University of New York Press.

Neville, R. C. (Ed.). (2001). *Ultimate realities. A volume in the comparative religious ideas project*. Albany, NY: State University of New York Press.

Neville, R. C. (2002). *Religion in late modernity*. Albany, NY: State University of New York Press.

Neville, R. C. (2013). *Ultimates. Philosophical theology* (Vol. 1). Albany, NY: State University of New York Press.

Nicol, D. (2015). *Subtle activism: The inner dimension of social and planetary transformation*. Albany, NY: State University of New York Press.

Nicolescu, B. (2002). *Manifesto of transdisciplinarity*. Albany, NY: State University of New York Press.

Northcote, J. (2004). Objectivity and the supernormal: The limitations of bracketing approaches in providing neutral accounts of supernormal claims. *Journal of Contemporary Religion, 19*(1), 85–98.

O'Connor, M. (2005). In the living spirit: Spirituality, psychic awareness, and creativity. *Transpersonal Psychology Review, 9*(1), 50–67.

O'Sullivan, E. V. (1999). *Transformative learning: Educational vision for the 21st century*. New York, NY: Zed Books.

O'Sullivan, E. V., Morrell, A., & O'Connor, M. A. (Eds.). (2002). *Expanding the boundaries of transformative learning: Essays on theory and praxis*. New York, NY: Palgrave.

Ogilvy, J. (2013). The new polytheism: Updating the dialogue between East and West. *East-West Affairs, 1*(2), 29–48.

Oldmeadow, H. (2000). *Traditionalism: Religion in the light of the perennial philosophy*. Colombo, Sri Lanka: Sri Lanka Institute of Traditional Studies.

Oldmeadow, H. (2004). *Journeys East: 20th century Western encounter with Eastern religious traditions*. Bloomington, IN: World Wisdom.

Olson, A. M., & Rouner, L. S. (Eds.). (1981). *Transcendence and the sacred*. Notre Dame, IN: University of Notre Dame Press.

Osterhold, H., Husserl, R. E., & Nicol, D. (2007). Rekindling the fire of transformative education: A participatory case study. *Journal of Transformative Education, 5*(3), 221–245.

Overzee, A. H. (1992). *The body divine: The symbol of the body in the works of Teilhard de Chardin and Rāmānuja*. New York, NY: Cambridge University Press.

Palmer, G., & Hastings, A. (2013). Exploring the nature of exceptional human experiences: Recognizing, understanding, and appreciating EHEs. In H. L. Friedman & G. Hartelius (Eds.), *The Wiley-Blackwell handbook of transpersonal psychology* (pp. 331–351). Malden, MA: John Wiley & Sons.

Palmer, H., & Hubbard, P. (2009). A contextual introduction to psychosynthesis. *Journal of Transpersonal Research, 1*(1), 29–33.

Palmer, P. J. (2000). *Let your life speak: Listening for the voice of vocation*. Hoboken,

NJ: John Wiley & Sons.

Panikkar, R. (1981). *The unknown Christ of Hinduism: Towards an ecumenical Christophany.* Maryknoll, NY: Orbis.

Panikkar, R. (1984). Religious pluralism: The metaphysical challenge. In L. S. Rouner (Ed.), *Religious pluralism* (pp. 97–115). Notre Dame, IN: University of Notre Dame Press.

Panikkar, R. (1987). The Jordan, the Tiber, and the Ganges: Three kairological moments of Christic self-consciousness. In J. Hick & P. F. Knitter (Eds.), *The myth of Christian uniqueness: Toward a pluralistic theology of religions* (pp. 89–116). Maryknoll, NY: Orbis.

Panikkar, R. (1988). The invisible harmony: A universal theory of religion or a cosmic confidence in reality? In L. J. Swidler (Ed.), *Toward a universal theology of religion* (pp. 118–153). Maryknoll, NY: Orbis.

Panikkar, R. (1993). *The cosmotheandric experience: Emerging religious consciousness* (S. Eastham, Ed.). Maryknoll, NY: Orbis.

Panikkar, R. (1995). *Invisible harmony: Essays on contemplation and responsibility.* (H. J. Cargas, Ed.). Minneapolis, MN: Fortress.

Panikkar, R. (1996). A self-critical dialogue. In J. Prabhu (Ed.), *The intercultural challenge of Raimon Panikkar* (pp. 227–291). Maryknoll, NY: Orbis.

Panikkar, R. (2014). *Mysticism and spirituality. Opera Omnia Series* (Vol 1). (Ed. M. C. Pavan). Maryknoll, NY: Orbis.

Paranjpe, A. C. (1998). *Self and identity in modern psychology and Indian thought.* New York, NY: Plenum Press.

Park, J. Y. (Ed.). (2006). *Buddhisms and deconstructions.* Lanham, MD: Rowman & Littlefield.

Parrinder, G. (1996). *Sexual morality in the world's religions.* Rockport, MA: Oneworld.

Parsons, W. B. (2003). Review of *Revisioning transpersonal theory: A participatory vision of human spirituality,* by Jorge N. Ferrer. *The Journal of Religion, 83*(4), 692–693.

Parsons, W. B. (Ed.). (2011). *Teaching mysticism.* American Academy of Religion Series. New York, NY: Oxford University Press.

Paul, R. W., & Elder, L. (2002). *Critical thinking: Tools for taking charge of your professional and personal life.* Upper Saddle River, NJ: Prentice-Hall.

Paulson, D. S. (2002). *Daryl Paulson on Jorge Ferrer's Revisioning transpersonal theory.* Retrieved from http://www.integralworld.net/abramson1.html.

Paulson, D. S. (2003). Amazon.com review of *Revisioning transpersonal theory: A participatory vision of human spirituality,* by Jorge N. Ferrer. Retrieved from http://www.amazon.com/Revisioning-Transpersonal-Theory-Participatory-Spirituality/dp/0791451682/ref=sr_1_1?ie=UTF8&s=books&qid=1302655607&sr=1-1.

Paulson, D. S. (2004). Toward a participative integral philosophy. *The International Journal of Transpersonal Studies, 23,* 135–140.

Peat, D. (1987). *Synchronicity*. New York: Bantam.

Peluso, D. (2014). Ayahuasca's attractions and distractions: Examining sexual seduction in shaman-participant interactions. In B. C. Labate & C. Cavnar (Eds.), *Ayahuasca shamanism in the Amazons and beyond* (pp. 231–255). New York, NY: Oxford University Press.

Perovich, A. N., Jr. (1985). Mysticism and the philosophy of science. *The Journal of Religion*, 63–82.

Perovich, A. N., Jr. (1990). Does the philosophy of mysticism rest on a mistake? In R. K. C. Forman (Ed.), *The problem of pure consciousness: Mysticism and philosophy* (pp. 237–253). New York, NY: Oxford University Press.

Péter, B. D. (2009). A transzperszonális pszichológia jelenlegi fejlődését legjobban befolyásoló elméleti megközelítések [The most influential approaches in the present development of transpersonal psychology]. *Pszichoterápia*, 18(4), 251–260.

Placher, W. C. (1996). *The domestication of transcendence: How modern thinking about God went wrong*. Louisville, KY: Westminster/John Knox.

Plantinga, A. (2011). *Where the conflict really lies: Science, religion, and naturalism*. New York, NY: Oxford University Press.

Pogge, T., & Horton, K. (Eds.). (2008). *Global ethics: Seminal essays*. New York, NY: Paragon House.

Polkinghorne, D. (1983). *Methodology for the human sciences: Systems of inquiry*. Albany, NY: State University of New York Press.

Popper, K. (1994). *The myth of the framework: In defense of science and rationality*. (M. A. Notturno, Ed.). New York, NY: Routledge.

Pourafzal, H., & Montgomery, R. (1998). *The spiritual wisdom of Haféz: Teachings of the philosopher of love*. Rochester, VT: Inner Traditions.

Preus, J. S. (1987). *Explaining religion: Criticism and theory from Bodin to Freud* (Vol. 16). New Haven, CT: Yale University Press.

Pryer, A. (2001). Breaking hearts: Towards an erotics of pedagogy. In B. Hocking, J. Haskell, & W. Linds (Eds.), *Unfolding bodymind: Exploring possibility through education* (pp. 132–141). Brandon, VT: Foundation for Educational Renewal.

Puhakka, K. (2008). Transpersonal perspective: An antidote to the postmodern malaise. *The Journal of Transpersonal Psychology*, 40(1), 6–19.

Quine, W. V. (1980). *From a logical point of view: 9 logico-philosophical essays* (Rev. ed.). Cambridge, MA: Harvard University Press. (Original work published 1953).

Quinn, W. W. (1997). *The only tradition*. Albany, NY: State University of New York Press.

Rabbání, S. E. (1973). *World Order of Bahá'u'lláh*. Wilmette, IL: Baha'i Publishing Trust.

Rachel, A. (2013). Daimonic ecologies: An inquiry into the relationships between the human and nonphysical species. In A. Voss & W. Rowlandson (Eds.), *Daimonic imagination: Uncanny intelligence* (pp. 321–338). Newcastle upon

Tyne, United Kingdom: Cambridge Scholars.

Rahner, K. (2001). Christianity and the non-Christian religions. In J. Hick & B. Hebblethwaite (Eds.), *Christianity and other religions* (pp. 19–38). (Rev. ed.). Rockport, MA: Oneworld.

Raskin, R., & Terry, H. (1988). A principal-components analysis of the Narcissistic Personality Inventory and further evidence of its construct validity. *Journal of Personality and Social Psychology, 54*(5), 890–902.

Rawlinson, A. (1997). *The book of enlightened masters: Western teachers in Eastern traditions.* Chicago, IL: Open Court.

Rawlinson, A. (2000). A model of experiential comparative religion. *International Journal of Transpersonal Studies, 19,* 99–108.

Ray, R. A. (2000). *Indestructible truth: The living spirituality of Tibetan Buddhism.* Boston, MA: Shambhala.

Ray, R. A. (2008). *Touching enlightenment: Finding realization in the body.* Louisville, KY: Sounds True.

Reason, P. (Ed.). (1994). *Participation in human inquiry.* Thousand Oaks, CA: SAGE.

Reason, P. (2010). A creative unfolding: Peter Reason explores participation in spiritual and religious studies. (Review of *The participatory turn: Spirituality, mysticism, religious studies,* edited by Jorge N. Ferrer and Jacob H. Sherman). *Resurgence, 260* (May/June) [web-exclusive]. Retrieved from http://www.resurgence.org/magazine/web-exclusives.html.

Reason, P., & Bradbury, H. (Eds.). (2008). *The SAGE handbook of action research: Participative inquiry and practice* (2nd ed.). Thousand Oaks, CA: SAGE.

Reason, P., & Torbert, W. R. (2001). Toward a participatory worldview, Part 2 [Monograph]. *ReVision: A Journal of Consciousness and Transformation, 23*(4).

Reichel-Dolmatoff, G. (1978). *Beyond the Milky Way: Hallucinatory imagery of the Tukano Indians* (Vol. 41, UCLA Latin American Series). Los Angeles, CA: UCLA Latin American Center Publications.

Rensma, R. (2009). *The innateness of myths: A new interpretation of Joseph Campbell's reception of C. G. Jung.* New York, NY: Continuum.

Repko, A. F. (2008). *Interdisciplinary research: Process and theory.* Thousand Oaks, CA: SAGE.

Rhie, M. M., & Thurman, R. (2000). *Wisdom and compassion: The sacred art of Tibet.* New York, NY: Henry N. Adams.

Roberts, T. B., & Hruby, P. J. (2002). Toward an entheogen research agenda. *Journal of Humanistic Psychology, 42*(1), 71–89.

Roberts, T. B., & Winkelman, M. J. (2013). Psychedelic induced transpersonal experiences, therapies, and their implications for transpersonal psychology. In H. L. Friedman & G. Hartelius (Eds.), *The Wiley-Blackwell handbook of transpersonal psychology* (pp. 459–479). Malden, MA: John Wiley & Sons.

Romanyshyn, R. D. (2007). *The wounded researcher: Research with soul in mind.*

New Orleans, LA: Spring Journal Books.

Romero, M. T., & Albareda, R. V. (2001). Born on Earth: Sexuality, spirituality, and human evolution, *ReVision: A Journal of Consciousness and Transformation*, 24(2), 5–14.

Roof, W. C. (2001). *Spiritual marketplace: Baby boomers and the remaking of American religion*. Princeton, NJ: Princeton University Press.

Roof, W. C., & Greer, B. (1993). *A generation of seekers: The spiritual lives of the baby boom generation*. San Francisco, CA: HarperSanFrancisco.

Rorty, R. (1979). *Philosophy and the mirror of nature*. Princeton, NJ: Princeton University Press.

Rorty, R. (1998). Pragmatism as romantic polytheism. In M. Dickstein (Ed.), *The revival of pragmatism: New essays on social thought, law, and culture* (pp. 21–36). Durham, NC: Duke University Press.

Rorty, R. (2004). A pragmatist view of contemporary analytical philosophy. In W. Egginton & M. Sandbothe (Eds.), *The pragmatic turn in philosophy: Contemporary engagements between analytic and continental thought* (pp. 131–144). Albany, NY: State University of New York Press.

Rose, K. (2013). *Pluralism: The future of religion*. New York, NY: Bloomsbury.

Rosemont, H., Jr. (1988). Against relativism. In G. J. Larson & E. Deutsch (Eds.), *Interpreting across boundaries: New essays in comparative philosophy* (pp. 36–70). Princeton, NJ: Princeton University Press.

Rosenthal, G. (1987). Inflated by the spirit. In D. Anthony, B. Ecker, & K. Wilber (Eds.), *Spiritual choices: The problem of recognizing authentic paths to inner transformation* (pp. 305–323). New York, NY: Paragon House.

Roth, H. D. (2008). Against cognitive imperialism: A call for a non-ethnocentric approach to cognitive science and religious studies. *Religion East and West, 8*, 1–26.

Rothberg, D. (1993). The crisis of modernity and the emergence of socially engaged spirituality. *ReVision: A Journal of Consciousness and Transformation, 15*(3), 105–114.

Rothberg, D. (1996). How straight is the spiritual path?: Conversations with Buddhist teachers Joseph Goldstein, Jack Kornfield, and Michelle McDonald-Smith. *Revision: A Journal of Consciousness and Transformation, 19*(1), 25–29.

Rothberg, D. (1998). Responding to the cries of the world: Socially engaged Buddhism in North America. In C. S. Prebish & K. K. Tanaka (Eds.), *The faces of Buddhism in America* (pp. 266–286). Berkeley, CA: University of California Press.

Rothberg, D. (1999). Transpersonal issues at the millennium. *The Journal of Transpersonal Psychology, 31*(1), 41–67.

Rothberg, D. (2000). Spiritual inquiry. In T. Hart, P. Nelson, & K. Puhakka (Eds.), *Transpersonal knowing: Exploring the horizon of consciousness* (pp. 161–184). Albany, NY: State University of New York Press.

Rothberg, D. (2006). *The engaged spiritual life: A Buddhist approach to transforming ourselves and the world*. Boston, MA: Beacon.

Rothberg, D. (2008). Connecting inner and outer transformation: Toward an extended model of Buddhist practice. In J. N. Ferrer & J. H. Sherman (Eds.), *The participatory turn: Spirituality, mysticism, religious studies* (pp. 349–370). Albany, NY: State University of New York Press.

Rothberg, D., & Kelly, S. (Eds.). (1998). *Ken Wilber in dialogue: Conversations with leading transpersonal thinkers*. Wheaton, IL: Theosophical Publishing House.

Rowan, J., Daniels, M., Fontana, D., & Walley, M. (2009). A dialogue on Ken Wilber's contribution to transpersonal psychology. *Transpersonal Psychology Review, 13*(2), 5–41.

Ruf, H. L. (Ed.). (1989). *Religion, ontotheology, and deconstruction*. New York, NY: Paragon House.

Sacks, O. W. (2012). *Hallucinations*. New York, NY: Alfred A. Knopf.

Said, E. (1979). *Orientalism*. New York, NY: Vintage Books.

Saler, B. (2000). *Conceptualizing religion: Immanent anthropologies, transcendent natives, and unbounded categories*. Brooklyn, NY: Berghahn.

Sarath, E. D. (2006). Meditation, creativity, and consciousness: Charting future terrain within higher education. *Columbia Teachers College Record, 108*(9), 1816–1841.

Sarath, E. (2013). *Improvisation, creativity, and consciousness: Jazz as integral template for music, education, and society*. Albany, NY: State University of New York Press.

Saso, M. (1997). The Taoist body and cosmic prayer. In S. Coakley (Ed.), *Religion and the body* (pp. 230–247). New York, NY: Cambridge University Press.

Satprem (1992). *The mind of the cells or willed mutation of our species* (F. Mahak & L. Venet, Trans.). Mt. Vernon, WA: Institute for Evolutionary Research.

Scafi, A. (2013). *Maps of paradise*. Chicago, IL: The University of Chicago Press.

Schafersman, S. D. (1997, February). *Naturalism is today an essential part of science*. Paper presented at the Conference on Naturalism, Theism, and the Scientific Enterprise sponsored by the Department of Philosophy, The University of Texas, Austin, TX. Retrieved from http://llanoestacado.org/freeinquiry/files/naturalism.html.

Schilbrack, K. (2014a). *Philosophy and the study of religions: A manifesto*. Malden, MA: Wiley Blackwell.

Schilbrack, K. (2014b). Religious pluralism: A check-up. *Religious Studies Review, 40*(1), 1–7.

Schipper, K. (1993). *The Taoist body*. Berkeley, CA: University of California Press.

Schlamm, L. (2001). Ken Wilber's spectrum model: Identifying alternative soteriological perspectives. *Religion, 31*(1), 19–39.

Schleiermacher, F. (1988). *On religion: Speeches to its cultural despisers*. (R. Crouter, Ed. & Trans.). New York, NY: Cambridge University Press.

(Original work published 1799).

Schrader, G. (1967). The thing in itself in Kantian philosophy. In R. P. Wolff (Ed.), *Kant: A collection of critical essays* (pp. 172–188). Garden City, NY: Anchor.

Schroeder, C. S. (1995). *Embodied prayer: Harmonizing body and soul.* Liguori, MO: Triumph.

Schroll, M. A., Krippner, S., Vich, M. A., Fadiman, J., & Mojeiko, V. (2009). Reflections on transpersonal psychology's 40th anniversary, ecopsychology, transpersonal science, and psychedelics: A conversation forum. *International Journal of Transpersonal Studies, 28,* 39–52.

Schumacher, E. F. (1977). *A guide for the perplexed.* New York, NY: Harper Perennial.

Schuon, F. (1984). *The transcendent unity of religions.* Wheaton, IL: Theosophical Publishing House.

Scott, A. (2004). Reductionism revisited. *Journal of Consciousness Studies, 11*(2), 51–68.

Scott, D. K. (2005). The scholarship of integration. In K. O'Meara & R. E. Rice (Eds.), *Faculty priorities reconsidered: Rewarding multiple forms of scholarship* (pp. 47–54). San Francisco, CA: Jossey-Bass.

Scotton, B. W., Chinen, A. B., & Battista, J. R. (Eds.). (1996). *Textbook of transpersonal psychiatry and psychology.* New York, NY: Basic Books.

Sedgwick, M. J. (2004). *Against the modern world: Traditionalism and the secret intellectual history of the twentieth century.* New York, NY: Oxford University Press.

Segal, R. A. (1992). *Explaining and interpreting religion: Essays on the issue.* New York, NY: Peter Lang.

Segall, M. (2013). Participatory psychedelia: Transpersonal theory, religious studies and chemically-altered (alchemical) consciousness. *Journal of Transpersonal Research, 5*(2), 86–94.

Seitz, D. D. (2009). *Integrating contemplative and student-centered education: A synergistic approach to deep learning* (Doctoral dissertation). University of Massachusetts, Boston, Massachusetts. (Order No. 3361091).

Sellars, W. (1963). *Science, perception, and reality.* New York, NY: Humanities Press.

Sells, M. A. (1994). *Mystical languages of unsaying.* Chicago, IL: University of Chicago Press.

Sen, A. (2006). *Identity and violence: The illusion of destiny.* New York: W. W. Norton.

Shah-Kazemi, R. (2006). *Paths to transcendence: According to Shankara, Ibn Arabi, and Meister Eckhart.* Bloomington, IN: World Wisdom.

Shanon, B. (2002). *The antipodes of the mind: Charting the phenomenology of the Ayahuasca experience.* New York, NY: Oxford University Press.

Shapin, S. (2010). *Never pure: Studies in science as if it was carried out by people with bodies, gender, situated in time and space, and struggling with credibility* and *authority*. Baltimore, MD: Johns Hopkins University Press.

Shapiro, D. H. Jr. (1992). Adverse effects of meditation: A preliminary investigation of long-term meditators. *International Journal of Psychosomatics*, 39(1–4), 62–67.

Shapiro, L. A. (Ed.). (2014). *The Routledge handbook of embodied cognition*. New York, NY: Routledge.

Shapiro, S. I., Lee, G. W., & Gross, P. L. (2002). The essence of transpersonal psychology: Contemporary views. *The International Journal of Transpersonal Studies*, 21, 19–32.

Sharf, R. H. (1995). Buddhist modernism and the rhetoric of meditative experience. *Numen*, 42(3), 228–283.

Sharf, R. H. (1998). Experience. In M. C. Taylor (Ed.), *Critical terms for religious studies* (pp. 94–116). Chicago, IL: University of Chicago Press.

Sharma, A. (2005). *Religious studies and comparative methodology: The case for reciprocal illumination*. Albany, NY: State University of New York Press.

Sharon, D. (1990). The San Pedro cactus in Peruvian folk healing. In P. T. Furst (Ed.), *Flesh of the gods: The ritual use of hallucinogens* (pp. 115–135). Prospect Heights, IL: Waveland.

Shaw, M. C. (1988). *The paradox of intention: Reaching the goal by giving up the attempt to reach it* (Studies in Religion/American Academy of Religion). New York, NY: Oxford University Press.

Shepard, G. H. Jr. (2014). Will the real shaman please stand up?: The recent adoption of Ayahuasca among indigenous groups of the Peruvian Amazon. In B. C. Labate & C. Canvar (Eds.), *Ayahuasca shamanism in the Amazon and beyond* (pp. 16–39). New York, NY: Oxford University Press.

Sherman, J. H. (2008). A genealogy of participation. In J. N. Ferrer & J. H. Sherman (Eds.), *The participatory turn: Spirituality, mysticism, religious studies* (pp. 81–112). Albany, NY: State University of New York Press.

Sherman, J. H. (2014a). *Partakers of the divine: Contemplation and the practice of philosophy*. Minneapolis, MN: Fortress Press.

Sherman, J. H. (2014b). On the emerging field of contemplative studies and its relationship to the study of spirituality. *Spiritus: A Journal of Christian Spirituality*, 14(2), 208–229.

Shirazi, B. A. K. (2001). Integral psychology: Metaphors and processes of integral transformation. In M. Cornelissen (Ed.), *Consciousness and its transformation* (pp. 29–53). Pondicherry, India: Sri Aurobindo International Center of Education.

Shirazi, B. A. K. (2005). Integral psychology: Psychology of the whole human being. In M. Schlitz, T. Amorok, & M. S. Micozzi (Eds.), *Consciousness and healing: Integral approaches to mind-body medicine* (pp. 233–247). Philadelphia, PA: Elsevier Churchill Livingstone.

Shirazi, B. A. K. (2012). Rethinking the future of world religion: A conversation with Jorge N. Ferrer. *Integral Review*, 8(1), 20–34. Retrieved from http://integral-review.org/documents/Shirazi,%20Vol%208,%20No%201,%20

CIIS%20Special%20Issue.pdf.

Shokek, S. (2001). *Kabbalah and the art of being: The Smithsonian lectures*. New York, NY: Routledge.

Siegel, R. K., & Jarvik, M. E. (1975). Drug-induced hallucinations in animals and man. In R. K. Siegel & L. J. West (Eds.), *Hallucinations: Behavior, experience and theory* (pp. 81–161). New York, NY: Wiley.

Simmer-Brown, J. (2002). *Dakini's warm breath: The feminine principle in Tibetan Buddhism*. Boston, MA: Shambhala.

Simmer-Brown, J., & Grace, F. (Eds.). (2011). *Meditation and the classroom: Contemplative pedagogy in religious studies*. Albany, NY: State University of New York Press.

Singleton, M. (2010). *Yoga body: The origins of modern posture practice*. New York, NY: Oxford University Press.

Skolimowski, H. (1994). *The participatory mind: A new theory of knowledge and of the universe*. New York, NY: Penguin.

Skoog, K. (1996). Is the Jivanmukti state possible?: Ramanuja's perspective. In A. O. Fort & P. Y. Mumme (Eds.), *Living liberation in Hindu thought* (pp. 63–90). Albany, NY: State University of New York Press.

Slattery, D. R. (2015). *Xenolinguistics: Psychedelics, language, and the evolution of consciousness*. Berkeley, CA: Evolver Editions.

Slife, B. D., & Williams, R. N. (1997). Toward a theoretical psychology: Should a subdiscipline be formally recognized? *American Psychologist, 52*(2), 117–129.

Slingerland, E. (2000). Effortless actions: The Chinese spiritual ideal of wu-wei. *Journal of the American Academy of Religion, 68*(2), 293–328.

Slingerland, E. (2008). *What science offers the humanities: Integrating body and culture*. New York, NY: Cambridge University Press.

Smart, N. (1980). Interpretation and mystical experience. In R. Woods (Ed), *Understanding mysticism* (pp. 78–91). Garden City, NY: Doubleday.

Smart, N. (2003). The global future of religion. In M. Juergensmeyer (Ed.), *Global religions: An introduction* (pp. 124–131). New York, NY: Oxford University Press.

Smith, B. H. (2005). *Scandalous knowledge: Science, truth, and the human*. Durham, NC: Duke University Press.

Smith, B. H. (2009). *Natural reflections: Human cognition and the nexus of science and religion*. New Haven, CT: Yale University Press.

Smith, H. (1976). *Forgotten truth: The primordial tradition*. New York, NY: Harper & Row.

Smith, H. (1987). Is there a perennial philosophy? *Journal of the American Academy of Religion, 55*(3), 553–566.

Smith, H. (1994). Spiritual personality types: The sacred spectrum. In S. H. Nasr & K. O'Brien (Eds.), *In quest of the sacred: The modern world in the light of tradition* (pp. 45–57). Oakton, VA: Foundation for Traditional Studies.

Smith, J. Z. (1982). *Imagining religion: From Babylon to Jonestown*. Chicago, IL: Chicago University Press.

Smith, W. C. (1978). *The meaning and end of religion: A revolutionary approach to the great religious traditions*. London, United Kingdom: SPCK.

Snow, C. P. (1964). *The two cultures and a second look*. New York, NY: Cambridge University Press. (Original work published 1959).

Sogyal Rinponche (1992). *The Tibetan book of living and dying*. New York, NY: HarperCollins.

Sohmer, O. R., Baumann, R., & Ferrer, J. N. (forthcoming). An embodied spiritual inquiry into the nature of human boundaries: Exploring the further reaches of integral education. *International Journal of Transpersonal Studies*.

Somé, M. P. (1995). *Of water and spirit: Ritual, magic, and initiation in the life of an African shaman*. New York, NY: Penguin Compass.

Sorell, T. (1991). *Scientism: Philosophy and the infatuation with science*. New York, NY: Routledge.

Sovatsky, S. (1994). *Passions of innocence: Tantric celibacy and the mysteries of eros*. Rochester, VT: Destiny.

Spangler, D. (2010). *Subtle worlds: An explorer's field notes*. Everett, WA: Lorian.

Spiegel, D. (Ed.). (1994). *Dissociation: Culture, mind, and body*. Washington, DC: American Psychiatric Press.

Staal, F. (1975). *Exploring mysticism: A methodological essay*. Berkeley, CA: University of California Press.

Stoddart, W. (2008). *Remembering in a world of forgetting: Thoughts on tradition and postmodernism*. Bloomington, IN: World Wisdom.

Stoeber, M. (1994). *Theo-monistic mysticism: A Hindu-Christian comparison*. New York, NY: St. Martin's Press.

Stoeber, M. (2015). The comparative study of mysticism. In J. Kostova (Ed.), *The Oxford research encyclopedia of religion.* Retrieved from http://religion.oxfordre.com/view/10.1093/acrefore/9780199340378.001.0001/acrefore-9780199340378-e-93#acrefore-9780199340378-e-93-note-65.

Stoller, P., & Olkes, C. (1987). *In sorcery's shadow: A memoir of apprenticeship among the Songhay of Niger*. Chicago, IL: University of Chicago Press.

Stone, J. A. (2008). *Religious naturalism today: The rebirth of a forgotten alternative*. Albany, NY: State University of New York Press.

Storr, A. (1996). *Feet of clay: Saints, sinners, and madmen: A study of gurus*. New York, NY: Free Press.

Strassman, R. (2001). *DMT: The spirit molecule: A doctor's revolutionary research into the biology of near-death and mystical experiences*. Rochester, VT: Park Street Press.

Streng, F. J. (1993). Mutual transformation: An answer to a religious question. *Buddhist-Christian Studies, 13*, 121–126.

Strenski, I. (2006). *Thinking about religion: An historical introduction to theories of religion*. Malden, MA: Blackwell.

Stroud, B. (2004). The charm of naturalism. In M. De Caro & D. Macarthur (Eds.), *Naturalism in question* (pp. 21–35). Cambridge, MA: Harvard University Press.

Stryker, S. (2008). *Transgender history*. Berkeley, CA: Seal Press.

Studstill, R. (2005). *The unity of mystical traditions: The transformation of con-*

sciousness in Tibetan and German mysticism. Leiden, The Netherlands: Brill.

Subbiondo, J. L. (2005). An approach to integral education. ReVision: A Journal of Consciousness and Transformation, 28(2), 18–23.

Subbiondo, J. L. (2006). Integrating religion and spirituality in higher education: Meeting the global challenges of the 21st Century. Religion and Education, 33(2), 20–38.

Subbiondo, J. L. (2011). CIIS and American higher education. Integral Review: A Transdisciplinary and Transcultural Journal for New Thought, Research, and Praxis, 7(1), 11–16.

Sugobono, N. (2013). Review of Revisioning transpersonal theory: A participatory vision of human spirituality, by Jorge N. Ferrer. In S. B. Sotillos (Ed.), Psychology and the perennial philosophy: Studies in comparative religion (Studies in Comparative Religion: World Wisdom, pp. 201–207). Bloomington, IN: World Wisdom.

Sullivan, G. (Ed.). (2010). Art practice as research: Inquiry in the visual arts (2nd ed.). Thousand Oaks, CA: SAGE.

Sutich, A. J. (1976). The emergence of the transpersonal orientation. The Journal of Transpersonal Psychology, 8(1), 5–19.

Suzuki, S. (1970). Zen mind, beginner's mind. New York, NY: Weatherhill.

Taber, J. A. (1983). Transformative philosophy: A study of Śaṅkara, Fichte, and Heidegger. Honolulu, HI: University of Hawaii Press.

Tacey, D. (2004). The spirituality revolution: The emergence of contemporary spirituality. New York, NY: Brunner-Routledge.

Tambiah, S. J. (1990). Magic, science, religion, and the scope of rationality. New York, NY: Cambridge University Press.

Tarnas, B. (2016). Iridescent infinity: Participatory theory and archetypal cosmology. Archai: The Journal of Archetypal Cosmology, 5, 87–104.

Tarnas, R. (1991). The passion of the Western mind: Understanding the ideas that have shaped our world view. New York, NY: Ballantine.

Tarnas, R. (2001). A new birth in freedom: A (p)review of Jorge Ferrer's Revisioning transpersonal theory: A participatory vision of human spirituality. The Journal of Transpersonal Psychology, 33(1), 64–71.

Tarnas, R. (2002). Foreword. In J. N. Ferrer, Revisioning transpersonal theory: A participatory vision of human spirituality (pp. vii–xvi). Albany, NY: State University of New York Press.

Tarnas, R. (2006). Cosmos and psyche: Intimations of a new world view. New York, NY: Viking.

Tarnas, R. (2007). Two suitors: A parable. ReVision: A Journal of Consciousness and Transformation, 29(4), 6–9.

Tarnas, R. (2012). Notes on archetypal dynamics and complex causality in astrology (Part I). Archai: The Journal of Archetypal Cosmology, 4, 39–60.

Tart, C. T. (1972). States of consciousness and state-specific sciences. Science, 176, 1203–1210.

Tart, C. T. (2006). Current status of transpersonal psychology. Journal of

Consciousness Studies, 13(4), 83–88.

Tauber, A. I. (2009). *Science and the quest for meaning.* Waco, TX: Baylor University Press.

Taves, A. (2003). Detachment and engagement in the study of "lived experience." *Spiritus: A Journal of Christian Spirituality, 3*(2), 186–208.

Taves, A. (2005). Michael Murphy and the natural history of supernormal human attributes. In J. J. Kripal & G. W. Shuck (Eds.), *On the edge of the future: Esalen and the evolution of American culture.* (pp. 224–249). Bloomington, IN: Indiana University Press.

Taylor, C. (1989). *Sources of the self: The making of the modern identity.* Cambridge, MA: Harvard University Press.

Taylor, C. (2007). *A secular age.* Cambridge, MA: Belknap.

Taylor, E., & Wozniak, R. H. (Eds.). *Pure experience: The response to William James.* Bristol, United Kingdom: Thoemmes.

Taylor, S. (2017). From philosophy to phenomenology: The argument for a "soft" perennialism. *International Journal of Transpersonal Studies, 35*(2).

Teasdale, W. (1999). *The mystic heart: Discovering a universal spirituality in the world's religions.* Novato, CA: New World Library.

Teilhard de Chardin, P. (1968). *Science and Christ.* New York, NY: Harper & Row.

Tenzin Gyatso (H. H. the XIVth Dalai Lama) (1988). *The Bodhgaya interviews: His Holiness the Dalai Lama.* (J. I. Cabezón, Ed.). Ithaca, NY: Snow Lion.

Teo, T. (2005). *The critique of psychology: From Kant to postcolonial theory.* New York, NY: Springer.

Thatamanil, J. J. (2006). *The immanent divine: God, creation, and the human predicament.* Minneapolis, MN: Fortress.

Thompson, E. (1996). The mindful body: Embodiment and cognitive science. In M. O'Donovan-Anderson (Ed.), *The incorporated self: Interdisciplinary perspectives of embodiment* (pp. 127–144). Lanham, MD: Rowman & Littlefield.

Thompson, E. (2007). *Mind in life: Biology, phenomenology, and the sciences of the mind.* Cambridge, MA: Harvard University Press.

Thurer, S. L. (2005). *The end of gender: A psychological autopsy.* New York, NY: Routledge.

Todorovic, N. (2002). *The mean green meme hypothesis: Fact or fiction?* Retrieved 22 March 2014 from https://www.academia.edu/2014906/Mean_Green_Meme_Boomeritis_Myth.

Torbert, W. R., & Reason, P. (2001). Toward a participatory worldview: Part 1. *Revision: A Journal of Consciousness and Transformation, 24*(1), 1–48.

Treleaven, D. (2010). Meditation, trauma, and contemplative dissociation. *Somatics, 16*(2), 20–22.

Treleaven, D. (2018). *Trauma-sensitive mindfulness: Practices for safe healing.* New York, NY: Norton.

Trungpa, C. (1987). *Cutting through spiritual materialism.* Boston, MA: Shambhala.

Turner, D. (1995). *The darkness of God: Negativity in Christian mysticism.* New

York, NY: Cambridge University Press.

Turner, E. L. B. (1992). *Experiencing ritual: A new interpretation of African healing.* Philadelphia, PA: University of Pennsylvania Press.

Turner, V. W. (1967). *The forest of symbols: Aspects of Ndembu ritual.* Ithaca, NY: Cornell University Press.

Twiss, S. B., & Grelle, B. (Eds.). (1998). *Explorations in global ethics: Comparative religious ethics and interreligious dialogue.* Boulder, CO: Westview.

Underhill, E. (1955). *Mysticism: A study in the nature and development of man's spiritual consciousness.* New York, NY: Noonday.

Urban, H. (2003). *Tantra: Sex, secrecy, politics, and power in the study of religion.* Berkeley, CA: University of California Press.

van Fraassen, B. C. (2002). *The empirical stance.* New Haven, CT: Yale University Press.

van Fraassen, B. C. (2008). *Scientific representation: Paradoxes of perspective.* New York, NY: Oxford University Press.

van Inwagen, P. (1998). The nature of metaphysics. In S. Laurence & C. Macdonald (Eds.), *Contemporary readings in the foundations of metaphysics* (pp. 11–21). Malden, MA: Blackwell.

van Manen, M. (1990). *Researching lived experience: Human science for an action sensitive pedagogy.* Albany, NY: State University of New York Press.

Van Ness, P. H. (Ed.). (1996). *Spirituality and the secular quest.* New York, NY: Crossroad.

Varela F. J., & Depraz, N. (2003). Imagining: Embodiment, phenomenology, and transformation. In B. A. Wallace (Ed.), *Buddhism and science: Breaking new ground* (pp. 195–230). New York, NY: Columbia University Press.

Varela, F. J., Thompson, E., & Rosch, E. (1991). *The embodied mind: Cognitive science and human experience.* Cambridge, MA: The MIT Press.

Vélez de Cea, A. (2013). *The Buddha and religious diversity.* New York, NY: Routledge.

Vennard, J. E. (1998). *Praying with body and soul: A way to intimacy with God.* Minneapolis, MN: Augsburg.

Vich, M. A. (1990). The origins and growth of transpersonal psychology. *Journal of Humanistic Psychology, 30*(2), 47–50.

Victoria, B. D. (2006). *Zen at war* (2nd ed.). New York, NY: Rowman & Littlefield.

Vieten, C., Cohen, A. B., Schiltz, M. M., Estrada, M., Radin, D., and Delorme, A. (2014). Engagement in a community-based integral practice program enhances well-being. *International Journal of Transpersonal Studies, 33*(2), 1–15.

Viveiros de Castro, E. (2014). *Cannibal metaphysics* (P. Skafish, Ed., Trans.). Minneapolis, MN: Univocal.

Viveiros de Castro, E. (2015). *The relative native: Essays on indigenous conceptual worlds.* Chicago, IL: Hau Books.

Voss, A. (2009). A methodology of the imagination. *Eye of the Heart: A Journal of Traditional Wisdom*, 3, 37–52.

Voss, A. (2013). Fireflies and shooting stars: Visual narratives of daimonic intelligence. In A. Voss & W. Rowlandson (Eds.), *Daimonic imagination: Uncanny intelligence* (pp. 244–265). Newcastle upon Tyne, United Kingdom: Cambridge Scholars.

Vroom, H. M. (1989). *Religions and the truth: Philosophical reflections and perspectives.* Grand Rapids, MI: William B. Eerdmans.

Vroom, H. M. (1996). *No other Gods: Christian belief in dialogue with Buddhism, Hinduism, and Islam.* Grand Rapids, MI: William B. Eerdmans.

Wade, J. (2004). *Transcendent sex: When lovemaking opens the veil.* New York, NY: Paraview Pocket Books.

Walach, H. (2013). Criticisms of transpersonal psychology and beyond—The future of transpersonal psychology. In H. L. Friedman & G. Hartelius (Eds.), *The Wiley-Blackwell handbook of transpersonal psychology* (pp. 62–87). Malden, MA: John Wiley & Sons.

Walach, H., & Runehov, A. L. C. (2010). The epistemological status of transpersonal psychology: The database argument revisited. *Journal of Consciousness Studies, 17*(1–2), 145–165.

Walker, H. (2012). On Marti Kheel's *Nature Ethics* and its implications for a more integrative approach to transpersonal psychology. *Restoration Earth: An Interdisciplinary Journal for the Study of Nature & Civilization, 1*(2), 49–60.

Walker, S. (Ed.). (1987). *Speaking of silence: Christians and Buddhists on the contemplative way.* New York, NY: Paulist.

Wall, K., Nye, F., & FitzMedrud, E. (2013). Psychospiritual integrative practice. In H. L. Friedman & G. Hartelius (Eds.), *The Wiley-Blackwell handbook of transpersonal psychology* (pp. 544–561). Malden, MA: John Wiley & Sons.

Wallace, B. A. (2000). *The taboo of subjectivity: Toward a new science of consciousness.* New York, NY: Oxford University Press.

Walsh, R. N. (1993). The transpersonal movement: A history and state of the art. *The Journal of Transpersonal Psychology, 25*(3), 123–139.

Walsh, R. N., & Roche, L. (1979). Precipitation of acute psychotic episodes by intensive meditation in individuals with a history of schizophrenia. *American Journal of Psychiatry, 136*(8), 1085–1086.

Walsh, R. N., & Vaughan, F. (1993). On transpersonal definitions. *The Journal of Transpersonal Psychology, 25*(2), 199–207.

Ward, S. C. (2002). *Modernizing the mind: Psychological knowledge and the remaking of society.* Westport, CT: Praeger.

Washburn, M. (1994). *Transpersonal psychology in psychoanalytic perspective.* Albany, NY: State University of New York Press.

Washburn, M. (1995). *The ego and the dynamic ground: A transpersonal theory of human development* (Rev. ed.). Albany, NY: State University of New York Press.

Washburn, M. (1998). The pre/trans fallacy reconsidered. In D. Rothberg & S. Kelly (Eds.), *Ken Wilber in dialogue: Conversations with leading transpersonal* thinkers (pp. 62–87). Wheaton, IL: Quest Books.

Washburn, M. (2003a). Embodied spirituality in a sacred world. Albany, NY: State University of New York Press.

Washburn, M. (2003b). Transpersonal dialogue: A new direction. The Journal of Transpersonal Psychology, 35(1), 1–20.

Watts, A. (2011). The book: On the taboo against knowing who you are. New York, NY: Vintage Books. (Original work published 1966).

Wayman, A. (1982). The human body as microcosm in India, Greek cosmology, and sixteenth-century Europe. History of Religions 22, 172–190.

Weiser-Hanks, M. E. (2000). Christianity and sexuality in the early modern world: Regulating desire, reforming practice. New York, NY: Routledge.

Welwood, J. (2000). Towards a psychology of awakening: Buddhism, psychotherapy, and the path of personal and spiritual transformation. Boston, MA: Shambhala.

West, C. (1999). The Cornel West reader. New York, NY: Basic.

Westheimer, R. K., & Mark, J. (1995). Heavenly sex: Sexuality in the Jewish tradition. New York, NY: New York University Press.

Wexler, J. G. (2004). Communication to the CIIS Integral Education Committee. California Institute of Integral Studies, San Francisco, California.

Wexler, J. G. (2005). Toward a model of integral education. ReVision: A Journal of Consciousness and Transformation, 28(2), 29–34.

Wexler, J. G. (2011). Evolving dimensions of integral education. Integral Review: A Transdisciplinary and Transcultural Journal for New Thought, Research, and Praxis, 7(1), 17–24.

Wezler, A. (2001). "Psychedelic" drugs as a mean to mystical experience: Aldous Huxley versus Indian reality. In C. C. Barfoot (Ed.), Aldous Huxley between East and West (pp. 191–220). New York, NY: Rodopi.

Whicher, I. (1998). The integrity of the yoga Darsana: A reconsideration of the classical yoga. Albany, NY: State University of New York Press.

White, D. G. (Ed.). (2000). Tantra in practice. Princeton, NJ: Princeton University Press.

Whomsley, S. (2014). Comments on John Abramson's paper: The misunderstanding and misinterpretation of key aspects of Ken Wilber's work in Hartelius and Ferrer's (2013) assessment. Transpersonal Psychology Review, 16(1), 13–14.

Widdows, H. (2014). Global ethics: An introduction. New York, NY: Routledge.

Wiebe, D. (1999). The politics of religious studies: The continuing conflict with theology in the academy (1st ed.). New York, NY: St. Martin's Press.

Wilber, K. (1995). Sex, ecology and spirituality: The spirit of evolution. Boston, MA: Shambhala.

Wilber, K. (1996a). Transpersonal art and literary theory. The Journal of Transpersonal Psychology, 28(1), 63–91.

Wilber, K. (1996b). The Atman project: A transpersonal view of human development (2nd ed.). Wheaton, IL: Quest Books.

Wilber, K. (1998). Response to Jorge Ferrer's "Speak now or forever hold your peace: A review essay of Ken Wilber's The marriage of sense and soul." The

Journal of Transpersonal Psychology, 30(1), 69–72.

Wilber, K. (1999). *One taste: Daily reflections on integral spirituality.* Boston, MA: Shambhala.

Wilber, K. (2000a). *A theory of everything: An integral vision for business, politics, science, and spirituality.* Boston, MA: Shambhala.

Wilber, K. (2000b). Integral transformative practice: In this world or out of it? *What Is Enlightenment,* 18, 34–39.

Wilber, K. (2000c). *Integral psychology: Consciousness, spirit, psychology, therapy.* Boston, MA: Shambhala.

Wilber, K. (2001). *The eye of spirit: An integral vision for a world gone slightly mad* (3rd ed.). Boston, MA: Shambhala.

Wilber, K. (2002). *Sidebar f: Participatory samsara: The green-meme approach to the mystery of the divine.* Retrieved 2 May 2014 from: http://wilber.shambhala. com/html/books/boomeritis/sidebar_f/index.cfm/.

Wilber, K. (2006). *Integral spirituality: A startling new role for religion in the modern and postmodern world.* Boston. MA: Integral Books.

Wilber, K., Patten, T., Leonard, A., & Morelli, M. (2008). *Integral life practice: A 21st-century blueprint for physical health, emotional balance, mental clarity, and spiritual awakening.* Boston, MA: Integral Books.

Wilczek, F. (2016). *A beautiful question: Findings nature's deep design.* New York, NY: Penguin.

Williams, A. (1997). Zoroastrianism and the body. In S. Coakley (Ed.), *Religion and the body* (pp. 155–166). New York, NY: Cambridge University Press.

Williams, L. (2006). Spirituality and Gestalt: A Gestalt-transpersonal perspective. *Gestalt Review,* 10(1), 6–21.

Williams, P. (1997). Some Mahayana perspectives on the body. In S. Coakley (Ed.), *Religion and the body* (pp. 205–230). New York, NY: Cambridge University Press.

Wilson, M. (2017). *Resource focused counseling and psychotherapy: An introduction.* London, United Kingdom: Routledge.

Wimbush, V. L., & Valantasis, R. (Eds.). (2002). *Asceticism.* New York, NY: Oxford University Press.

Winkelman, M. (2013). Shamanism and psychedelics: A biogenetic structuralist paradigm of ecopsychology. *European Journal of Ecopsychology,* 4, 90–115.

Winter, M. (1995). Islamic attitudes toward the human body. In J. M. Law (Ed.), *Religious reflections on the human body* (pp. 36–45). Bloomington, IN: Indiana University Press.

Wrathall, M. A. (Ed.). (2003). *Religion after metaphysics.* New York, NY: Cambridge University Press.

Yandell, K. E. (1993). Some varieties of religious pluralism. In J. Kellenberger (Ed.), *Inter-religious models and criteria* (pp. 187–211). New York, NY: St. Martin's Press.

Yasuo, Y. (1987). *The body: Toward an Eastern mind-body theory* (T. P. Kasulis, Ed., S. Nagatomo & M. S. Hull, Trans.). Albany, NY: State University of New York Press.

Yasuo, Y. (1993). *The body, self-cultivation, and ki-energy* (S. Nagatomo & M. S. Hull, Trans.). Albany, NY: State University of New York Press.

Zaehner, R. C. (1980). *Mysticism sacred and profane: An inquiry into some varieties of preternatural experience.* New York, NY: Oxford University Press. (Original work published 1957).

Ziolkowski, T. (2007). *Modes of faith: Secular surrogates for lost religious belief.* Chicago, IL: The University of Chicago Press.

Zuleski, C. (1987). *Otherworld journeys: Accounts of near-death experience in medieval and modern times.* New York, NY: Oxford University Press.

INDEX

Printed in Great Britain
by Amazon